AND STILL THE WATERS RUN

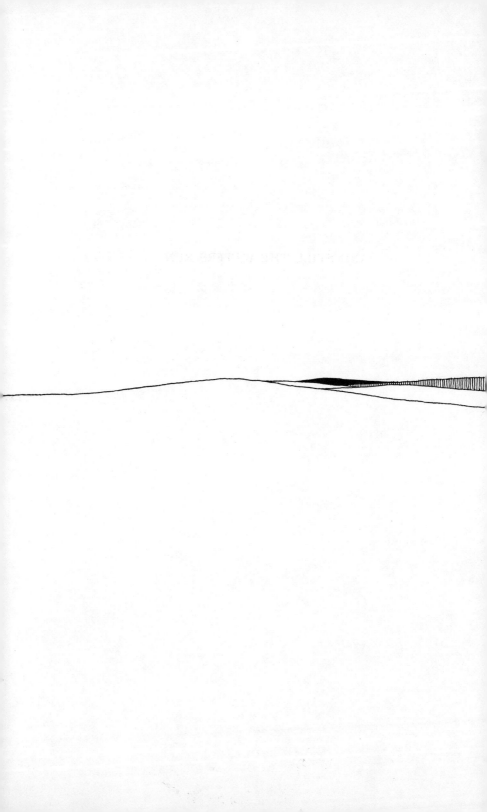

# And Still the Waters Run

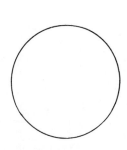

## THE BETRAYAL OF THE FIVE CIVILIZED TRIBES

*Angie Debo*

PRINCETON
UNIVERSITY
PRESS

LCC 72–6098

ISBN 0–691–00578–8 (*paperback edition*)

ISBN 0–691–04615–8 (*hardcover edition*)

Printed in the United States of America
by Princeton University Press, Princeton, N.J.

TO MY PARENTS

EDWARD P. AND LINA DEBO

WHOSE CONSTANT INTEREST IN THIS BOOK

AND WHOSE PATIENCE AND FORBEARANCE DURING ITS PROGRESS

HAVE LIGHTENED THE LABORS OF AUTHORSHIP

# CONTENTS

## MAPS

# ILLUSTRATIONS

# PREFACE

EVERY schoolboy knows that from the settlement of James-
town to the 1870's Indian warfare was a perpetual
accompaniment of American pioneering, but the second
stage in dispossessing the Indians is not so generally and
romantically known. The age of military conquest was succeeded by the age of economic absorption, when the long rifle of
the frontiersman was displaced by the legislative enactment
and court decree of the legal exploiter, and the lease, mortgage,
and deed of the land shark. As a preliminary to this process
the Indians were persuaded or forced to surrender their tribal
organization and accept United States citizenship and to divide
their communal holdings into individual allotments.

Because of the magnitude of the plunder and the rapidity
of the spoliation the most spectacular development of this
policy occurred with the Five Civilized Tribes of the Indian
Territory. At the beginning of the present century about seventy
thousand of these Indians owned the eastern half of the area
that now constitutes the state of Oklahoma, a territory im-
mensely wealthy in farmland and forest and coal mines, and
with untapped oil pools of incalculable value. They ruled
themselves and controlled this tribal property under constitutional governments of their own choosing, and they had attained a degree of civilization that made them at once the boast
of the Indian Office and living examples of the benefits of
travelling in the white man's road. Their political and economic
tenure was guaranteed by treaties and patents from the Federal
Government, and warned by the tragic fate of all Indians who
had lost their homes, they insisted upon the observance of these
conditions. But white people began to settle among them, and
by 1890 these immigrants were overwhelmingly in the majority.
Congress therefore abrogated the treaties, and the Indians

received their land under individual tenure and became citizens of Oklahoma when it was admitted to the Union in 1907.

The orgy of exploitation that resulted is almost beyond belief. Within a generation these Indians, who had owned and governed a region greater in area and potential wealth than many an American state, were almost stripped of their holdings, and were rescued from starvation only through public charity. Such treatment of an independent people by a great imperial power would have aroused international condemnation; but these Indian republics were—to quote John Marshall's famous opinion—"domestic dependent nations," and the destruction of their autonomy was a matter of internal policy. Even as a real estate transaction this transfer of property would have attracted wide attention, but the Indians had been forced to accept the perilous gift of American citizenship and they were despoiled individually under the forms of existing law; hence no writer of American history devotes even a sentence to their wrongs, students of Indian life are interested only in their inspiring achievements under the tribal régime, and their plight during the generation of their exploitation has been consistently ignored by the press.

Obviously the rapidity of the spoliation called for crude methods, in many cases even criminal methods, and the immense value of the loot exerted a powerful influence upon contemporary opinion and standards of conduct. It should not be necessary to point out that Oklahomans are no worse than their neighbors, for this is only one episode—although the most dramatic episode—in a process that constitutes an unrecorded chapter in the history of every American frontier. But the reaction of this process upon the ideals and standards of successive frontier communities is a factor in the formation of the American character that should no longer be disregarded by students of social institutions.

Fortunately the historian is not expected to prescribe remedies. The policy of the United States in liquidating the institutions of the Five Tribes was a gigantic blunder that ended a hopeful experiment in Indian development, destroyed a unique civilization, and degraded thousands of individuals. As the story unfolds, the reader may formulate policies that might have averted this disaster if adopted, or he may conclude that the catastrophe was inevitable.

This study was undertaken before the election of 1932, and if its findings support the tenets of the present Indian administration the circumstance is accidental. The research was carried on independently and with no preconceived theories of Indian policy. The facts uncovered during the investigation were a revelation to the writer, who had grown up in Oklahoma without knowing that these things were so.

The manuscript was completed in 1936 only a few days after the passage of the Oklahoma Indian Welfare Act; but publication has been delayed and it has been decided to include some new material to bring the subject up to date as far as possible. This portion of the research has been necessarily superficial, for it is too early to reach conclusions as to the effect of such a radical change in Indian policy. It is believed, however, that the revision will be a convenience to the reader in the relatively unimportant matter of statistical information.

The author is under obligations to Dr. E. E. Dale, head of the history department of the University of Oklahoma, for awakening in student days an interest in Indian institutions; to Mr. Frank Phillips of Bartlesville, whose public spirit in establishing a collection of historical material at the University has provided facilities for research; to Mrs. Mabel Bassett, Commissioner of Charities and Corrections of the State of Oklahoma, for free access to her files; to Miss Margaret Camp of Albuquerque, New Mexico, for secretarial help that amounted to collaboration; to Commissioner John Collier and the employees of the Indian Office at Washington and in Oklahoma for unlimited access to current files and the opportunity of observing the work of the field service; to the librarians and

archivists at the University of Oklahoma and the Oklahoma
State Historical Society; and above all to the Social Science
Research Council for a grant-in-aid without which the research
could not have been completed.

ANGIE DEBO

*Marshall, Oklahoma*
May 28, 1940

### THIRTY-TWO YEARS AFTER

I welcome the opportunity provided by the reissue of this book
to clarify one expression I used unthinkingly in the original
edition. The term "restricted Indian" had passed into common
speech as a convenient designation for the owner of restricted
land, and I used it without realizing that is was subject to misinterpretation. Actually there is no such thing as a "restricted
Indian." Only the land obtained from the tribe carries this
protection against alienation; and the ownership of restricted
land no more restricts an Indian's personal freedom than does
the ownership of trust property or tax-free bonds by any other
citizen. This distinction is important in view of the slogans
of exploiters who would "set the Indians free." I regret that I
have blurred it by my loose terminology.

I also welcome the opportunity to answer the question with
which my book closed in 1940: Could the lost fullbloods of the
Five Tribes be saved? Nine years later I made a survey to
answer that question at the request of the Indian Rights Association, which published my findings under the title *The
Five Civilized Tribes of Oklahoma: Report on Social and
Economic Conditions*. To bring the reader up to date, I shall
draw on this sequel and—with the permission of my publisher
—from *A History of the Indians of the United States*, which
includes insights I gained from another survey made in 1956
at the request of the Association on American Indian Affairs.
(At the time of the 1949 survey the Indians still owned

930,833 acres of allotted land, and 326,935 acres of inherited land was still in the possession of the heirs. Of this land, 223,284 acres were in the Cherokee Ozark counties; 141,496 lay in the cut-over pine area of the Choctaw mountains; and most of the remainder consisted of the blackjack-postoak jungle that covered the belt of ragged hills stretching between the rivers to the west. Except in the Creek country—and to a certain extent even there—one could be fairly certain in approaching an Indian settlement to find only worthless land. A good many Choctaw and Chickasaw hill dwellers owned some of their good prairie "surplus," but the idea of migrating to that distant region was completely foreign to their experience And because the rolls had been closed on March 4, 1906 th youngest allottees were well along in their forties. Thos younger than that were completely landless except for inherited land still in family possession. And the law enacted January 27, 1933 extending restrictions on inherited land until 1956 had been repealed through Oklahoma initiative on August 4, 1947. Thus if one grandchild decided to sell his 1/24 interest in the family estate, the other heirs had no recourse. The purchase of his interest was entirely beyond their financial resources.)

At the time my book was published loans had recently become available under the Oklahoma Indian Welfare Act. In practice this meant that the agricultural agents of the Indian service known as farm management supervisors drew up the plans, and the credit associations were guided by their recommendations. This made a perfect combination of expert planning, adequate capital, Indian labor, and educative guidance. At the end of the fiscal year 1948 (the 1949 figures had not yet been computed) the Indians had borrowed in cumulative figures $906,864.93, of which $590,454.99 had been repaid ($24,578.01 through foreclosure), $312,709.43 was still outstanding, and $3,700.51 had been charged off as lost. Most of these loans had been made on farming ventures; and the lending agency took the risk that a poverty-stricken

Indian without experience or capital would succeed if given a chance. Truly a remarkable record of repayment.

I spent some time in the Superintendent's office at Muskogee collecting such statistical information, but I did most of my work in the field. Many interviews took place on rustic porches or inside rude dwellings where chickens wandered in and out through unscreened doors, or sudden showers dripped into every available vessel through leaky roofs. Initial contacts were made through persons the Indians knew and trusted— home economists and farm management supervisors of the Indian service and religious leaders—and no attempt was made to explain the purpose of my visit. But in this relaxed atmosphere of friendly conversation many facts emerged that made up the fabric of the Indians' lives. As the interviews multiplied, these facts began to fit into a pattern.

These Indians were living in appalling poverty, which varied somewhat from tribe to tribe. The Cherokees were the hardest hit; the Choctaws and Chickasaws owned more property, but they made the poorest use of their resources; the Creeks, with their more compact land holdings, had retained more of their capacity for self-support; the Seminoles had less economic skill, but they were still supported to a cretain extent by the spectacular oil development of their country.

Throughout the hills the Indians were living in log cabins as their ancestors had done a century before. Most of them raised gardens, and the women knew how to can vegetables and fruit; but the orchards that had surrounded their dwellings in tribal days had disappeared. They carried their water from springs and did their laundry in the back yard. Although a few of the women were slatterns, the majority kept their crowded, dilapidated houses surprisingly neat. The washings that hung on their lines were clean, their beds were clean, and there were flowers blooming in their yards. And although flies were not plentiful—probably because they had no stables or privies as breeding places—their sleeping babies were invariably protected with mosquito nets.

Thanks to the opportunities of war and post-war industry, most of these families had some members working in an Oklahoma or a West Coast city. Some of them had been sustaining themselves outside for many years. And of those who remained in the hills, many of the men—at least in the summer when the survey was made—found some work as unskilled laborers cutting timber, building electric power lines, constructing flood control dams. The women and children and some of the men worked in the commercial truck gardens and berry patches of the area, or even picked wild berries for sale. Apparently none of them lacked for food when I saw them.

When the extension service of the Indian Bureau was established in 1930, the agricultural agents in those desperate depression years *talked* farming to Indians who did not own a single farm implement or one head of livestock, and distributed the Red Cross and other relief that alone kept them from starving to death. (I mean *to death.*) Then came the passage of the Oklahoma Indian Welfare Act. Young Herbert Kinnard, a recent graduate of the state agricultural college, came to the Cherokee hills in 1937 just before credit under the Act became available.

He made a revealing survey of a community around Nicut, a tiny village northeast of Sallisaw. It had been one of the first settlements made by the Cherokees when they came to Oklahoma more than a century before, only five or six miles from the cabin where the great Sequoyah had lived and taught his people to read and write their language. The first settlers had cleared the level places and practiced a subsistence agriculture, raising cotton for their homespun garments, and corn for their food and feed for their livestock running the range. Later, as white enterprise began to penetrate the hills, the land was placed under more intensive cultivation and lumbering became important. Now the marketable timber was gone, and the soil was gone.

One hundred families were receiving their mail at the vil-

lage post office. Seventy-five of these were Indian families, all
with a high degree of Indian blood. Most of these belonged to
the landless generation, and were squatting on the allotments
of friends or relatives. Only about one-fifth of the six-mile-
square township remained in Indian hands. A map of the area
showed a graphic picture of Indian dwellings crowded on these
contracted holdings. One generous old woman was furnishing asylum to six families living in miserable log cabins on her
sixty acres. One of the cabins housed sixteen people. Much of
of the land lost to the Indians had been bought by non-
residents, who were fencing it for cattle. They estimated twenty
acres to the animal—a larger per capita acreage than the
Indians had. Needless to say, it was not supporting them. Half
of the families were living on public assistance.

In another community I saw five families living on their
deceased father's allotment—sixty acres that would hardly
have supported one family. Their families were large—one
with eleven children, almost unbelievably ragged. The five
houses were poverty-stricken hovels, but family pride still existed there, for flowers were blooming in the yards. Even this
land base was breaking up, for there were fifteen heirs and a
forced sale was imminent. (The mother's land had gone
three months before.) An honest county judge—a Cherokee
himself who looked like a fullblood—would see that the land
sold for its full three dollars an acre value, but five families
would still be homeless.

Herbert Kinnard had some dramatic successes with families
still owning land. He began with the strawberry-growing operation that had barely started when I wrote this book in the
late 1930's. Now I had the opportunity to learn the whole
story. The work animals of the entire settlement totaled one
horse owned by an old preacher, and even if farm equipment
had been available, the land was too rough for cultivation.
Mr. Kinnard analysed the mantle of loose rock that covers
those "flint hills" and concluded that it would grow strawberries; he analysed just as closely the character of the

Indians and decided they were adapted to the painstaking hand work. He held many meetings with them and helped them organize. They borrowed $2,800 with which they bought a team and paid some other necessary expenses, but much of the money was advanced to the members for food and to be deducted from their share of the profits. They set out twenty acres, which was later increased to forty.

The first year was crucial: back-breaking work, with only the promise of a next year's crop to a people who had never experienced success. (A survey had shown that the average cash income of these families was $54 a year.) But the co-operative cleared its debt and paid each of its member families an average annual profit of $600. It was dissolved in 1946 with complete goodwill, and the members branched out on their own.

By the time of my survey strawberry-raising had been taken up by white growers around Stilwell, and it had become an important Oklahoma industry. But the local banker estimated that over half of the proceeds went to Indians. Although some of this no doubt was wages paid to Indian pickers by white growers, Mr. Kinnard had 150 families growing berries and expected to have 300 the next year. All these ventures had been started with small loans, usually about $500.

The required equipment was "a Georgia stock, a crook-necked hoe, and a fifteen-year-old mule." First the scrub timber was cleared off, but soil erosion could never be a problem for the hills are nothing but rock piles. In planting, the Indian carried a pail of soil and a pail of water. He pushed the stones aside with a blow of a dull ax to form a triangular hole, and placed a handful of soil in this depression; then he set his plant and watered it. The roots eventually found their way between the rock fragments, but commercial fertilizer was necessary.

Fearing the effects of a one-crop agriculture, Mr. Kinnard also encouraged the growth of cattle herds, the raising and canning of food, and the commercial growing of beans, cu-

cumbers, tomatoes, and boysenberries. But obviously his work could extend only to Indians with available land, and it had the obvious limitation of one man's time and strength. He was helping only four or five hundred Cherokees out of a needy six thousand. (The Nicut community, for example, had not even been touched.) At the end of the fiscal year 1948 there had been 363 loans made in Adair County since the program started, and about half that number in each of the adjoining hill counties. These 363 loans totaled $168,567.49, of which $120,329.94 had been repaid ($2,773.57 through foreclosure), $47,821.11 was still outstanding, and only $416.44 had been charged off as lost. A remarkable record by adding machine standards, but more remarkable in establishing people in self-support.

I found fewer successful loan clients in the Choctaw and Chickasaw country. Here the landless Indian had developed a special form of squatting, collecting on their church grounds, using the camp houses built in tribal days for their week-end or week-long meetings; and their chief support came from public assistance or veterans' benefits.

In one Choctaw region a disillusioned director of the county credit association, a very able and prominent Choctaw, said he had known only one Indian who had profited by the loan policy. The others had used the money for living expenses, paid it back with sweat and tears, and reverted to their former status. This county had made a total of thirty-nine loans, but all the fullblood settlements I saw were grouped around the churches or hidden in scrub timber, untouched by the rehabilitation program. It required a demonstration, but how could one start the initial effort? In the mountains of Pushmataha County was a Choctaw community with total agricultural assets of one wagon, owned by a widow. The whole neighborhood used it—when it was in condition to use. These Indians owned good land far to the west and lived inadequately on rentals.

But in some Choctaw areas were excellent farmers who had

got their start through the loan fund. In the comparatively
level land around Idabel, where wealthy mixed bloods more
than a century before had laid out their great cotton plantations, there were leached-out, eroded, abandoned fields grown
up to brush, and requiring extensive fertilization to bring them
back into production. Here I talked with fullblood, or apparently fullblood, Choctaws who were producing good field
crops, raising beef or dairy herds, and reclaiming their land
through scientific conservation practices.

It was a revelation to hear a Choctaw settled on eighty acres
of family land talk in this wise to the farm management supervisor. "I'm getting ready to improve that pasture. I'm going
to start at the far end and clear out the brush and make it
good. I need to mow this end to kill the weeds. I'm going to get
a mower. And what do you think of putting fertilizer and
sowing it to lespedeza?" He had accumulated a good dairy
herd, was raising a fine bunch of shoats in an enclosure he had
fenced, and had enlarged his house and built a porch. His
wife was canning fruit. The house was neat. The yard also
was neat, though in the absence of a mower they had stretched
a wire around it and were cropping the grass by mule power.
And yet before they embarked on the loan program, their farming experience had been limited to planting a patch of corn
for the native hominy dish.

In the mountains other Choctaw fullbloods had gone into
the cattle business, raising their feed in the valleys and using
the free range then permitted under Oklahoma law. An initial
loan of seven or eight hundred dollars bought a team and some
farm implements, three or four cows, and perhaps a sewing
machine and a stove for the wife. Some with this start had accumulated good herds; a few had even bought land of their
own.

I found the best farmers of all among the Creeks. These
Indians, with better land, had never reached the poverty and
despair of the Cherokee hill dwellers; and they had escaped
the sterile homestead and distant "surplus" combination that

had taught the Choctaws to starve on rentals. Most of them had been farming on a scale too small for profit, but they *were* farming. The loans gave them the required start. One example will illustrate the progress I saw repeated numerous times.

At the time the loan policy started, a young landless Creek with a high degree of Indian blood was living on a fine forty-acre tract belonging to another Creek, farming inadequately with one team. Then one of his horses died in the midst of the busy season, and he came diffidently to the farm management supervisor, Al Feighny of Holdenville.

In the ten years since that time he had bought the forty acres and rented another eighty. He was growing peanuts, cotton, and corn; and his terraced fields were beautifully culti-vated. He lived with his thrifty wife and well-dressed children in a comfortable house with butane fuel and electricity, set in a well-kept lawn. There was a tractor and other farm ma-chinery under shelter and a sturdy old car in the garage. The barnyard was covered with chickens, and the cream check was a weekly asset. All this he and his wife had earned through the judicious use of borrowed capital and the advice of an expert in the beginning years. Now he made his own plans and talked to Mr. Feighny man to man. In fact, when I visited him Mr. Feighny was asking *his* advice about a beginning client.

Of course not all the Creeks had access to good land. And many, like Indians of the other tribes, were completely land-less. A start had been made in helping this class by the pur-chase under the Oklahoma Indian Welfare Act of a few tracts for the tribes, which with the small areas left over from allotment brought the total up to 36,000 acres. It was in the fullblood settlements, and much of it was of sub-marginal quality. Every tribe except the Seminole received a share. Small, snug houses were built on some of the tracts by Indian Relief and Rehabilitation (Indian counterpart of WPA) la-bor. Management by incorporated groups as envisioned by the

Act failed to develop, but the land was there and could be used.

The Cherokees in their desperate need simply started to move on. When I visited them, 57 families were living on about 9,000 mountainous acres south of Stilwell, and Herbert Kinnard was helping them with agricultural planning and credit. Their attainments varied, but all were far removed from the hopeless poverty of their landless brethren.

One would never find a more attractive place in town or country than the small newly-built house occupied by one Indian couple. They were of early middle age, fullbloods of limited education. Both were landless; they had been crowded into the cabin of the wife's mother, a good woman, who in spite of difficulties had trained her daughter in the old-time Cherokee housekeeping. Now their yard was carefully kept, their house was modern in taste and furnishings, and beautifully canned fruit and vegetables were on the shelves. The man did his farming with one small well-cared-for horse, raising fine patches of strawberries and beans. They paid their tribe sixty-five dollars a year rental, but their feeling was that of owners, not tenants.

Farther down the road was a log cabin with a few surrounding acres in a rich spot of valley, the home of an elderly couple, speaking very little English, farming in the old way and filling a log storehouse with food. They paid fifteen dollars a year rental, and felt a security they had not experienced since through some sort of legal legerdemain they lost their allotments. On the edge of a wider valley lived a middle-aged son of Redbird Smith. He and his numerous brothers and sisters were landless, for in their youth at the behest of their father they got the restrictions removed from their allotments, and mortgaged and subsequently lost them in an ill-conceived effort to set up a community co-operative and to finance some fruitless appeals to Washington to restore the old order. Now Redbird's son was using 160 acres of this tribal land, for which—with much grumbling, for he felt it was *his* land—he paid eighty dollars a year. Half was in cultivation, the rest in range. He was a good farmer, as his father had been before him, raising corn and potatoes and feed for his livestock and running a sorghum mill. He held many friendly arguments with Mr. Kinnard as to the relative merits of college agriculture and Cherokee signs and nature lore. His son lived close by in one of the newly-built houses, and he too was prospering.

In general, the Choctaws were not making effective use of their purchased land, though I found a few exceptions. But a landless group of Chickasaws, too often content to lease their allotments, was making a notable success of subsistence farming on 569 acres of broken land along a creek east of Ada. Some of the purchases for the Creeks proved to be unsuitable land subject to overflow, but they had placed the best of it under power-operated efficiency.

The progress of two landless brothers furnishes a good case study. In the desperate poverty of the 1930s they had paid eight dollars for tax title to sixty acres of worthless wooded hillside along the North Canadian, where they built cabins for their families and lived precariously by trapping, cutting wood, or finding a few days' work in the neighborhood. Mr. Feighny settled them on the tract acquired by their town—Alabama-Quassarte—and started them off with a loan. When I saw them, they were successful farmers by any man's standards. Two young sons of one of them were cutting hay. A boy about ten was driving the tractor with expert mastery, while his sixteen-year-old brother was following on the mower, laying the tall bluestem grass out in long, even swaths. They were handsome lads, farm boys who would have been a credit to any community in the United States.

But the success of the agricultural program was curtailed by the shortage of farm management supervisors—only fifteen for the whole Five Tribes area. At the close of my 1949 survey I answered the question with which I had closed my book nine years before: The lost fullbloods could indeed be saved. But I raised another question: Would sufficient effort be made to save them? The answer was not long in coming.

In 1950 the policy known as "termination" was launched by the Indian Bureau under Commissioner Dillon S. Myer, and it was followed throughout the eight years of the Eisenhower administration by Myer's successor, Glenn L. Emmons. It was advocated by both party platforms in the presidential campaign of 1952, and was officially adopted by the following Congress. In practice it meant: pull the land out from under the Indians and break up their communities. The uprooted Indians were to be shipped to distant cities and assisted in finding work and adjusting themselves to urban life. This migration had long existed among Indians, just as it had with white Americans, but when the "relocation" was joined with the drive of the Myer and Emmons era to make rural life untenable, it became part of the pattern. With the Five Tribes most of it could be carried out administratively.

In 1956 the Association on American Indian Affairs under a grant from the Field Foundation made an objective study of the relocation policy, and it became my duty to investigate its operation in Oklahoma. For the Five Tribes I found that, according to the statistics of the preceding fiscal year, 144 "units" (i.e., wage earners) totaling with their families 440 persons had been relocated, mainly in Los Angeles. Of these, 23 "units" totaling 58 persons had returned. These figures indicated that even at its best—and I saw it at its best—relocation had barely scratched the surface of the Five Tribes Indians' economic problems.

I was impressed by the dedicated spirit of the Indian service employees in charge. The Muskogee Area Director (new title for the superintendent) had assigned to the program people known and trusted by the Indians, either as members of the tribes or as white people with a long record of field service among them. They made every effort to prepare the relocatees for their new experiences, and tried to follow them up by friendly letters, many written at home on their own typewriters during weekends.

In general, the Indians regarded relocation as an opportunity. Even those who had given up and returned said it was "all right." But in a deeper sense this support came from the realization that it was the only prospect in sight. I tried to discover why, with the almost universal approval of relocation, that more did not avail themselves of it and that some returned. The answer seemed to lie in the realm of imponderables: the forces that had kept them in the same communities for fifty or sixty years after they were supposedly distributed among the general population. There was a security in knowing that if one person in the neighborhood sold a piece of land or cashed a relief check, all would share. There was a sense of history that united them and their ancestors who had lived on this same soil. I had a strange feeling that many of the successful relocatees would come back eventually.

These community ties were purposely severed by the administration. I attended a half-hour meeting of Indian leaders called by Carl Beck, who had headed the relocation program of the Washington office. They were not unfriendly, but one of them asked, "Why do you send them so far away?" He answered that if they were in nearby cities they would "get homesick" and would go back to visit their old neighbors on weekends. Later I talked with Richard Chuculate, a young Cherokee who was making an intensive study of a fullblood Cherokee community for his master's thesis in a school of social service. He was not aware of Beck's statement, but he volunteered the information that Indians working in Tulsa or Muskogee regularly returned to their old homes to attend church, and that they needed this steadying influence—"without those church ties they drift to the taverns."

Another way to separate the Indians from their communities was the discontinuance of agricultural assistance. In 1954 the Indian Bureau had made a determined attempt to persuade

Congress to turn this work over to the state agricultural colleges. In the hearings on the bill the tie-up of credit and
agricultural guidance was mentioned with disfavor by Assistant Secretary of the Interior Orme Lewis; and a clear explanation and defense of the connection was expressed in
Indian protests against the transfer. But Congress failed to
act, and the change was thereupon made administratively
under the Johnson-O'Malley Act of 1934 by which the Indian
Bureau could make contracts with state or local agencies to
carry on its work. The Oklahoma contract, involving agricultural and home economics extension, was made March 1,
1956. The farm management supervisors were given the opportunity of transferring to the state service; but in the Five
Tribes area all except one refused, saying that credit was the
heart of the program, and separated from that, they could
give no help to the most needy Indians.

Not only were they separated from the credit branch of the
Indian service, but the credit itself was discontinued. The
credit division at the Area Office became simply a collection
agency. The theory was that other sources of credit were available. This was simply not true, when the Indians had only
restricted land and no other property as security for a loan.

There was one adverse condition for which the Bureau was
not responsible. Oklahoma agriculture had become mechanized
to the extent that large-scale operations were displacing the
small farmer, both Indian and white. I was careful to check
the Indians I had seen successfully farming in 1949, and
found that virtually all of them had continued to prosper.
Having made their start, they had adjusted themselves to this
development. But by 1956 it required too much land and
capital and too much managerial skill on the part of a beginning Indian to launch him in so large an enterprise. Even so,
all informed people in touch with the situation were convinced
that there was need for a sound credit program to enable
Indians working part time for wages to supplement their in-

come by what they could produce on land units too small for full-time farming. The Indians were desperately unhappy over the cutting off of credit.

It required four more years for me to uncover the status of the revolving loan fund. Finally, Albert Huber, chief of the credit branch of the Indian Bureau, furnished the information that on April 30, 1960 the Oklahoma balance was $1,212,501.03. It was lying idle in the Federal treasury, and not an Indian could touch it.

Meanwhile, at the time of my survey in 1956 the new men of the state agricultural extension service were earnestly trying to make their work productive. There were nine of them for the entire state whereas fifteen had been working in the Five Tribes half. They could tell a successful Indian farmer the newest way of fighting boll weevils or explain the provisions of Federal parity payments, but beyond that they could not go. And the poverty was unrelieved. I sat in the public welfare office of a Five Tribes county and watched the people come in for surplus commodities. Three-fourths of them were Indians, apparently able bodied, and—in spite of their needs—upright and self-respecting. The director, himself an Indian, said that they were not lazy, but that their land and the work they could pick up simply would not buy their food. He had found their integrity remarkable: if one ever got a chance to better his situation, he came in at once and reported, to have the relief stopped.

It will be remembered that the restrictions on Five Tribes allotments had been extended to 1956. As this date approached, Congressman Ed Edmondson, whose district included the Cherokee fullblood settlements, introduced a bill to extend them for the lifetime of the original allottee. (Oklahoma by this time had reached a state of maturity where its Congressional delegation worked to protect the Indians rather than to exploit them.) Orme Lewis testified that "a large number" of the allottees did not need this protection, and that "it would be unwise" to extend it except by the Secretary of

the Interior in individual cases. But the bill passed late in the
session of 1955 through the efforts of the Oklahoma delegation. At that time the restricted land had shrunk to 750,000
acres.

In the presidential election of 1960 both party platforms
repudiated the termination dogma, and both candidates made
enlightened personal commitments. A constructive Indian
policy has accordingly been carried out through the Kennedy,
Johnson, and Nixon administrations. The revolving loan fund
was reactivated, though usually, with the Five Tribes, for
small business ventures rather than for agriculture. In fiscal
year 1971 the land base totaled 285,599 acres of restricted
allotments, 288,591 acres owned by heirs of allottees, 39,246
acres owned by the Tribes and 20,484 acres of Government
land assigned to Indian use. This shrinkage, plus the continued increase in agricultural mechanization and the aging of
the allottees (the youngest now being sixty-six), has discouraged new farming undertakings. Only two agricultural
extension agents are now employed—at Idabel and Stilwell—
and they concentrate mainly on youth work and family life.
Three home economists work with Indian women—at Holdenville, Stilwell, and Jay.

The Muskogee office still has to devote too much time to
technicalities growing out of the tribal liquidation. For example, the Government finally bought the Choctaw-Chickasaw
coal and asphalt land in 1948 for eight and a half million
dollars, which the Superintendent had to pay out per capita to
the enrolled tribal citizens and their heirs, hopefully the last
act in dividing their estates. The winning of several claims
against the Government for actions far back in tribal history
has involved similar office work in the disbursement.

One reversal of the tribal liquidation was the election of
Principal Chiefs (Chickasaw, Governor) in 1971 under an
act passed by Congress the previous year upon the urging of
the Indians. All enrolled members of the tribes and their
descendants who had registered for the election were eligible to

vote; and voting was by secret ballot under the supervision of committees appointed by the Tribes. Two of those elected had long been serving as appointed Chiefs: of the Cherokees, W. W. Keeler, chairman of the board of directors of Phillips Petroleum Corporation, who had given much time to the economic problems of the hill people; and of the Choctaws, Harry J. W. Belvin, a prominent rancher of Durant, who had been very aggressive in defending Indian rights.

With the depletion of the oil fields in Eastern Oklahoma the Muskogee office no longer has to cope with the problems of wealthy Indians and their guardians. Under the present Area Director, Virgil N. Harrington, the office is oriented towards the uplift of the economically depressed. Its services are concentrated mainly on welfare, industrial development in retarded communities, education, and vocational training.

An active housing program is in process in rural areas and small towns, principally through contacts with the Department of Housing and Urban Development. The Area Office has been involved in the location of thirty-one industrial plants employing six hundred Indian workers with a total income in 1971 of $2,064,192. The education of Indian children is carried out mainly in the public schools under a Johnson-O'Malley contract made in 1947. Only orphans and children with an intolerable home situation are maintained in boarding schools. Seventeen hundred students received financial assistance to attend colleges and universities during the 1971–72 school year. There were approximately two hundred graduates, fifty of whom received master's degrees, one a doctorate. Vocational training is available under Public Law 959 passed in 1956 through the efforts of Congressman Edmondson. There are now 565 "units" enrolled. Three hundred of these are at Okmulgee Tech, a branch of Oklahoma State University without academic entrance requirements. According to a study I made in 1963 the most popular course there was auto mechanics, with auto body work and diesel mechanics running close, and printing and drafting not far behind. The graduates were having no difficulty in finding employment in Oklahoma, though a few took advantage of the relocation program, now truly voluntary.

Since 1967 relocation services have been provided in Tulsa and Oklahoma City. Two hundred "units" are now being served in Tulsa (favored by its East Side location). But 135 "units" are in cities outside the state, the reason for their choice being higher wages or the presence of relatives relocated in those places under the old program. The present financial assistance is now $360 for a single person, and up to $100 for a large family.

The problems of Indians in the backwash settlements are receiving more sympathy than in previous years from the general population. Oklahoma had been slow to admit that the liquidation of tribes and tribal holdings to which it owed its existence had not brought all the separated individuals into happy participation in the dominant society. Even prominent state leaders of noticeable Indian blood were unaware of the situation or brushed it aside as a reproach to their pride of race. But recently the universities have become interested in Indian studies and concerned about Indian welfare. Out of this trend grew an important movement at the University of Oklahoma.

In 1963 the University launched an effort to enlist in unified community programs white civic leaders and Indians living apart somewhere on the edge of the towns in Western Oklahoma. Through the leadership of a member of the Comanche tribe, Mrs. LaDonna Harris, the wife of Senator Fred R. Harris, this grew into a statewide organization, Oklahomans for Indian Opportunity. In 1966 it received a grant of $240,733 from the Office of Economic Opportunity, and employed an able Indian woman as full-time director and a number of Indian field workers. It chose locations of Indian concentration and developed (1) programs of community improvement carried out by Indians and non-Indians working together, (2) work orientation, enlisting employers in training Indian workers, and (3) youth activities, helping Indian high school students acquire qualities of leadership.

The organization expanded its work through grass roots activity, culminating in annual Indian Achievement Conferences and Indian Youth Conferences at the University of Oklahoma with nationally known speakers and awards to communities and individuals. In 1968 it received an OEO grant of $470,277 to conduct a comprehensive three-year Rural Development Program in ten Cherokee and Choctaw hill counties. This was carried out by ten neighborhood workers, whose required qualifications included residence in the county and ability to speak the local Indian language.

Out of these experiences have grown small loans, often through referral to the Small Business Administration—for equipment to set up an Indian as a house painter, assistance to an Indian television repair man to open a shop, and similar undertakings. An important project is the Lost City Cooperative Marketing Association organized in the hills of Cherokee County with twenty family members in August 1969 to raise feeder pigs. Now it has 155 members in thirteen Cherokee, Creek, and Choctaw counties, and has raised and shipped a total of 21,152 pigs at a value of $333,529. It is the largest shipper and seller of pigs in Oklahoma, shipping to feed lots within the state and in Nebraska, Kansas, and Iowa. Another enterprise is the Cherokee Forest Industries organized by the Indians of Bull Hollow in Delaware County in January 1971. About forty Cherokee woodcutters furnish the cordwood, and three other employees work full time at the kiln to produce charcoal, which is sold to a Missouri firm.

It is no longer possible for me to drive through the hills and blackjacks to observe the results of the present policy. Probably I should still find pockets of social and economic stagnation. Also I might find sections in the cities of Oklahoma where Indians unable to adjust have gravitated to urban slums. But, looking from the outside, it seems possible that educational and economic opportunities may be developing a generation of Five Tribes fullbloods drawing strength and security from their past but equipped to face the present. Thus with an enlightened Federal policy, a dedicated Area Office, and a growing public awareness, I am even daring to hope that the lost fullbloods are being saved.

ANGIE DEBO

*Marshall, Oklahoma*
June 10, 1972

AND STILL THE WATERS RUN

CHAPTER I

# The Indians' Country

EVERY American of middle age can remember when his
school geography showed to the south of Kansas a large
unmarred expanse of map designated as the Indian
Territory. While never a territory in the political sense, it was
owned and ruled by the five autonomous Indian republics
known as the Cherokee, Choctaw, Chickasaw, Creek or Muskogee, and Seminole nations.

Although they were fiercely and passionately devoted to
their homes, these Indians had only recently settled in the West.
Their ancestors when discovered by De Soto were living east
of the Mississippi in the Gulf and southern Appalachian
region. When first visited by Europeans they were an agricultural people, raising corn, beans, squashes, and tobacco; but
they also depended largely upon hunting and fishing. They
soon began trading with the English settled along the Atlantic
seaboard, the Spanish in Florida, and the French in Louisiana;
and they learned to plant European grains and garden vegetables, and to raise horses, cattle, hogs, and barnyard fowls.

When the United States succeeded to European colonial
influence in the Gulf region, the new government followed a
custom established by its predecessors of making alliances and
treaties with the Indian tribes, but from 1800 on a new problem
arose through the encroachments of its advancing settlements.
One important result of this closer intercourse was the rapidity
with which the Indians, especially the Cherokees and Choctaws, began to adopt the white man's institutions. They invited
Christian missionaries to their country and established
churches and schools, they adopted constitutions and legal
codes, and some of their leaders began to operate plantations

worked by Negro slaves. The progress of the Cherokees was especially rapid at this time, because Sequoyah, one of the greatest geniuses ever produced by any race, invented a phonetic alphabet that enabled the whole tribe to become within a few months a literate people.

But this advancement in civilization served only to provoke the frontiersmen to increased hostility, because it enabled the Indians to contest their encroachments more effectively. The United States, to relieve its Western settlers, began to purchase outlying portions of the Indians' territory in exchange for money and annuities and wild tracts of land beyond the Mississippi. A gradual emigration took place to these new lands, but it was apparent that most of the Indians were determined to strengthen their institutions and remain in their ancestral homes. The period of forcible removal began when Andrew Jackson became President in 1829. His policy was embodied in the Indian Removal Act of 1830, which expressed the settled purpose of the Government to locate the Eastern tribes beyond the frontier.[1]

At the same time there was a feverish and speculative development of the rich Gulf cotton lands, and reports of gold discovery in the Cherokee country in Georgia caused prospectors to rush in, tearing down the Indians' fences and destroying their crops. The states began to pass laws breaking down the tribal autonomy of these unwelcome independent communities that were obstructing their settlement. In 1829 Mississippi extended her state laws over Choctaw and Chickasaw lands joining organized counties, and in 1830 the Indians were made citizens of Mississippi and forbidden under penalty of fine and imprisonment to hold any tribal office. Georgia also extended her jurisdiction over the Cherokee country, forbade the tribal legislature to meet except for the purpose of ratifying land cessions, and invited her citizens to rob and plunder their Indian neighbors at will by making it illegal for an Indian to bring suit or testify against a white man. When President

---

[1] *Statutes at Large of the United States of America* (Boston, Washington, 1854-1934), IV, 411-12, May 28, 1830.

Jackson began to negotiate with the Indians under authority of the Indian Removal Act, he pointed to the inability of the Federal Government to prevent this extension of state sovereignty, and held out a guarantee of perpetual autonomy in the West as the strongest incentive to emigration.

By a combination of bribery, trickery, and intimidation the Federal agents induced all five tribes during the 1830's to cede the remainder of their Eastern lands to the United States and to agree to migrate beyond the Mississippi. All these removal treaties contained the most solemn guarantees that the Indians' titles to these new lands should be perpetual and that no territorial or state government should ever be erected over them without their consent. Some of the treaties also contained provisions by which individual Indians might accept allotments in the land they had ceded and hold them under the white man's laws.

The tragic suffering of the exiles on the "Trail of Tears" is familiar to all students of American history. It is matched only by the saturnalia of exploitation to which they were subjected by land speculators who crowded them from their homes before the time fixed for their emigration, and who possessed themselves of their individual allotments by every possible combination of violence and fraud.[2] The Indians emerged from this experience with the most invincible determination to maintain their tribal autonomy in the West against the encroachments of territorial or state government, and to guard their tribal holdings against the white man's system of land tenure, when history should begin to repeat itself upon their new frontier.

As soon as they were settled in their new homes these Indians made such remarkable social and political progress that they soon became known as the Five Civilized Tribes to distinguish them from their wild neighbors of the plains.[3] At first they owned all of the present state of Oklahoma except the "Pan-

---

[2] Grant Foreman, *Indian Removal* (Norman, Oklahoma, 1932).
[3] *Idem, The Five Civilized Tribes* (Norman, Oklahoma, 1934).

handle," but they made alliances with the Confederacy at the outbreak of the Civil War, and when they resumed treaty relations with the United States they were compelled to surrender the western half of their territory as a penalty for their "rebellion."[4] Part of this ceded land was used by the Federal Government for the settlement of other Indian tribes, and the remainder by a series of "Openings" from 1889 on was thrown open to white homesteaders and became the Territory of Oklahoma.

The land retained by the Five Civilized Tribes continued to be known as the Indian Territory. It consisted of 19,525,966 acres divided as follows: the Choctaws controlled 6,953,048 acres in the southeastern part; the Chickasaws exercised jurisdiction over 4,707,903 acres west of the Choctaws; the Cherokees owned 4,420,068 acres in the northeast; the Creeks owned a 3,079,095-acre tract southwest of the Cherokees; and the Seminoles were settled on 365,852 acres which they had purchased from their near kinsmen, the Creeks. The Choctaws and Chickasaws, who are very closely related, owned their lands jointly, but their settlements were fairly distinct and each tribe exercised complete jurisdiction over its own district.[5]

In spite of the losses and spoliations which they had sustained, the Indians still owned a princely domain. Larger than several of the Atlantic states, the Indian Territory was approximately the size of South Carolina, and almost as large as Indiana. The Creek and Chickasaw nations contained some of the best agricultural land of the present state of Oklahoma; much of the Choctaw country was covered with valuable timber, and extensive coal fields were opened soon after the Civil War; and the Cherokee, Creek, Chickasaw, and Seminole lands were destined to produce a large share of that flowing gold that was to make Oklahoma famous for its fantastic wealth.

---

[4] Annie Heloise Abel, *The American Indian as Slaveholder and Secessionist* (Cleveland, Ohio, 1915); *The American Indian as Participant in the Civil War* (Cleveland, Ohio, 1919); *The American Indian under Reconstruction* (Cleveland, Ohio, 1925).

[5] Department of the Interior, *Annual Report,* 1919, II, 342.

Each tribe also owned a large sum of money derived from the sale of its Eastern lands and held in trust by the United States. The income formed a considerable part of the revenue of the tribes and was appropriated by their legislatures for the support of their governments and schools. These trust funds in 1894 were:[6]

| Cherokee | $2,716,979.98 |
|---|---|
| Choctaw | 975,258.91 |
| Chickasaw | 1,206,695.66 |
| Creek | 2,275,168.00 |
| Seminole | 2,070,000.00 |

Each tribe formed an intensely nationalistic small republic with distinctive customs and institutions. The Creeks and Seminoles were conservative, but the other three tribes were eagerly receptive of any custom which they considered superior to their own.

The conversion of all the tribes to Christianity had been effected rapidly after the Removal. There was some brief hostility especially among the Creeks to the work of the missionaries, but upon the whole the new religion was readily and gladly accepted. Naturally a devout people with deep mystical feeling and a strong sense of moral obligation and family and group solidarity, they found Christian teachings fitted to their own way of thought. Every remote settlement had its Presbyterian, Methodist, or Baptist church, and the Indians combined their religious zeal with their love for community gatherings in the brush arbor camp meeting with its all-day services. A few missionaries continued to work among them, but most of their preachers were Indians, often college trained.[7]

Each tribe maintained a complete school system under its own administrative officials. Elementary education was carried on in the neighborhood schools, which in their irregular at-

[6] Commissioner of Indian Affairs, *Annual Report*, 1894, pp. 475-78.

[7] *Report of the Select Committee to Investigate Matters Connected with Affairs in the Indian Territory* (*Senate Reports*, 59 Cong. 2 Sess., No. 5013), I, 690-91, 696; Angie Debo, *The Rise and Fall of the Choctaw Republic* (Norman, Oklahoma, 1934), pp. 63-65, 229-32.

tendance and inadequate instruction, corresponded to the rural schools of the adjoining states. Each tribe also maintained several boarding schools with highly qualified faculties, and at least one tribe paid the expenses of a selected group of young people in the great universities of the country. As a result of this boarding school and college training there was a larger proportion of educated people among the Cherokees, Choctaws, and Chickasaws than among the white people of the neighboring states. Some of the children, however, failed to profit from these educational opportunities, and there was considerable illiteracy so far as knowledge of English is concerned.[8]

It is apparent that with the possible exception of the Seminoles, about whom little is known, practically all the Indians were accustomed to reading books and newspapers in their own language.[9] The Presbyterian missionaries, who began their work among the Choctaws in Mississippi in 1818, began to translate books into Choctaw and to hold native language schools for the adult Indians. Later, although their spoken dialect differs somewhat from the Choctaw, the Chickasaws were able to use this same written language. After the Removal, the missionaries reduced the Creek-Seminole language to a simple written form. As a result of Sequoyah's great invention the Cherokees established a national newspaper in 1828. Under the name of the *Cherokee Phoenix* and the *Cherokee Advocate* this paper continued through most of the tribal period, and served to keep even the most conservative fullbloods well informed on all public questions. The Choctaws and the Creeks also made some attempt to maintain national newspapers, but in general they were not successful.[10] Of the privately owned papers a few were owned and edited by Indian citizens, but the great majority were published by white residents and advocated a policy inimical to Indian interests. Even these foreign

[8] *Select Committee,* I, 1051; II, 1169, 1172; Debo, *op. cit.,* pp. 42-45, 60-63, 236-43; Commissioner of Indian Affairs, *Annual Report,* 1893, pp. 146-48.

[9] *Select Committee,* I, 318, 690-91.

[10] Debo, *op. cit.,* pp. 226-28; Carolyn Thomas Foreman, *Oklahoma Imprints* (Norman, Oklahoma, 1936), pp. 55, 76-85, 190-94.

publications, however, usually carried columns in the local Indian language.

The United States maintained a protectorate over these Indian republics. The rights of each were based upon an elaborate system of treaties extending from the beginning of the American Government to the agreements negotiated at the close of the Civil War; and although it had long been a recognized principle of law that Congress had the legal right to abrogate a treaty by statute, the Federal officials up to 1890 showed some decent hesitation about breaking the pledges to the Five Civilized Tribes. The Indian leaders quoted the treaties with such skill and fluency that they invariably outdebated their white opponents, and even the most conservative fullbloods knew their terms and insisted upon their fulfilment.

The United States maintained a representative to the tribes, known as the Union Agent with offices at Muskogee, in the Creek Nation. He was assisted by two clerks, and he used a small force of Indian police, citizens of the various nations, as enforcement officers. His duties were purely diplomatic and advisory, and few men who held the office made a serious attempt to inform themselves regarding the internal affairs of the tribes.[11]

Each of the tribes had a constitutional government with a Principal Chief (Chickasaw Governor) and other executive officers; a General Council, bicameral except for the Seminole; and a system of courts. The ancient Creek "town" and the Seminole "band" still formed the local governing unit for these two tribes, but the political divisions of the other three were largely artificial and geographical.[12]

The Indians had a natural genius for politics. Trained through countless generations in the proud democracy of primitive councils, they found their borrowed Anglo-American institutions in perfect harmony with their native development.

[11] This is shown in the agent's annual reports. The Choctaws, for instance, took a periodic census, but the reports are filled with the wildest guesses regarding population and economic statistics; for example, Debo, *op. cit.*, pp. 111n., 114n., 221-22.

[12] Department of the Interior, *Annual Report*, 1900, pp. 85, 118-20, 145-46; Debo, *op. cit.*, pp. 151-63, 236.

Their parliamentary assemblies were models of decorum, and their orators spoke with the disciplined eloquence of a restrained but passionate race. In a political unit so small that it was possible for every voter to have a personal knowledge of candidates and issues, the elections and inaugural ceremonies and the deliberations of the legislatures furnished recreation and excitement for the entire populace. Few communities have ever equalled these small Indian republics in political skill.

But the Indians were noticeably deficient in practical judgment and in business ability, and they showed a tendency to settle every question by making an eloquent speech, adopting a well-worded resolution, or passing a law; and their law enforcement did not correspond with their legal ability or with their elaborate system of courts.

Their legal codes show a curious mixture of primitive custom and Anglo-Saxon law. The punishments were fine, whipping, or death by shooting or hanging. The enforcement officers consisted of sheriffs and a special group of hardy mounted Indians known as lighthorsemen.[13]

The jurisdiction of the courts and participation in the government was limited to citizens. Citizens by blood consisted mainly of those Indians and their descendants who had settled in the Indian Territory at the time of the Removal and had lived there continuously ever since. People of recognized Indian descent who had remained behind or who had been living as white citizens of various states occasionally came to the Territory and were admitted to citizenship by special act of the tribal governments.

The Cherokees, Creeks, and Seminoles had been induced to grant full citizenship to their former slaves at the close of the Civil War. The Choctaws and Chickasaws had secured an optional provision in their peace treaty, and the United States agreed to remove the freedmen within two years and colonize them elsewhere if the Indians should decide against adoption.

[13] Debo, *op. cit.*, pp. 175-78.

Both tribes promptly voted for their removal, but the United States failed to take action. Finally, after twenty years, the Choctaws adopted their freedmen and gave them the limited economic, educational, and political privileges permissable under the treaty; but the Chickasaws, except for a temporary weakening in 1873, continued to petition for the fulfilment of the treaty during the remainder of the tribal period.[14]

The Cherokees, Choctaws, and Chickasaws also admitted intermarried whites to citizenship. There had been considerable admixture of white blood in all the tribes before the Removal, but for a time after the settlement in the West white influence almost disappeared. After the Civil War, with the construction of the first railroads across the Indian Territory and the rapid settlement of the Western frontier, this immigration and intermarriage began again.

The Chickasaws had been recklessly generous to their intermarried citizens, and as a result these white men monopolized the best agricultural lands in the Nation. In 1890 the Indians attempted to protect themselves by enacting a law providing that intermarried citizenship should confer no property or political rights, but the white men held meetings and defiantly resolved that if any attempt were made to dispossess them they would "exterminate every member of this council from the chief down."[15] The Choctaws began to regulate intermarried citizenship before it assumed such serious proportions. They required the applicant to furnish a certificate of good moral character signed by ten Choctaw citizens, to pay a license fee of one hundred dollars, and to renounce the protection of the laws and courts of the United States.[16] The Cherokees conferred no property rights upon those citizens who intermarried after 1877.[17]

There was a certain amount of overlapping settlement beyond the borders of the various tribes and of intermarriage

---

[14] *Ibid.*, pp. 99-109; *United States Supreme Court Reports* (Lawyers' Edition, Rochester, New York, 1904), XLVIII, 640-45.

[15] *Report of the Commission Appointed to Negotiate with the Five Civilized Tribes of Indians, Known as the Dawes Commission* (*Senate Docs.*, 54 Cong., 1 Sess., No. 12), 1895, p. 59. Law enacted October 1, 1890.

[16] Debo, *op. cit.*, pp. 106, 179-80.     [17] *Supreme Court Reports*, LI, 96-105.

between their citizens. This condition was especially noticeable between the Choctaws and Chickasaws and the Creeks and Seminoles. A considerable number of Cherokees and a few Creeks who had been driven from their homes by Northern armies during the Civil War settled in the Choctaw country and made permanent homes there. There was also some exchange of tribal populations across the Creek-Cherokee border.

This intermingling of tribes seldom caused any difficulty. The Choctaws and Chickasaws had a treaty by which the members of either tribe were entitled to all the privileges of citizenship in the other when residing within its jurisdiction. Citizenship in the other tribes was regulated largely by mutual tolerance, but an intertribal code was drawn up in 1859. This agreement provided for the requisition of escaped criminals, made Indians living under a foreign jurisdiction subject to the local courts and laws, and provided for naturalization. It appears from contemporary records that a considerable amount of this naturalization took place.[18]

A more serious problem than white or intertribal citizenship was the non-citizen white immigration, which began to trickle into the Indian Territory soon after the Civil War and became a deluge that engulfed the Indian settlements by the close of the century. A large number of Negroes also came in as laborers in the mines or as tenants on the Indians' farms. Many of the white immigrants were intruders, who had entered the country in defiance of tribal law and had fastened themselves upon the Indians' possessions with a grip that it seemed impossible to break. The most troublesome of the intruders were those who had advanced some fantastic claim to citizenship, and who loudly demanded every privilege enjoyed by the Indians in spite of repeated denials of their claims by the tribal authorities. A large number of the immigrants, however, were legal residents, who conformed to the tribal laws, and whose productive labor was wanted by the Indians. But regardless of status the non-citizens came in such hordes that they soon out-

[18] Debo, *op. cit.*, pp. 66, 71.

numbered the Indians, and the tribal communities as minority governments found it increasingly difficult to maintain their authority.

The first United States census of the Indian Territory, which was made in 1890, shows the approximate racial composition. It classed the inhabitants according to physical appearance without regard to citizenship, but it reveals in a startling way how the Indians were crowded in their last refuge by the pressure of other races. The statistics are as follows:[19]

| NATION | WHITES | NEGROES | INDIANS | TOTAL | PERCENTAGE OF INDIANS |
|--------|--------|---------|---------|-------|-----------------------|
| Cherokee | 29,166 | 5,127 | 22,015 | 56,309 | 39.1 |
| Choctaw | 28,345 | 4,406 | 11,057 | 43,808 | 25.24 |
| Chickasaw | 48,421 | 3,676 | 5,223 | 57,329 | 9.11 |
| Creek | 3,287 | 4,621 | 9,999 | 17,912 | 55.82 |
| Seminole | 172 | 806 | 1,761 | 2,739 | 64.29 |
| TOTAL | 109,393 | 18,636 | 50,055 | 178,097 | 28.11 |

Pleasant Porter, the great and wise Chief of the Creeks, more than any other man of his generation attempted in a detached and philosophic way to analyze the problems of his people. Speaking before a Senatorial committee visiting the Indian Territory in 1906, the old man told of the idyllic conditions of the untroubled life he had known in his boyhood and of their disappearance under the pressure of the new invasion. The unwelcome immigrants "got pretty smart and they wanted taxes and big lots of cattle—they wanted everything that way, and if we didn't do it we were in the soup anyway . . . but we wouldn't listen to them at first, but took them and turned them loose up here on the borders of Kansas and Missouri, but they would come back, and others would come, and we could not keep them out, so they would flow all over us. . . . We have striven in our own way for our elevation and uplifting, and for a time it seemed that we were actually going to evolve a sort of civilization that would suit our temperament; and we prob-

[19] Bureau of the Census, *Extra Census Bulletin, The Five Civilized Tribes of the Indian Territory* (Washington, 1894), pp. 3-5.

ably would if it had not been for this white and black invasion."[20]

According to ancient Indian custom the land was held in all the tribes under communal tenure. Any citizen might cultivate as much land as he wanted and the tribal laws protected him in his right of occupancy and in the possession of his improvements, but as soon as he ceased to use it the title reverted to the Nation. With a natural gift for collective enterprise the Indians were contented and prosperous under a system that seemed actually sacrilegious to the individualistic and acquisitive white man. Pleasant Porter's description presents an accurate picture of the simple but sufficient economic life of the old Indian country, and the way in which it broke down before the restless energy of the invading whites.

"In those days they always raised enough to eat, and that was all we wanted. We had little farms, and we raised patches of corn and potatoes, and poultry and pigs, horses and cattle, and a little of everything, and the country was prosperous. In fact in my early life I don't know that I ever knew of an Indian family that were paupers. There is plenty of them now; there was none then. They were all prosperous and happy and contented in their way, and what more could they want? I say I don't know of an Indian family in my early life that were paupers. In those days the ones that would be paupers if they lived now stayed with their kin folks and they made them work. Now, back of that the custom of the Creeks was that everybody had to work or live on the town, and the town had taskmasters who took care of him and saw that he worked. There was not a skulker or one who shirked amongst us then; quite different from what it is now. We had a kind of an Arcadian government then. If anyone was sick or unable to work, the neighbors came in and planted his crop, and they took care of it—saw that the fences were all right—and the women took care of the garden, and wood was got for him, and so on. In fact, everything was done under the care of the people—they

[20] *Select Committee*, I, 624-25.

1. Dwelling of Creek Fullblood. "We had little farms, and we raised patches of corn and potatoes, and poultry and pigs, horses and cattle."

did everything and looked after the welfare of everything. The Creek had that much knowledge, that they cared for each other in that way; and while they used to live in towns [in Alabama], out here in this peaceful country they had scattered out just like white men, and each one had gone to his farm, . . .

". . . In those days, you know, a hog ran wild in the woods— went just where he liked—only they would be fed regularly a little corn or something to keep them kind of tame and domesticated; but now you have to keep him under fence, you can't leave him out now like then. He is just as unsafe outside to-day as a squirrel is."[21]

By 1890 ranching had changed the character of the Creek country. Under the grazing law of 1889 any Creek head of a family could enclose one square mile of the public domain for pasture purposes without making any payment to the tribe. Then, under the theory that fencing the land along the frontier would keep out the cattle from adjoining tribes, the law contained express provisions for large enclosures there. The citizen who wanted to secure control of a large pasture was required to present a petition to the judge of the district, who would then call an election and submit the question to the voters. If he was successful in this referendum, the enterprising Creek then secured the land under a three-year lease, with the privilege of renewal. He was required to fence it and to pay the Nation an annual rental of five cents an acre. He would then sub-lease it to cattlemen, usually from Texas, and make considerable profit on the transaction.[22]

Under this law most of the prominent Creek families acquired holdings of from thirty thousand to sixty-eight thousand acres. A study made of the leasing situation in 1896 gave a list of sixty-one individual citizens or companies of citizens whose holdings totaled 1,072,215 acres—approximately one-third of

21 *Ibid.,* I, 23, 624-25. Miss Alice M. Robertson, who had a lifelong familiarity with Creek life, also testified regarding neighborhood cooperation and the cultivation of the "town" farms (*ibid.,* I, 688, 693-96). For Choctaw economic life see Debo, *op. cit.,* pp. 110-15.

22 *Muskogee Times-Democrat,* July 9, 1909; *Muskogee Phoenix,* January 19, 1919.

the entire area of the Creek Nation. The Perryman family received an annual rental of $25,000 for their pastures, and the firm of Turner and Porter (Pleasant Porter and Clarence W. Turner, a white man married to a Creek citizen)[23] was next with an income of $16,000.[24]

Among the Cherokees also, large tracts of land were monopolized by a few citizens, usually mixed bloods, for farming or ranching purposes. The same study showed a list of twenty-three Cherokees who controlled a total of 174,000 acres. The eight citizens whose names were at the head of the list each held from ten thousand to twenty thousand acres.[25] But the Cherokees' greatest difficulty was with the intruders, who seized their land, erected improvements, and proved impossible to dislodge. Since they were not recognized as citizens, they were outside tribal jurisdiction, and the Cherokees were unable to secure their expulsion by the Federal authorities.

The Chickasaw tribe, with its small population and its rich agricultural land, had the most serious problem of all. Nearly all the best land was held by intermarried white men or leased to white non-citizens. About 1867 the Nation had tried to prevent this condition by enacting a law, with severe penalties, forbidding a Chickasaw to lease land to a non-citizen for a longer period than a year; but the law was generally evaded by secret agreements between the parties, and although many Chickasaw citizens were indicted for its violation, the practice was so common that it was virtually impossible to find a jury that would convict. As a result, land was leased all over the country for agricultural purposes for terms of from two to fifteen years, and in a few instances even for the lifetime of the parties.[26]

The Choctaws regulated their immigration and the use of their land and natural resources more successfully. It was

[23] *Muskogee Phoenix, loc. cit.*

[24] *Senate Docs.*, 54 Cong., 1 Sess., No. 182, pp. 27-31, testimony of Archibald S. McKennon of the Dawes Commission before the Committee on Indian Affairs.

[25] *Ibid.*, p. 8.

[26] *Ibid.*, p. 38; Overton Love to Dawes Commission, Dawes Commission, *Report,* 1896, pp. 112-13.

made illegal in 1870 to lease the public domain for grazing purposes and in 1877, for agricultural purposes; and in 1880 non-citizens were forbidden to own livestock except a limited number under permit for family use. In 1880 the size of a pasture that could be enclosed by a citizen was limited to one square mile, but two citizens who already held larger pastures continued to use them. These laws were evaded to a certain extent, but the Choctaw country was never monopolized by non-citizen farmers or cattlemen.[27]

The Choctaws were usually classed as the best business men of the Five Tribes, and some of their wealthiest citizens belonged to fullblood or nearly fullblood families. The richest Choctaw, Wilson N. Jones, was said to hold 17,600 acres under fence, of which 550 acres was under cultivation, and to own 5,000 cattle, 75 horses, several coal mines, a store, and a cotton gin. It was not illegal for a citizen to lease his personal holdings to non-citizens, and most of the labor on these great farms was performed by white or Negro tenants.[28]

The rich coal mines, of course, belonged to the Nation, but Choctaw law recognized the right of a citizen to stake out a mining claim that covered a radius of one mile from the point of discovery. The canny Choctaws often employed mining experts to assist them in discovering coal veins, and most of the well-to-do citizens owned mines. A tribal official, the National Agent, leased these mines to operators under strict public regulation, and collected the royalties, which were divided equally between the Nation and the citizen who owned the mine. In 1890 the National Treasurer's report showed that $57,839.49 in royalty had been turned into the tribal treasury that year. Timber sales also were placed exclusively under the control of the National Agent, and, as the lumbering industry developed, these royalties became another important source of public revenue.[29]

27 *Senate Docs.*, 54 Cong., 1 Sess., No. 182, p. 39; Debo, *op. cit.*, pp. 110-11, 144-45.
28 Debo, *op. cit.*, pp. 110-11.                                     29 *Ibid.*, pp. 128, 134-39, 145.

All the tribes except the Seminole secured additional revenue by taxing non-citizens through their right to control immigration. There was a tax on business conducted by non-citizens, a per caput annual permit fee to be paid by all employers for their non-citizen laborers, and an annual license fee to be paid by skilled laborers and professional men.[30]

The presence of this alien population and the consequent industrial development caused thriving white men's towns to grow up throughout the Indian Territory, except in the Seminole Nation where there were only a few trading stations owned by the wealthy mixed-blood Brown family. These towns were important shipping centers for coal, timber, cattle, and agricultural products, but only the Cherokees provided for their incorporation. As a result the physical appearance of Indian Territory towns presented a shocking contrast to their real prosperity. There were no city taxes except in the Cherokee Nation, hence no schools except voluntary subscription schools, no police or fire protection, and no sewers, city lighting, or paving; and no title could be secured to the lots upon which the business houses and dwellings were erected.[31]

This enterprising non-citizen life was carried on almost without legal protection or restraint, for the tribal governments had no authority over United States citizens and Federal courts were created very slowly. The United States Court for the Western District of Arkansas at Fort Smith had criminal jurisdiction, but there was no civil jurisdiction of any kind until the first Indian Territory court was established at Muskogee in 1889. After this the Federal courts were rapidly extended, and in 1895 three judicial districts were created, with a court of appeals sitting at McAlester, in the Choctaw

[30] Debo, *op. cit.*, pp. 140-43, 145-46; Department of the Interior, *Annual Report*, 1891, pp. 83-84; 1899, I, 107, 118-19; 1900, pp. 93, 95, 106-7, 141-42, 180-86; 1901, I, 226-27; Cherokee Papers (Phillips Collection, University of Oklahoma), Reply of Cherokee Delegation to Ex. Doc. No. 86, Washington, March 8, 1884; Lee Mills, Personal Interview (Pryor, Oklahoma, September 27, 1935).

[31] Debo, *op. cit.*, pp. 222-23; Department of the Interior, *Annual Report*, 1899, I, 128, 197; 1901, I, 226; Mills, Personal Interview; Cherokee Papers, handbill dated Tahlequah, March 7, 1872, advertising the sale of occupancy titles to town lots in stations along the Atlantic and Pacific Railroad.

Nation. These courts now had complete civil and criminal jurisdiction over United States citizens and over tribal citizens in mixed cases where United States citizens were involved. The laws of Arkansas were placed in effect by the acts of Congress creating these courts.

Because of the limited application of Federal law during most of the period, crime flourished in the Indian Territory. Judge Isaac C. Parker, who presided over the Fort Smith court from 1875 to 1896, established a record of 172 sentenced to death and 88 actually hanged, nearly all of whom were Indian Territory "bad men." Little attempt was made to arrest any but the most depraved criminals against whom the evidence was overwhelming. Less spectacular than the frequent commission of serious crimes, but more annoying to the hundred thousand white residents of the Indian Territory was the complete absence of civil law. There was no way of enforcing the payment of debts, and people who had a dispute over property had no recourse except to "shoot it out," or to refer it to the arbitration of the Indian Agent.[32]

In other respects also the large white population was living under conditions never before encountered by any considerable body of United States citizens. Thousands of children were growing up with no educational opportunities of any kind, a large body of tenants were cultivating land to which they could never secure title, and the proud and self-assertive white Americans were paying taxes to support a government in which they had no voice and a school system from which they received no benefits. The inhabitants of this fierce frontier did not even consider the fact that the Indian tenure rested upon the most solemn commitments by the Federal Government, and that by settling in the Indian Territory they had voluntarily subjected themselves to these conditions; and they set up a constant clamor for the abolition of the tribal govern-

[32] S. W. Harman, *Hell on the Border* (Fort Smith, Arkansas, 1898); Debo, *op. cit.*, pp. 184-91; *Statutes at Large*, XXVI, 93-100; Commissioner of Indian Affairs, *Annual Report*, 1895, pp. 445-50; Secretary of the Interior, *Annual Report*, 1896, II, 151.

ments and the establishment of a system representative of the entire population, and for the breaking up of the communal holdings into an individual tenure that would pass easily into the hands of the whites. This demand was echoed by the people of the neighboring states, who were distressed by the spectacle of rich agricultural land that had never felt the plow, and towns that could not anticipate in the very near future the erection of skyscrapers.

From the date of the Removal the Indians had been confronted with these proposals, the treaties signed at the close of the Civil War contained optional provisions for allotment and territorial organization, and during the following generation Congress had been deluged with bills for the forcible abolition of the tribal tenure.[33] By the opening of Oklahoma in 1889 and the creation of its territorial government a year later, a new and lusty voice was added to the popular clamor. Although the Indians managed to defeat this legislation through the extraordinary diplomatic skill and legal ability of their leaders and the determined opposition of their entire citizenship, it became apparent by 1890 that the treaties would not be allowed much longer to block the path of "progress."

The Indian Office opposed in principle the communal land tenure, and the Union agents—with the single exception of Robert L. Owen, a Virginian of Cherokee descent who had been admitted to tribal citizenship—filled their annual reports with condemnation of the system. For a time the Indian Office depended upon persuasion, but in 1886 the Commissioner of Indian Affairs recommended the forcible allotment of a quarter-section to each citizen and the purchase of the remainder for white settlement. In 1890 the *Special Census Bulletin* for the Indian Territory departed from its statistical impartiality to advocate a similar policy.[34]

---

[33] Annie Heloise Abel, "Proposals for an Indian State," *Annual Report of the American Historical Association,* 1907, I, 95-100; Grant Foreman, *Advancing the Frontier* (Norman, Oklahoma, 1933), pp. 180-94; Debo, *op. cit.,* pp. 212-17.

[34] *Extra Census Bulletin,* pp. 23-24, 32-33; Commissioner of Indian Affairs, *Annual Report,* 1886, pp. v, viii, x-xii.

At the same time Eastern philanthropic friends of the Indians added their dignified voices to the clamor of the turbulent frontiersmen. For some time these theorists had professed an almost mystical faith in the value of private ownership and its power to transform the nature of any Indian who could be persuaded or forced to accept it.

The Board of Indian Commissioners was created in 1869. It was supposed to be made up of distinguished philanthropists, who were to serve without pay, and whose reports would operate as a check upon vicious legislation or administration. After a year of study this board made its first report, recommending, as a general Indian policy, allotment with restrictions on alienation of the land, and specifically that members of the Five Tribes should be made United States citizens and taxed as soon as possible. From that time on the Board commonly regarded the extent of allotment as the measure of progress in Indian advancement.[35]

In 1883 a small group of Eastern humanitarians began to meet annually at Lake Mohonk, where with an agreeable background of natural beauty, congenial companionship, and crusading motive, they discussed the Indian problem. At their third meeting Senator Henry L. Dawes of Massachusetts, a distinguished Indian theorist, gave a glowing description of a visit of inspection he had recently made to the Indian Territory. The most partisan Indian would hardly have painted such an idealized picture of his people's happiness and prosperity and culture, but, illogically, the Senator advocated a change in this perfect society because it held the wrong principles of property ownership. Speaking apparently of the Cherokees, he said: "The head chief told us that there was not a family in that whole nation that had not a home of its own. There was not a pauper in that nation, and the nation did not owe a dollar. It built its own capitol, in which we had this examination, and it built its schools and its hospitals.

---

[35] Board of Indian Commissioners, *Annual Report,* 1902, pp. 3-7.

Yet the defect of the system was apparent. They have got as far as they can go, because they own their land in common. It is Henry George's system, and under that there is no enterprise to make your home any better than that of your neighbors. There is no selfishness, which is at the bottom of civilization. Till this people will consent to give up their lands, and divide them among their citizens so that each can own the land he cultivates, they will not make much more progress."[36]

The Conference accepted this viewpoint, and continued to advocate "reform" with all the earnestness of a moral crusade. Like Senator Dawes, the members based their opposition purely upon theoretical belief in the sanctity of private ownership rather than upon any understanding of the Indian nature or any investigation of actual conditions. With regard to Indians in general, their program in 1903 comprised: the abolition of the Indian Bureau and all Indian agencies, and the extension of state authority over all Indian tribes; the extinction of tribal governments and the granting of full United States citizenship with its privileges and obligations; and the division of the communal holdings among the individual Indians, to be held under the same conditions of taxation and freedom to alienate as the white man's farm.[37]

With these respectable groups influencing public opinion it is not strange that the articles about the Indian Territory appearing in the serious magazines were almost unanimous in their condemnation of tribal control. These accounts were widely divergent, and most of them were grossly inaccurate; but whether the writers described an impossibly utopian society and sought a method to improve perfection, or whether they slandered the Indians' character and achievements and urged a remedy for an intolerable condition, they united in demanding abolition of the tribal tenure. Only the National Indian Defense Association, formed at Washington in 1885, opposed

[36] *Ibid.*, 1885, pp. 90-91.
[37] *Ibid.*, 1900, pp. 25-32; Lake Mohonk Conference, *Report*, 1904, pp. 5-6; Department of the Interior, *Annual Report*, 1900, pp. 655-735.

the change, and its warning was hardly heard in the general clamor.[38]

In response to this faith in private ownership, Congress passed the Dawes Severalty Act in 1887. It provided that Indian reservations should be allotted in 160-acre tracts to heads of families, 80 acres to unmarried adults, and 40 acres to children; and that the remainder should be purchased by the Government and thrown open to homestead entry.[39] The Five Tribes were exempted from its provisions, but they rightly interpreted it as an expression of public policy dangerous to their institutions.

Every session of Congress in the early Nineties was charged with menace, but when the dreaded legislation was enacted, March 3, 1893, it provided only for negotiation. The President was authorized to appoint three commissioners who should have great discretionary power in making agreements with the Indians for the extinction of their communal titles and the eventual creation of a state.[40] Fortunately for the Indians Grover Cleveland came into office the following day. Like nearly all white men of his time he believed in allotment, but he was one of the three or four Presidents of the United States most conspicuously friendly to Indian aspirations.[41]

Dawes, who had retired from the Senate, became chairman of the Commission, and Meredith H. Kidd of Indiana and Archibald S. McKennon of Arkansas were appointed as the other members. It was officially designated as the Commission to the Five Civilized Tribes, but so great was the prestige of the venerable chairman in Indian affairs that it was universally known as the Dawes Commission.

Soon after their appointment the members proceeded to the Indian Territory and invited the tribes to negotiate. They were deeply incensed at the concerted resistance they encountered,

[38] Anna Laurens Dawes, "An Unknown Nation," *Harper's Magazine*, LXXVI (1888); Rezin W. McAdam, "An Indian Commonwealth," *Harper's Magazine*, LXXXVII (1893).
[39] *Statutes at Large*, XXIV, 388-91.
[40] Commissioner of Indian Affairs, *Annual Report*, 1893, pp. 512-13.
[41] Dawes Commission, *Report*, 1895, pp. 60-61.

and they advised Congress to disregard the treaties and abolish the tribal status without waiting for the Indians' consent. But Congress authorized them to continue the negotiation, and after three years of patient effort they persuaded the first tribe—the Choctaws—to treat with them. During the entire period they published annual reports, appeared before committees of Congress, and made speeches before various public gatherings describing the conditions they found in the Indian Territory and pointing out the necessity for a change.

These statements were naturally accepted by Congress and the country at large as authentic, and are still generally quoted uncritically by even the most careful students of Indian history; but they are no more objective than the manifestoes issued by the average government before entering upon a war of conquest. Unquestionably land hunger was the real motive behind most of the agitation to terminate the tribal régime, and a fairly good case could have been made out in the name of "manifest destiny," or the right of the strong to dispossess seventy thousand easy-going Indians in favor of a million white people who could occupy and develop their rich holdings; but civilized men have seldom been willing to state their motives so baldly. The reports of the Dawes Commission, therefore, are couched in a high moral tone often rising to impassioned eloquence condemning the exploitation of the fullblood Indians under the existing régime and painting glowing descriptions of the deliverance awaiting them.

They portrayed the inconveniences suffered by the white residents, the appalling number of crimes of violence, and the great natural resources of the Indian Territory, which were lying undeveloped. These were the white man's arguments, and in all this they told the truth. But they presented a completely unfair picture of the poor Indian crowded back in the hills and living in abject poverty while the rich leaders of the tribe monopolized the productive land that belonged equally to all. Thirty-nine Choctaws, they said, had collected $65,000 in coal royalties in 1894, and with great moral indignation they condemned these selfish individuals for thus seizing the common property. It is evident that in this argument they were attempting to hold the Indians to abstract and ideal rather than comparative standards, for certainly the poor Indian had a better chance to become a prosperous farmer than the landless member of the white man's society; such public attempts to regulate the size of holdings as the Choctaw pasture limitation and the Creek referendum on proposed enclosures went further in preventing land monopoly than any law ever passed by an American state; and a garbled misrepresentation of the Choctaws' system of public control of natural resources came with especially bad grace from the members of a race that in the short space of a century had seen the greatest natural wealth in the possession of any people pass into private and often rapacious hands. They characterized the Indian governments as hopelessly venal. It is true that some Indian politicians were corrupt, but no serious student of the tribal governments familiar with subsequent developments in Oklahoma would contend that they were any more dishonest than the state government that supplanted them, or that official corruption was any more general than it was at that very time in the surrounding states. The Commissioners constantly asserted that only the greedy monopolists resisted the allotment of the communal holdings and that only the dishonest officials opposed the dissolution of the tribal governments. No doubt they were sincere in these misstatements, but the sequel was to show that the tribal leaders finally submitted to the inevitable while the ignorant fullbloods clung to their institutions with a despairing tenacity that refused to accept the logic of events. No such charitable allowance can be made regarding their statements about the freedmen. They condemned the Choctaws for the limited citizenship granted their Negroes, and asserted that the United States was "bound by solemn treaty" to place the Chickasaw freedmen "securely in the enjoyment of their rights as Chickasaw citizens, and cannot with honor ignore the obligation." The Choctaws had been most generous in extending favors to their freedmen beyond the stipulations of the Treaty of 1866, and for thirty years the United States, with or without honor, had "ignored the obligation" of that treaty to remove these unwelcome residents from the Chickasaw country. This misinformation was apparently obtained from attorneys who were trying to secure for the freedmen equal shares of the tribal property, but for the members of the Dawes Commission, who were paid an adequate salary to devote their entire time to an important public assignment, ignorance in such a matter is as inexcusable as intentional falsehood.[42]

A speech made by Chairman Dawes at the Lake Mohonk Conference in 1896 furnishes an example of the influence of such irresponsible statements. Seventy-seven years old at the time of his appointment and afflicted by an increasing deafness, which had troubled him during his last months in the Senate,[43] he had not been active in the work of the Commission. But apparently he had conferred with the other members or had read their reports, for his description of the hopeless misery of the fullblood Indians crowded out of their heritage sounds strangely different from the ideal conditions which he had found in the Indian Territory eleven years before. Referring, of course, to Judge Parker's 172 death sentences in 21 years, he said, "One judge who has been there ten or fifteen years has sentenced something like 1,000 men to be hanged for crimes committed in that Territory." Such vague charges may have satisfied his audience; one must examine the court records to find that he had requested exact statistics and that the court clerk had sent him a carefully compiled list of the death sentences for each year since 1875. In the same speech he also said that the treaties of 1866 had provided for allotment and the creation of a territorial government, but he neglected to state that those provisions had been optional, and that the tribes had overwhelmingly rejected them.[44]

[42] Dawes Commission, *Report*, 1894, pp. 15-19, 23-53, 82, 88; 1895, pp. 55-63; 1896, pp. 8, 28-30, 38-40; 1899, p. 7.

[43] *Dictionary of American Biography.*

[44] Charles F. Meserve, *The Dawes Commission and the Five Civilized Tribes of the Indian Territory* (Philadelphia, 1896), pp. 41-44; Fort Smith Papers, United States Court and Indian Territory (Phillips Collection, University of Oklahoma), Vol. II, Nos. 1 and 2.

As head of the Commission, Dawes was naturally accepted as an authority on Indian Territory conditions, and these naïve misstatements had a most mischievous effect. The Indian Rights Association sent Charles F. Meserve, the president of Shaw University, to the Indian Territory to investigate. His report, which was a terrible indictment of the Indian régime and an unqualified endorsement of the Dawes Commission, contained this misleading speech in full.[45]

Subject to the clamor of an irresistible white immigration and deserted by public sentiment, the situation of the Indians was indeed hopeless. A letter written to Chief Mayes by the Cherokee delegation in Washington in 1895 presents such an accurate and comprehensive and yet restrained analysis of conditions that it deserves to be quoted at length. The delegates said that the Dawes Commission had just presented the written report of the fruitless negotiations with the Indians, and had also made an oral argument before a joint meeting of the Committee on Territories and the Judiciary Committee of the House of Representatives. The Cherokees also had been invited to appear and make a refutation, which they hoped had made an impression.

"Yet, in the struggle to shield our country from the calamities which the scheme contemplated by the friends of the Dawes report would certainly bring upon it, we had to labor under great disadvantages. It did seem as if the world was about to rise in arms against us. We saw that even the press had been largely subsidized in favor of the dissolution of our government and the invasion of our rights. Before the committee on territories of the House, in order to make the impression on members of Congress that the people of the several tribes were in favor of a territorial government, it was stated by lobbyists sent from Ardmore that there were fifty-five newspapers in Indian Territory, and that all of them excepting five were in favor of a territorial government. But care was taken not to let it be known that all these papers favoring a territorial government had been

[45] Meserve, *The Dawes Commission, loc. cit.* See also *Senate Reports,* 53 Cong., 2 Sess., No. 377.

mounted [?] in the Indian Territory either by intruders or non-citizen white men for the express purpose of subverting the governments of the Indians and turning the country over into the hands of speculators and inferior politicians, who imagine that, in event of such change as they contemplate for the Indian country, they would be importuned to fill the territorial offices, and possibly to represent the dear people in the halls of Congress. Nevertheless, these papers have their influence. They are circulated at Washington as well as throughout the country at large. We met with some of them in the Department of Justice, where officers of the Government appeared to have formed their opinions in reference to our country from the stories told in their columns. . . . While we on our side of the great debate between the United States and the Cherokee Nation, have, for the most part, supinely rested in the belief that all was peace and safety, they with a zeal which knew no pause, have been sapping the very foundations of our government.

"Furthermore, many of the great dailies that a few years ago pleaded so persistently for the liberation of the slaves, are now insisting upon 'opening' our country for the settlement and occupancy of the whites. Still further, as an evidence of the influence which the press has against us, even benevolent associations which were organized a few year[s] ago to urge Congress to keep the treaties which had been made with Indian tribes, are now advising the erection of a territorial government in our country and allotment of our lands in violation of our treaties and without our consent. It is worthy of remark, too, as indicating the course of public sentiment in relation to our country, that even the pulpit, which some time ago, was so exuberant of love for the slave has no good word to speak in behalf of the Indians of Indian Territory. No church assembly now passes resolutions against a violation of our treaties, the abrogation of our government and an invasion of our right of property. . . .

"Under these circumstances, we cannot refrain from the indulgence of a reflection. The history of human affairs convinces us that it is always a misfortune to hold the position of a weaker party. East of the Mississippi we were a happy people. The United States wanted our country there; reluctantly we parted with it, and to this day have not received all that was promised us for it. The Government wanted the six million acres of our strip lands;[46] we agreed to part with those lands, but the terms of the agreement entered into at Tahlequah and ratified by act of the National Council, were changed by act of Congress without our consent, and yet, after changing those terms to its own liking, the Government has not complied with them. And now, they want us to enter into another agreement—an agreement with the Dawes Commission. But what assurance have we, even if we were disposed to come to an agreement with that Commission, that the terms of such agreement would not be swept aside and others, to which we could never assent, imposed upon us? We think it would be but fair on [the] part of the Government to comply with the agreements already made with our people, before asking us to enter into others of a nature more serious in their character than any hitherto proposed.

". . . [With regard to the failure of the United States to carry out a recent pledge to remove the intruders—] The newspapers, too, are interesting themselves in the matter. The question has been raised as to where the intruders can go, if they are to be removed from our country, as if their were no space on the continent outside of our lands, where even millions can find homes, if they only have a desire to do so. . . . We opine, however, that the same energy which they have displayed in their efforts to wrest from us a large portion of our property, will enable them to acquire homes even amongst the most astute of their fellow citizens. But there seems to be a sinister motive for keeping the intruders in our country. It was the contents of the wooden horse emptied inside the walls of Troy, that enabled the Greeks to take that ancient city.

". . . [In view of the great potential wealth of the Indian Territory the real motive of the plan is to secure the Indians' property.] It is seen by the keen eye of speculation, that, if our country were revolutionized as contemplated in the scheme

---

[46] Lands in Oklahoma Territory opened to white settlement in 1893.

of the Dawes Commission, it would become easy for capitalists and monied men of less degree to soon become the owners of millions. But what about the other side? What about our people, who are, now, the legal owners and sovereigns of these lands? Why the question is [e]asy of answer. Crushed to earth under the hoofs of business gread, they would soon become a homeless throng, more scoffed at and abused than a Coxey's army. No territorial or state legislation can protect the Indian in his rights. Business has no moral consciousness; when a statute comes in its way, it will invoke the aid of a 'higher law' and grasp the Indian's property anyhow.

". . . It is wonderful, too, to see with what unanimity the papers exclaim that *'Carthage must be destroye[d].'* . . . Even the heavy Quarterlies, such as the *North American Review,* are being operated in the interests of our enemies. . . .

". . . As far as the Indian people are concerned, the present are days to try men's souls; and he who is made of stuff so lofty of nature, as to rise superior to all selfish considerations, and, in face of the popular clamor of the times, boldly speak out in favor of the rights and freedom of the Indians, becomes an object worthy to be venerated by the good and great in all lands."[47]

This report, written hastily by hand, was but an informal letter from the delegates to their friend, the Chief; but it shows an insight strangely lacking in the voluminous publications of white writers and Government officials. It has an even more uncanny accuracy as a prophecy of the future.

---

[47] Cherokee Papers, Report of S. W. Gray, Roach Young, and J. F. Thompson to Hon. S. H. Mayes, 1895.

# CHAPTER II

# The White Man's Land System

THE final surrender of the tribal institutions came only after prolonged negotiations, with the threat of force always in the background. The division of the tribal property was carried out partly under agreements made with the Dawes Commission and partly under Federal legislation. Even after the agreements were secured, Congress changed the terms so freely and arbitrarily that the apprehensions of the Cherokee delegates were fully realized.

Few public officials in the United States ever conducted a transaction of such magnitude as fell to the lot of the Dawes Commissioners, for it became their duty to determine the heirship and to divide estates with a total value equal to that of many an American state. So far as property interests were concerned, they conducted their tremendous task with a high degree of honesty and efficiency, but unexpected complications prolonged the process for many years. At the same time the change was accomplished at a terrible and unregarded cost of human suffering.

The membership of the Commission changed with bewildering frequency, but Dawes remained as nominal chairman until his death in 1903. Tams Bixby of Minnesota, who had served on the Commission since 1897, and who had been acting as chairman, was then formally appointed to the position. The Commission was abolished in 1905, and Bixby carried on the work as sole Commissioner. He resigned in 1907, and was succeeded by J. George Wright, who continued to serve until the office was abolished in 1914.[1] The Commission employed

---

[1] Department of the Interior, *Annual Report,* 1914, II, 5-6.

hundreds of clerks, appraisers, surveyors, etc., who worked in specialized fields throughout the Five Tribes area.

During the century that the Indians had witnessed the constant shrinking of their territory before the land hunger of the white man, they had developed a horror of land cessions; and it became apparent at the very beginning of the negotiations that they "would not under any circumstances agree to cede any portion of their land to the Government, but would insist that if any agreements were made for allotment of their lands it should all be divided equally among them." The Commissioners accordingly abandoned the idea of purchase, and proposed the reservation of the townsites and the Choctaw coal and the asphalt deposits of the Chickasaw district and the division of all the remainder among the citizens. They also suggested that the individual allottee should be protected by making "Sufficient land for a good home for each citizen . . . inalienable for twenty-five years, or such longer period as may be agreed upon."[2]

For three years the Indian nations separately and in intertribal conventions steadfastly refused to treat. But Congress in 1895 authorized a survey of the land, and in 1896 directed the Dawes Commission to make a complete roll of the citizens of each tribe, and gave rejected citizenship claimants the right of appeal to Federal courts. Bills were also introduced at each session providing for forcible abolition of the tribal status. Finally the more progressive Indian leaders, realizing that only by a negotiated settlement could they avoid a dictated one, began to use their influence in favor of an agreement.[3]

All the tribes but the Cherokees accordingly consented to treat. They appointed delegations to negotiate with the Dawes Commission, and by 1898 compacts had been drawn up, and one, the Seminole Agreement, had been ratified by the tribe. There was every prospect, however, that the other settlements would be rejected. Congress, therefore, in the Curtis Act of

[2] Dawes Commission, *Report*, 1894, pp. 82-87.
[3] *Ibid.*, 1894, p. 81; 1895, pp. 47-55, 64-65; Debo, *op. cit.*, pp. 253-55; *Statutes at Large*, XXIX, 321.

June 28, 1898, enacted the long-threatened legislation terminating the tribal tenure without the Indians' consent. This law did not apply to the Seminoles, since they had already come to terms with the Government; and the agreements negotiated with the other three tribes were amended somewhat and embodied in the act with the stipulation that if they should be accepted by the Indians within a specified period they would be substituted for the more drastic general provisions.[4]

The Creeks, however, rejected the agreement at a special election, and the Curtis Act went into effect in their country. The Cherokees also, who had steadfastly refused to treat, came under its provisions. Because they owned their land in common, the Choctaws and Chickasaws had negotiated their agreement—the so-called Atoka Agreement—jointly, and now they voted individually rather than by tribes. The more conservative citizens refrained from voting and the measure carried. The division of the Choctaw-Chickasaw estate was therefore carried out largely under its provisions.[5]

The Creeks were so anxious to escape the terms of the Curtis Act that the next attempt to effect a settlement with them was successful. This agreement was ratified by the tribe May 25, 1901. Pleasant Porter afterwards explained the reasons that motivated the Creeks. There were only three ways to resist, he said: by fighting, which would have meant destruction; by emigration, by which they would have lost their country and would have found no place to go; and by passive resistance, which would have been futile. The leaders discussed the situation and decided upon surrender, and Porter consented to accept the office of Chief in order that he might carry the plan through and use his influence to secure, as far as possible under the circumstances, the rights of each citizen. "I will tell you what I have felt and I ought not to have felt that way. I have said that I was conscious that I was compelled under the ad-

---

[4] Department of the Interior, *Annual Report*, 1897, pp. 409-15; Charles J. Kappler, *Indian Affairs, Laws and Treaties* (Washington, 1904), I, 92-99, 656-65.

[5] Commissioner of Indian Affairs, *Annual Report*, 1898, p. 435; *Indian Citizen*, September 1, 1898.

vance of civilization to sign the paper now that I know [that I now know] took the lifeblood of my people."[6]

But the Cherokees still remained without a written settlement. That numerous and able people had rejected all proposals as long as they retained any freedom of action. Then, when the Curtis Act abolished their institutions, they bargained for more favorable terms than Congress was willing to accept. The first negotiations took place during the winter following the passage of the Curtis Act. The proposals submitted by the tribal delegates contained the provision that all land should be non-taxable for thirty-five years. The Federal Commissioners sought to modify this condition, but the counter-proposals they submitted were more generous in the protection of the individual allottee against alienation than were to be found in any of the agreements with the other tribes. The Cherokees also stipulated that their freedmen should be limited to forty-acre allotments and should not share in the distribution of the tribal funds, and the Dawes Commission embodied this proposal in the draft agreement. But the most significant Cherokee proposal was labelled, "Plan for preserving in effect the continuity of the Tribal Relations of the full blood Indian." It provided that as many fullbloods as desired might take adjacent allotments within an area subject to the approval of the Dawes Commission and hold it as a corporation for their joint use under communal title.[7] Apparently this proposal was not even considered by the Federal officials; but barely a generation was to pass until the whole machinery of Indian administration would be set in motion to bring about this identical result.

The agreement drawn up through this negotiation was apparently not sufficiently favorable to the white man, for although it was accepted by the tribe it failed of ratification by

[6] Kappler, *Laws and Treaties*, I, 729-39; Department of the Interior, *Annual Report*, 1901, p. 143; *Select Committee*, I, 649. Isparhecher, an unlettered fullblood elected upon an anti-Dawes platform, served as Chief until 1899.

[7] Cherokee Papers, Joint Session United States Commission and Cherokee Commission. These stenographic reports do not indicate the authorship of the last proposition, but it was certainly submitted by the Cherokee delegation.

Congress. After several other fruitless attempts to reach a settlement, an agreement was finally adopted in 1902. Until that time the Cherokees remained under the Curtis Act.[8]

As the allotment proceeded under the various agreements, it became apparent that details had been overlooked or that policies had been adopted that proved unacceptable. Supplemental agreements were accordingly made with the Seminoles in 1900 and with the Creeks and the Choctaws and Chickasaws in 1902.[9]

An examination of all these agreements shows some modification of Indian thought during the period from 1896—the date of the first Choctaw negotiation—to 1902. The Curtis Act had provided for the retention of mineral rights by the tribes—a policy that would have had important results when the Indian country became one of the great oil fields of the world—but the Creeks and Cherokees repealed this provision in their agreements and the minerals were allotted with the land. Under the Atoka Agreement the Choctaw-Chickasaw coal and asphalt were to be reserved and the royalties were to be collected under the supervision of the Secretary of the Interior and used for the tribal schools; but the Supplemental Agreement changed this policy to segregation and sale of the coal and asphalt land and the distribution of the proceeds among the citizens. The earliest agreements—with the Choctaws and Chickasaws and the Seminoles—provided for a school fund. This policy was not adopted in the later settlements, and was abandoned by the Choctaws and Chickasaws when they decided upon the sale of their mineral land.

All these changes indicate that the Indians, though slow to surrender their communal system, came eventually to desire the complete liquidation of all their tribal assets. This was partly owing to the acceptance of the new system by their leaders, and the natural desire to make the process complete; but it was

---

[8] Department of the Interior, *Annual Report*, 1900, p. 105; Dawes Commission, *Report*, 1901, p. 156; 1902, p. 202. The text of the first agreement will no doubt be discovered by some future writer of Cherokee history.

[9] Commissioner of Indian Affairs, *Annual Report*, 1902, p. 122; Dawes Commission, *Report*, 1902, p. 201; Kappler, *Laws and Treaties*, I, 702-3, 761-65, 771-87

caused mainly by dissatisfaction with Federal administration of their estates. If they were not to control their property, they wished to have it divided as completely as possible.

The terms under which the Indian was to hold his allotment differed in the various agreements, but all of them contained provisions to protect the inexperienced allottee in his new title. It was recognized that the Indian under communal tenure had developed no familiarity with written contracts, deeds, mortgages, taxes, and other methods of alienating his holdings. A limited portion of the allotment, designated as the "homestead," was accordingly guarded by restrictions against alienation, while the remainder, which came to be known as the "surplus," would soon pass freely into the Indian's control. It was expected that the Indian would immediately sell his surplus, and that living on his homestead he would be surrounded with white neighbors. This would satisfy the land hunger of the white men, would open the country to the development of its resources, and would distribute the Indian population among the general citizenship of the community. All the objectives of the general allotment policy would thus be attained as effectively as though the Indian tribes had been willing to accept small allotments and sell large tracts of their land to the United States.

The agreements also varied as to the closing of the tribal rolls. None of the tribes had consented to negotiate when enrolment began by Federal mandate under the law of 1896. The Indians resented the division of their property among a list of citizens whom they did not recognize; but the Supreme Court upheld the authority of the Dawes Commission to make the rolls, and they were compelled to acquiesce. When they began to make agreements, however, they secured provisions in some cases protecting them against the more indefensible raids upon their property, and regulating the closing of the rolls. But while completion of the enrolment was delayed by intricate problems of detail and disputed points of law, the natural Indian birth rate continued, and Congress in response to requests from all the tribes provided for these new arrivals.

The final rolls, therefore, do not indicate the population of the tribes, but the totals formed by adding the numbers living on a series of designated dates. The Creeks in particular had five of these enrolment periods; hence it is obvious that the roll of this tribe was very much larger than the population at any one time.[10]

The work proved to be complicated far beyond the expectations of the Federal or tribal authorities. The tribes all possessed rolls and census lists, but these had been carelessly kept. In a community as small and informal as these Indian republics the recognition of citizenship rested more upon family and neighborhood knowledge than upon official registration. The Dawes Commission, moreover, charged—apparently with some truth—that the tribal politicians had manipulated the rolls according to corrupt or personal motives. They attempted, therefore, to check these lists by personal identification of every citizen and to supplement them by the addition of any omitted names. They found the conservative fullbloods, driven to this last desperate stand against allotment, extremely reluctant to enroll. At the same time they were besieged by white and Negro claimants, usually prompted by scheming attorneys, who were determined to share in the tribal property. Since they had everything to gain and nothing to lose by a judicial settlement, these applicants carried their claims to the last tribunal, and the enrolment was delayed for many years by litigation.

The Commission began to receive the applications of citizenship claimants at Vinita, in the Cherokee Nation, immediately after the passage of the law of 1896. But the work of enrolling the real Indians was carried out in the field, and the employees of the Commission visited every remote settlement of the Five Tribes.

[10] Kappler, *Laws and Treaties*, I, 119, 702-3, 737, 762-63, 791-92; III, 148, 170; Dawes Commission, *Report*, 1899, pp. 160-78; Commissioner of Indian Affairs, *Annual Report*, 1902, p. 519; 1904, pp. 117-18; United States Department of the Interior, Indian Territory Division Files, 16716/05, Enclosures No. 4, 13; Acts of the Choctaw Nation (Phillips Collection, University of Oklahoma), November 22, 1905; *Congressional Record*, LI, 11919.

They began enrolling the Seminoles immediately upon the ratification of the agreement with that tribe in 1898. The work was simple. Intermarried citizenship was not recognized, and most of the citizens were fullblood Indians or freedmen who had become completely incorporated within the tribal community. The Commissioners found the tribal rolls crude but free from irregularities and evidence of corruption. They took this list, subtracted for deaths and duplications, and added the names of children born since it had been compiled and seven names that had been omitted. The work was virtually completed within two months, except that it was necessary to add the names of "newborns" in 1905. Only seven applications were rejected during the entire period.[11]

As soon as the Atoka Agreement was ratified, the Dawes Commission, having completed its field work among the Seminoles, entered the Chickasaw country. It began working in the Choctaw Nation the following spring and continued there through most of the summer. Each nation had appointed a citizenship commission of capable and well informed men, whose knowledge of the neighborhood and family history was of great assistance to the Dawes Commission. By the fall of 1899 most of the citizens on the tribal rolls had been identified, but the Indian governments continued for several years to seek out humble members of their race who might have been overlooked during the registration.[12]

At the same time the tribes were greatly aroused over the prospect of dividing their property with a horde of claimants whose citizenship was not recognized by their law. Most of the applicants were rejected by the Dawes Commission, but they appealed to the Federal courts of the Indian Territory and although many were excluded, thousands were admitted to citizenship. The Choctaws and Chickasaws were thrown into angry confusion. With more zeal than system, they began to employ

11 Dawes Commission, *Report,* 1899, p. 13; 1900, p. 14.

12 *Ibid.,* 1902, pp. 15-17; Five Tribes Papers (Oklahoma State Historical Society, Oklahoma City), Choctaw—Citizenship, report of citizenship commission to Council, October, 1899; Acts of the Choctaw Nation, November 1, 1899; October 22, 31, 1900; November 6, 1901, October 22, 1903.

2. Enrollment of Citizens in the Choctaw Nation. By the fall of 1899 most of the citizens on the tribal rolls had been identified.

attorneys under extravagant and overlapping contracts to fight this menace to their landed interests. The amount they spent in litigation is impossible to determine, but it was amply justified by its results.[13]

The most important services were rendered by the firm of Mansfield, McMurray, and Cornish. These attorneys assisted the tribes in negotiating the Supplemental Agreement with the Dawes Commission, and they managed to secure a provision for a special tribunal to which the Indians might appeal the cases of the "court citizens."[14]

President Roosevelt appointed Judge Spencer B. Adams of North Carolina, Judge Henry S. Foote of California, and Judge Walter L. Weaver of Ohio as members of this court. It began its work in the fall of 1902 and continued until the close of 1904. It ruled against the constitutionality of a tribal law by which intermarried citizenship was forfeited upon subsequent marriage to a non-citizen, but it rejected the unconscionable claim that a white person once admitted into the tribe by marriage to an Indian could confer citizenship upon any white person whom he might afterwards marry and upon his white descendants. It also uncovered a great mass of nauseous evidence, and rejected a large number of claims upon the ground that they had been advanced through perjury and forgery. In 263 suits involving about 3,403 claimants admitted by the Indian Territory courts, all but about 156 claimants were excluded, and property valued at $16,000,000 was thereby recovered for the recognized citizens of the tribes.[15]

[13] Department of the Interior, *Annual Report*, 1898, pp. 459-73; Dawes Commission, *Report*, 1899, p. 15; 1900, pp. 15-18; 1902, p. 17; *Indian Citizen*, December, 1896—January, 1897; Acts of the Choctaw Nation, September 18, 1896; October 22, November 4, 1897; November 5, 1901; October 22, December 19, 1902; October 30, 1903; Five Tribes Papers, Choctaw—Attorneys; *ibid.*, Choctaw—Citizenship; Debo, *op. cit.*, pp. 269-71; *Cases Decided in the Court of Claims of the United States* (Washington, 1927), LXII, 501.

[14] Acts of the Choctaw Nation, January 7, November 5, 1901; December 19, 1902; *Court of Claims Reports*, LXII, 460, 466-67, 470-71, 480-81; Indian Territory Division Files, 4412/04; *House Reports*, 61 Cong., 2 Sess., No. 2273, Vol. I, pp. 369, 539, 699, 795.

[15] *Chickasaw Capital*, December 8, 1904; Indian Territory Division Files, File C, 1903-4; *Court of Claims Reports*, LXII, 471.

Mansfield, McMurray, and Cornish, of course, represented the tribes before the citizenship court. They had been employed under contracts carrying a 9 per cent contingent fee; but the Indian governments had lost their independence of action by the Atoka Agreement, and such contracts were subject to Federal approval. The Secretary of the Interior attempted to reduce the fee, but the firm refused to accept this modification and continued to work without an approved contract. The determination of the fee was then referred by Congress to the citizenship court, which reduced it to $750,000, about 4.5 per cent of the amount recovered.[16]

The payment of this fee aroused more virtuous-sounding condemnation than any other event in the liquidation of the Five Tribes estates. The Indian Office was highly incensed and started an investigation, a grand jury indicted the members of the firm and the two tribal executives, and civil proceedings were instituted to recover the fee: but all these actions failed. Accusations of bribery—entirely unsupported by evidence—were freely circulated against the judges of the citizenship court, and much Congressional eloquence was expended in denouncing the transaction as the greatest of Indian Territory scandals.

It is fairly evident that a great deal of this moral outcry originated with the citizenship claimants and their attorneys and the members of Congress who numbered them among their constituents; and that these over-zealous defenders of the Indians overlooked several important facts. Congress by its legislation had created a situation by which the two Indian tribes could be plundered of a large share of their inheritance, and the Department of the Interior had supinely permitted this spoliation. The tribal officials had made reckless commitments at a time when the case seemed hopeless, and the firm had undertaken the work when recovery was extremely doubtful. There is, moreover, no evidence to indicate that any undue influence was used to secure the contracts from the tribal officials. The fee, large as it was, was an excellent investment, for the amount recovered represented one-eighth of the Indians' possessions. The real blame rests with a Federal policy that drove the tribes to such ruinous measures of defense.[17]

Only a little less serious was the difficulty which the two tribes experienced with their freedmen. According to the Treaty of 1866, under which the Choctaw freedmen had been adopted, their final shares in the event of allotment were restricted to forty acres of average land with no participation in any per caput distribution; and this provision had been embodied in the Atoka Agreement. The Chickasaw freedmen had, of course, no legal or economic status, but attorneys had presented their plight so well that not only the Dawes Commission but many committees of Congress had been influenced to the extent of misrepresenting the facts in their official reports. Congress therefore amended the agreement by providing for the allotment of the Chickasaw freedmen upon the same terms as the Choctaw, and the Indians had only the alternatives of accepting or rejecting the entire settlement. But they secured a provision in the Supplemental Agreement that the case would be referred to the Court of Claims, and that if the court should decide that the Chickasaw freedmen had no right to allotment independent of the Atoka Agreement, the Dawes Commission would appraise the land and the tribes would be compensated by the United States.[18]

The Indians won their case. At last the white man had taken the trouble to read the plain provisions of this oft-misquoted Treaty of 1866. Congress appropriated $606,936.08 to compensate the two tribes, but this computation was based upon comparative estimates used for convenience in allotting and represented only a small fraction of the value of the land.[19] A curious result of the joint ownership arrangement was that the individual Chickasaw suffered the same reduction in the value

[17] *Ibid.*, LXII, 513-15; *Congressional Record*, LI, 3302-3; *Muskogee Phoenix*, November 17, 1907.

[18] Dawes Commission, *Report*, 1894, pp. 93-123; Kappler, *Laws and Treaties*, I, 780.

[19] *Supreme Court Reports*, XLVIII, 640-45, case decided February 23, 1904; *Statutes at Large*, XXXVI, 809, June 25, 1910.

of his share of the common property as did the Choctaw when the Choctaws adopted their freedmen, and that the Choctaw benefited to the same extent as the Chickasaw by the Chickasaws' refusal to adopt.

The Indians also had trouble because of the Negroes' attempts to secure full shares of the tribal property by transfer from the freedman to the Indian rolls. Apparently at the time of the enrolment the Dawes Commission regularly enrolled all with apparent Negro blood as freedmen. If any of them had Indian blood they were not recognized as Indians by tribal law, for there was no way by which a valid marriage could be contracted. Illegitimate children of white fathers and Negro mothers are, of course, uniformly classed as Negroes by white Americans, and the Indians had followed the same rule.[20]

Attorneys who were said to hold contracts giving them 50 per cent of all the property they should secure for the freedmen made a determined effort to change their enrolment. But the so-called Five Tribes Act passed in 1906 for the conclusion of tribal affairs provided that no freedman should be transferred to the Indian roll unless he had applied during the enrolment period, and that all illegitimate "newborns" should take the status of their mothers. The attorneys continued to lobby for legislation, but Mansfield, McMurray, and Cornish were equally vigilant and the transfer was never effected.[21]

Even more helpless pawns in the hands of white men were the Mississippi Choctaws. By the Removal Treaty of 1830 the Choctaws were given the option of remaining in Mississippi, selecting an allotment, and becoming citizens of the United States. A large number had elected to remain, but the Federal Government had defrauded them of the allotment provision and the Mississippians had crowded them to remote districts or reduced them to peonage on the cotton plantations. The Choctaws in the West during their entire history had been most

---

[20] Acts of the Choctaw Nation, November 6, 1885; September 18, 1896.

[21] Kappler, *Laws and Treaties*, III, 170-71; *Select Committee*, I, 524-45, 937-45, 962-63; II, 1497-1623; *Muskogee Phoenix*, January 26, 1907; *Senate Docs.*, 59 Cong., 2 Sess., No. 257; Department of the Interior, *Annual Report*, 1907, II, 106-7; 1909, II, 378; *Federal Reporter* (St. Paul, 1908), CLXIV, 670-73.

generous in inviting these exploited people to share their prosperity, had sent committees to induce them to remove, and had even made appropriations for their support after their arrival; but although groups did emigrate from time to time, thousands still remained in Mississippi.

As soon as the Dawes Commission was authorized to make the tribal rolls, Robert L. Owen and Charles F. Winton became convinced that the Mississippi Choctaws were entitled to share in the tribal property without removing to the Indian Territory. Winton accordingly went to Mississippi and secured approximately a thousand contracts carrying a 50 per cent contingent fee, while Owen presented their case to the Dawes Commission and committees of Congress. They enlisted the support of John Sharp Williams, who was then a member of the House of Representatives from the district where most of the Choctaws lived, and Williams began to present memorials to Congress prepared by Owen and Winton, setting forth the claims of his newly-discovered constituents. The immediate result of such a construction of the treaty would have been the transfer of several million dollars' worth of tribal property to the temporary possession of the Mississippi fullbloods before half of it passed to Owen and Winton and the remaining half, by the natural gravitation of Indian money, passed to the white residents of Williams' district.

But in the fall of 1896 the Dawes Commission refused to enroll the Mississippi Choctaws, upon the ground that Choctaw blood of itself did not constitute citizenship in the Nation, and when Owen appealed to the Indian Territory courts he was again refused. The Curtis Act then directed the Dawes Commission to identify the Mississippi Choctaws; and the Indian Appropriation Act of 1900 gave them the right to settle in the Choctaw country and receive allotments, but specifically invalidated all prior liens upon their property. The law thus proved to be a disappointment to its sponsors; it invalidated the Owen-Winton contracts, and John Sharp Williams for years afterward bewailed the fact that a clause had been slipped in disinheriting his constituents who remained in Mississippi.

Meanwhile the Dawes Commission attempted the enrolment. They found a people industrious and law-abiding, but ignorant and helpless and destitute, and so suspicious that they withdrew in fear from the Federal officials. But the field workers camped near the fullblood settlements, sent interpreters into the homes, and slowly secured these reluctant allottees in their inheritance. They finally enrolled 2,534, most of whom were fullbloods, but only 1,578 established a residence in the Indian Territory and received allotments. A few others who had settled in the Nation in 1891 in response to a tribal invitation were also carried on the rolls as Mississippi Choctaws. They were too primitive to manage their property after they received it, and many soon returned to Mississippi, leaving their allotments in the hands of trespassers.

The holders of the contracts secured legislation in 1906 and 1908 referring their interests to the Court of Claims, and in 1922 they received an award of $175,000 upon the principle of *quantum meruit*. The Federal officials paid the judgment partly from individual funds on hand belonging to Mississippi Choctaws and partly from the tribal treasury, and for years thereafter meager sums coming into the possession of the Mississippi Choctaws were requisitioned to pay their debt to the tribe.[22]

Presenting fewer legal complications than the Choctaw and Chickasaw, the Creek enrolment caused the greatest difficulty of all in actual registration. When the Dawes Commission attempted to prepare rolls under the Act of 1896, the tribal officials refused to turn over the rolls in their possession and the conservative fullbloods refused to register. Finally the Curtis Act provided that the Federal courts might compel tribal officials to surrender their rolls and require citizens to register.

[22] Kappler, *Laws and Treaties*, I, 106; II, 311, 313; III, 172, 370; IV, 367-68; *House Docs.*, 58 Cong., 2 Sess., No. 614; *Senate Docs.*, 70 Cong., 2 Sess., No. 263; Debo, *op. cit.*, pp. 70-71, 181; *Select Committee*, I, 1126-27; *Court of Claims Reports*, LI, 290-334; LVII, 617; *Supreme Court Reports*, LXIV, 690-91; LXV, 304-34, 684-97; Department of the Interior, *Annual Report*, 1898, pp. 459-65, text of decision, *Jack Amos* et al. v. *Choctaw Nation*; 1909, II, 376; 1919, II, 51; Dawes Commission, *Report*, 1899, appendix, pp. 36, 74-80; 1902, pp. 24-30; *Congressional Record*, LI, 308; LII, 5152-53; LXXII, 11100.

The Creek government then appointed a citizenship commission to assist, and the work proceeded more smoothly.

Rejected claimants appealed to the Federal courts, but not so many secured enrolment as in the Choctaw and Chickasaw nations. Their failure to grant intermarried citizenship protected the Creeks against white claimants, but there was a general feeling that too many Negroes had been admitted. As Pleasant Porter said, "our freedmen have increased wonderfully. . . . They come forth from the four quarters of the earth and employ a lawyer here to assist them, and they and the lawyer will get up the proof that slides them through." Creek freedmen shared equally with the Indians, hence there was no inducement for them to claim Indian blood.

But the primitive Creeks had never adopted a systematic nomenclature, and identification was almost impossible. One John Buch appeared before the Dawes Commission for enrolment. They searched the tribal rolls in vain for John Buch, but he was finally located as Co-e-cath-tahny Yah-lah-pon-co-conthlany. Later events were to disclose many irregularities in the Creek rolls as compiled by the Dawes Commission.[23]

The Cherokee enrolment came last and resulted in nearly as many legal tangles as the Choctaw-Chickasaw, and almost as much resistance as the Creek.

The Dawes Commission worked on the enrolment during 1901, checking their work against a tribal census roll of 1896. But when the field parties came to a fullblood settlement, they found amusements planned in remote places to call the Indians away. When they tried to secure the names of delinquents from their neighbors, the witnesses were threatened with bodily harm; and it was finally necessary to obtain a court order compelling the leading recalcitrants to come in with their families and submit to enrolment, and special deputy marshals went to hunt them out. Redbird Smith, a fullblood Cherokee, subsequently related his experience to a Senatorial committee:

[23] Dawes Commission, *Report*, 1900, pp. 21-25; Kappler, *Laws and Treaties*, I, 99; *Select Committee*, I, 648.

"When the Dawes Commission was here for the purpose of making the enrollment for final settlement by the allotment of the land, I stood up for my rights. I stood for the treaties and agreements that were made by my fathers with the Government of the United States; and I was at home enjoying myself in peace when I was arrested and taken to prison. I and several other Indians were arrested and taken together to the Muskogee jail for standing up for our rights—my old treaty with the United States Government—as I have always stood for it without violating any part of it, nor have I violated any law.

"By SENATOR LONG:

"Q. How long did they keep you there?—A. One night. On Saturday evening they put me in jail and they kept me all night in jail and on Sunday morning they let me out, and then they took me to the commissioner's office and made me enroll against my will."[24]

While the Cherokees were resisting enrolment, thousands of white applicants carried their claims to the United States Supreme Court. Their case was decided in 1906, and the Cherokee citizenship laws were upheld in every particular. White people who had intermarried with Cherokees after 1877 were denied any share of the tribal property. Unlike the Choctaw-Chickasaw citizenship court in a parallel case, the Supreme Court also upheld the forfeiture provisions of Cherokee law. The Cherokees had made no provision conferring intermarried citizenship upon one who should marry a Cherokee citizen not of Indian blood, hence the court ruled against such claims. A law of 1839 by which a Cherokee moving out of the Nation lost his citizenship unless readmitted by the Council was also sustained. Of the 3,627 claimants only 286 who had intermarried before 1877 were admitted.[25]

Additional litigation arose when a group of Cherokee citizens challenged the right of Congress to reopen the rolls after they had been closed by the Cherokee Agreement. The case was

[24] Dawes Commission, *Report*, 1902, pp. 31-34; *Select Committee*, I, 98.
[25] Kappler, *Laws and Treaties*, III, 54; Department of the Interior, *Annual Report*, 1906, II, 291; *Supreme Court Reports*, LI, 96-105.

carried to the United States Supreme Court, and the rights of
the 5,605 "newborns" were upheld in 1912. The same year
the court decided against 1,720 freedmen who based their
claims on a roll not recognized by the tribe.[26]

The Five Tribes Act provided that all the rolls should close
March 4, 1907. But some duplications were afterwards canceled, and 312 names were added by act of Congress in 1914.
The rolls included several small groups that had been incorporated into the tribes, especially about seven hundred Euchees,
who formed a part of the Creek Nation, and about a thousand
Delawares, who had purchased the right to Cherokee citizenship in 1867. The quantum of blood indicated by the rolls is
somewhat misleading, partly because of inaccuracies in a matter that at the time seemed unimportant, and partly because
fullblood Indians of mixed tribal descent were classed as mixed
bloods. The final rolls are as follows:[27]

|  | INDIANS | | | WHITES | FREEDMEN | TOTAL |
|---|---|---|---|---|---|---|
|  | fullbloods | mixed | total |  |  |  |
| Cherokees | 8,703 | 27,916 | 36,619 | 286 | 4,919 | 41,824 |
| Choctaws | 7,087 | 10,401 | 17,488 | 1,651 | 6,029 | 25,168 |
| Miss. Choc. | 1,357 | 303 | 1,660 |  |  | 1,660 |
| Chickasaws | 1,515 | 4,144 | 5,659 | 645 | 4,662 | 10,966 |
| Creeks | 6,858 | 5,094 | 11,952 |  | 6,809 | 18,761 |
| Seminoles | 1,254 | 887 | 2,141 |  | 996 | 3,127 |
| TOTAL | 26,774 | 48,745 | 75,519 | 2,582 | 23,405 | 101,506 |

While the enrolment was going on, other employees of the
Dawes Commission were appraising the land. They divided
the small Seminole area into three classes according to comparative value, but the rest of the land was listed under eighteen
or nineteen descriptive classifications such as "best black
prairie," "bottom subject to overflow," "rough mountain land,"

[26] *Supreme Court Reports*, LVI, 928-34; Department of the Interior, *Annual Report*, 1912, II, 427-31.
[27] Superintendent for the Five Civilized Tribes, Office Files (Muskogee, Okla-homa), Report of A. M. Landman, 1935, p. 54; Department of the Interior, *Annual Report*, 1905, I, 128, 141-42; 1916, II, 73, 79; 1917, II, 50; *Select Committee*, II, 1316.

etc. The timbered section of the Choctaw Nation was appraised last, and the standing pine was estimated by timber experts.[28] The work was honestly and carefully done, and the appraisement made at this time furnished the basis of all future computations regarding the value of Indian property.

As soon as the field parties had completed the classification, an arbitrary monetary valuation was placed upon each class. These figures were comparative only; since all the land was to be divided among the citizens there was no attempt to estimate the actual valuation. It was a convenient and fair method of equalizing the property among the allottees, but it had the unfortunate result of arousing the cupidity of the white man, who could not bear to see good land pass to Indians at such bargain prices. The tribes accordingly had to combat many schemes upon the part of individuals and the Federal Government for forced sale of the land "at the appraised valuation," a phrase that sounded honest yet was equivalent to legalized robbery. When the United States used this valuation to pay the Supreme Court judgment for lands allotted to the Chickasaw freedmen, it was an act of national dishonesty amounting to confiscation.

Before the allotment began, the Dawes Commission segregated the townsites, the Choctaw-Chickasaw coal and asphalt land, the land occupied by schools and tribal buildings, and small tracts needed for cemeteries and churches. The Interior Department took over the management of this property, which was to be sold in order to distribute the proceeds among the citizens. The only exception was the Seminole townsite of Wewoka, which was to be platted and sold by the tribal officials.

The Seminole allotment was completed with little difficulty. The three classes of land were valued at $5.00, $2.50 and $1.25 an acre. The total landed wealth of the Nation was secured by multiplying the number of acres in each class by this valuation. This sum when divided by the number of citizens gave each Seminole a share of about $300, which he might invest in

[28] Dawes Commission, *Report,* 1899, pp. 22-25; 1900, pp. 28-29, 130; 1901, pp. 32-37; 1903, pp. 31-32.

3. Opening of the Creek Land Office at Muskogee, April 1, 1899. Creek citizens were invited to register their selection of allotments.

any kind of land he chose. The Seminole allotment, therefore, varied from 60 to 240 acres.

The Dawes Commission established a land office at Wewoka, June 1, 1901, and the Seminoles began choosing their allotments. The work progressed rapidly in this small and compact settlement, and within two months the allotment to citizens on the current roll was virtually completed. But the per caput share had run slightly above $300, and the fraction had been discarded, so that some allotted land was left. The "newborns" were then added to the rolls, but they were restricted to forty-acre allotments. This completed the division, with the exception of a very small acreage, which was afterwards sold.[29]

The Commission did not succeed so well in an equitable distribution of the Creek property. For some reason this most recalcitrant of all the tribes was the first to which allotments were made, and the only one for which the work was begun under the Curtis Act without any negotiated agreement. The Commissioners, therefore followed the Government's general Indian policy by allotting a quarter-section to each citizen with the ultimate intention of purchasing the remainder for white settlement; but the Creeks steadfastly refused to sell any of their land, and when the agreement was finally negotiated with the tribe it carried the so-called "equalization" plan.

The land office was opened in Muskogee April 1, 1899, and Creek citizens were invited to register their selections. Then according to the equalization plan the value of the best land was set at $6.50 an acre, or $1,040 for a quarter section; and citizens whose land fell below this standard were to be compensated by enough additional land or money to equal it. Any tribal funds remaining were to be distributed per caput.[30]

But with the additions of "newborns" to the rolls, virtually all the land was required for these 160-acre allotments, and the tribal funds proved insufficient for equalization. The Creeks refused to discharge the United States from further

29 *Ibid.*, 1900, p. 28; 1901, pp. 153-54; 1902, pp. 43-45; 1914, p. 214.

30 *Ibid.*, 1899, pp. 20-21; Department of the Interior, *Annual Report*, 1899, I, 124; Indian Territory Division Files, 4412/04, pp. 126-27.

obligation, and the matter stood at a deadlock until 1914, when Congress authorized the distribution of tribal funds upon an equalization basis of $800. An additional distribution took place under legislation enacted in 1918, and the equalization was brought up to $860.[31]

But the Cherokees suffered an even more serious shortage, for many citizens of that tribe failed to receive any land at all. The Cherokee Agreement had fixed 110 acres of average land as the individual share. According to the comparative values placed upon the different classes of land by the Commission, this provision meant that every Cherokee had an allotment credit of $325.60, which he might invest in land.[32] As the allotment progressed, it became apparent that the Cherokees were running short of land, and Congress therefore provided that each citizen who failed to receive his share should be paid $651.20 from tribal funds, an amount equal to twice the appraised value of the land. In 1910 the Department officials listed 1,522 for this payment, and 1,205 of the "newborns" who won their right to enrolment in 1912 received no land. The Federal officials usually purchased and improved a small tract of land with this money, and the Indian held it under a special deed restricting it against alienation, but there was no way by which it could be made tax exempt. Allottees who failed to receive the full amount of land to which they were entitled were also compensated by a cash payment of twice the appraised value of the shortage.[33]

The Choctaw-Chickasaw allotment was carried on at the same time as the Cherokee. Land offices were established April 15, 1903, at Atoka for the Choctaw Nation and at Tishomingo for the Chickasaw. A citizen might select his allotment in either nation or in both, but he was required to apply at the office

---

[31] Department of the Interior, *Annual Report*, 1907, II, 305; 1909, II, 45-46, 180, 385; 1915, II, 378-80; 1919, II, 368; Kappler, *Laws and Treaties*, III, 412; IV, 24-25, 166; *Congressional Record*, LI, 11019, 11918-25, 13768, appendix, 706-7.

[32] Department of the Interior, *Annual Report*, 1910, II, 170; Kappler, *Laws and Treaties*, I, 788.

[33] Department of the Interior, *Annual Report*, 1907, II, 104-5; 1909, II, 377; 1910, II, 170; 1912, II, 303, 431; 1913, II, 494; 1914, II, 295-96; Kappler, *Laws and Treaties*, III, 170, 412.

where the land was located. Under the Supplemental Agreement the Choctaws and Chickasaws, alone of the tribes, had modified their original demand for the division of *all* their land, and had consented to allotments of 320 acres of average land and the sale of the remainder. According to the comparative values placed upon the nineteen classes of land by the Dawes Commission, 320 acres of average land would vary in actual area from 160 to 4,165 acres, and the freedmen's limited shares would run from 20 to 521 acres. In the case of timber land the estimated value of the pine—in this instance the actual value—had been added to the appraisement. The allotments of these rich tribes were larger than the easy-going Indians could conveniently use, and many of them showed little interest in selecting their full acreage; hence Congress provided in 1909 that money payments of twice the appraisement might be substituted for remnants not exceeding fifty dollars in allotment value.[34]

Although the allotments could not be entirely completed as long as there was any legal complication or any irregularity in the rolls, the work was virtually over in all the tribes by 1910. The following table will show the final disposition of the land in the Five Tribes area:[35]

| | TOTAL ACREAGE | ALLOTTED ACREAGE | SEGREGATED AND UNALLOTTED ACREAGE |
|---|---|---|---|
| Choctaw-Chickasaw | 11,660,951 | 8,091,517.48 | 3,569,432.52 |
| Cherokee | 4,420,068 | 4,346,145 | 73,923 |
| Creek | 3,079,095 | 2,997,114 | 81,981 |
| Seminole | 365,852 | 359,575 | 6,277 |
| TOTAL | 19,525,966 | 15,794,351.48 | 3,731,613.52 |

These immense tracts were not partitioned without conflicts. One of the most difficult tasks of the whole allotment process

---

[34] Dawes Commission, *Report*, 1903, p. 53; 1904, pp. 41-43; Kappler, *Laws and Treaties*, III, 412; Department of the Interior, *Annual Report*, 1910, II, 179.

[35] Superintendent, Office Files, Report of A. M. Landman, 1935, pp. 56-60.

was an obligation assumed by the Federal Government in the agreements "to place the allottee in possession." This duty was performed by the Union agent with his Indian police. Often the trespassers were mere intruders claiming no right but difficult to dislodge. Others were rejected citizenship claimants, who refused to surrender the land they had formerly occupied. More often they were owners of occupancy titles purchased from a former claimant or from a land baron whose great holdings were in excess of his own share and the shares of his family. There were many involved contests between two Indians claiming the right to allot the same land. In such cases a regular trial would ensue, with the taking of testimony and the rendering of formal judgments. Collisions were most frequent in the northwest portion of the Cherokee Nation, which was believed to be valuable oil territory. Five contests, for instance, were filed on one ten-acre tract in this region.[36]

The Missouri, Kansas, and Texas Railroad also contested the division of the land among the Indian owners. When this corporation secured a franchise to build a north-south line across the Indian Territory shortly after the Civil War, Congress in spite of the guarantees of perpetual ownership made to the tribes, had granted it alternate sections in a ten-mile strip on each side of the right-of-way in the event that "said lands become a part of the public lands of the United States." The railroad followed the coal outcrop across the Choctaw Nation, hence the ratification of this iniquitous grant would have been equivalent to a gift of many millions of dollars.

It is apparent that any method of allotment by which the land would pass even temporarily into the possession of the United States might automatically validate this grant; hence it was to the interest of the railway officials to oppose any plan for the direct division of the tribal estates among the citizens. When the Choctaw agreement was negotiated in the fall of 1896, the railroad attorney hurried to Washington to protest against its ratification. As soon as the Cherokees opened nego-

36 Dawes Commission, *Report*, 1899, pp. 20-21; 1904, p. 35; Department of the Interior, *Annual Report*, 1906, I, 230-31; 1907, II, 370.

tiations, he appeared before the joint meeting of the Dawes Commission and the Cherokee delegates and submitted the views of his company. But the Indians were alert to prevent this spoliation; the Dawes Commission maintained the utmost vigilance lest the wording of a law or an agreement might fulfill the conditions; and the Five Tribes Act of 1906 specifically stated that the tribal lands should never become the public property of the United States but should be held in trust for the benefit of the Indians and their heirs. The railroad then sued to force the grant, and in 1914 the United States Supreme Court decided that the conditions had never been consummated.[37]

Less noticeable at the time than the legal difficulties, because carried on in subterranean channels, but more serious from the standpoint of human values, was the uncompromising resistance of the more conservative Indians to the allotment policy. The exploited fullblood of the earlier Dawes reports, who was to be restored to his heritage by equitable division of the land, refused to accept his deliverance and clung to the old order with the stubbornness of despair. When the more progressive element surrendered to the threat of the Curtis Act and other coercive measures, these conservatives withdrew to form a tribal organization that would not misrepresent them.

In October of 1900 the Creek fullbloods chose a Principal Chief, a Second Chief, an advisory council of twelve, a legislative body of two houses, and a judicial tribunal. They made their capital the "Old Hickory Stomp Ground," long a ceremonial meeting place of the Creeks. Here they reenacted their old laws, and appointed lighthorsemen to enforce them, especially against the apostates of the tribe who were accepting allotments. The Choctaws had a similar band, which elected a Chief and Council and exercised governmental functions. With a touching belief in the inviolability of treaties, they insisted that the Dawes Commission had no lawful authority, and

[37] *Statutes at Large,* XLV, 236-39; *Indian Citizen,* January 14, 1897; Cherokee Papers, Joint Session Cherokee Commission and United States Commission; Kappler, *Laws and Treaties,* III, 181; *Supreme Court Reports,* LIX, 116-21.

that the United States would protect them from its illegal acts. No corresponding organization was reported among the Chickasaws, but the irreconcilables worked with the Choctaws in presenting memorials and petitions to the Federal Government. Among the Cherokees the old fullblood society, the Kee-too-wahs, divided and the dissenters formed the Nighthawk organization. No unified resistance was reported among the Seminoles.[38]

With the Indian genius for collective action, the Creek, Cherokee, Choctaw, and Chickasaw irreconcilables formed the Four Mothers Society, said at one time to have twenty-four thousand members. It probably originated at least as early as 1895, and although its existence was apparently unknown to Federal officials, it was functioning actively in 1906. Eufaula Harjo, a fullblood Creek, was one of the leaders, and Redbird Smith seems also to have been active in the organization. The society sent frequent delegations to Washington to secure a restoration of the old ways, and employed a white man representing himself to be an attorney to secure legislation to that effect. The work was supported by monthly dues of $1 for the men, 25 cents or more for the women, and 5 cents or more for each child. At least part of the members made these payments regularly from 1895 to 1915, and probably continued them for a long time thereafter.[39]

The only open result of this determined opposition was the widely reported "Snake Uprising" of 1901. Chitto Harjo, or Crazy Snake, the leader, was a typical defender of the old order. Intelligent and industrious in his primitive way, he lived in a little log cabin in a clearing, plowed a little patch of corn with a pony, filled his smokehouse with meat, and sharpened the neighbors' plowshares and wrought rings and ornaments in silver at a little forge he had constructed.[40] With all the

[38] Department of the Interior, *Annual Report,* 1901, I, 235; Acts of the Choctaw Nation, October 22, 1903; Dawes Commission, *Report,* 1902, pp. 31-32; *Select Committee,* I, 299, 956-61.

[39] *Select Committee,* I, 89-100; Commissioner of Indian Affairs, Office Files, 82904/10.

[40] *Select Committee,* I, 689, testimony of Miss Alice M. Robertson.

eloquence of an intense and ardent nature he urged that the guarantees of the removal treaties should be fulfilled. Picturing the conflicting races as two individuals, he summed up the long controversy between the Indians and the whites in the form of a dramatic dialogue:

"He told me that as long as the sun shone and the sky is up yonder these agreements will be kept. . . . He said as long as the sun rises it shall last; as long as the waters run it shall last; as long as grass grows it shall last. . . . He said, 'Just as long as you see light here, just as long as you see this light glimmering over us, shall these agreements be kept, and not until all these things cease and pass away shall our agreement pass away.' That is what he said, and we believed it. . . . We have kept every turn of that agreement. The grass is growing, the waters run, the sun shines, the light is with us, and the agreement is with us yet, for the God that is above us all witnessed that agreement."[41]

The "Snakes," as Chitto Harjo's followers were called, became such a menace to the more progressive Indians that Chief Porter called on Dr. Leo E. Bennett, the United States marshal, for protection. The Snakes dispersed at Bennett's order, but the following January they reconvened their "Council" and prepared to enforce their "laws" restoring the tribal régime. Their "Principal Chief" sent a notification to the President, and copies of their "laws" were posted throughout the Nation, warning all Creeks not to take allotments, rent land to noncitizens, or employ white labor in any capacity. Their "lighthorsemen" arrested and whipped several persons who had violated these orders; they also commanded all who had received allotment certificates from the Dawes Commission to surrender them, and they secured a large number, which they turned over to the "Chief."

This action caused widespread alarm throughout the Indian Territory, and the movement was reported to be spreading among the Cherokees, Choctaws, and Seminoles. Bennett and

---

[41] *Ibid.*, I, 1248, speech of Chitto Harjo to a Senatorial committee in 1906, interpreted by David Hodge.

Agent Shoenfelt in alarm called for a troop of cavalry, but before the soldiers arrived, Bennett went with a posse to a log cabin in the foothills along the South Canadian, where he found twenty or thirty armed Indians. He warned them to disband. They made no attempt to harm him, and he returned to Muskogee the following day. When the soldiers arrived, Bennett with several deputies and Indian police accompanied them and arrested 94 Indians, 67 of whom were placed in jail at Muskogee. They were tried before Judge John R. Thomas and sentenced to long terms in prison; but Thomas, who sympathized with the bewildered fullbloods, lectured them and set them free upon their promise to drop their opposition. Their helplessness and their pathetic trust in the United States is shown in their own account of the affair, which they sent to President McKinley. It was written immediately after Bennett's invasion of their settlement, and its purpose was to claim protection under the treaties.

Hickory-town, I. T.

Prestitent McKinley                            Jan. 26, 1901
    Washington D. C.

DEAR SIR:

As I want you to hear from me Hickory-town Muskogee Indian as we full-bloods as we held a meeting there as this the treaty between U. S. government & Indians was made long along a I am under the treaty raise my children a I have already told to you. I have made elect the chief and also light horsemen ready all together made my sign through the Indian nation but your citizen is what trouble me so. cause my citizen in trouble your citizen arrest my citizen without any cause, I know of. I am doind perfectly right as what treaty was. I am not disturb any U. S. government nor break any law whatever. I am right line. but your citizen what trouble me so I am you said to let know what cause you to trouble so. I wrote to you about it but it is your citizen. you have perfecly right to tend right away, as I ask to you. as you said any-one bother in your nation I would tend to that clear out of my nation as you said as this gentleman what bothers so his name Dr. Bennett. U. S. marshall suppose to be. As you see this letter to please answer it right away.

    I am friendly worker for Muskogee Nation

LARTER MEKKO[42]

---

[42] Department of the Interior, *Annual Report,* 1901, I, 235-37; Five Tribes Papers, Creek, 34546 A.

This Creek attempt to resist allotment by constitutional forms, and its bloodless outcome became an "Indian Uprising" to a generation hungering for its lost frontier. It had no other result except to halt the Creek appraisement for a few weeks.

The Snake resistance in the other tribes did not receive so much publicity, but the same sort of difficulty developed. In 1903 the Federal officials seem to have requested Chief Mc-Curtain to suppress the Snake band of Choctaws, which through a similar governmental organization was intimidating many citizens of the tribe and preventing them from selecting allotments, but the Council declared that any attempt by the Chief to suppress the Snakes would result in bloodshed, and formally requested the Indian agent to take action.[43]

It proved impossible, however, to compel the Snakes and Nighthawks to accept allotments. When they refused to register their choice, the Dawes Commission made the selection for them, trying conscientiously to include the Indian's little cabin in his allotment; but the Indians refused to accept the selections, and when the certificates and patents were mailed to them, they returned them. Eufaula Harjo explained it in 1906:

"After our country was divided they would send the half breeds around—the half breed Indians—they would go out and hunt for the names of the full-blood Indians without their consent, and they would take the names down and go and present them before the Dawes Commission, and these half breeds that brought these names before the Dawes Commission would go and take an oath over it. That was the way it was done, and the Dawes Commission itself has taken an oath for the Indians. . . . These people would not know anything about it, but they would find a certificate sent to them at the postoffice. . . . When I went to the store one day the postmaster handed me this certificate, but he did not tell me what it was. I took it because I didn't know what it was, but when I found out what it was I returned the certificate back again to the Indian agent. The Indian people did not want these certificates,

[43] Acts of the Choctaw Nation, October 22, 1903.

so they gathered up a whole lot of them and brought them to me and I took them to the Indian agent. The Indian people are still sending these certificates back again, for they don't want them."[44]

As late as 1912 nearly two thousand members of the Cherokee tribe alone steadfastly refused to claim their allotments, and their land was lying idle or in the possession of trespassers. These fullbloods lived in the "Cherokee hills" in the most extreme destitution, but they refused to accept the per caput payments to which they had become entitled in the final distribution of their property. When the great Cushing oil pool was opened in the Creek country, it was reported that seventy or eighty Snakes who had been arbitrarily allotted in that region refused for a time to claim their tremendous wealth. In 1915 Indians were still returning checks mailed to them from the Agency.[45]

The more educated of these irreconcilables realized, however, that even a treaty that was to endure "as long as the waters run" could not induce water to run uphill. They recognized the new order as an accomplished fact that had been accepted by the tribe over their protest, and they planned to accept their undesired allotments, sell them to the land-hungry white man, and purchase a tract of land in Mexico or South America, where they might resume again their tribal life and their communal tenure. Large numbers of Cherokees, Choctaws, Chickasaws, and Creeks were interested in this project, which assumed at one time an official character. They began to advocate it at least as early as 1895, and as late as 1908 they still hoped to secure Congressional action to remove the restrictions against the alienation of their allotments so that they might be free to carry it out.[46]

---

[44] *Select Committee,* I, 90-91.

[45] *Muskogee Phoenix,* December 27, 1912; April 3, July 29, 1914; May 21, 1915; Department of the Interior, *Annual Report,* 1912, II, 474.

[46] Commissioner of Indian Affairs, *Annual Report,* 1895, p. 160; 1897, p. 141; *Muskogee Phoenix,* July 8, August 29, 1905; February 25, 1906; February 5, 1908; *Muskogee Times-Democrat,* October 31, 1908.

A paper expressing the aims of the Choctaws and Chickasaws who desired removal was presented to a Senatorial committee that visited the Indian Territory in 1906, by Jacob B. Jackson, an elderly Choctaw fullblood who had been sent to college by the Nation and had long been prominent in tribal politics.

"Surely a race of people, desiring to preserve the integrity of that race, who love it by reason of its traditions and their common ancestors and blood, who are proud of the fact that they belong to it may be permitted to protect themselves, if in no other way by emigration. Our educated people inform us that the white man came to this country to avoid conditions which to him were not as bad as the present conditions are to us; that he went across the great ocean and sought new homes in order to avoid things which to him were distasteful and wrong. All we ask is that we may be permitted to exercise the same privilege. We do not ask any aid from the Government of the United States in so doing. We do ask that we may be permitted, in a proper way, by protecting our own, to dispose of that which the Government says is ours, and which has been given us over our protest against the distribution, to the end that another home may be furnished, and another nation established.

". . . We ask consideration of this prayer for these reasons: First, it is our desire, and we make the request with a full knowledge of its importance, both to us and to our children. Second, we believe, if it were known, it would be the desire of the white man. He does not want the Indian any more than we want him, and by carrying out this plan he will get that which he wants—the Indian land. We will leave and trouble him no longer. Third, it is right—it is just. Over our protest a majority, or what is said to be a majority, of voters approved an agreement with the United States changing our social, political, and personal conditions. There is nothing left for us to do but accept conditions as they are. There is no remedy for us except removal.

"If the Choctaw and Chickasaw people as a whole were willing to lose their racial status, to become by a slow process of blood mixture, and through changed conditions, white men in fact, . . . we do not oppose the carrying out of their desires; but, in addition to the reasons given, we believe that the Great Father of all men created the Indian to fill a proper place in this world. That as an Indian he had certain rights, among which is a right to exist as a race, and that in the protection of that right, it is our belief that we are fulfilling the purpose of the Divine Creator of mankind."[47]

The Senators received Jackson's appeal with ridicule. The project, indeed, seems never to have been seriously considered by the Federal officials, and it was definitely discouraged in 1908 by Secretary Garfield.[48] It is doubtful if the white man's conscience could have permitted the Indians to be driven a second time into exile. He could convince himself that by allotment he was conferring a real boon on the Indians, but to save his own self-respect he could not permit them to flee from his benefactions. He was happier not to be confronted with the spiritual wastage that he had wrought.

But the division of the land among the Indians was only one phase of the immense task of liquidating the tribal régime. The Federal officials also assumed the management of four great estates and the political and social control of a numerous Indian and white population.

[47] *Select Committee,* I, 960-62.
[48] *Muskogee Phoenix,* February 12, 1908.

# CHAPTER III

# The White Man's Guardianship

WHILE the Dawes Commission was engaged in making the rolls and appraising and allotting the land, other agencies of the Government were entrusted with the administration of the undivided property and the protection of the individual allottees.

All these activities were under the supervision of Secretary of the Interior Hitchcock. As a conservationist, Hitchcock made an honest attempt to guard the tribal property from the predatory private interests that began to snatch it as soon as the tribal control was relaxed; but he never grasped the elemental fact that he was administering four great estates belonging to a hundred thousand individuals, rather than the public domain. He had no scruples against using the property for the supposed benefit of the owners without their consent, or even for the benefit of other Indian tribes or the general public, and he never felt the slightest obligation to render an accounting.

The Curtis Act had provided for an Indian Inspector to act as the direct representative of the Secretary. This officer supervised the Union agency, the tribal governments and schools, the collection of the tribal revenues, the Choctaw-Chickasaw coal and asphalt mines, the platting and sale of the townsites, and the general administration of all undivided tribal property. J. George Wright, an inspector in the Indian service, was detailed to this position and established his office at Muskogee. He served until 1907, when his office was consolidated with that of Commissioner to the Five Civilized Tribes and he took over the combined work.[1]

---

[1] Kappler, *Laws and Treaties*, I, 100; Department of the Interior, *Annual Report,* 1899, I, 85-86; 1900, pp. 84-85; 1908, II, 191.

The most important office under Wright's supervision was the Union agency. When the tribal governments began to lose their power, the agent had to deal not with five political units but with thousands of bewildered individuals attempting to adjust themselves to new conditions. As the work increased in complexity, Congress made larger appropriations; and the two clerks, who had once constituted an adequate office force, were joined by hundreds of employees working in specialized departments.

J. Blair Shoenfelt was serving as agent when the duties of the office first became important. Without going into the truth or falsity of charges that were brought against him, it is evident that he was sluggish in the administration of his duties.[2] He was succeeded by Dana H. Kelsey in 1905. Barely thirty years old when first entrusted with his tremendous responsibility, Kelsey had spent eleven years in the Indian service—five in Oklahoma Territory, and the last six in Wright's office. His integrity was never questioned, and he was conscientious in trying to protect the vast property interests of his inexperienced charges. In the more important—and possibly insuperable—task of aiding the Indians to make the necessary spiritual adjustment, he was not so successful. The year after he took over the work he accounted for more than three million dollars that passed through his hands, but the disintegration of Indian character that took place during the same time was unrecorded.[3]

Political patronage was freely employed in selecting the personnel of the new Governmental agencies in the Indian Territory. Republican Senators and Representatives from the forty-five states flooded the Secretary's office with recommendations for the employment of the faithful among their con-

[2] This is evident in tracing individual transactions. For example, the involved correspondence between Shoenfelt and the Choctaw officials regarding the expulsion of an intruder physician (Five Tribes Papers, Choctaw—Intruders; Indian Territory Division Files, 4412/04).

[3] *Muskogee Phoenix,* May 13, 1905; Department of the Interior, *Annual Report,* 1907, II, 99-100. For Kelsey's honest admission of his difficulty, see *Select Committee,* I, 583-84, 588-90.

stituents, and frequent requests for their promotion, watching the payrolls of the various agencies with a solicitous care that extended from administrative leaders to the humblest employees.[4]

A. P. Murphy of Missouri explained frankly to an investigator in 1903 the tortuous method which he had found necessary to employ to secure appointment as attorney for the Creek Nation. Chief Porter had already made two selections which had been rejected by Secretary Hitchcock. When Murphy applied, the Chief refused to recommend him until he should first secure proof that his appointment would be acceptable. Murphy was not personally acquainted with the Secretary, but he secured the endorsement of the chairman of the Missouri State Committee and other political friends, and recommendations as to his character and ability, and forwarded them to Hitchcock. Hitchcock then gave his consent and the Chief made the appointment.[5]

Some attempt, however, was made by the Agency and the Dawes Commission to select and retain employees because of their qualifications, and many complaints arose from local Republican newspapers that too many undeserving Democrats and lukewarm Republicans secured employment. According to the investigation made in 1903, the 240 employees of the Dawes Commission owed their positions to a haphazard combination of political patronage, a real appraisal of their qualifications, and an accidental selection to supply an immediate need.[6] In 1908 an executive order of Theodore Roosevelt conferred civil service status upon 126 employees of the Union agency without examination, and their tenure from that time on was fairly permanent.[7]

As the Federal agencies increased in administrative authority, the tribal governments declined. The Indians had hoped that by yielding to allotment they might retain their govern-

[4] Indian Office Files, *passim.*

[5] Indian Territory Division Files, 4412/04, pp. 268-70, 300.

[6] *Ibid.,* 4412/04, p. 164; *Senate Docs.,* 58 Cong., 2 Sess., No. 189, p. 32; *Muskogee Phoenix,* December 14, 1905.

[7] *Congressional Record,* LI, 10925-27, 12834-35.

mental functions,[8] but they were not successful. In 1897 Congress made all tribal legislation subject to Presidential veto, and the Atoka, the Creek, and the Cherokee agreements set the date for the end of the tribal régime at March 4, 1906.[9] Only the Seminoles retained for a time a measure of independence; under their agreement they continued to pass laws without supervision, but in 1903 Congress provided that their government also should end March 4, 1906. The acts of the other Councils were submitted to Inspector Wright, who transmitted them with his recommendations to the Secretary. The President always acted upon his advice.[10]

Apparently by common consent the different tribes ceased to hold elections, and the last elected Councils and executive officers continued to serve. W. C. Rogers, Green McCurtain, Douglas H. Johnston, and Pleasant Porter were at the head of the administration in the Cherokee, Choctaw, Chickasaw, and Creek tribes, respectively. Hulbutta Micco (Alligator King), an illiterate fullblood, served as Chief of the Seminoles from 1901 until his death in 1905. John F. Brown, who had served as Chief for twenty years prior to the administration of Hulbutta Micco, was elected to succeed him.[11] All these executives except Green McCurtain, who chose to ignore some distant white ancestors and class himself as a fullblood, were of mixed blood, and all of them represented the element in their respective tribes that realized the inevitability of surrendering to the Dawes Commission.

When it became apparent that the tribal estates would not be divided by 1906, the Indians began to request some provision for the extension of their governments. The Five Tribes Act therefore authorized the continuance of the governments in an attenuated form, but the Councils soon ceased to meet and

[8] *Indian Citizen,* November 12, 19, 1896; Dawes Commission *Report,* 1896, pp. 99-106.

[9] Department of the Interior, *Annual Report,* 1897, pp. 400-1, 414; Kappler, *Laws and Treaties,* I, 739, 796.

[10] Indian Office Files, Correspondence Land Division, Letter Book, DCCXXXVII, 170; Kappler, *Laws and Treaties,* III, 24; Acts of the Choctaw Nation, 1898 ff.

[11] *Seminole Capital,* May 11, 1905; Indian Office Files, Correspondence Land Division, Letter Book, DCCXXXVII, 170-72.

the executives and attorneys became Presidential appointees.[12]

The decline of the tribal courts was even more rapid. Congress in 1897 extended Federal law over tribal citizens, and the next year by the Curtis Act abolished the tribal courts. These laws went into effect in the Cherokee, Creek, and Seminole nations, but the jurisdiction of the Choctaw and Chickasaw courts was continued by the Atoka Agreement except in cases involving real estate titles and certain serious crimes. In 1904 Congress extended Federal jurisdiction over estates and guardianships in these two tribes, but the courts were not abolished until 1907.[13] During the same period the United States courts were progressively enlarged to take care of this extension of jurisdiction and of the growing needs of the white population. The Indians opposed the abolition of the tribal courts less than any of the other changes, for their leaders admitted the seriousness of the crime situation.[14]

The United States also assumed gradual control over the tribal revenues. By the Atoka Agreement the Choctaw-Chickasaw coal and asphalt royalties, and by the Curtis Act all the revenues of the Cherokees and Creeks were paid into the Federal treasury. The Department of the Interior had complete control of Cherokee and Creek disbursements, but the Choctaws and Chickasaws continued to issue, circulate, and pay tribal warrants. For a short time in 1898 the Agency collected the revenues of all the tribes, but in general the Choctaw and Chickasaw officials continued to collect all but the coal and asphalt royalties and a grazing tax that they had entrusted to the Federal officials in 1903 because of the defiance of intruder cattlemen. The Seminoles controlled their own finances until the Five Tribes Act of 1906.[15]

[12] Indian Territory Division Files, 16716/05, Enclosure No. 13; *ibid.*, Special File 39c, 15732/05; Acts of the Choctaw Nation, July 3, November 25, 1905; Kappler, *Laws and Treaties*, III, 171, 181; *infra*, pp. 258-59.

[13] Kappler, *Laws and Treaties*, I, 87-88, 100; III, 278, 647, 653-54.

[14] Department of the Interior, *Annual Report*, 1897, pp. 142, 401; 1902, II, 91, 487, 497-99; 1904, I, 184, 521-22; Debo, *op. cit.*, p. 253.

[15] Kappler, *Laws and Treaties*, III, 97, 652-53; Department of the Interior, *Annual Report*, 1899, I, 112-13, 120; 1903, I, 167-68; 1904, I, 209; Acts of the Choctaw Nation, October 23, 1903; Five Tribes Papers, Choctaw—Cattle.

In 1905 with the tribal governments rapidly approaching dissolution, the non-citizens made a determined effort to resist paying the tribal taxes, and many brave speeches were made reminiscent of Bunker Hill and the Boston Tea Party. But Hitchcock insisted that in the absence of any repeal by Congress the taxes were still in effect, and President Roosevelt supported him in this position. The agent prepared to expel all delinquents from the Territory as intruders, and at least a portion of the tribal revenues was collected.[16]

The Five Tribes Act retroactively abolished all tribal taxes from December 31, 1905. It provided that a special official appointed by the Department of the Interior should receive all tribal revenues and should pay tribal warrants and other debts against the tribes. No tribal treasurer received or disbursed any moneys after the passage of this law.[17]

At the same time the Indians lost control of their revenues, they inadvertently lost control of education; for the Secretary of the Interior ruled that his control over the Choctaw-Chickasaw royalties and all Cherokee and Creek revenues invested him with the management of the schools. Under this interpretation he appointed a superintendent of schools for the Indian Territory, and a supervisor for each of the tribes except the Seminole. The schools were not incorporated into the regular Indian school service, but the Indian Office formulated regulations for the guidance of the administrators.[18]

John D. Benedict of Danville, Illinois, was appointed as superintendent February 10, 1899. He owed his position to the patronage of Joseph G. Cannon, who continued to show an interest in his welfare even to the extent of requesting his retention when the Department was investigating charges against him. He engaged at once in numerous business activities and became a leader in Republican politics in the Indian

---

[16] Department of the Interior, *Annual Report,* 1899, I, 119; 1903, I, 163-72; Dawes Commission, *Report,* 1900, pp. 93-95, 123-24; Five Tribes Papers, Choctaw—Intruders; *ibid.,* Choctaw—Doctors; *Muskogee Phoenix,* June 3, 4, 7, 13, 21, 1905.

[17] Kappler, *Laws and Treaties,* III, 173-74; Department of the Interior, *Annual Report,* 1907, II, 366; Indian Office Files, 5642/09 Five Tribes 013.

[18] Department of the Interior, *Annual Report,* 1899, I, 86-87.

Territory. The four supervisors, who were appointed April 30, 1899, were also from distant Northern states and as unfamiliar as Benedict with the Indians' institutions.[19]

Even before Benedict took charge of the schools, he reported to Commissioner Jones concerning the deplorable conditions of nepotism and waste and inefficiency that he found there. It was asserted that a child would better remain illiterate than to come in contact with such corruption at an early age. He declared that not more than four superintendents of the twenty-one boarding schools were competent to teach the ordinary English branches, and that they were even guilty of conversing with the children in the native language. He also deplored the emphasis given to academic training; the boys were trained for college and the professions instead of industry, and the girls studied Latin and mathematics instead of learning to keep house.[20]

It is difficult to evaluate Benedict's condemnation of the Indian schools. The Indian republics were so small and their people so closely interrelated that appointment to positions was somewhat a family and neighborhood matter, and a sort of uncritical nepotism was generally accepted in the management of the tribal schools. It is also true that Indian politicians, like their white brethren, often used educational appointments for political patronage, and that as a result there was some corruption and inefficiency. But nobody who is familiar with the fine culture attained by the Indian leaders can fail to respect the educational system that produced it. It is true that the superior intellectual attainments of the leaders were not matched by the literacy of the general population, but Benedict himself testified before a Federal investigator in 1903 that a great majority of the Indians could read and write,[21] an achievement for which the schools must be given great credit, for

[19] *Ibid.*, 1899, I, 86-89; Indian Office Files, 2272/10 Indian Territory Schools 150; Indian Territory Division Files, 4412/04, pp. 119-20, 201, 334-37, Enclosure No. 2; *Muskogee Times-Democrat*, December 8, 1909. In the face of continued charges Cannon finally withdrew his request.

[20] Department of the Interior, *Annual Report*, 1899, I, 87-92.

[21] Indian Territory Division Files, 4412/04, p. 341.

Indian literacy as recognized by the white man meant learning to speak and read and write a foreign language.

Benedict's condemnation of the curricula is even more difficult to evaluate. Indian society was distinguished by intellectual and artistic achievement, but very few Indians showed the restless acquisitiveness or the practical business sense of the white man. Their schools during the period of tribal control reflected these native traits. Benedict was too ignorant of the Indians' history to realize his rashness in attempting to change by an omnipotent gesture the genius of a people.

His most serious mistake was his failure to understand the devotion of the Indians to their schools. Some of the tribes had educational systems older than his own state of Illinois, and even yet had a larger proportion of college-trained men and women. Benedict's glowing reports of the great educational progress under his administration and of his success in arousing an interest in education must have been very offensive to a people accustomed for many years to regard their schools as their highest creative achievement.[22] He seems honestly to have thought the Indians would be glad to turn their educational systems over to his superior management, and when trouble later developed, he attributed it solely to the disappointment of tribal politicians accustomed to using the schools for patronage.

During the first summer he held examinations and appointed teachers. It is probably true that the educational standards of the Indian rural schools were too low, and that their teachers were unable to qualify. Whatever the reason, he soon had a corps of teachers, very few of whom were Indians, and most of whom were newcomers to the Territory.[23]

Benedict's troubles began as soon as the Councils convened in the fall. The Choctaws protested against the "interference of the said Secretary of the Interior without authority of law,"

[22] Debo, *op. cit.*, pp. 240-42; Department of the Interior, *Annual Report,* 1904, II, 274-75; 1908, II, 247-54.

[23] Department of the Interior, *Annual Report,* 1900, pp. 155-56; 1904, II, 290-93; Indian Territory Division Files, 4412/04, pp. 279-80, testimony of Miss Alice M. Robertson in 1903 that few Creeks secured positions because they were unable to qualify.

4. Nuyaka, Creek Boarding School. The Indians regarded their schools as their highest creative achievement.

and demanded "restitution" of tribal funds "illegally" expended for the support of Benedict's office. But they soon surrendered; their coal and asphalt royalties had passed from their hands by the Atoka Agreement and if the Secretary chose arbitrarily to disburse their other funds they had no means of defense.[24] The Chickasaws had no stronger economic position, but they were more determined in their opposition; they continued to manage their own schools, depending apparently upon tribal warrants to meet their financial obligations while their money was expended by the Secretary for the unused administrative machinery he was attempting to force upon them.[25] The Creeks displayed the same resentment, but they were entirely helpless in view of the complete control of the revenues conferred upon the Secretary by the Curtis Act; and they finally accepted the situation in the Creek Agreement. But this surrender did not prevent the Council from passing a unanimous resolution abolishing the supervisor's office, an action which, of course, had no legal effect.[26] Strangely enough the proud and independent Cherokees made the least resistance; their Board of Education worked in harmony with the new administrative officials, and D. F. Redd, the supervisor, showed a sincere appreciation of the great and noble history of the tribal schools.[27]

The Five Tribes Act of 1906 definitely placed the schools under Federal management. The Chickasaws then relinquished their control, but from that time on they began to send their children to private or state institutions and constantly demanded the discontinuance of the tribal schools. The Semi-

[24] Acts of the Choctaw Nation, October 11, 1899; October 24, 26, 31, 1900; October 29, 30, November 4, 1901; October 23, 1903; November 30, 1905; Department of the Interior, *Annual Report,* 1900, pp. 156-57; 1901, I, 127-28; 1903, I, 77, 79.

[25] Indian Office Files, 2272/10 Indian Territory Schools 150, statement by Benedict.

[26] Indian Territory Division Files, 4412/10, pp. 113-34, 266-67, 278-80; Kappler, *Laws and Treaties,* I, 738; *Select Committee,* I, 640.

[27] Indian Territory Division Files, 16716/05, Enclosures No. 4, 13; *Select Committee,* I, 235-37.

noles now for the first time came under Federal administration. They resisted so strongly that for a while the supervisor was unable to exercise his authority, but the Secretary now had complete control of their finances and their opposition was hopeless.[28]

It seems fairly obvious that the real reason for the Secretary's policy in assuming control of the schools under the doubtful authorization of the Atoka Agreement and the Curtis Act was the plight of the white children in the Territory. The Negroes also were in great need: there was a large non-citizen colored population; the Chickasaw Negroes had never received any educational provision; and although the Choctaw freedmen had been given schools at the time of their adoption they were now receiving the forty-acre allotments, which was their share of the tribal property, and were thereby precluded from any further benefits from tribal revenues.

As soon as Benedict and his supervisors took charge, they began to admit white children upon the payment of tuition by their parents. In 1904 Congress appropriated $100,000 from the Federal treasury, which was followed by an additional $100,000 in 1905, by $150,000 and an undetermined amount of surplus court fees in 1906, and by $300,000 in 1907.[29] Although these appropriations were usually referred to as gratuities to the Indians, their real purpose was the creation of educational opportunities for non-citizens. The money was used for the payment of tuition for the attendance of white children in existing schools, and for the establishment of additional rural schools—mixed schools for whites and Indians and separate schools for Negroes. Communities desiring a school were required to erect and equip a building, and the Department provided the teacher. The buildings were usually

[28] Kappler, *Laws and Treaties*, I, 663; III, 172-73; Department of the Interior, *Annual Report*, 1907, II, 307; *Select Committee*, I, 245; Indian Office Files, 2272/10 Indian Territory Schools 150.

[29] Kappler, *Laws and Treaties*, III, 277; Department of the Interior, *Annual Report*, 1902, I, 127; 1904, I, 90-91; 1904, II, 222-23.

of rough logs and the benches homemade, but the people were pathetically eager for educational opportunities.[30]

Benedict found the Snake settlements so hostile that he considered it unsafe to attempt the admission of white children. The Chickasaws also refused to admit non-citizen children during the period of tribal control. Eufaula Harjo, in explaining the opposition of his people, pointed out an inherent racial quality that placed them at a disadvantage:

"In the Indian Territory there is lots of schools in the Territory. There has always been lots of schools among the Indians ever since we came here, and we were proud of our schools, and our children went to them until the white man came in and crowded us out and took our schools away from us, and it seems to me that the little white children and the little negro children should not be made to go to the Indian schools that the Indians made with their own money. . . .

". . . I came in here a good while ago, and I was sitting back there a long time, but I couldn't understand what was going on only from what my interpreter would tell me. You saw me sitting back there, and I don't like to come forward. Now, when I take a little Indian child to school the white man and the negroes will go before me to school with their children and they will put their children first and they will push mine out of school, and that is the way it will go."[31]

It was certainly imperative that something be done for the non-citizen children; but the Indians resented the assumption that the Government in making the appropriation was bestowing a largesse upon *them*, and they strongly suspected that their own money was being used to educate the non-citizens. As Pleasant Porter said, "Yes, gentlemen, they took our funds and applied it to the education of white children, and now they come before you and make the plea of poverty for the

[30] Department of the Interior, *Annual Report*, 1902, I, 127; 1904, I, 90-92; 1904, II, 222-23, 273-74; 1905, I, 113-14; 1905, II, 221; 1907, II, 349-62; *Select Committee*, I, 220-33, 257-70.

[31] *Select Committee*, I, 92-93, James L. Gray, interpreter.

cause of education, and I want it distinctly understood that
the Indian is making no such plea. If he had his own he is
amply provided with funds to take care of his own."[32]

The great administrative cost represented by the generous
salaries of Benedict and the four supervisors and their liberal
office allowances could be justified only on the ground that these
officials were creating a Territorial school system. In that case
it certainly should not have been borne by the Indians, but it
was regularly paid from the revenues even of those tribes
that were successfully resisting their authority.

It is impossible to escape the conviction that the published
financial statements were intentionally ambiguous; but for the
school year 1907-1908, the last year under the Territorial
arrangement, it is possible by making numerous computations
to discover the number of Indians attending the rural schools
and the sums spent for their education. The boarding school
enrolment and expenditures may be disregarded because
the expense was borne entirely by the tribes and only Indians
were in attendance. The rural schools were maintained by
$272,576.83 of the Congressional appropriation, $41,811.86
from surplus court fees, and $90,366.40 from tribal funds. The
Indians, therefore, paid 22 per cent of the expense. A portion of
the money went to maintain schools for Negroes, of whom
11,556 were enrolled. The report makes no distinction between
citizen and non-citizen Negroes, but in 1907 the Indian Territory had a colored population of 80,649 while the Cherokee,
Creek, and Seminole rolls with their overlapping enumerations
of "newborns" carried the names of only 12,624 freedmen. It
is obvious, therefore, that the Negroes entitled to share in the
tribal funds constituted far less than 22 per cent of the total
colored population. The Indian enrolment in the rural schools
was 10,041, and the white was 54,853, a proportion of only
15 per cent Indian enrolment. It is therefore apparent that the
tribes not only paid the entire administrative cost of establish-

[32] *Select Committee,* I, 640.

ing a Territorial school system, but that they paid a disproportionate share of its maintenance.[33]

By this time Benedict had made ten glowing reports describing his success in arousing the Indians to an interest in education. But his enrolment of the Choctaws, for instance, contrasts
unfavorably with the report of the tribal officials for the school
year 1892-1893, the year the Dawes Commission was created.
In justice to Benedict it should be mentioned that the latter
figures include the Choctaw freedmen, but the number is negligible. These enrolments are as follows:[34]

|                      | 1907-1908 | 1892-1893 |
|----------------------|-----------|-----------|
| Rural schools        | 2,165     | 3,819     |
| Boarding schools     | 751       | 490       |
| Maintained in college |          | 40        |
|                      |           |           |
| TOTAL                | 2,915     | 3,439     |

In the fall of 1909 Inspector E. B. Linnen and other Indian
Office agents visited the Indian Territory boarding schools.
They reported the plants to be in an almost unbelievable condition of filth and dilapidation, the food insufficient, and sani-
tation and medical care entirely neglected. They found some
good teaching, but they reported a complete absence of vocational training—the very field in which Benedict had claimed
such revolutionary achievements. They found that Benedict
had until very recently been president of the Guarantee State
Bank of Muskogee, and had other extensive private interests,
and that "He has wholly neglected these schools, and is not
now familiar with their deplorable conditions."

When confronted with these charges, Benedict made no
attempt to deny the conditions reported by the inspectors. He
stated that the plants had been in a run-down condition when

---

[33] Department of the Interior, *Annual Report*, 1908, II, 241; Bureau of the Census, *Population of Oklahoma and Indian Territory 1907* (*Bulletin No. 89,* Washington, 1907), p. 9. Benedict's tables may possibly include the administrative expenses.

[34] Department of the Interior, *Annual Report*, 1893, p. 146; 1908, II, 241-46.

he assumed charge, and he pointed out the fact that the Government had never adopted a permanent policy regarding the boarding schools, but had continued their existence only during the transition from a tribal to a state school system, and that he had consequently not felt justified in making expensive repairs. This perfectly reasonable defense would be more convincing, however, if he had frankly stated his difficulties in his reports.

The school administration was completely reorganized as a result of this investigation. Benedict's office and the offices of the supervisors were abolished and regular Indian service employees were placed in charge; and the administrative cost was cut from $24,210 a year to $13,250. Of the twenty-four boarding schools, twelve that had fallen into the most serious dilapidation were abandoned, and the remaining twelve were rendered habitable by extensive repairs. The rural schools were taken over by the state government that had been established, and the Congressional appropriation from this time on was used to pay tuition for the Indian children who attended.[35]

The Department's treatment of Benedict furnishes material for ironical reflection. There can be little doubt that in creating a Territorial school system for non-citizens he was carrying out the real purpose of his superiors, but that purpose had been so deeply concealed under professions of benevolence to the Indians that in the end his administration was judged solely by its effect upon Indian education. But whatever the reason for the mismanagement of the tribal schools, the Indians had been seriously wronged. Enormous expenditures had been made, not only from their current revenues but from their trust funds, to maintain their schools, without a corresponding benefit.

In 1933 one tribe—the Creek—secured an accounting by the Court of Claims; but of course this judicial determination took into account only the legality of disbursements under acts of Congress rather than the moral justification. The Creek

---

[35] Department of the Interior, *Annual Report*, 1910, II, 223-30; 1911, II, 459-68; Indian Office Files, 2272/10 Indian Territory Schools 150.

Nation had spent $76,468.40 for education the last year of its control. The Department raised this amount to $155,218.91 in 1899-1900 and $102,208.95 in 1900-1901, but the latter sum was authorized by the Council. Both these sums were legal in the absence of any limitation, but the Creek Agreement of 1901 set $76,468.40 as the legal limit. The Secretary ignored this provision, and spent $20,021.85 more than the legal limit in 1901-1902, $10,800.87 in 1903-1904, and $29,024.66 in 1904-1905. The Five Tribes Act then limited the disbursements to the amount spent in 1904-1905. Since the Secretary had that year misappropriated $29,024.66 of Creek funds, this law had the curious result of perpetuating an annual expenditure of $105,493.06. Apparently this figure was high enough to relieve the Department officials from further temptation, for they exceeded it only once—$5,175.97 in 1906-1907. The Court of Claims decision returned $65,023.35 to the Creek treasury, but obviously this restitution represented only a small fraction of the sum lost through Departmental extravagance.[36]

Perhaps this reckless spending was encouraged by the large sums of money coming into the tribal treasuries from the sale of town lots. The important work of establishing the towns was carried on at the same time as the making of the tribal rolls, the appraisal and allotment of the land, and the gradual extension of Federal administration over the Indians. It was supervised by the Dawes Commission until 1901, when Congress placed it under the authority of the Indian Inspector. The actual platting, appraisal, and sale was carried out under the direction of a townsite commission upon which the tribe was represented.[37]

The platting began in 1899 and was nearly completed by 1903. Sales were conducted on a cash deposit and deferred payment plan. The payments began to assume immense proportions by 1902. They reached the peak in 1908 with

[36] *Court of Claims Reports,* LXXVIII, 496-98; Kappler, *Laws and Treaties,* I, 739.

[37] Kappler, *Laws and Treaties,* I, 94-96, 105-7, 731-36, 739, 751, 771-87, 794-95; Department of the Interior, *Annual Report,* 1897, p. 411; 1898, p. 436.

$975,228.92. Small amounts continued to come in for a long time, but the payments were practically completed by 1915. The total receipts from sales are as follows:[38]

| | |
|---|---:|
| Creek | $ 924,689.84 |
| Cherokee | 773,302.40 |
| Choctaw and Chickasaw | 3,097,257.33 |
| TOTAL | $4,795,249.57 |

In 1903 Congress provided that private parties might plat and sell townsites at their own expense, with the approval of the Dawes Commission. From that time on most of the towns were laid out by this method on land that had been allotted to individual Indians. The Dawes Commission held a regular hearing and examined witnesses regarding the location of the town, the education and business experience of the allottee, and whether the sale of the land to the townsite promoter would be to his best interest; and made recommendations to the Department for the removal of the restrictions on alienation. By 1907 individual allottees had received $2,020,829.61 for land sold as townsites.[39]

The various laws and agreements had provided that the towns might be incorporated and might levy taxes on all property except town lots still owned by the tribes. Provision was also made for bond elections under the supervision of the Secretary of the Interior. The municipalities began to establish schools, build electric light plants, construct water systems and sewers, and lay down paving and sidewalks. So far as the towns were concerned, the long-desired "development" had at last come to the Indian Territory.[40]

While the towns and the allotted land were passing under individual tenure, the Federal Government was administering a decreasing but still immense amount of undivided property.

---

[38] Department of the Interior, *Annual Report*, 1915, II, 342; Superintendent, Office Files, Report of A. M. Landman, 1935, p. 64.

[39] Department of the Interior, *Annual Report*, 1904, I, 110, 112; 1904, II, 24-25; 1907, II, 322.

[40] Kappler, *Laws and Treaties*, I, 95, 118-19, 734, 736, 783, 795.

Each citizen, of course, occupied his individual holdings until he received them in his allotment; but a great deal of land had never been placed under cultivation, and until it was allotted it was simply the public domain of the tribes. It was exploited to a considerable extent by trespassers, but the Federal Government made some attempt to expel intruders, to collect a grazing fee, and to prevent depredations of timber thieves. The capitols, jails, courthouses, and other public buildings also passed into the custody of the Secretary when they were no longer used by the tribal governments.[41]

A small amount of Seminole land remained after each citizen had received his share. Even in the Cherokee and Creek nations in spite of the shortage of land, a certain amount remained unallotted either because it was of no value or because it was in inconvenient small tracts. The Five Tribes Act provided for the sale of this land by the Secretary.[42]

When the Choctaws and Chickasaws decided to limit their allotments to an average of 320 acres, it was apparent that about three million acres of surplus would be subject to sale. As a large part of the Choctaw country was mountainous, unfit for agriculture, and covered with valuable timber, the Federal officials decided that it should be set aside as a forest reserve.

Before the allotment began, the Dawes Commission pointed out the advantage of this policy; and eight days after they opened the land office at Atoka they withdrew from allotment almost a million acres upon the pretext that timber speculators were prompting ignorant fullbloods to select their land in the forested area. This segregation was subsequently released, but the Department of Agriculture then sent out an investigator, who reported favorably upon the value of the timber, the need of a forested watershed to prevent flooding of the lower Red and Arkansas rivers, and the possibilities of this beautiful region as a public playground. Its purchase, he said, would be a "good bargain," for only the pine had been appraised and the Government would thus secure without cost an immense

---

[41] *Ibid.*, III, 173-74; Department of the Interior, *Annual Report*, 1906, I, 138-40.
[42] Kappler, *Laws and Treaties*, III, 175-76.

amount of hardwood. He recommended the segregation of a small amount of Cherokee land and all the Choctaw land east of the Missouri, Kansas, and Texas Railroad—a policy that would have increased the Cherokee land shortage and excluded almost the entire Choctaw population from their homes, and would have validated at least half of the land grant to the railroad. Secretary Hitchcock then drew up a plan for the consideration of Congress. His plan contemplated a careful appraisement of all the timber, but it would have been nevertheless a "good bargain" for the Government; for he proposed that the Indians should receive the gross proceeds from timber sales until the appraised value without interest should be paid. The United States would thereby secure a valuable forest reserve without a cent of cost.

The Choctaw Council indignantly rejected the overtures of the Federal officials for the purchase of the land. The full-bloods had settled in that region when they immigrated from Mississippi more than two generations before, and in accordance with their strong sentiment for their homes and their indifference to agricultural values, they desired to select their allotments in the neighborhoods where they lived. At the same time the members of the Council showed an uncritical willingness to grant valuable property to a favored individual, for they decided to sell a hundred thousand acres of their timber land for a private fish and game preserve; but this rash transaction was not permitted by the Federal officials.

In the meantime commercial clubs throughout the Indian Territory protested vigorously against the creation of a Federal forest reserve as a hindrance to their plans for exploitation. Members of Congress from the Western states who were already bitterly hostile to Hitchcock because his conservation policy had checked the wholesale looting of the public domain refused to sanction the reservation. The Cherokee segregation was soon abandoned, but 1,373,324.62 acres of Choctaw land was finally and definitely withdrawn from allotment. The Choctaws continued to petition for relief, and Congress withheld its authorization, but the project was not abandoned until 1911.[43] The soundness of the plan from the standpoint of conservation is hardly open to question; but the whole incident illustrates the tendency of Federal officials to forget that the property held by Indians under patent from the Government was not a part of the public domain.

The segregation of the Choctaw-Chickasaw timber land without the consent of the owners was almost exactly paralleled by the administration of their coal and asphalt. The Supplemental Agreement had stipulated that the land containing these minerals should be segregated by the Secretary and sold within three years at public auction, the leased land under the terms of the leases. Citizens whose farms should fall within the segregated area were to be paid from tribal funds for their improvements and permitted to select allotments elsewhere. Any mineral deposits in unsegregated land were to be the property of the allottee.[44]

The segregation was made by following the coal outcrops, but no drilling or even digging was undertaken; hence the value of the mineral was undetermined. With two tracts subsequently set aside by Congress, a total of 438,302 acres of coal and 7,240 acres of asphalt was segregated. About one-third of the coal and nearly all the asphalt was under lease.[45]

Secretary Hitchcock, however, was unwilling to sell the land under the Supplemental Agreement. In 1904 he drafted a bill, which was subsequently adopted by Congress, providing for the sale of only the unleased land in 960-acre tracts under sealed bids. Some land was placed on the market during 1904 and 1905, but no adequate offers were received. As the time

43 Kappler, Laws and Treaties, III, 171-72; Select Committee, II, 1715, 1717-18, 1734-36, 1743-57, 1953-56; House Docs., 58 Cong., 2 Sess., No. 575; Dawes Commission, Report, 1904, II, 38, 41-42; Acts of the Choctaw Nation, October 28, 1903; November 25, 1905; February 21, October 15, 1907; Indian Territory Division Files, 16716/05, Enclosure No. 21, pp. 19-23; Department of the Interior, Annual Report, 1906, p. 146; 1908, II, 196; 1911, II, 395-96; 1912, II, 440; Antlers News, November 30, 1906; Indian Office Files, 5642/09 Five Tribes 013.
44 Department of the Interior, Annual Report, 1897, pp. 409, 412-13; 1898, p. 440; 1899, I, 102; 1900, p. 88; Kappler, Laws and Treaties, I, 783-85.
45 Select Committee, I, 715-25, 756, 889-90, 905-6, 1155-56.

approached for the termination of the tribal governments, the Indians became greatly aroused over this failure. McCurtain addressed a special message to the Council in the fall of 1905 asking advice. He stated that he had an unofficial offer of fifteen million dollars for the entire tract. The Council adopted a resolution condemning the method of sale employed by the Department, and declaring for public auction or private sale with no limitation upon the amount purchased by one individual. But the Progressives in Congress were determined that the coal should not fall into monopolistic hands, and the Five Tribes Act withdrew the entire area from sale until the expiration of the leases or further legislation by Congress, and appropriated $50,000 of tribal funds to make an exhaustive investigation and appraisal.[46]

Meanwhile the withdrawal of this large tract, much of it rich agricultural land, offered a serious temptation to trespassers. As soon as the Supplemental Agreement was adopted, the Choctaws attempted to lease the surface, but the Department ruled that such a policy was illegal. The land was soon covered with squatters, and commercial clubs throughout the Territory began to urge Congress to relieve the situation by selling the surface in small tracts to actual settlers.[47]

The Indians opposed this plan because they believed that it would indefinitely delay the sale of the minerals. They said they could sell the entire tract within six months at a satisfactory price; if the United States objected to this sale through fear of monopoly, it could buy the land, but it was unjust to destroy their market through considerations unrelated to their interests. They presented these arguments before a Senatorial committee that visited the Indian Territory in 1906; but although the Senators were very scornful of the suggestion that the United States should purchase the land, they warned the

[46] *House Docs.*, 58 Cong., 2 Sess., No. 556, p. 3; Kappler, *Laws and Treaties*, III, 54-55, 174, 214; Acts of the Choctaw Nation, November 25, 1905.

[47] *Select Committee*, I, 181-86, 257-70, 468-69, 711-12, 809-55, 933, 996; II, 1965; Acts of the Choctaw Nation, December 13, 1902.

Indians that no bill permitting the coal to pass into the hands of a monopoly would ever be accepted by Congress.[48]

There was a strong desire throughout the Indian Territory for the purchase of the segregated land by the Federal Government as a permanent school endowment for the new state to be created. Bixby drafted a bill to that effect in the fall of 1905, setting the price at ten million dollars—another "good bargain" for the Government. When the Senators made their investigation, the Enabling Act had already been passed, carrying a grant of five million dollars to the state as a permanent school fund. Suggestions were made that this sum or an additional appropriation by Congress should be invested in the coal land. The people would thus be assured of a fuel supply free from monopolistic control and the royalties would assist in supporting the state schools. The Senators emphatically rejected this suggestion also.[49]

The Department officials had various plans for the segregated land. Francis E. Leupp, Commissioner of Indian Affairs, favored the creation of a corporation with Government officials and tribal representatives as officers and directors, and with the citizens of the tribes as stockholders. Hitchcock favored the sale of the surface in small tracts, but he believed that the coal should be held and the royalties used to "educate the children of the several tribes," apparently not realizing that he was dealing with the private property of the Choctaws and Chickasaws.[50]

In the meantime the mining industry developed very rapidly during this period of Federal management. Many new mines were opened, and large royalties came into the Federal treasury to the credit of the tribes. By 1906 the oil and gas of the Cherokee and Creek nations were beginning to take the place

[48] *Select Committee,* I, 885-95, 902-4; II, 1178-79; Acts of the Choctaw Nation, February 9, 1906; October 15, 1907.

[49] Indian Office Files, 16716/05, Enclosure No. 2, pp. 18-19; Enclosure No. 19, pp. 11-13; Enclosure No. 21, pp. 28-29; Enclosure No. 23, pp. 14-15; *Statutes at Large,* XXXIV, 272; *Select Committee,* I, 139; II, 1178, 1183, 1851-53.

[50] *Ibid.,* II, 1647-50, 1658-59; Secretary of the Interior, *Annual Report,* 1907, II, 96-99; Francis E. Leupp, *The Indian and his Problem* (New York, 1910), pp. 338-40.

of coal, but the competition did not appear serious at the time. The royalty collections began at $110,145.25 during the fiscal year 1898-1899, reached the peak of $277,811.60 during 1903-1904, and stood at $273,196.82 in 1907-1908.[51]

With such a satisfactory income from their mineral lands the Indians probably would not have been so anxious to dispose of them if they had not had more than a suspicion that their funds were being misappropriated. All the tribes but the Seminoles were spending immense sums in litigation to defend their rolls and property; most of them also had outstanding indebtedness, and when their estates were liquidated large disbursements were required to redeem their tribal warrants; and the usual running expenses of the governments were greatly increased by the extraordinary responsibilities of the allotment period; but even after making allowances for these emergency expenditures, they realized that large sums were being collected from townsite sales, royalties, and other sources, with no corresponding increase in tribal funds. The division of their property had been forced upon the Indians against their united opposition for the benefit of the white man; consequently the agreements had provided that the entire cost of the change should be borne by the Federal Government. But this fact was easily forgotten by the Federal officials, and there was an increasing tendency to regard the complicated duties of the various agencies as the free gift of a paternal government to the Indian people. Since the Indians had large sums of money to their credit, it was easy to charge them for these services, first by unauthorized administrative procedure, and later by specific Congressional appropriations of tribal funds.[52]

The agreements contained provisions for the settlement of numerous claims against the United States. The Indians won several Court of Claims decisions, and received at least partial restitution for losses sometimes dating as far back as the Removal. The money was appropriated by Congress, and paid

[51] *Select Committee,* I, iii-iv, 836; Department of the Interior, *Annual Report,* 1908, II, 216.

[52] See for example, Department of the Interior, *Annual Report,* 1900, p. 143; 1902, I, 203; 1903, I, 169; Kappler, *Laws and Treaties,* III, 173.

out by the Agency to individual claimants or distributed per caput among the citizens.[53] The agreements had also provided for the per caput distribution of the townsite money and the trust funds at an early date; but because of unforeseen delays in liquidating the tribal estates and authorized and unauthorized drains on the tribal funds, only two of these payments were made to any of the tribes during the Territorial period. The Choctaws and Chickasaws, after repeated requests, finally received a $40 payment in 1904 and $35 in 1906.[54]

The annual reports published by the Department of the Interior show in elaborate detail the receipts and disbursements of the various Federal agencies in the Indian Territory, but no attempt is made to differentiate between Federal and tribal funds. Large sums of money came in from Governmental appropriations and tribal collections, and apparently were paid out at random without regard to the source.[55] The reports also carry tables in the back, showing the trust funds and invested funds of all Indian tribes in the United States. During the tribal period it was possible to trace the Federal accounting with the Indians by specific explanations in case any fund was increased or diminished. But from 1897 to 1907, although the same heading was employed—"The changes in the statement of funds . . . are accounted for as follows:"—the explanation degenerated to a mere, "Decreased by $693,061.79," "Decreased by $346,364.74," which indicates only that the Federal officials were able to subtract correctly. In only one instance during the entire period was any attempt made at correct accounting; a trust fund of $390,257.92, which the Choctaws had secured from a land lease in 1855, was dropped in 1906 with the usual hypocritical evasion, and restored by the Indian Appropriation Act of the following year. In 1907

[53] Kappler, *Laws and Treaties,* I, 655, 700-1, 736, 786; II, 172; Department of the Interior, *Annual Report,* 1901, II, 233-35; 1904, II, 247; 1906, I, 223; *Court of Claims Reports,* LXXVIII, 502-3.

[54] Department of the Interior, *Annual Report,* 1904, I, 520-21; 1906, I, 224, 232; 1907, II, 367-68; Acts of the Choctaw Nation, December 18, 1902; October 22, 1903; November 28, 1905; February 2, 1906.

[55] Department of the Interior, *Annual Report,* 1908, II, 226-28.

the solemn farce, "accounted for as follows:" was abandoned, and from that time on the funds were progressively decreased with no pretense at explanation. Only the Seminole funds remained intact during the whole period.[56]

The Indians vainly attempted to secure an accounting. The method varied from the acts of the Choctaw Council directing the Chief to "take steps to recover" various amounts expended "without authority of law," to the tactful and reasonable requests of the Creeks for the accounting usually required of the administrator of an estate. These acts were vetoed by the President or ignored by the Department officials. The bill drafted in 1905 by Hitchcock for the final settlement of tribal affairs provided that any funds of the Five Tribes except the Choctaw-Chickasaw mineral royalties, which had been set apart for education, might be expended by the Secretary with the approval of the President "for any purpose deemed by him to be for the best interests of the tribe." The Five Tribes Act carried no such specific authorization, but the only limit to the Secretary's control of finances was with regard to the educational expenditure.[57]

As soon as the Indian Territory secured representation in Congress, the Cherokee citizen, Robert L. Owen, then a member of the United States Senate, secured the passage of a resolution directing the Secretary to prepare a detailed statement of Five Tribes revenues for the ten years subsequent to the passage of the Curtis Act.[58] When this statement was published in 1909, it confirmed the worst suspicions of the Indians, who had seen their funds melting away in the hands of their administrator.

There is nothing systematic about this record. Expenditures of varying amounts are simply listed chronologically, as a child might keep account of how he spent his allowance. Large sums

[56] Department of the Interior, *Annual Report*, 1897, pp. 417-18; 1898, pp. 555-56; 1901, I, 642-43; 1902, I, 559-60; 1903, I, 483-84; 1904, I, 535-36; II, 143-44; Kappler, *Laws and Treaties*, III, 278.

[57] Acts of the Choctaw Nation, October 26, 1900; February 2, 1906; Indian Territory Division Files, Special File 39c, 284/05; *House Docs.*, 58 Cong., 2 Sess., No. 556, pp. 8-9; Kappler, *Laws and Treaties*, III, 172-73.

[58] *Congressional Record*, XLII, 6383.

were spent for legitimate purposes, such as the redemption of tribal warrants and the running expenses of the governments, but numerous items pertain to the office expenses of the Agency, the advertising of town lots, the expense of making per caput payments, and the extravagant cost of education. A large portion of the administrative cost of closing out the tribal régime was borne by the Indians.[59] Considering the unlimited control of tribal funds given to the Secretary by the Curtis Act this maladministration was probably legal, but it has no other defense.

The Federal Government also assumed the administration of the affairs of the individual allottee. Because of their inexperience in the control of real estate, the agreements and the various acts of Congress had attempted to safeguard the Indians in the leasing and sale of their allotments.

Leases for agricultural and grazing purposes were restricted in all the tribes. The Seminole Agreement contained regulations to protect the allottee, and gave the Chief supervisory authority. The Atoka Agreement contained similar safeguards, but its enforcement was left to the Federal courts. The Creek Supplemental Agreement and the Cherokee Agreement specified that grazing leases for more than one year and agricultural leases for longer than five years should be subject to Departmental approval. In 1905 Congress authorized the Secretary to investigate any lease of allotted land in the Indian Territory, and to refer cases of apparent fraud to the Attorney-General. The Five Tribes Act provided that all lease contracts longer than one year for the surplus of fullbloods were subject to Departmental approval, and that the homesteads of fullbloods could be leased only in cases of old age or infirmity through special authorization by the Secretary.[60]

The Department made elaborate regulations for the approval of long-tenure Creek and Cherokee leases under the agreements

[59] *Senate Docs.,* 60 Cong., 2 Sess., No. 707.

[60] Kappler, *Laws and Treaties,* I, 649, 765, 798; III, 136-37, 177; Indian Office Files, Correspondence Land Division, Letter Book, DCXXXVII, 170-72; Department of the Interior, *Annual Report,* 1904, I, 101-2; 1904, II, 475-76; *House Docs.,* 58 Cong., 2 Sess., No. 556, p. 4.

of 1902, but few were submitted. Most lessees preferred to secure contracts from the individual allottee by taking chances on a fraudulent lease or making a legal lease for a shorter period. In 1906, 1,740 leases were rewritten by the Agency, doubling or even trebling the amount of the rental contract, and fifty were referred to the courts for cancellation; but this number constituted only a small proportion of the hundred thousand allotments.[61]

The Department exercised greater supervision over mineral leases. No important leasing occurred in the Choctaw, Chickasaw, and Seminole nations, but the oil and gas development of the Cherokee and Creek country was one of the spectacular consequences of allotment.

The Creeks and Cherokees were so strongly opposed to the tribal ownership of minerals provided by the Curtis Act that the Department rejected all applications for leases, except in special cases, until agreements could be adopted in accordance with the Indians' desires. A few informal permits were granted to Cherokee citizens to mine coal, chiefly for local consumption; a few coal operators working in the Creek Nation were allowed to continue; and finally in 1902 thirteen oil and gas leases were approved because the lessees showed that they had secured them from the Cherokee government before the passage of the Curtis Act. After the ratification of the Cherokee Agreement these tribal leases were changed to the individual form.[62]

The first oil in the Indian Territory was discovered west of Chelsea by Edward Byrd, who had secured a contract from the Cherokee Nation. He had six wells, drilled to a depth of 165 feet, and each produced a barrel a day. Oil in paying quantities was discovered in the Red Fork section of the Creek Nation in 1901, and great excitement resulted. By that time the Curtis Act had been superseded by the Creek Agreement. This com-

[61] Department of the Interior, *Annual Report*, 1903, I, 86; 1904, II, 410; 1907, II, 371-72; *Select Committee*, I, 461; *infra*, pp. 99-102.

[62] Kappler, *Laws and Treaties*, I, 663, 765; *Select Committee*, II, 1146-54; Department of the Interior, *Annual Report*, 1901, I, 144; 1902, I, 132-33; 1902, II, 120, 180-81; 1904, II, 211, 226.

pact provided for the individual ownership of minerals, but since it contained no regulations for leasing and forbade the allottee to alienate his land, the Department ruled that all leasing was illegal. The oil development was accordingly halted, but the town lots in Red Fork and Tulsa were appraised and sold in 1902 and drilling was resumed within the townsites.[63]

Just at that time the Department was given complete control of mineral leasing by the ratification of the Creek Supplemental and the Cherokee agreements. Detailed regulations were adopted in 1903, and leasing developed rapidly. By 1907 there were 4,366 oil and gas leases in effect, covering about 363,000 acres. A deep field extended from the Kansas line along the western boundary of the Cherokee Nation through the Bartlesville and Dewey district, and reached sixty-five miles south to Tulsa in the Creek Nation. A shallow field included Chelsea and Coody's Bluff in the Cherokee Nation, and extended up the Verdigris River almost to the Kansas line. The Glenn Pool, a small tract south of Tulsa discovered in 1905, had become one of the most spectacular producing pools in the world.[64]

The lessees began to bid against each other by offering bonuses to the allottees. This amount usually ran from three to five dollars an acre, but in 1907 one minor Creek received $43,000 for the lease of a twenty-acre tract in the Glenn Pool. In 1907 one Indian was receiving over $3,000 a month in royalty, several were receiving more than $2,000 each, and many had monthly incomes of over $300. Ironically enough, the main Creek development occurred in the fullblood sections, especially in the broken country where the Snakes had been arbitrarily allotted and where the "newborns" had received the worthless land that remained after the desirable allotments were taken. The grotesque tricks of chance that were to attract

[63] Department of the Interior, *Annual Report,* 1902, II, 180; *Muskogee Phoenix,* February 17, 1924, statement by Shade Wallen.

[64] Kappler, *Laws and Treaties,* I, 756, 798; Department of the Interior, *Annual Report,* 1904, I, 99-100, 202; 1904, II, 212, 226-27, 410-11; 1907, II, 375-76; *Select Committee,* I, 162; II, 1234-35.

national attention to the Five Tribes Indians were already apparent.[65]

The Department collected the royalty from the lessee and paid it to the fortunate Indian by a monthly check. The collections began with $1,300 from the first thirteen leases in 1903-1904, rose to $91,624 in 1904-1905, and soared to $323,555.40 in 1905-1906 and $775,489.15 in 1906-1907.[66]

Oil men complained loudly of the delay occasioned by Departmental "red tape" in securing approval of a lease, but apparently the industry was not seriously retarded. The regulations aimed to prevent monopoly control, by limits on acreage and strict supervision of transfers; and judging from the alternate expressions of approval and complaint, and the failure of certain attempts to evade them, they were eminently successful. As a result the oil industry was a free-for-all scramble, with the great Mellon and Standard interests, the young oil worker who could scrape together enough money to drill a well of his own, and the gambler who must try one more "sure thing," all entering into the most unrestricted rivalry. The wild, speculative, active spirit of the oil field gave a lurid phase to the early development of the Indian Territory.[67]

The Department also assisted the individual allottee in the sale of his land. The first sales took place under the Creek Supplemental Agreement, which provided that the restrictions against alienation might be removed by the Secretary. The Federal officials "desired, as far as practicable, to leave the sale of land to individual Creek citizens, in order that they might become proficient in business transactions," but they drew up regulations requiring appraisal and description of the land, forbidding any sale at a price lower than the comparative Dawes appraisal, and placing safeguards to insure the payment of the full consideration to the allottee. It soon became apparent, however, that the Indians were paying too dearly

---

[65] Department of the Interior, *Annual Report*, 1906, I, 227-28; 1907, II, 378-79; *Select Committee*, I, 577, 563; II, 1302-3, 1417-18, 1430-31.

[66] Department of the Interior, *Annual Report*, 1907, II, 333.

[67] *Select Committee*, I, II, *passim*; *Federal Reporter*, CC, 519-22.

for their experience, for a suspicious number of deeds carried the minimum consideration—the $6.50 or less fixed by the Dawes Commission simply for convenience in allotment. The Department accordingly rejected all deeds and adopted a sealed bid system. The first sale took place in the fall of 1903, and from the standpoint of securing an adequate price it was a marked success. Within the next four years a total of 73,379.64 acres of Creek land was sold by this method for $1,153,-748.39.[68]

Fullbloods were usually allowed to sell only eighty acres of their allotments. At first the Indian received a check for the entire amount as soon as the sale was consummated, but this method proved disastrous. In 1904 Departmental regulations provided that the money should be retained by the Agency and doled out in ten-dollar monthly payments. In special cases where competence was established, larger sums were turned over to the Indian upon authorization by the Agent. Every effort was made to persuade the allottee to improve the remainder of his farm, and to buy livestock and farm machinery.[69]

Legal alienation under the agreements could take place only in the Creek Nation, but Congress changed the terms in 1904. This law removed the restrictions from all land but the homestead of adult white and Negro allottees, and authorized the Secretary to remove them at his discretion from the surplus of adult Indians. More than a million and a half acres was automatically thrown on the market in the Five Tribes by this law. Under regulations prepared by the Department each Indian applying for the removal of his restrictions was required to state his age, sex, quantum of Indian blood, and business experience; and if his request was granted he was released from all supervision regarding the sale of his surplus land.

[68] W. A. Jones, *Regulations* (Approved by E. A. Hitchcock, December 5, 1902); *Select Committee*, II, 1655; Indian Office Files, Correspondence Land Division, Letter Book, DCXXIII, *passim;* Department of the Interior, *Annual Report,* 1903, I, 84-86; 1904, I, 201; 1904, II, 408-10, 413; 1907, II, 102.

[69] Department of the Interior, *Annual Report,* 1905, I, 118, 218; 1906, p. 233.

About six thousand Indians secured this exemption during the first three years that the law was in effect.[70]

Under the agreements the surplus land in all the tribes would have become alienable as follows: Creek, five years from the ratification of the Supplemental Agreement; Cherokee, five years from the issuance of the patent; Choctaw-Chickasaw, 25 per cent in one year, 25 per cent in three years, and the remainder in five years from the date of the patent; and Seminole, upon the expiration of the tribal government.[71] But the so-called McCumber Amendment to the Five Tribes Act of April 26, 1906 extended the inalienability of the entire allotment of fullbloods for twenty-five years from the passage of the law, and provided that these restrictions could be removed only by act of Congress. The Dawes rolls were to be accepted as conclusive in determining the quantum of Indian blood.[72]

In 1907, according to this cumbersome and complicated legislation, the following classes of allottees were free to sell their surplus: adult whites of the Cherokee, Choctaw, and Chickasaw nations; adult Cherokee and Seminole freedmen; all Creeks except fullbloods; all mixed bloods of the five tribes from whom restrictions had been removed; and all fullbloods from whom restrictions had been removed prior to April 26, 1906. In addition a small number of Choctaw and Chickasaw mixed bloods who had received their patents early were free to sell 25 per cent of their surplus. All inherited land was alienable, but Departmental approval was required for conveyances by fullblood heirs. The homesteads of the different tribes were as follows: Cherokee, a varying amount equal in value to 40 acres of average land; Choctaw-Chickasaw, 160 acres in average value for whites and Indians, the entire allotments of freedmen; Creek, 40 acres; and Seminole, 40 acres. The Choctaw-Chickasaw and Cherokee homesteads were inalienable for

[70] Department of the Interior, *Annual Report,* 1904, I, 102-3; 1905, I, 138, 217; 1906, p. 232; 1907, II, 340, 343, 372-73; *Select Committee,* I, 582-85; Kappler, *Laws and Treaties,* III, 50.

[71] Kappler, *Laws and Treaties,* I, 649, 663-64, 764, 772, 788.

[72] *Ibid.,* III, 176-77.

twenty-one years "during the lifetime of the allottee," the Creek
for twenty-one years, and the Seminole "in perpetuity."[73]

The Federal administration of the tribal estates had not
always been to the best interests of the owners, but there was a
genuine desire to protect the individual allottee. As the Federal
officials began to realize the vast helplessness and inexperience
of the average Indian, they began, through a blundering process
of experimentation, to try to guard his property. But because
of the lack of a definite and constructive policy, and most of all
because of the inherent difficulty of the task itself, the general
effect of allotment was an orgy of plunder and exploitation
probably unparalleled in American history.

[73] *Ibid.*, I, 120, 664, 764, 783; III, 178.

# CHAPTER IV

# The Grafters' Share

**D**URING the decade that elapsed from the abolition of tribal status by the Curtis Act to the creation of a state government, the bulk of the landed wealth of the Indians passed into individual hands. The Indians had been independent and self-sustaining under an economic order which they understood, but to a great majority the new status carried conceptions of property entirely foreign to their previous experience. As the business incapacity of the allottees became apparent, a horde of despoilers fastened themselves upon their property.

The Dawes Commission proceeded carefully and conscientiously with the physical task of dividing the vast Indian Territory estates among the owners; but every step in the process involved so many unanticipated problems of human adjustment that it created a new opportunity for exploitation. As the various Federal administrators were confronted with the disastrous effects of their policy, they attempted to correct errors, to revise their regulations, only to find that they had made new mistakes. The plunder of Indians was so closely joined with pride in the creation of a great new commonwealth that it received little condemnation. The term "grafter" was applied as a matter of course to dealers in Indian land, and was frankly accepted by them. The speculative fever also affected Government employees so that it was almost impossible to prevent them from making personal investments.

The period was dominated by a frenzy of development. The 109,393 white people enumerated by the census of 1890 had increased to 339,560 in 1900 and 538,512 in 1907, while the

Indian population remained stationary.[1] Most of this increase
was the result of the immigration of the young, restless, adven-
turous element naturally attracted to a developing frontier.
These newcomers had no knowledge of Indian tradition, no
respect for Indian institutions. In the excitement of discovering
oil fields, building cities, and placing rich land under the plow,
they created a philosophy in which personal greed and public
spirit were almost inextricably joined. If they could build their
personal fortunes and create a great state by destroying the
Indian, they would destroy him in the name of all that was
selfish and all that was holy.

A real estate dealer of Ardmore explained this point of view
to the Senatorial committee in 1906. He was arguing for the
removal of the alienation restrictions so that white homeseekers could purchase and settle the land. As for the Indians,
he admitted that under such a policy "Some of them will go to
the wall," but he went on to express his convictions as follows:
"His status would be the same as the status of every man in
this free country ought to be . . . he would find his own level,
just as you found yours and I find mine. . . . My opinion is that
he might just as well find it now as in fifty years from now, for
until he does it his presence, enjoying these special favors and
exemptions, will be a terrible drag on this country.

". . . I would like—oh, more probably than anybody here—
to see conditions so arranged and settled once for all so that
this country could go ahead and take the place that is its true
portion; and the only way that can ever be arrived at is to have
things so absolutely settled that outsiders can come in here and
look abroad over the country and see how fair it is, and know
that the time of turmoil and change is gone forever. . . . First
provide the land for the home seekers and then have such a title
that he will know when he buys a piece of land that he is getting
the best title in all this world; and if you will do that, gentlemen, you need have no fears as to the future of this country.
It will work out its own salvation without assistance from any-

[1] *Population of Oklahoma and Indian Territory 1907*, p. 9; *Thirteenth Census
of the United States*, 1910, III, 464.

one, and in this process the Indians will find their own level, which they will do despite all the legislation you have ever enacted or will enact. All you can do is to hurry along the course of events, but as to retarding them permanently, you might as well try to dam the course of the Mississippi."[2]

At first the Indians did not feel resentful toward the grafter. He usually understood their psychology, and they trusted him. If he kept his word with them, and doled out the unconscionably small payments he had promised, he found that they would voluntarily keep illegal contracts impossible of enforcement except through their strong sense of personal honesty.[3] It was a bitter lesson for the Indians and involved an unreckoned amount of moral deterioration, when they learned that they had been tricked, that a bad bargain need not be kept, and that the courts and the Agency would assist them to break their word.

But although the average untutored Indian was, to use the expression of a notorious grafter, "painfully honest," a few were the grafters' willing tools. It was they who went out among their people and secured names and signatures. In some cases they probably did not realize the extent of their betrayal of their people, but too often they were educated Indians who had absorbed too much of the white man's acquisitiveness. As Pleasant Porter said, "they see that he [the grafter] is making money, and as that seems to be the chief end and aim of existence they try to do likewise."[4]

The allotting of the land gave the grafters their first opportunity. The Dawes Commission made every effort to see that the Indian's selection included his little holdings in the hills, and they exercised the same care in the case of the Snakes and Nighthawks, whose allotments had to be chosen for them; but in order to give every fullblood his share of the good land they tried to include some choice prairie or valley land in his

[2] Select Committee, I, 1117, 1120-25; House Docs., 58 Cong., 2 Sess., No. 528, p. 21.

[3] Select Committee, I, 141-42, 651-72, 1025-26; Indian Territory Division Files, 4412/04, p. 212.

[4] Select Committee, I, 625-26; II, 1191-92, 1268, 1299; Lake Mohonk Conference, Report, 1913, p. 21.

surplus.[5] This accorded exactly with the ideas of the grafter, who expected to secure this surplus land and was anxious, therefore, to see the fullblood receive a good allotment. No better plan could have been devised to strip the Indians of their most valuable possessions. It was soon apparent that the sympathy expressed for the dispossessed fullbloods in the earlier Dawes reports had been misplaced, for their small holdings were as large as they cared to cultivate. When a piece of paper gave them the exclusive possession of some extra acres, they were willing to bestow it upon the first person who approached them.[6]

The allotment grafters worked most actively among the Choctaws. The fullbloods lived in the mountains in the eastern part of their country, some of them more than ninety miles from the Choctaw land office at Atoka and an even greater distance from the Chickasaw office at Tishomingo. The rich agricultural land lay along the Washita valley in the Chickasaw district. Most of it had been controlled by white people—intermarried citizens, citizenship claimants, or lessees. When they were obliged to surrender all or a part of their great holdings, these people usually sold the occupancy title and improvements to real estate speculators. In other cases the real estate dealers simply seized the land and held it, with no shadow of title.

The Indians were too poor to travel the long distance to the land office and maintain themselves there for several days awaiting their turn. In selecting their allotments they had, of course, no conception of the surveyors' numerical descriptions and could not identify their own holdings. The ubiquitous grafter, who furnished them transportation, board and lodging, and assistance in selecting their allotments, performed a real service.

Enterprising scouts went into the fullblood settlements, gathered up the Indians, loaded them on trains and brought them in, and sold them to the highest bidder among the real

<hr/>

[5] Indian Office Files, Land, 31640/01.

[6] *Select Committee,* I, 104-5; II, 1319-20; Department of the Interior, *Annual Report,* 1912, II, 484.

estate dealers, at ten, twenty-five, or even thirty dollars a head. The purchaser then coached his Indians to choose as their surplus the land to which he claimed some sort of possessory title, and secured a lease that was a virtual gift; and the allottee returned to his distant mountain home, content to be relieved of all responsibility for his new possessions. To make matters worse, there was corruption in the Chickasaw land office, and by paying a five dollar bribe for each of his Indians the grafter could allot them out of turn. When Bixby learned of this condition, he went to Tishomingo and conducted an investigation; and as a result two Federal employees were dismissed and one attorney was disbarred from practice before the Dawes Commission. This seems to have ended the most flagrant abuses in the Tishomingo office, but until this reform was effected it was very difficult for an Indian not sponsored by a grafter to reach the allotment desk.[7]

Lumber dealers gained immense plunder by assisting Choctaws to select allotments and immediately purchasing the timber for a grossly inadequate consideration, thus leaving the victim with a tract of stripped and worthless land. The Choctaw officials requested legislation placing timber sales under Departmental supervision, but the Dawes Commission used the request merely as a pretext to further its own plan for a forest reserve, and Hitchcock drafted a bill providing for the sale of the timber by the Department for the benefit of the tribe—a policy that would have placed the money realized from timber sales under the same irresponsible control as the mineral royalties and the invested funds.[8]

The Choctaw government made repeated attempts to deal with the whole allotment problem in a statesmanlike and constructive manner, but for some reason it was forbidden to act. Four months before the allotment began, the Council attempted

[7] Indian Teritory Division Files, File E, 6504, 9242, 9244, 12820, 13002, 14494; *ibid.*, 4412/04, pp. 28-30, 311-17; *Select Committee*, I, 909-10, 976, 1023-24, 1083-94, 1111-18, 1128-30; *Muskogee Democrat*, September 11, 1905; *Caddo Herald*, September 22, 1905.

[8] *Select Committee*, II, 1747-49; Dawes Commission, *Report*, 1904, pp. 38-42, 223, 233; *House Docs.*, 58 Cong., 2 Sess., No. 575; Acts of the Choctaw Nation, October 28, 1903.

to create a commission to visit every township with maps, plats, and field notes, and furnish information to the citizens to assist them in selecting their land. This act was vetoed by President Roosevelt upon the advice of J. W. Zevely, who was acting temporarily in Wright's place as Inspector, upon the ground that the Dawes Commission would not require assistance. While the allotment was in progress, Chief McCurtain wrote to the Indian Office describing the manner in which his people were being over-reached, but his communication was simply referred to the Dawes Commission and no action was taken. The Council then in desperation tried again to create an allotment commission, but this act also was vetoed by the President.[9]

It is difficult to see why this intelligent plan was not adopted. No agency of the entire allotment period had carried out its work with more efficiency and public spirit than the Choctaw citizenship commission that had been created to assist in the enrolment. It was the duty of the Dawes Commission to carry out the allotment; but if the Choctaws wished to create machinery to prevent the perpetration of monstrous abuses and to pay for it with their own money, there was no apparent reason for denying them this measure of defense. The Choctaws also attempted to secure an early distribution of the townsite money according to the terms of the Atoka Agreement, so that the poorer members of the tribe might have funds for the expenses of allotment and would not be thrown upon the mercy of the grafters, but these requests also were disregarded.[10]

The most ambitious traffic in Indians was the transportation and allotment of the Mississippi Choctaws. Congress appropriated $20,000, and 420 were brought on special trains. Camps were established in the localities where they received their allotments, and each family was furnished with food, a tent, and tools, and encouraged to build a house on its own land. But most of the Mississippi Choctaws were imported by

[9] Acts of the Choctaw Nation, December 12, 1902; October 29, 1903; Indian Office Files, Land, 81640/01, 54314/03; Indian Territory Division Files, 4412/04, Enclosure No. 2.

[10] Acts of the Choctaw Nation, December 18, 1902; October 22, 1903; Indian Territory Division Files, 4412/04, pp. 28-30; ibid., Enclosure No. 2.

land companies. They were packed into box cars like cattle and shipped to Ardmore where they were housed in insanitary barracks and allotted on choice land in that vicinity. They were entirely helpless in the hands of the speculators, but because of the McCumber Amendment restricting the alienation of their land, they proved to be an unprofitable investment.[11]

The Chickasaw fullbloods were subjected to the same influences in the selection of their allotments as the Choctaw, but they were not numerous enough for wholesale exploitation. The small and comparatively valueless Seminole country was allotted too early and too rapidly for the grafters to awake to its possibilities. The Creek allotment also began early, and the choice land was immediately selected by the well-to-do citizens, who understood its value. The rich valley land around Muskogee was largely taken by freedmen, who had settled in that vicinity when their masters had fled from Northern armies during the Civil War.[12] The Snakes and the "newborns" received the rugged land that was left.

The fullblood Cherokees were brought from the remote hill settlements and guided through the land office by the real estate speculators in the same manner as the Choctaws.[13] Excess landholders within the tribe also used the same method to retain control of their large farms and ranches when their holdings were reduced to the common level through allotment.

Robert L. Owen, who had controlled ten thousand acres in the Little Caney Valley, explained and defended this latter procedure when the transaction was afterwards called in question. He had established and improved this property in 1887, and had put into it the earnings of his young manhood. Then the Curtis Act had "confiscated" his land by forcing the divi-

[11] Kappler, *Laws and Treaties,* III, 17; Indian Office Files, Land, 31640/01; Warren K. Moorehead, *The American Indian in the United States* (Andover, Massachusetts, 1914), p. 167; *Select Committee,* I, 1018, 1118; *House Reports,* 61 Cong., 3 Sess., No. 2273, II, 818-28; *Court of Claims Reports,* LI, 293, 303-19; *Supreme Court Reports,* LXV, 684-97; Department of the Interior, *Annual Report,* 1915, II, 359.

[12] *Select Committee,* I, 697.

[13] Indian Office Files, Land 31640/01; Dawes Commission, *Report,* 1904, pp. 38-40; *Vinita Weekly Chieftain,* September 3, 1903; *Select Committee,* I, 300-7.

sion of the Cherokee estate with no compensation for the investments of excess holders. He accordingly instructed his agents to
allot the land inside his old fences to Cherokee citizens who in
most cases lived nearly a hundred miles away and had no land
that they cared to take as surplus. The agents made rental
contracts with the allottees, which guaranteed the delivery of
warranty deeds as soon as the land should become alienable,
and which carried "every security which they could devise to
insure good faith in carrying out the contract."[14]

An investigation of the allotment process was carried out in
1903 under the direction of Charles J. Bonaparte, at that time
a member of the Board of Indian Commissioners. The investigators concluded that the allotting should have been done in
the field and carried on simultaneously with the improvement
survey and the enrolment; that each district should have been
completed before moving to the next, and that the land should
have been all in one tract, or at least within a day's journey of
the Indian's home. The Dawes Commission answered that
allotment by field parties would have been impossible because
of the difficulty of moving a carload of records from place to
place, and the impossibility of storing them in fireproof
vaults.[15] It must be admitted, however, that the members of the
Commission, who were so conscientious in carrying out the
purely mechanical task of dividing the tribal property, seemed
to feel no responsibility for the effect of their action upon the
Indians.

Allottees who made their selections without the assistance
of grafters also lost the use of their land through entangling
contracts. The most ambitious dealings in Indian land were
carried on in the Creek and Chickasaw nations.[16]

Real estate dealers secured immense tracts of the rich undeveloped Creek land that had formerly been leased to cattlemen,
and erected improvements, put it under cultivation, and advertised widely for settlers. Investigators of the Department of

[14] Indian Office Files, 53683/08 Cherokee 311.
[15] *Senate Docs.*, 58 Cong., 2 Sess., pp. 30-32, 52-54.
[16] Department of the Interior, *Annual Report*, 1902, I, 201-2; 1903, I, 176-77.

Justice published a copy of a lease given by a Creek allottee in 1903 which illustrates the wide latitude given the real estate dealers in carrying out this type of contract. The Indian surrendered his entire allotment of 160 acres for "one dollar and other valuable considerations," and the land company engaged to establish "such improvements as may be necessary for the maintenance of the premises."[17] The president of this company stated to the Bonaparte investigators the same year that he had eighty thousand acres of Creek land under lease.[18]

Most leases of Chickasaw land nominally carried an annual rental of thirty to sixty dollars for two hundred acres of rich land, but the improvements—a tumble-down log house, a rusted wire fence, and a shallow well—were given a greatly inflated valuation and charged to the Indian as part of the consideration. Usually the Indian actually received nothing for the lease except an initial payment of ten or fifteen dollars, which was used to induce him to sign the contract. Many speculators were said to control ten thousand acres each under such leases, and a few controlled as much as a hundred thousand acres. The farmer usually paid an annual rental of $1.50 to $3.00 an acre. He had no facilities for seeking out the allottee and making a fair rental bargain; he rented from the real estate dealer and seldom knew even the name of the owner.[19]

The Seminoles had less trouble with leasing than any other tribe. It will be remembered that their agreement had provided for supervision by the Chief, which in actual practice meant that all leases were approved by the tribal attorney. This responsibility fell to A. S. McKennon, who had retired from the Dawes Commission and accepted the appointment in 1901.[20]

[17] *House Docs.,* 58 Cong., 2 Sess., No. 528, p. 18; *Muskogee Phoenix,* June 7, 1905.

[18] *House Docs.,* 58 Cong., 2 Sess., No. 528, p. 17; *Select Committee,* I, 650-72; Indian Territory Division Files, 4412/04, p. 203.

[19] *House Docs.,* 58 Cong., 2 Sess., No. 528, pp. 4-6; *Select Committee,* I, 976, 1023-34, 1040-48, 1089-1110, 1128-30; II, 1872-79, 1985-87; Indian Territory Division Files, 4412/04, Enclosure No. 2.

[20] Indian Office Files, Correspondence Land Division, Letter Book, DCCXXXVII, 170-72; *Wewoka Herald,* August 8, 1905; *Select Committee,* I, 624, 1010, 1100; Indian Territory Division Files, 4412/04, pp. 249-50.

The Creeks vainly tried to obtain the same protection. Their Supplemental Agreement as originally drafted had provided for close Departmental supervision of leases, but it was amended by Congress before ratification at the request of the Muskogee Chamber of Commerce. As soon as it went into effect, the Creeks attempted to create a tribal lease inspector; but Acting Inspector Zevely advised the President to veto the act on the ground that such regulation of leases was in violation of the Agreement. The Creeks continued to request supervision by Federal or tribal officials, but their protests were ineffective.[21]

Various devices were employed to evade the alienation restrictions and give these leases the effect of deeds. Except for a small cash bonus the payment of the rental was postponed and made contingent upon the delivery of a deed at the expiration of the restrictions; and large damages were stipulated to be paid upon any failure of the allottee to fulfill the contract. Other leases were made for ninety-nine years with no provision for payment, aside from the cash bonus, except upon execution of a deed.[22]

Other dealers were content with oral agreements; they trusted the innate honesty of the Indian for the fulfilment of the obligation. One man explained his methods with amazing truthfulness to the Senatorial committee in 1906. His company held about five hundred agreements by which allottees had promised to deed their land. He doled out small sums of money from time to time as advance payments and furnished each allottee with an account book in which these amounts were carefully recorded. He was careful to keep his word, and the Indians trusted him and recommended him to their neighbors.

21 Indian Territory Division Files, Special File 39c, 68/03; 4412/04, 15736/05, 16716/05; Department of the Interior, *Annual Report,* 1903, I, 176; 1905, I, 127; 1906, p. 231; 1907, II, 343; *Senate Docs.,* 58 Cong., 2 Sess., No. 189, pp. 37-38; *Muskogee Phoenix,* October 4, 1905; *Select Committee,* I, 461.

22 Muskogee County (Oklahoma) Register of Deeds, Miscellaneous Record, Book V, 386-95; *ibid.,* Record Book of the United States Court for the Western District of the Indian Territory, Book G2, pp. 148-73. See also Indian Territory Division Files, 4412/04, pp. 61-71, 136-43; Indian Office Files, Land, 81640/01.

It was not even necessary for him to visit the land, for he depended upon the appraisement made by the Dawes Commission.[23]

Another method of securing a deed to the Indian's land was through the use of the power of attorney. One Kansas firm obtained hundreds of such instruments from Choctaw fullbloods. A copy placed in the *Congressional Record* by Senator Curtis shows that the allottee signed by mark April 26, 1907. The published contract shows that it was signed in blank and that the numerical description of the land was filled in later. The Indian gave his agents complete possession of his land, and the right to sell it as soon as it should become alienable. The contract was to remain in force until December 31, 1939, and in the event of the Indian's death was to be binding upon his heirs.

Curtis quoted a mixed blood Choctaw, who stated that he had been employed to go among his people to secure signatures. He said that he himself did not understand the nature of the instruments, but that he told the Indians that they were leases and would enable them to receive higher rents for their land. He said that each Indian received one dollar for his signature, and that he himself was paid $2.50 for every contract he turned in.[24]

Other speculators used less tortuous methods in their illegal purchases of restricted land. In 1901 Congress had conferred United States citizenship upon every Indian in the Territory. The land dealers then contended that the restrictions in the agreements were invalid, because they restricted the freedom of contract of a United States citizen. They began openly to secure warranty deeds to Creek land almost as soon as the allotment began, and many such deeds were secured to the Choctaw-Chickasaw surplus. When the McCumber Amendment extended the restrictions of fullbloods beyond the period

[23] *Select Committee*, I, 650-72.

[24] *Congressional Record*, XLVIII, 11153; United States District Court, Eastern District of Oklahoma (Muskogee, Oklahoma), Court Records, Thirty Thousand Land Suits, Journals XXII, XXIV, XXXIV, XLII, XLIX, LVI.

specified in the agreements, many of the leading attorneys of the Territory believed it to be unconstitutional.[25]

The Creek government seems to have been the most active in seeking to protect the land of its citizens against these illegal conveyances. In the fall of 1905, when it was still expected that the tribal governments would end the following March, Chief Porter informed the Council that the efforts of the Department to protect the Creeks in their allotments had been largely ineffective, and recommended that if possible an agreement should be secured with the United States for a complete investigation of fraudulent conveyances and the removal of all clouds upon the titles of allotments. The Council then instructed the Creek delegates at Washington to urge legislation to void all deeds and conveyances upon restricted land and to penalize every grantee who should fail to quitclaim by March 4 by a $50 fine for every day of his delinquency. The delegation worked actively to carry out these instructions, but without result.[26]

Governor Johnston of the Chickasaw Nation recommended the opposite policy—the removal of the restrictions from the surplus land without waiting for the expiration of the time specified in the agreements. He said that ignorant citizens were inveigled into signing deeds that, whether legal or illegal, clouded the title and depreciated the value of the land. The removal of restrictions would allow allottees to sell in the open market to honest buyers at a fair price.[27]

The most revolting phase of the grafter's activities was his plundering of children. The system arose from a series of perfectly legitimate administrative actions and court decisions, but it soon became a lucrative and highly specialized branch of the grafting industry. The division of the tribal property

[25] *Vinita Weekly Chieftain,* September 24, 1903; *Muskogee Phoenix,* May 4, 1905; July 2, 23, 1907; *Supreme Court Reports,* XXV, 506-12; Indian Territory Division Files, Special File 39c, 15730/05; Kappler, *Laws and Treaties,* III, 279; *Select Committee,* I, 393-95, 411, 633-34, 650-72, 1091-92, 1100-3; II, 1968-72.

[26] Indian Territory Division Files, Special File 39c, 15730/05; *ibid.,* 16716/05, Enclosure No. 12; *Muskogee Phoenix,* October 4, 1905.

[27] *Muskogee Phoenix,* September 9, 1905.

equally among all the citizens had created a situation unparalleled in the history of jurisprudence. Every minor possessed an estate varying in value from an average farm to the great and speculative wealth represented by an oil allotment. No other children had ever been so rich or so defenseless.

Under their own system the strong Indian affection for children had shown itself not only in parental love, but in a sense of responsibility for all children. Any Indian family would make room for a needy child, and the orphans received the most generous educational provision by the tribal governments.[28] But when the land was allotted, the average parent was entirely irresponsible in dealing with his children's property; he was ready to sign it away for any bauble or appropriate the entire income for family expenses. At the same time the Agency was besieged by requests to be "placed in possession" on the part of parents who had innocently leased their children's land, possibly to several different parties, and spent the money.

It was evident by 1903 that the enterprising grafter was aware of the value of orphans. "Professional guardians" began to appear, thrifty geniuses who had secured appointment through the Federal courts in order that they might control the orphans' property.[29] This system was unintentionally extended by a court decision in the case of *The Indian Land and Trust Company* vs. *Shoenfelt*.

In 1902 this company made a lease contract with the parents of a Creek minor. The parents then requested the Agency to expel the lessee and "place the allottee in possession," and the company claiming under its lease carried the case to the courts. It was decided August 7, 1903, by Judge Raymond that natural guardians could not lease a minor's land without a court order, that they were in every way accountable to the court, and that the lease was therefore invalid. This decision was upheld by the Court of Appeals for Indian Territory, February 20, 1904. It was hailed as a great victory for the chil-

[28] Roy M. Johnson, *Oklahoma History South of the Canadian* (Chicago, 1925), I, 410.

[29] *Vinita Weekly Chieftain*, September 3, 1903.

dren, but Owen, the president of the company, reasonably
pointed out at the time that Judge Raymond had thirteen hundred cases on his criminal docket of which fifty or sixty were
murder cases, and an immense number of civil cases, and that it
would be impossible for him to pass upon twelve thousand
minor cases besides.[30]

After this decision the Department ruled that the agent
should have a legal guardian appointed before entering any
complaint to put the minor in possession of an allotment leased
by his parents without authority. The same ruling also applied
to the sale of timber from the allotments of Choctaw children.
The Department specifically notified each parent that he could
not legally dispose of the timber without formal appointment
by the court. In cases where the parents failed to qualify, the
court was requested to appoint another guardian. A representative of the Inspector's office visited the pine district to
insure that no timber was sold except from the allotments of
adults or by legally appointed guardians. Oil leases also were
made through a guardian appointed by the court, but in this
case the Department maintained some supervision through the
control of mineral leases provided by the Creek Supplementary
and the Cherokee agreements. The royalty was collected by the
Department and placed in a bank to draw interest, and the
guardian was permitted to draw out only fifty dollars a month,
with the approval of the Indian agent. Larger sums could be
drawn only through a court order.[31]

The act of March 3, 1905, which authorized the Department to investigate fraudulent agricultural leases, provided
that no lease made by a guardian should be binding without
the approval of the court. In directing the Department to turn
fraudulent leases over to the Attorney-General for prosecution,
it specifically exempted leases made by a guardian under court

[30] *Ibid.,* February 25, 1904; Department of the Interior, *Annual Report,* 1904,
II, 231-32, 479-84; Indian Territory Division Files, 4412/04, pp. 147-48; *Indian
Territory Reports* (Parsons, Kansas, 1906), V, 41-47; Muskogee County Register
of Deeds, Miscellaneous Record, Book V, 386-95; Book G2, pp. 148-73.
[31] Department of the Interior, *Annual Report,* 1904, II, 196-97, 223, 225, 231;
1907, II, 379.

order. The Department, therefore, investigated no leases except upon request of the guardian himself.[32]

This new policy forced the versatile grafters to change their methods. Before 1903 they had plundered the children through unconscionable contracts with their parents; now they made haste to secure appointment as guardians. It is difficult to see how any other result could have followed. A large number of allottees were too inexperienced to qualify as guardians of their own children, and sufficient men could not be found who were willing to undertake the responsibility of administering tens of thousands of estates through motives of pure philanthropy. The Department officials had gladly turned the whole matter over to the courts; the courts were too busy to give any supervision except to see that certain legal formalities were carried out; and the grafter soon reckoned his property by the number of guardianships he owned.

This class of real estate dealers employed representatives, usually young Indians who could speak English, to make a house-to-house canvass of the fullblood settlements and secure waivers from the parents, which they presented to the court. These children usually cost from five to twenty-five dollars each, but they were well worth the price. Dr. J. S. Murrow, veteran Baptist missionary to the Choctaws and Chickasaws, stated that he once sat in the courtroom at Antlers and heard a land speculator and lumber dealer apply to the judge for 161 Choctaw children who had not yet received their allotments. His purpose was to locate his wards in the pine belt, and he would have been the virtual owner of a tract of timber that would have made him many times a millionaire. In this particular case the judge rejected the application, but schemes only a little less ambitious were successful.[33]

The guardianship method was worked out most systematically in the making of agricultural leases. One man secured the appointment as guardian of a large number of children; he

[32] Kappler, *Laws and Treaties*, III, 136-37; *Select Committee*, I, 1099, 1112.
[33] Johnson, *Oklahoma History South of the Canadian*, I, 410; *Select Committee*, I, 868, 974-76, 1091-92; II, 1131, 1167-69.

then leased the land at a very small figure to a real estate dealer with whom he was in collusion; and the real estate dealer sub-leased it to farmers at an enormous profit. The real estate dealer thus continued to control large tracts of land under the same conditions of inadequate rental as he did before the guardianship was established. The guardian through various legal fictions involving expenses, charges for his services, etc., managed to retain the rental paid him by the real estate dealer; and although the amount in each case was small he received a large sum in the aggregate. The child received nothing for his allotment; he was supported by his parents if they were living, or he was maintained by the tribe in an orphan asylum if they were dead. The guardians almost invariably considered themselves agents of the lessees rather than officers of the court; legal leases could not be made without a guardian, and in most cases the appointment had been made solely for that purpose.[34]

Nelson H. McCoy, chief clerk of the court at Ardmore, who supervised the appointment of guardians, explained the procedure to the Senatorial committee in 1906:

"THE CHAIRMAN. Do you think there was any complicity or collusion between the guardian and the grafter to share in the profits of these deals?

"MR. MCCOY. I have no doubt of it. . . .

"THE CHAIRMAN. If you found a man coming to you and making application after application to you to be made the guardian of minor Indian children, which would be sufficient to put you on your inquiry on that very proposition, would you not be inclined to take some steps looking toward a discontinuance of that practice and seeing that some one else was appointed guardian of these children who had more interest in their welfare, who would administer their estates to the very best advantage of the children?

"MR. MCCOY. I presume so, but that is not the condition here. In cases where the parents of the minor had made a special request that a certain man be appointed as guardian for

<hr>

[34] *Select Committee,* I, 135-36, 869, 1030-35, 1049-50, 1112-33; II, 1188-95.

his child, we in every instance granted that request and made the appointment.

"THE CHAIRMAN. Do you think that the parents of these minors knew what they were doing? I understand that they are mostly full bloods and ignorant; would they know what they were signing when they would sign a request of that kind?

"MR. MCCOY. I don't know. A man is presumed to know what he is signing. I would not know them, and I take it that it is no part of my duty to make a personal investigation into the circumstances surrounding these matters. If I did I would be doing nothing else. I haven't the time nor the money to do that work. When a person brings in such a request properly prepared, certified, and witnessed, I have no option in the matter— the way I look at it—but make the appointment.

"THE CHAIRMAN. In that case do you not think the parent of the child was approached by the grafter and requested by him to make application that a certain party be appointed guardian of his child?

"MR. MCCOY. I don't know sir; but I presume in many instances that was done. I expect that the grafter was getting through the guardian the improved farm of this child, which in five years would be turned over to the child and would become a valuable allotment, which the child would not have had had it not been for the enterprise of the grafter. These men called 'grafters' are not such bad fellows. . . . They spend a lot of money in getting these allotments made to these ignorant Indians. They hunted up the land and got it identified and classified and arranged, and then they hunted up the Indian, who would never have known of the existence of this good land if it had not been for the grafter, and the grafter took the Indians to it and showed it to them, and then took them to the land office and had it allotted to them all at his own expense, for there was not one in a hundred of these Indians who had a cent to do that with, and I think it is right that these people called 'grafters' should have a chance to get their money back and a lot more along with it. . . .

"THE CHAIRMAN. Is the guardian required to make an annual report?

"MR. MCCOY. Yes, sir.

"THE CHAIRMAN. When he makes that annual report is there any effort made by the court, or by you or the other clerks, to ascertain whether the amounts that he returns as the proceeds of the leasing of the estates of his wards are the amounts he received, and whether or not they are the fair and reasonable amounts that should have been realized as the proceeds of these estates, or any one of them?

"MR. MCCOY. Yes, sir. Every detail of the matter is gone into very carefully and thoroughly.

"THE CHAIRMAN. Is any attempt made to ascertain what the tenant actually pays to the real estate man for the land?

"MR. MCCOY. No, sir. . . .

"THE CHAIRMAN. An attempt is made to ascertain what is paid on the lease direct from the guardian to the grafter?

"MR. MCCOY. Yes, sir.

"THE CHAIRMAN. But no attempt is made to ascertain what is paid by the tenant who actually works the land to the grafter who leases it from the guardian?

"MR. MCCOY. No, sir. . . .

"THE CHAIRMAN. Does the court or the clerk or the party who approves of the guardian's account, know what that land ought to bring annually in rental?

"MR. MCCOY. That matter was determined when the lease was approved. After the lease is approved the guardian is only responsible for the amount of money he receives under that lease, and that is all he reports. . . .

"THE CHAIRMAN. But he receives it from the farmer through the grafter, does he not?

"MR. MCCOY. Certainly; yes, sir. . . .

"THE CHAIRMAN. . . . is there any effectual means taken to ascertain that the helpless little Indian ward is receiving the full value for the use of his land?

"MR. MCCOY. By the court?

"THE CHAIRMAN. Yes, or by you or by anybody else connected in any way with the appointment of the guardian?

"MR. MCCOY. No, sir.

"THE CHAIRMAN. So then if the guardian really wants to betray his trust to the grafter (unless he betrays the grafter, which is impossible, or the grafter betrays him, which is improbable) there is not much chance of finding it out, is there, so far as the little Indian is concerned?

"MR. MCCOY. The minor is protected by the bond.

"THE CHAIRMAN. I know that; he is supposed to be.

"MR. MCCOY. He is; the bonds are good.

"THE CHAIRMAN. I am not disputing that, but the minor does not know anything about it, does he? And if he did, is incapable, in law, of doing anything direct himself. He is there relying on his guardian to protect his interests?

"MR. MCCOY. As I said before, the report of the guardian recites his expenditures and is scanned very closely, and gone into item by item.

"THE CHAIRMAN. The face of the papers is looked into, and it is seen that the columns of figures add up correctly and that they balance each other, but what I want to find out is whether any care is taken to see that the actual figures on the paper represent the actual facts?

"MR. MCCOY. Yes, sir; the guardian is closely questioned.

"THE CHAIRMAN. Is the question ever asked him, what the tenant pays for this ward's property; what the man actually on the place, and working it, actually pays for it in the way of rent?

"MR. MCCOY. No, sir.

"THE CHAIRMAN. Why not?

"MR. MCCOY. That is not within the province of the court.

"THE CHAIRMAN. Do you not think that that would be a material question?

"MR. MCCOY. No, sir; not after the contract is made.

"THE CHAIRMAN. Not after the contract is made between the guardian and the grafter?

"MR. MCCOY. No, sir; not after the contract is made, it is nobody's business what the tenant pays. . . .

"SENATOR BRANDEGEE. Did you ever know of a suit being brought on the bond in the trust company or bond company that a guardian gave for the faithful performance of duty?

"MR. MCCOY. No, sir."[35]

The committee attempted to discover the amount which the guardian was allowed for his services, but McCoy refused to make an estimate. James A. Veasey, an attorney of Bartlesville, testified, however, that he had personally investigated about three hundred Cherokee guardianships at the instance of a trust company. The children had owned their allotments for about three years, and during that period not a single cent of agricultural rental had come to one of the three hundred. About two-thirds of the children in this group were fortunate in owning oil property, and they had received some income from oil leases and bonuses.[36]

It would be possible to cite many striking instances of exploitation, such as the case of the little fullblood orphan girl, who had received through allotment and inheritance about a thousand acres of improved land in the Chickasaw Nation. This land was leased to farmers for an annual rental of $2.50 an acre, but the child was boarded in an Indian family for ten dollars a month and not even sent to school, while her guardian appropriated all the rest of her income. Specific instances, however, are not so convincing as the fact that large expenditures were made from Federal, tribal, and private funds for the maintenance of orphans' homes; and that it was the universal experience of those in charge of the work that the inmates contributed nothing to their own support.[37] With the exception of some of the last Cherokees and Seminoles to receive allotments, there was hardly an Indian child in the Territory, whether orphaned or not, who could not have been supported from his own estate if it had been properly administered.

---

[35] *Select Committee*, I, 1052-73.    [36] *Ibid.*, II, 1458-59.

[37] *Ibid.*, I, 135-36, 241-42; Kappler, *Laws and Treaties*, III, 277, 338; Department of the Interior, *Annual Report*, 1908, II, 241, 245.

W. B. Johnson, formerly United States attorney for the
Southern District, testified before the Senatorial committee
at Ardmore. He mentioned a real estate dealer in the room at
the time who had secured the court's approval in one lot of 175
leases made by guardians. He told the Senators that if they
would go over to the courtroom he was convinced they would
find less than half a dozen men as guardians for two hundred
to three hundred children. He had called the matter to the attention of the Department of Justice when he was in Washington
during the previous winter, but he believed that as soon as a
state government would be established the system would be corrected. The Senators evaded responsibility by accepting the
same solution.[38]

The tribes reacted in various ways to the situation. The
Cherokee officials at first were inclined to trust the courts, but
by 1906 the general sentiment seemed to be in favor of placing
agricultural leasing under the control of the parents without
court procedure.[39] The Creeks made the strongest objection to
the legal guardianships. They tried repeatedly to amend the
Creek Agreement or to secure legislation by Congress placing
guardianship in the hands of the parents and providing supervision by the tribe or the Agency to curb the grafter; but the
acts of their Council were vetoed by the President and their
memorials and recommendations were ignored by the Department.[40] The Choctaws alone took legal steps to protect their
children; they appointed the firm of McCurtain and Hill
(D. C. McCurtain, son of Green McCurtain, and E. P. Hill)
to represent the Nation in guardianship cases in the Federal
courts. These attorneys undertook to check the reports presented by guardians and administrators, but they were not
able to effect much improvement in probate administration.

[38] *Select Committee*, I, 882, 1033.

[39] Indian Territory Division Files, 16716/05, Enclosure No. 13, p. 10; *Select
Committee*, I, 289-91, 311-12; II, 1480-81; *Vinita Weekly Chieftain*, November
16, 1904.

[40] Kappler, *Laws and Treaties*, I, 738; Indian Territory Division Files, Special
File 39c, 2763/04, 15734/05; *ibid.*, 16716/05, Enclosure No. 12; *Muskogee Phoenix*,
October 4, 1905; July 30, 1907; *Select Committee*, I, 243-44, 429-30.

The Council also adopted a memorial to be presented to President Roosevelt in person requesting him to point out the evils of the guardianship system in his message to Congress. This communication was disregarded.[41]

But although the guardian could cut the timber, squander the rents, and collect and spend the per caput payments of his wards, in most cases he could not actually sell their allotments. The restrictions remained on nearly all the land of minors during the Territorial period, and although the land was greatly abused and it deteriorated in value, the title still remained with the minor. There was little, however, to prevent the guardian from selling inherited land and squandering the proceeds.

A brisk traffic grew up in "dead claims," land that had become alienable through the death of the allottee. The real estate dealer secured the names of enrolled citizens who had died before receiving allotments. He then sought out the heirs and secured their consent to the appointment of a prospective purchaser as administrator. The administrator then selected as the allotment a fine piece of improved land to which the real estate dealer had secured the occupancy title from an excess holder or rejected citizenship claimant. The land was then sold through the court to the real estate dealer, and it passed immediately into the hands of the administrator. It was common for the rejected citizenship claimants to regain control of their holdings by such manipulated purchases.[42]

Speculators also attempted to secure allotments by means of wills, but this method proved unprofitable. One large-scale importer of Mississippi Choctaws, attempted to reimburse himself in this manner. In a typical will, admitted to probate in 1906, a Mississippi Choctaw bequeathed five dollars "to my dear wife," and to the speculator "the balance of my allotment." The Department brought the situation to the attention of the Attorney-General, and suits were instituted to test the

[41] Acts of the Choctaw Nation, October 27, November 2, 1904; October 30, 1905; October 15, 1907; Five Tribes Papers, Choctaw—Attorneys, 13361, 13362.

[42] Indian Territory Division Files, File E, 12820, 13002; Indian Office Files, 107395/06; *Select Committee*, II, 1269.

validity of such wills. Judge Hosea Townsend of the Southern District, in a case decided in 1907, refused to admit them to probate. It was currently reported at the time that this decision invalidated nearly a thousand such instruments. After a state government had been created, the Supreme Court ruled in the case of a Chickasaw allottee that all restrictions against alienation applied also to wills, and the decision was upheld by the United States Supreme Court.[43]

The grafters were the main beneficiaries when Congress removed the restrictions from the surplus of adult whites and Negroes in 1904. The act released 1,523,380 acres, distributed as follows: Cherokee, 313,500 acres; Choctaw, 317,400 acres, Chickasaw, 299,000 acres; Creek, 549,480 acres; and Seminole, 44,000 acres.[44] The white citizens saved or squandered their property according to their individual business capacity, which was equivalent to that of the average citizens of any other community; but the Creek and Seminole freedmen were as simple and credulous as the fullblood Indians. An educated Creek Negro, who later became active in land transactions, stated that he personally knew of several instances where one buyer secured from fifteen to twenty of the 120-acre surplus tracts before noon of the day when the law went into effect. In most instances the land went to lessees who were holding illegal contracts of sale, and the consideration was merely nominal. It was by this method that much of the rich land in the Arkansas valley passed into the hands of the whites.[45]

Another class of land became subject to legal purchase by the expiration of the restrictions in the agreements. The Cherokee and the Seminole restrictions did not expire during the Territorial period; the Choctaw-Chickasaw allotment had begun late and the issuance of patents had been delayed, consequently only a small portion of the first 25 per cent of the

[43] Kappler, *Laws and Treaties*, III, 178; Department of the Interior, *Annual Report*, 1907, II, 371-72; *Select Committee*, I, 494-95, 882; *Muskogee Times-Democrat*, June 7, 1907; *Supreme Court Reports*, LIX, 121-23, decision November 16, 1914.

[44] Superintendent, Office Files, Report of A. M. Landman, 1935, p. 47.

[45] *Select Committee*, I, 441, 592-93, 688-89, 697; II, 1264-65.

5. Type of Creek Freedman. The Creek and Seminole freedmen were as credulous as the fullblood Indians.

surplus came on the market; but the restrictions on the Creek surplus expired August 8, 1907. The fullbloods were protected by the McCumber Amendment, but 437,790 acres of land belonging to mixed blood Creeks became alienable.[46]

Many of the Creeks were mixed bloods only in the technical sense that they were descended from fullblood Creek mothers and fullblood Seminole fathers. Others who had a small quantum of white blood were as inexperienced as the average fullblood. During the night of August 7-8 crowds of these Indians were brought into Muskogee and entertained by the land buyers. The buying began at midnight, and the statement was made by one entirely familiar with the situation that at the end of the first hour one-half the entire amount of land released from restrictions was delivered to the real estate dealers. The buyers also purchased freely from fullbloods, trusting to the unconstitutionality of the McCumber Amendment. The recording of the deeds at the Federal clerk's office was a nerve-racking experience, for in a number of cases the purchaser found that a rival had also secured the Indian's signature and recorded his instrument first. When the wild orgy of buying was over, it was left to the courts to untangle the inextricable confusion of legal and illegal conveyances and duplicate and conflicting deeds.[47]

The removal of restrictions by the Department after special investigation of individual cases also offered opportunities for the grafter. Many of the applications were made without the Indian's knowledge at the instance of a real estate dealer who held a sale contract, or a merchant who had extended extravagant credit trusting to the honesty of the Indian for the payment of an uncollectable debt. The practice also furnished easy fees for attorneys, who regularly charged $50 to $100 for filling out the simple application blanks, and sometimes as much as $500 or half the proceeds of the sale. Kelsey exercised the

---

[46] Superintendent, Office Files, Report of A. M. Landman, 1935, p. 47; *Federal Reporter*, CCXXXV, 97; S. T. Bledsoe, *Indian Land Titles* (Kansas City, 1909), pp. 138-41; *Muskogee Phoenix*, July 2, 23, August 9, 1907.

[47] *Muskogee Phoenix*, August 9, 1907; Moorehead, *The American Indian*, pp. 142-43.

utmost vigilance in passing upon these applications, but many allottees were over-reached. In 1906 the Department reserved a tract of land within the oil and gas area and refused to remove any further restrictions there. A great protest went up from the speculators, and lachrymose appeals were made to the Senatorial committee in 1906 for the supposed relief of allottees living in dire poverty because the grafters were not able to purchase their oil land.[48]

One of the most diabolical methods of securing oil property was the removal of restrictions by special act of Congress without the knowledge of the Indian. The same method was used to obtain townsite or other land that the speculator particularly desired. Most of the victims were fullbloods, and the restrictions were usually removed from both homestead and surplus. The legislation was in the form of "riders" to Indian appropriation bills.[49]

In 1906 Inspector Wright's office investigated the status of individual allottees whose restrictions had been removed by the Indian Appropriation Act of that year. No attempt was made to select unusual cases. A field worker simply took the names of Cherokee allottees as they appeared in the law, and followed down the list. The findings were shocking beyond description.

Several of the transactions centered in Pryor Creek, and two merchants who had been extending credit to Indians were the most active beneficiaries. One of these men obtained powers of attorney from the Indians, and as soon as their names were included in the act he gave a deed through his power of attorney to his associate. Apparently for the purpose of making sure, a second deed was then procured from the allottee himself for a small consideration paid partly in cash and partly in credit at the stores. Evidently these instruments had not

[48] Department of the Interior, *Annual Report*, 1904, I, 206-7; Indian Territory Division Files, Land File G, 37192/06; Indian Office Files, 72545/08 Five Tribes 311; *Select Committee*, I, 419, 422-23, 448-49, 585, 588-96, 1122; II, 1170, 1229-30, 1459.

[49] *Select Committee*, I, 340-41; Kappler, *Laws and Treaties*, III, 64, 213, 279, 482.

been difficult to obtain. In this simple society the trusted trader served as banker, legal and financial adviser, and friend; and the Indians were accustomed to meeting their obligations with scrupulous honesty. But in this case when the field agent interviewed the Indians who had given deeds he found some of them under a mistaken impression as to the amount and location of the land they had conveyed. In two transactions involving the most valuable oil land the first dealers had been outwitted by others who obtained the confidence of the allottees, placed them on the train, and spirited them from place to place until the law went into effect and they could make a valid deed. In another case a real estate dealer of Ramona secured the removal of restrictions from a minor's allotment and purchased the property through the guardian without even the knowledge of the child's father. The minor afterwards attempted to recover the land through the state courts, but the Supreme Court of Oklahoma ruled that a private sale was valid under the Arkansas statutes in force at the time and that all legal formalities had been observed.[50]

In this feverish period when wealth in land and forest and minerals was passing from hands too inexperienced to hold it, it is perhaps not strange that the Federal officials also found it impossible to refrain from real estate investments. A vast number of mushroom companies sprang into existence, almost without capital but with boundless plans for shaping the future of a rich and growing region. Some aimed to carry on legitimate activities of development; others were frankly organized for systematic and wholesale exploitation of the Indian through evasion or defiance of the law.

In August 1903, nation-wide publicity was given to charges made by S. M. Brosius, agent of the Indian Rights Association, that members and employees of the Dawes Commission and other Federal agencies in the Indian Territory were speculating in Indian land. This publication was a signal for a deluge of

---

[50] *Select Committtee*, I, 451-60; Indian Office Files, 24746/17 Cherokee 306; Indian Territory Division Files, File G, 23136/06, 23560/06; *ibid.*, Letter Book, CCCVI, 161; *Pacific Reporter*, CXIV, 724-30.

complaints from humble citizens who had watched the frauds with helpless indignation, and now found an outlet by writing letters to the Department, or the President, or the Indian Rights Association. Two investigations took place in the fall of 1903 as the result of these charges: that of the Dawes Commission and Interior Department agencies by Charles J. Bonaparte, and of the courts and court employees by three examiners from the Department of Justice.[51]

It was found that numerous court officials had been connected with land companies; but several of them had hastily severed their connection as soon as the Brosius report was published, and in other cases the companies had been organized too recently for the nature of their activities to be matters of record. Several court officials were removed for drunkenness, immorality, and inattention to duty; several were severely censured for their investments, but no dismissals were recommended; and Attorney-General Knox determined to have the connection of Department of Justice officials with land companies investigated from time to time.[52]

Every member of the Dawes Commission and nearly every high Interior Department official in the Territory was credited with stock in one or more of these companies, and most of them were listed as officers and directors; and apparently almost everyone down to the humblest clerk in a Government office had purchased a share. They defended their investments on the ground that that particular company was not dealing in Indian land, or that the stock had been issued to them without their knowledge and had not been paid for, and that they had been elected as officers and directors without their consent.[53] The investigation occurred so soon after the companies were organized that this defense in some cases sounds reasonable enough; but the whole situation contributed to the uncertainty and restlessness and suspicion that were a natural accom-

---

[51] Indian Territory Division Files, 4412/04, Enclosures No. 3, 4, 8; *Senate Docs.*, 58 Cong., 2 Sess., No. 189, pp. 5-7, 13-14.

[52] *House Docs.*, 58 Cong., 2 Sess., No. 528, pp. 4-35.

[53] *Senate Docs.*, 58 Cong., 2 Sess., No. 189, pp. 12-22; Indian Territory Division Files, 4412/04, pp. 116, 119, 201, 235-36, 313, 335; *ibid.*, Enclosure No. 6.

paniment to the gigantic frauds that were going on in the Indian Territory.

Bonaparte found that Tams Bixby was buying many town lots, securing possessory rights before the lots were scheduled, and even before the townsite was established. Bixby protested that these investments did not conflict with his official duties; that the Dawes Commission was administering *tribal* property, and that the townsites no longer belonged to the tribe. This reasoning, however, did not satisfy the investigators, for they pointed out that it was the duty of the Dawes Commission to pass upon the segregation of townsites established on allotted land by private promoters. Nearly all the Federal employees seemed to be purchasing lots, but it was difficult to distinguish between legitimate purchases for residence purposes, legitimate investments in town property after it had passed completely into the hands of white people, and speculation in possessory titles to land still owned by the Indians.[54]

As a result of this investigation Secretary Hitchcock directed Wright to forbid the leasing or purchase of Indian land or the purchase of town lots for speculation, on the part of Federal employees, and notified the members of the Dawes Commission that their own activities should cease; and the Indian Appropriation Act of 1904 contained a prohibition sufficiently comprehensive to cover all possible dealings in Indian property. A cynical Indian Territory newspaper expressed some anxiety lest the release of all these holdings at once would glut the market, and there were whispers that certain high officials continued their investments in the names of friends and relatives, but the matter never again became an open scandal.[55] It will probably never be known to what extent the private investments of Federal officials in land companies may have in-

[54] *Senate Docs.*, 58 Cong., 2 Sess., No. 106; No. 189, pp. 14-15, 22-23; Indian Territory Division Files, 4412/04, pp. 104-5, 121-22, 161-63, 243-46, 273-75, 322-23; *ibid.*, Enclosure No. 6; Indian Office Files, Land, 31640/01.

[55] *Senate Docs.*, 58 Cong., 2 Sess., No. 189; Indian Territory Division Files, File E, 11488, 11593, 11608; Indian Office Files, Land, 31640/01; *Vinita Weekly Chieftain*, February 25, March 24, 1904; *Statutes at Large*, XXX, 205; Department of the Interior, *Annual Report*, 1904, I, 118.

fluenced them to condone the plundering of Indians. In view of the fact that the whole allotment policy had been undertaken for the real, though unexpressed, purpose of "developing the country" it is perhaps not strange that most Government employees felt that their obligations to the Indians ended with the equitable division of the tribal property.

The Department completely ignored one serious instance of misconduct on the part of Federal officials—the town lot frauds.

All the laws and agreements had recognized the interests of those non-citizens who had created the property values in the towns. The lots were appraised without regard to improvements; and the holder of improved lots was allowed to purchase them at a fraction of the appraised valuation, or if he failed to purchase, his lots were sold at auction and he received all in excess of the appraisement. But this concession was not sufficient to satisfy the holders of occupancy titles, who apparently had expected to receive the lots as a gift from the Government; and as soon as they learned the terms of the agreements they protested loudly that their property had been confiscated for the benefit of the Indians. As they began to make their influence felt in Congress, every change in legislation gave them greater concessions in the amount of reduction they received and the number of lots they were allowed to purchase at reduced rates.

Obviously all concessions to actual owners of town property presented an invitation to speculators. The lots were appraised at a very low figure, and the country was developing and values were rising very rapidly; therefore the one who could hold a lot by planting a tree or digging a well received the option of purchasing it at a greatly reduced price or selling it at a highly inflated valuation. Within a month from the passage of the Curtis Act the most feverish activity was displayed all over the Territory in seizing lots and erecting "improvements."[56]

The most serious frauds occurred in the Creek Nation. Apparently they began innocently enough through the natural

[56] Department of the Interior, *Annual Report*, 1899, I, 125.

desire of legitimate owners of land within the segregated limits of Muskogee to protect their holdings. The townsite included a shipping pen and a pasture of about one hundred acres which Turner and Porter had owned for about ten years. Porter also owned half a block of business property and a valuable improved residence tract. Other large pastures owned by Captain F. B. Severs and his partner and son-in-law, A. Z. English, were also included within the city limits.[57]

The Curtis Act had given the owner of an improved lot the right to purchase it at half the appraised value, but the Creek Agreement, negotiated under the leadership of Pleasant Porter, contained vaguely-worded provisions appearing to mean that any person having the occupancy title had the right to purchase four acres at half the appraised valuation, or one-fourth the lots in the entire tract at two-thirds the appraised valuation.

Muskogee was platted under the Curtis Act while the Creek government was still negotiating with the Dawes Commission. The work was done under the direction of a townsite commission composed of three members: Dwight W. Tuttle, a protégé of Senator Platt of Connecticut, representing the United States; John Quincy Adams, representing the city of Muskogee; and Benjamin F. Marshall, representing the Creeks, but chosen by the Secretary of the Interior because Chief Isparhecher, Porter's conservative predecessor, refused to make an appointment. Adams naturally considered it his duty to secure the most favorable terms possible for the people of Muskogee, and even Marshall, who was a real estate dealer, was influenced by the "booster" spirit. The appointment of Tuttle was most unfortunate, for many of the towns of the Territory were afterwards platted under his direction; and it was the conclusion of subsequent investigators that he was incompetent.[58]

The sale of the Muskogee townsite was carried out by a new commission after the ratification of the Creek Agreement.

---

[57] Indian Territory Division Files, 4412/04, Enclosures No. 3, 4, 8; *ibid.,* 10614/07, pp. 57-62, 151-61.

[58] *Ibid.,* 10614/07, pp. 10, 31-33, 57, 66, 119-29; *ibid.,* 4412/04, pp. 36-38, 135, 193, 265, 322, 345-47.

Muskogee was a rapidly-growing and progressive town in a very fertile country, with a population in 1900 of 4,254. The segregated area of 2,383 acres was given a total appraisement of $238,835 by the townsite commission. Inspector Wright reported at the time that the appraisement was extremely low, but since it had received the unanimous concurrence of the commissioners, he recommended that it be approved. It was accordingly approved by the Department, August 10, 1901. Six months later the first tax assessment, always a low estimate, placed the value of the lots apart from the improvements at $1,063,366. The next year the assessment totalled $1,584,788. The difference between the last two figures represents the normal increase in value during a year of rapid growth, and contrasts sharply with the vast disparity between the appraised valuation and the assessed valuation six months later.[59]

The appraisement also presents a striking contrast with the price which speculators were willing to pay for the occupancy title giving them the right to purchase the lot at half price or benefit by its sale at auction. Tams Bixby, for instance, stated that he had paid Turner about $660 for the occupancy title of lots appraised at $300, and had purchased a lot in the English block for $2,000 which was appraised at $326. He said the improvements in both cases were negligible.[60]

Because of the immense advantage given to them by this low appraisement, holders of possessory titles found it extremely profitable to evade the four-acre limit. They secured the names of persons in Muskogee or of friends and relatives from all parts of the United States and filed them as the owners of their excess holdings. The townsite commission then scheduled the lots to these "dummies," who in most cases did not even know that they were the owners of property. The excess holder made the payments and attended to all the business, and when the property was clear the nominal owner nearly always proved "honest" enough to deed it to him. If the "dummy" lived in Muskogee, he was usually given one lot out of the tract to

[59] Indian Territory Division Files, 10614/07, pp. 24-25, 29.
[60] Ibid., 10614/07, pp. 27, 34, 68-69.

reward him for the use of his name. This method was practised not only by people like Severs and Porter who actually
owned land within the townsite and may have thought they
had a moral right to benefit, but by recent purchasers who
secured possessory rights purely for speculation.[61]

Naturally only undesirable lots remained unclaimed, and
were sold at auction for the Nation, but the price which this
property brought is another indication of the extent to which
the Creeks were defrauded. For a townsite worth over a million
dollars for tax assessment, the Creeks received the following
amount:[62]

|  | APPRAISED VALUATION | SALE PRICE |
|---|---|---|
| Sold at half price | $228,056 | $114,028 |
| Sold at two-thirds price | 2,796 | 1,864 |
| Sold at auction | 7,983 | 22,595 |
| Parks, cemeteries, etc. |  | 2,740 |
| TOTAL | $238,835 | $141,227 |

The town of Wagoner was also segregated and platted under
the Curtis Act, and the same methods were employed. The
other Creek towns were laid out after the ratification of the
Creek Agreement, but the same system of counterfeit development and false scheduling apparently went on in Tulsa,
Holdenville, Wetumka, Okmulgee, Sapulpa, and other towns
in the Creek Nation.[63]

The erection of temporary improvements was notorious at
Fort Gibson in the Cherokee Nation,[64] but no investigation of
the Cherokee townsites was ever made; and there is every
indication that the same process went on in some of the Choctaw and Chickasaw towns. The agreements with these tribes,
however, offered smaller inducements than the Creek Agree-

[61] *Ibid.*, 10614/07, pp. 1-62; *Muskogee Phoenix*, January 29, May 9, 1909;
*Muskogee Times-Democrat*, September 15, 1910.

[62] Indian Territory Division Files, 10614/07, p. 67.

[63] *Ibid.*, 10614/07, pp. xii-xiii, 30, 67-83, 134-36, 169-73; *ibid.*, 4412/04, p. 265;
*Muskogee Phoenix*, May 9, 1909; *Muskogee Times-Democrat*, September 15, 1910.

[64] Indian Territory Division Files, 4412/04, p. 321; Indian Office Files, Land,
31640/01.

ment to speculators to secure valuable property at the expense of the Indians.

Overwhelming evidence of the dishonest scheduling of townsites was presented to the Bonaparte investigators in 1903, and several Federal employees truthfully admitted their participation in the speculation; but all mention of the subject was suppressed in the published report.[65] But M. L. Mott, who had succeeded Murphy as Creek attorney, kept the matter before the Council and influenced the legislators to pass resolutions demanding a Federal investigation or authorizing him to bring suit. Finally in 1906 the Department sent William Dudley Foulke to investigate.

Foulke visited the city hall at Muskogee and found the discrepancy between the appraised and assessed value of the townsite. Then he examined the notices of appraisement that had been mailed to the persons to whom the lots had been scheduled, and found that 632 had been acknowledged by A. Z. English. He decided, therefore, to confine the investigation to the Severs and English property, since it represented the largest tract so scheduled. He sent out notices to the "dummies" and asked them to appear and testify. Most of them lived in distant states, but twenty-four who lived in Muskogee voluntarily gave their testimony. English also assisted the investigation by a completely honest and truthful statement of the whole transaction. He said, "We believe this to have been the general plan carried out throughout the Territory. There was nothing hidden or secret about it. It was a matter of general knowledge."[66]

Through a communication from a law firm Foulke learned of a similar instance of false scheduling in Tulsa, but he was not able to follow up this information. He reported to the Department that the fraud seemed to be widespread, and he recommended that suits should be brought throughout the Creek Nation. The scheduling of the other townsites was never inves-

[65] Indian Territory Division Files, 4412/04, pp. 295-98, for example; *Senate Docs.*, 58 Cong., 2 Sess., No. 189.

[66] Indian Territory Division Files, 10614/07, pp. 1-66; Indian Office Files, Correspondence Land Division, Letter Book, CMXVII, 217-23.

tigated, however; but the prosecution of the town lot frauds in Tulsa and Muskogee was to be the occasion of nation-wide publicity when one of the beneficiaries became Governor of the state.[67]

The whole period of wholesale exploitation of Indians, feverish and speculative development, and confused and sometimes corrupt administration created a feeling of uneasiness and strain. The Bonaparte report gave an accurate summary when it characterized conditions as "exceedingly unfortunate. They involve imminent danger of ruin to the genuine Indian population and profound discredit to the United States, excite reasonable discontent on the part of all classes of the population, and demand prompt and drastic remedies on the part of Congress."[68] But a frontier population seldom suffers in silence; and during the entire period a discordant clamor arose from the Indian Territory, demanding diverse but immediate measures of relief.

[67] Indian Territory Division Files, 10614/07, pp. 51-53, 169-73, *infra,* pp. 203-5.
[68] *Senate Docs.,* 58 Cong., 2 Sess., No. 189.

# CHAPTER V

# The Voice of the Indian Territory

A CROSS-SECTION of Indian Territory opinion shows that the diverse elements of the population had not yet been welded into a common society. The recent settlers were the most uncritical and therefore the most vocal in their demands for reform; rejoicing in the opportunity for individual enterprise, whether large-scale swindling or the building of a commonwealth, they felt a vast impatience with all obstacles that stood in the way of their ambitions. The leaders of the old Indian Territory, whether Indian or white, were puzzled and distressed; nothing worked out as it had been planned, and every attempt to correct conditions brought fresh disaster. The Federal officials were torn between their instinctive desire to develop the virgin resources of a rich new land and their duty to protect the owners. The unassimilated Indians, bewildered and disheartened, withdrew in fear and silence from the alien society that had displaced the old simple order in which they had proudly borne their part. The most unfriended were the freedmen, coddled by speculators eager to protect their "rights" in the division of the tribal property, and regarded by the general populace with hate and envy while they owned their allotments, and with hate and contempt after they lost them.

A large number of Indians who had adopted the white man's acquisitive ways adjusted themselves without difficulty to the new society. The same group that had cultivated extensive fields and owned stores and mines and large herds of cattle in tribal days continued to prosper under the new conditions. This adaptability was not entirely a matter of blood, for some fullblood families had always been wealthy, nor was it altogether a matter of intelligence or even of education. It seemed to be a combination of native aptitude and business experience; those Indians, whether fullbloods or mixed-bloods, who had cared to acquire property in the old days had developed a knowledge of commercial transactions.

But the Indians who had been content to live simply on the products of a little cultivated patch in the hills and the livestock running loose in the woods were unable to make the adjustment. They had been thrifty and self-reliant in their way, frugal in the expenditure of the small sums they earned, and shrewd traders in their simple business transactions. No white person ever understood the spiritual shock which they suffered when their land was allotted. Logically the white man argued that each Indian had received his full share of the tribal property, more land and better land than he had ever owned before; why should he not rejoice in his good fortune, take care of his allotment and be satisfied? But the Indian grieved deeply as a man without a country; he cared nothing for the few paltry acres in his own name that had replaced the wide sweep of mountain and prairie, the winding rivers, and the deep forests that had all been his. Shy and distrustful as any wild thing, he hid from the enrolment parties, and he returned his allotment certificate to the Agency.

The allotment period brought financial loss to all classes of Indian citizens. The wealthy were reduced to the common level through the loss of their excess holdings. The poorer citizens found the expenses incident to the selection of their allotments a severe strain on their slender resources. Those who were forced to move because their homes had been included in townsite or timber segregations found themselves with raw land on their hands and with no means to improve it. With the settlement of the country and the more efficient development of agriculture, their free range was gone and their livestock lost or stolen. Worst of all, their apathy and hopelessness in the face of the general uncertainty prevented them from making their usual effort. During the entire allotment period the humbler citizens were in a state of extreme destitution.

The condition of those who refused to accept allotments was the most unfortunate of all. In cases where the Dawes Commission had succeeded in allotting their own land to them, they continued to live in their little cabins in constant fear of dispossession, not knowing that they were protected by the patent they had refused to accept. In other cases mistakes had been made, and their holdings passed into the possession of others, and often were sold or leased to white people. Sometimes they continued to occupy their houses temporarily through the tolerance of the new tenant; in other cases they were completely homeless. The fact that they owned an adequate tract of land somewhere, upon which they should settle, was not even considered; they had not consented to the division of the property, and they would never accept an allotment. The statements of several Snakes who testified through an interpreter before the Senatorial committee in November 1906, give a glimpse of the experiences of this forgotten group.[1]

Eufaula Harjo, Creek fullblood, explained it as follows: ". . . We are pushed out of all that we had. The full-blood Indian people are pushed out today, and they have left their homes and taken what they have, and everything, and are camped out in the woods today. The half breeds and negroes are the ones that have taken all the land, and there is nothing left for the full-blood Indian at all. Their homes and lands are all taken, and now the Indians are all outside nearly—the full bloods—and they don't know what to do or where to go. It is going to be cold weather after a while, and there is the women and the little children and the old people, and we don't know what to do with them or where to get a house to put them in. All the property such as cattle and hogs and horses—it is all gone, and we have not got anything left. We used to have plenty and more than we wanted and now we haven't got anything.

[1] *Select Committee*, I, 92-105.

"Q. Is not that because you have declined to take your allotment, or make your allotments on the land you have occupied, and having declined to make the allotments on that land, it has been allotted to someone else?—A. They have taken it away from us, and they are in the houses that we built and that are ours."

Samuel Leslie, Creek fullblood, stated: ". . . This is no free country, and I haven't any farm any more. . . . Another woman got my farm, and she has sold it to a white man, and they have that farm and have been working on it for two years, so I haven't any farm today, and that is the way they are treating the poor Indian people to-day. I am very sad, and I hope my fathers will help the poor Indians.

"Q. Why don't you take your allotment?—A. The reason I did not take it was because I wanted my right and property interest, for I loved them. I love the old treaty, and I want it. . . .

"Q. How long did you work that farm?—A. I had that farm and worked it for a good while. It was about fourteen years that I worked it. . . .

"Q. Well, do you live there in the same place that you lived for fourteen years?—A. On the same place.

"Q. . . . has anyone tried to put you out of your farm?— A. Yes, sir; they tried to put me out, but they never put me out, for I am still there yet; but they sold my farm, and this lady has it and is working it today. . . .

"Q. It was allotted to this woman, was it?—A. I don't know. It must have been for she has got it. A white man told me that he had bought that farm, and he would put me out. . . .

"Q. Well, he has not put you out?—A. No, sir; not out of the house, but they have taken my land away."

Osway Porter, fullblood Chickasaw, testified as follows:

"Q. Have you taken your allotment?—No, sir.

"Q. Do you live in the same place you have been living on for the past ten or fifteen years?—A. I am still living on the same place now for twenty-four years. I just had a little patch of my own.

"Q. And you still are there in the same place?—A. Yes, sir; I never depended on no big farm or any thing of that kind.

"Q. Have you been interfered with in the possession of that home?—A. I have been under fear all the time about that home.

"BY THE CHAIRMAN:

"Q. Well, why don't you take this allotment—why don't you take your allotment and so remove this fear?—A. I believe the old treaty between the United States and the Indians never told me that I must take a piece of ground."

In their poverty and bewilderment it is not strange that the Indians were glad to earn a few dollars by the simple process of making their mark on a paper. Usually they had no idea of the commitments they made. In other cases they realized they had leased or sold their land, but they had no use for it, they knew nothing of real estate values, and the pittance they received seemed like a great windfall. Since they did not understand the rules of the new economic society, they had no incentive to be thrifty as they had formerly been with the few dollars they had earned, and the money was spent as quickly as it came. Probably another white man would come with a paper for them to sign, or a windfall would descend from some other unexpected quarter.

The carefully safeguarded sales conducted by the Agency brought the Indians more money, but the disintegration of character was the same. The temporary relief of the Indian's destitution by the sale and dissipation of his property was hardly a constructive solution of a complex spiritual problem. When the dole system was adopted, it prolonged the process but did not change the result. Moreover, as some people pointed out at the time, it was a bad business policy, for the Indian's money was held without interest and gradually spent, whereas by retaining and renting his land, he could have secured an equal income with no diminution of capital. When the Indians of the Five Tribes, who had been self-sustaining and self-respecting during their entire history, began to depend for support upon a monthly dole from the Agency, it represented a certain moral degradation. The Creek Council protested that it was a "system similar to that in vogue among the blanket Indians of the West, who are supported by periodical issuance of rations by the Government."[2]

It was easier, however, to condemn the existing arrangement than to discover a proper remedy, for the bewildered Indians seemed unable to make a living, or to hold their land, or to use their money wisely. M. L. Mott appraised their knowledge of business when he said, "It is an absolute and utterly hopeless and impossible task to make them understand it. Their heads are not built right."[3] The Choctaw and Chickasaw leaders believed at the time, and have continued to believe, that if the Government had proceeded quickly with the allotment, and had sold the undivided property and distributed the proceeds without waste or delay while the allottees were moving upon their new land, they would have spent the money thriftily in establishing themselves on their farms. There is no doubt that the prolonged transition period had a bad psychological effect, but it is difficult to see how some of the delays could have been avoided.

The fact is that while the Indians' immense property losses attracted some attention, their greater spiritual injuries received little notice. Only a person in close touch with the situation could have described it with the insight of Dr. Murrow: "The fullbloods are slow. They are timid. They are conscious of their ignorance and helplessness, hence they are afraid of progress. They are discouraged and have lost all heart. . . . It is hard to work for them. . . . Their disposition has changed. They lack the sense of gratitude they once possessed. But they are needy, they are abused, they are wronged."[4]

Pleasant Porter, with his discerning and sensitive understanding, described the plight of his people to the Bonaparte investigators, but he had no remedy to offer: ". . . It was a

---

[2] Indian Territory Division Files, Special File 39c, 12502/04; *Proceedings of the Oklahoma Bankers' Association*, 1904, p. 54.

[3] *Select Committee*, II, 1265.

[4] Johnson, *Oklahoma History South of the Canadian*, I, 411.

mistake to have changed these people's relations with the government. . . . The Indians . . . haven't had time to grow up to that individuality which is necessary to merge them with the American citizen. The change came too soon for them. . . . There will be a remnant that will survive, but the balance is bound to perish, do what you may for them. There is that sense of right and wrong which will bind men together and preserve the peace and maintain virtue and provide for offense without. That is the institution out of which a nation grows. Each of these groups [the Five Tribes] must have had that; but you rub that out, you transplant them into what they have no knowledge of; . . . there is no life in the people that have lost their institutions. Evolving a thing out of itself is natural, transplanting it is a matter of dissolution, not growth. There may be a few that will grow . . . but the growth will not be natural; and I don't see anything now that it has gone this far but to come to it heroically and pay no regard now to our prejudices or sentiment; do the matter up in a businesslike way, for every delay changes conditions. . . .

"If we had our own way we would be living with lands in common, and we would have these prairies all open, and our little bunches of cattle, and would have bands of deer that would jump up from the head of every hollow, and flocks of turkeys running up every hillside, and every stream would be full of sun perch. Those things are what we were used to in our early life. That is what we would have; and not so much corn and wheat growing, and things of that kind. But we came up against it; this civilization came up against us and we had no place to go.

"Q. You told us a moment ago they were dying off pretty fast?

"A. Yes, sir, the older people are.

"Q. Is there any special cause for that?

"A. Nothing; there is no new disease; I don't see anything other than the want of hope."[5]

[5] Indian Territory Division Files, 4412/04, pp. 127-31.

6. Pleasant Porter, Chief of the Creeks. With discerning and sensitive understanding, he described the plight of his people.

These despairing words of the wise old Chief contrast strangely with the active, buoyant, hopeful spirit of the white inhabitants of the Territory. The latter class were in an overwhelming majority. A special Federal census, taken in 1907 because of approaching statehood, showed the following racial distribution: white, 538,512, or 79.1 per cent; Negro (tribal and immigrant), 80,649, or 11.8 per cent; and Indian, 61,925, or 9.1 per cent. Muskogee increased in population from 4,254 in 1900, to 14,814 in 1907, and 25,278 in 1910, an increase of 494.2 per cent in ten years. The growth of Tulsa was even more spectacular, with a population of 1,930 in 1900, 7,298 in 1907, and 18,132 in 1910.[6]

Only in the cities was there any oportunity for self-government. There was a universal protest against the "carpetbag" administration, arising partly from the natural desire of a large American population to be self-governing, and partly from a vast hunger for the spoils of the many Federal agencies in the Territory that were monopolized by Northern Republican politicians. Bad as the spoils system was, it was not bad enough to suit local Republicans. They condemned the higher officials of the Dawes Commission, the Inspector's office, the Agency, and the courts for their failure to fill all subordinate positions with "loyal, working Republicans." These administrative officials, they insisted, were overlooking their "solemn duty" to strengthen the party against the day of statehood; they were offering no encouragement to the untried voter to join the Republican ranks.

There was universal dissatisfaction with the inconveniences of long distance government. The impatient promoter of a legitimate enterprise chafed against the vexatious delay occasioned by the unwinding of Departmental red tape, and demanded that more authority be given to local Federal administrators. The grafter raised his voice in righteous-sounding protest against the regulations that retarded his activities. Few American officials were ever so execrated by half a million of

---

[6] *Population of Oklahoma and Indian Territory 1907*, p. 9; *Thirteenth Census of the United States, Abstract with Supplement for Oklahoma*, p. 592.

their fellow citizens as was Secretary Hitchcock. Civic bodies passed resolutions against him, newspapers of both parties condemned him, and the average citizen responded joyfully to any slur cast upon him. The witty speaker who said in referring to the large Arkansas element in the population that the Indian Territory had been "sired by Arkansas and damned by Hitchcock" met with delighted response. The Secretary was blamed at once for every mistaken policy of his administration, and for every impediment that he placed in the way of the most predatory grafter.[7] Above all, these enthusiastic builders of a new commonwealth united in opposing the restrictions on Indian land.

The effort to defeat the restrictions was exerted even in the negotiation of the agreements. During the first conversations between the Cherokee delegates and the Dawes Commission, C. L. Jackson, attorney for the Missouri, Kansas, and Texas Railroad, appeared in behalf of his company and insisted that the titles to the allotments should be as unrestricted as the land titles in adjoining states—"Only by such system will there be a full development of the Territory."[8] When the Creek Supplemental Agreement was before Congress, the Muskogee Chamber of Commerce sent Thomas P. Smith to Washington to lobby for its amendment. He presented the following resolutions:

". . . It should be borne in mind that 5,000 of these allottees are freedmen of the colored race, who are industrious and fully competent to care for themselves, while of the 9,000 having Indian blood a great part are of predominant white or negro blood.

"Regardless of the condition of blood, the people who received allotments in the Creek tribe, which has for seventy-five years and over been known as one of the Five Civilized Tribes,

[7] *Muskogee Phoenix,* December 14, 1905; *Muskogee Times-Democrat,* May 6, 1907; *Select Committee,* I, 288, 316-18, 1010; II, 1464-65, 1479-80, 1493-94, 1866, 1984; *Senate Docs.,* 58 Cong., 2 Sess., No. 189, pp. 28-30, 38-40.

[8] Cherokee Papers, Joint Session United States Commission and Cherokee Commission.

are as fully competent to care for themselves as any ordinary community of people are."

It has been noticed in another connection that Smith was able to defeat the provision so greatly desired by the Creeks for supervision of agricultural leases, but he failed in an attempt to advance the alienation date.[9]

The feeling was general among white citizens of the Territory that the Negroes had never been entitled to Indian land. The Federal officials shared this attitude and hastily withdrew all supervision from this class of allottees.[10] It was unfortunate for the Indians that the United States did not make this discovery earlier. The freedmen had been the special favorites of the Government from the negotiation of the peace treaties in 1866, through an entire generation of threatened division of the land, to the compulsory allotments to freedmen provided by the various agreements with the Dawes Commission. The extreme solicitude with which the Federal Government forced the Indians to divide their property with the Negroes, the haste with which all protection was removed, and the rapidity with which the land passed out of their temporary possession is suspiciously equivalent to the usual policy of throwing an Indian reservation open to white settlement. Keen-minded old Chitto Harjo expressed very clearly the ultimate results of this policy: "I hear that the Government is cutting up my land and is giving it away to black people. I want to know if this is so. . . . These black people, who are they? They are negroes that came in here as slaves. They have no right to this land. It never was given to them. It was given to me and my people and we paid for it with our land back in Alabama. . . . Then can it be that the Government is giving it—my land—to the negro? I hear it is, and they are selling it. . . . I am informed and believe it to be true that some citizens of the United States have titles to land that was given to my fathers and my people by the Government."[11]

---

[9] *Senate Docs.*, 57 Cong., 1 Sess., No. 381, p. 2; Indian Territory Division Files, 4412/04, p. 236.

[10] Indian Territory Division Files, File G, 1655/05, 2965/05.

[11] *Select Committee*, II, 1251-52.

But the result that the old conservative feared was exactly what the progressive element in the Territory desired. Although the sole purpose of the Bonaparte investigation was to discover the connection of Departmental employees with land speculations, several of the witnesses introduced the subject of removing the restrictions, especially from the surplus and even more particularly from the surplus of freedmen. As Judge Thomas expressed it, "The Indian Territory is now held by a grasp at the throat which is literally killing it and stifling all business, it is killing all improvement, it is killing every business enterprise here. If the restrictions on the sale of land were removed this country would blossom like a rose and the material condition of the people would be vastly improved. These negroes won't work if they can avoid it and as long as they have one hundred and sixty acres of land, they won't work." Even Pleasant Porter said that although the freedmen were so ignorant about business transactions that many would lose their land, he saw no reason why they should be protected.[12]

The investigators concluded that it had been a mistake to allot the land in larger tracts than the Indians cared to occupy; small allotments should have been made, inalienable either by sale or lease except through court procedure, and the Government should have sold the remainder. And the "freedmen, who constitute, on the whole, an uninteresting and unpromising class of the population, seem to need the care of the Government no more than the other people of their race throughout the Union."[13]

It will be remembered that at this very time the Lake Mohonk Conference was advocating a policy of unrestricted land tenure and local control of Indian administration that would have satisfied the extreme demands of Indian Territory "boosters."[14] But some of the latter were willing to accept less. A notable attempt to influence Congress to release the surplus land was undertaken by a special committee of the Muskogee Chamber of Commerce.

---

[12] Indian Territory Division Files, 4412/04, pp. 128-29, 147, 320.
[13] *Senate Docs.*, 58 Cong., 2 Sess., No. 189, pp. 35-37.     [14] See *supra*, p. 22.

Charles N. Haskell, a recently arrived railroad builder, was the chairman of this committee; and A. P. McKellop, a prominent mixed-blood Creek, P. B. Hopkins, a former employee of the Dawes Commission, who was one of the organizers of a land company, and Robert L. Owen were among the other members. The Bonaparte investigators had visited Muskogee in December. The first week of the following January the committee began to take depositions of leading citizens of the town regarding the necessity of removing the restrictions upon the sale and lease of all allotted land except the homesteads. Among these deponents were: Alexander Posey, the talented young mixed-blood Creek who was city editor of the *Muskogee Times;* Dew M. Wisdom, former Union Agent; William T. Hutchings, chairman of the Muskogee Bar Association; J. H. Scott, president of Bacone College, a school established by the Baptists for the higher education of Indians; Rev. A. Grant Evans, president of Henry Kendall College, a Presbyterian institution; and A. P. McKellop. Under the influence of the committee similar depositions were taken also at Catoosa, Fort Gibson, Sulphur, Muldrow, and Bokchito; and the Vinita Commercial Club prepared a petition to Congress to the same effect.[15]

A general convention was held at Okmulgee, the Creek capital, January 19, and resolutions were unanimously adopted for the removal of restrictions upon the sale and leasing of all Indian land. Dissatisfaction was expressed with the sealed bid system recently adopted by the Department in the Creek land sales, which at the current rate of progress would require, it was argued, 120 years to give each allottee his statutory right of sale. As for protection to the Indian: "It is the sincere conviction of this convention that the best thing which can be done for even our most helpless Indian fellow-citizens is to place their protection with the courts, which normally protects the interests of the helpless and incompetent, and in all respects to place them as rapidly as possible in the position of ordinary citizens, so that instead of being American Indians, these

15 *Select Committee*, II, 1898-1930; *Vinita Weekly Chieftain*, January 14, 1904.

people who surely have the fullest right to the title, may become in name and fact American citizens." A draft resolution was prepared for adoption by municipal organizations, preachers, and other groups of citizens. The Rev. A. Grant Evans was appointed to proceed to Washington and lobby for the desired legislation.[16]

The prepared resolutions were endorsed by twenty-two preachers, by another group of "undersigned residents of the Indian Territory," and by the officers of the Republican Club of Welch. They declared that "The idea that the Indian citizen is an innocent victim of the rapacity and craft of the white race in Indian Territory is ludicrous to those familiar with both classes," and that "the same freedom of transacting business should prevail in this country as in the other states of the Union." A similar set of resolutions was adopted by the mayors and members of the town council, the postmaster, or the commercial clubs of twenty-one towns. They asserted that the Indians had "been a Christian, civilized, agricultural people for five generations, and with full school privileges and constitutional laws for over half a century. They are as competent to manage their own affairs as the people in any of the other states of the nation, whether east or west. The per cent of incompetence, whether from minority or from other cause, is as low among the members of this former so-called Five Civilized Tribes as among citizens of the older states."[17]

Evans collected these resolutions and a great number of newspaper editorials, and presented them to Congress; but he was more modest in his requests than some of the people he represented, for he was willing that the restrictions should remain upon the land of the non-English speaking Indians. The Congressional delegations from Texas, Arkansas, and Kansas were understood to be favorable to the legislation, and the bill was introduced by Little of Arkansas. The result of this effort was the act of 1904 removing the restrictions from the surplus of adult whites and Negroes and authorizing the De-

---

[16] *Senate Docs.*, 58 Cong., 2 Sess., No. 169, pp. 8-11.    [17] *Ibid.*, pp. 45-52.

partment to pass upon individual applications from Indians. It was a disappointment to its sponsors, but it was hailed throughout the Territory as "a good beginning."[18]

The agitation for the removal of more restrictions continued. Late in the year the Inter-Territorial Republican Press Association met at Guthrie, the capital of Oklahoma Territory, with Colonel Clarence B. Douglas, editor of the *Muskogee Phoenix*, as presiding officer. This gathering adopted resolutions asking Congress to protect the Indian's homestead and remove the restrictions from his surplus.[19] In the summer of 1905 the newspapers published a petition which was being circulated among the Cherokees asking Congress to remove "the greatest burden that ever rested on a people." This petition stated that some of the signatories wanted to sell their land and return to their ancient homes in North Carolina or to emigrate to Mexico; that others were of mixed blood, and could not lose the freedom of contract which had descended to them from white ancestors; that all of them believed they should be allowed to sell their children's land, since the children had received the right of allotment from their parents; and that they desired the removal of all restrictions, because they were amply able to cope with the white man in business transactions. Incidentally the man who was sponsoring the petition was a white merchant who had secured control of Indian land through the extension of credit in his store.[20]

The same summer, during the tax controversy, an incident occurred showing the pressure that Indian Territory as an important market was able to bring upon the bordering states that supplied its needs. Representatives from twenty-seven towns met in Okmulgee and formed the Indian Territory Commercial League. Caustic resolutions were adopted condemning Hitchcock for his stand on the tax matter and demanding the removal of restrictions. For some time Kansas City had been showing a gratifying hostility to the Secretary, and St. Louis,

---

[18] *Ibid.*, pp. 1-7, 52-55; *Select Committee*, II, 1940; *Muskogee Evening Times*, March 7, 1904.

[19] *Seminole Capital*, December 1, 1904.    [20] *Muskogee Phoenix*, August 27, 1905.

as Hitchcock's home, was believed to be somewhat lukewarm in its opposition. A committee was therefore appointed to interview the St. Louis wholesale dealers and warn them that if they did not join in the demand for Hitchcock's removal they would be boycotted and all orders for goods would be canceled in favor of Kansas City and other towns.[21]

During the winter of 1905-1906, with the approach of the date set in the agreements for the end of all the tribal governments, the Chiefs and Councils and the Departmental officials worked systematically to draft legislation for the final settlement of tribal affairs and the limited continuance of the tribal governments. Some of the tribes took action at this time upon the restriction matter: the Chickasaw Council upon the advice of Governor Johnston memorialized Congress to remove the restrictions from the surplus of all adults; the Choctaw Council declared that the restrictions gave the speculator a monopoly of the land market, enabling him to secure large tracts at inadequate prices, and asked for their removal from all surplus land; and the Creek delegation requested the continuance of Departmental supervision of sales and the removal of restrictions from inherited land.[22] Bixby advised the removal of restrictions from the surplus of all allottees of less than one-half Indian blood. Wright reported that many mixed-blood Indians had shown themselves to be incompetent and he advised that the method of special examination of each individual case should continue; but he "earnestly" recommended that the restrictions upon fullbloods should be extended so that no land could be alienated except with the consent of the Secretary. Commissioner Leupp combined these opposite opinions of Bixby and Wright in his recommendation; he advised the extension of restrictions upon fullbloods, and the removal from the surplus of all adult mixed-bloods. Leupp's suggestion was embodied in the bill prepared by a special committee of the

---

[21] *Muskogee Phoenix,* June 7, 21, 1905.

[22] *Ibid.,* September 9, 1905; Acts of the Choctaw Nation, February 9, 1906; *Select Committee,* I, 912; Indian Territory Division Files, 16716/05, Enclosure No. 12.

Department appointed to draft legislation for the final settlement of Five Tribes affairs.[23]

While the legislation was before Congress, J. W. Zevely, Tams Bixby, Robert L. Owen, Clarence B. Douglas, and J. Blair Shoenfelt went to Washington and worked diligently for the removal of restrictions. Bixby was, of course, Commissioner to the Five Civilized Tribes, and all the others except Owen had recently been connected with the Indian service. Their recommendations naturally carried weight, and they were extensively quoted in Washington newspapers. Governor Frank Frantz, former Governor Cassius M. Barnes, and Henry Asp of Oklahoma Territory actively assisted them, and the fight in the House of Representatives was led by Bird S. McGuire, territorial delegate from Oklahoma, A. P. Murphy, now a Congressman from Missouri, and John H. Stephens of Texas. It was a great disappointment to the Indian Territory and its helpful neighbors when the Five Tribes Act as finally passed not only failed to remove any restrictions but extended them in the case of fullbloods by the McCumber Amendment and gave the Department complete control of fullblood leasing.[24]

The special committee of the Senate visited the Territory the following November. The members were Clarence D. Clark of Wyoming, chairman, Chester I. Long of Kansas, Frank B. Brandegee of Connecticut, Henry M. Teller of Colorado, and William A. Clark of Montana. Most of these men were actively sympathetic toward Indian Territory aspirations, and had worked unsuccessfully during the preceding session of Congress for the removal of restrictions.

The committee worked hard, visiting Vinita, Muskogee, McAlester, Ardmore, Tulsa, and Bartlesville, holding day and night sessions and even taking testimony on the train, and secured an imposing mass of evidence, opinion, and propaganda from all classes of people. They sent word in advance to the commercial clubs of the towns they intended to visit, and

[23] Indian Territory Division Files, 16716/05, Enclosure No. 2, pp. 24-25; No. 6, pp. 8-9; No. 19; No. 21, pp. 18-19; No. 22, pp. 13-14; No. 23, p. 9.
[24] *Muskogee Phoenix*, February 23, April 13, 15, 17, 29, May 1, July 22, 1906.

the commercial clubs planned for their accommodation and organized the presentation of their arguments by assigning topics to leading citizens. The Creeks, Choctaws, and Chickasaws also drew up declarations of policy and chose official delegations to present them, and even such fullblood organizations as the Kee-too-wahs and the Four Mothers selected representatives to present their views. The leading Federal officials were questioned as to their experiences in dealing with allottees. Many individual citizens appeared voluntarily and expressed their opinions, towns which the committee was not able to visit presented resolutions, and farmers' unions, bar associations, and other organized groups of citizens drew up memorials. The published hearings of this committee thus show a fairly complete cross-section of Indian Territory opinion in the fall of 1906.[25]

The business and professional men argued that the Indians were as competent as other citizens or that it was impracticable to protect an incompetent class by legislation; that enterprising homeseekers were passing through the Indian Territory and settling in Oklahoma, Texas, and New Mexico, leaving the country undeveloped in the hands of an undesirable tenant class; and that it would be impossible to establish roads, schools, a state government, and other institutions of civilized living without taxation. A large number believed that all restrictions should be swept away; but there seemed to be a general admission that they might remain on the homesteads of fullbloods and possibly of all minors, either to protect the Indian or merely as a concession to public sentiment. Many advocated the dangerous policy of placing all incompetent fullbloods under guardianship and permitting the sale of all minor and fullblood land by the guardians under court supervision. There was a general belief that with statehood all questions of competency and protection could safely be left to the local courts.[26]

[25] *Muskogee Phoenix*, November 11, 1906; *Select Committee*, I, II.
[26] *Select Committee*, I, 141-44, 181-90, 392-424, 1009, 1083-89, 1119-21; II, 1327-50, 1383-84, 1458-59, 1491-94, 1866-67, 1894, 1965-66.

Some attempt had been made to influence the Indians to reinforce these arguments. A few petitions for the removal of restrictions, often signed by mark and purporting to represent an entire Indian neighborhood, were presented by white "boosters" who appeared before the committee. Samuel J. Haynes, Creek fullblood member of the House of Kings, exhibited a revealing letter. It was written on the stationery of a land company; signed by a Creek who said he had been appointed by the Muskogee Commercial Club to take up with his people the matter of removing the restrictions; and directed to a selected group of Indians, inviting them to "lay our little matters" before the Senators at Muskogee, and promising free hotel accommodations and "all the cigars that we can smoke up." But apparently none of the Creeks accepted the invitation, and one of them turned his letter over to Haynes.[27]

Strangely enough the farmers, who suffered more than any other class except the Indians from the vicious leasing system, had very little to say. A Farmers' Union convention at Ardmore drew up resolutions calling for the removal of restrictions upon surplus land, and supervised sales of the surplus and leases of the restricted land in not more than 160-acre tracts to actual settlers. If such a plan could not be adopted, they preferred that the restrictions remain as they were; almost all the land sold so far, they said, had been seized by the grafter, and they preferred to have it owned by Indians rather than by the grafter.[28]

Except for this expression from the farmers there was a general agreement that if the restrictions were removed the land would be thrown on the open market, the speculator's monopoly would be abolished, and grafting schemes would become unprofitable. Frank and unashamed grafters openly boasted that the restrictions aided their business. Prominent people whose grafting operations were more or less secret held illegal deeds and sale contracts against fullblood land that would be automatically validated by the removal of restrictions. Their specu-

27 *Ibid.*, I, 196-97, 432; II, 1342, 1472; *Muskogee Phoenix*, July 4, 1906.
28 *Select Committee*, I, 1073-74; II, 1890.

lative investments carried a possibility of enormous profits, but they might prove to be a total loss if Congress should become sentimental. These respectable leaders of Indian Territory opinion insisted in such righteous tones that the removal of restrictions would magically end all grafting that their real motives were not always apparent. The average citizen, sickened by a vast evil which he hardly understood and was helpless to prevent, accepted this specious argument. Its fallacy, however, is apparent. The grafters monopolized agricultural leases, although leasing until 1906 was virtually unrestricted, and they had secured practically all the freedman land from which restrictions were removed in 1904. Moreover they controlled the children's land through guardianships, and awaited only a legal opportunity to dispossess their wards through purchase.

While the grafters and the builders of a new commonwealth and all recent arrivals were urging their solution with such uncritical unanimity, the older settlers who understood and loved the Indians had no glib remedy to offer. They were uncertain and puzzled, and generally hopeless of the Indians' future.

William Johnson, an oil operator of Bartlesville, who had come into the Cherokee country in 1876 and intermarried too late for enrolment, seems typical of this class. Questioned as to his opinion of the restrictions, he said, "There are two sides to that question. There is the Indian side to it and there is the commercial side to it. There is the side that affects the Indians and there is a side that affects the material progress of the country." He advocated the removal of restrictions on mixed-bloods and on the surplus of fullbloods after examination before some competent tribunal; but he thought the fullbloods' homestead should remain inalienable, not because they were necessarily more incompetent than many mixed-bloods, but "because I want them to have a home in this country forever. It is their country, and if I had my way every last man, woman, and child of them would have a home here forever and a home that they could not dispossess themselves of either."[29]

[29] Select Committee, II, 1463-66.

Dr. Murrow expressed the most solemn warning against turning the problem over to local control—a warning that viewed in the light of subsequent events seems charged with prophetic insight. When Senator Teller urged his favorite thesis that the evils of the system were only temporary and that the proposed state of Oklahoma would soon correct all abuses, the old man stoutly asserted: "That is where the danger lies. . . . If we look to the people who will be running the State of Oklahoma, we will be looking to people who don't care a snap for the Indians.

.   .   .        .   .   .        .   .   .

"THE CHAIRMAN. Well, you don't think, do you Doctor, . . . that the people . . . of this great new State . . . would deliberately stand back of a policy of robbery practiced against these full bloods, and would not see that they were afforded the full protection of the laws, and safeguarding their interests in the same manner that they protect and safeguard the interest of any other of its citizens? You don't mean to say that you believe that, Doctor?

"MR. MURROW. I think inside of a year that these full bloods would be deprived of almost every bit of their property.

"THE CHAIRMAN. Then I understand you to say that you believe you can get together 1,200,000 white citizens in any State or section of this country that would deliberately set about the robbery of some of their defenseless and helpless fellow-citizens?

"MR. MURROW. As God is my judge, I do believe it.

"THE CHAIRMAN. I don't believe it.

"MR. MURROW. I do believe it.

"THE CHAIRMAN. I don't believe it. It is a slander on the State of Oklahoma to make such a statement.

"MR. MURROW. I believe as firmly as I believe I am standing here before you that the State of Oklahoma will rob these Indians of every foot of land they own, if the opportunity is given it to do so. . . .

"SENATOR TELLER. I think you are wrong, Doctor. . . .

"MR. MURROW. Well, I don't believe I am, and I appeal to the developments of the future to show whether I am or not."[30]

No other person of either race in Indian Territory or Washington or the country at large made such a sincere attempt to view the problem objectively as did Pleasant Porter. His hesitancy in expressing an opinion contrasted sharply with the fluent readiness with which the six months' resident could solve the whole problem in a few minutes: "I have taken almost every side of this matter that anybody else has taken for the past seven or eight years—I have been on all sides of it—and I have been so sure so often that I was right only to come to the conclusion that I was wrong that I hardly know what to say. . . . It was all new to me when it commenced. I did not know anything about allotting lands, excepting that I saw the history of the allotments that were made for the past forty or fifty years, and I saw that each of them proved to be a complete failure, as far as securing the Indian a home and making him a carpenter or a farmer. . . . I am satisfied that the Government of the United States from the time of its organization has tried in good faith to protect the Indians. . . . I have no fault to find. I have made mistakes myself, and I am one of them [the Indians], for I have been for things which I honestly believed were for the good of my race, but that plan when put in operation has proved by its results to have been a bad thing; so how could I blame the Government for doing things that turned out badly when many of the very things that I advocated turned out badly. It is a complex problem, gentlemen. It is something that never was tried before, this trying to educate a people up to a form of government and conditions alien to all their habits of thought and action. . . .

". . . It is not so much a question of capacity as it is of time. . . . You are the evolution of thousands of years, and we the evolution of thousands of years, perhaps. . . . We both probably started at the same point, but our paths diverged, and the influences to which we were subjected varied, and we see the result. Who can say but that we would finally have reached a

[30] *Select Committee,* I, 883-84.

stage of civilization toward which we were progressing slowly, but none the less surely, which would have suited our life better than the civilization which has been so violently and suddenly thrust upon us—a civilization which in the matter of the care and disposition of property would have suited us far better than the cumbrous and intricate methods which you have of adjusting property interests amongst you.

". . . In conclusion I would say that I would like to see this country become a great and prosperous State . . . and see the day when all these questions which so vex us now would be settled in such a manner as to show that the designs of Providence are always good, though at times inscrutable. Above all things, I would like to live to see the day when, in the great State that will inevitably be here, I would see my people and the white man living side by side in a prosperous land on terms of perfect intellectual and political equality, and each doing his share toward the maintenance and support of that state; . . . but I don't want to rush it at such a rate that the Indian would be lost in the transformation.

"Now I must close. . . . I don't know that I have said anything that would suggest remedial legislation, and that, I apprehend, is what you wanted. I have advised so often in the past and been wrong that I am a little loath to give advice in these days even when it is asked."[31]

Young Dana H. Kelsey was as hesitant as the old Chief in prescribing a solution. He frankly admitted that he had made many regrettable mistakes; he had removed restrictions after the most careful investigation, and dire poverty had resulted. He could not recall a single instance where such action had benefited a fullblood. He was positive that if the Indians were thrown upon their own resources they would be completely dispossessed and degraded. On the other hand, he was emphatically in favor of some plan by which the Indians could dispose of their surplus; they would never use it themselves, and as long as it remained in their possession, the progress of the Territory would be retarded. But he was unable to reconcile

[31] *Ibid.*, I, 623-29.

the welfare of the Indians with the future of the state—"while I have thought over the matter very deeply, I confess that I have been unable to see my way to a solution of the problem."[32]

Many educated Indians who appeared before the committee were under the influence of a somewhat emotional pride in their new United States citizenship, and a strong sense of personal humiliation at their restricted status. Some demanded the immediate abolition of all racial discrimination, but others were willing to surrender their own sense of personal dignity in view of their people's undoubted need of protection.[33]

The Cherokees expressed no official opinion, but David Muskrat, acting head captain of the Kee-too-wah Society, stated emphatically through an interpreter that he wished the restrictions to remain on all fullblood land, that he did not consider himself competent, and that nearly all fullbloods felt as he did. It seemed to be the general desire of the Cherokees that the restrictions should remain as they were except in individual cases.[34]

The Choctaw-Chickasaw delegates had been appointed to urge the sale of their undivided property and the closing of their estate, and their discussion of the restrictions was unofficial. But the Choctaws always opposed any arbitrary repeal of the negotiated agreements by act of Congress; hence they objected alike to the McCumber Amendment and the removal of restrictions from any homestead.[35] The Chickasaw delegates did not show the same unanimity, and the opinions expressed by individual citizens showed the greatest possible variation.[36]

In view of his subsequent prominence, the policy advocated by Charles D. Carter is of special interest. Descended from a white man captured in childhood at the Wyoming Valley Massacre and adopted by the Cherokees, Carter was of mixed

[32] *Select Committee,* I, 582-97. See I, 461-62; II, 1664-72, 1699-1700, 1846-47 for the opinions of Inspector Wright and Secretary Hitchcock.

[33] *Ibid.,* I, 321-37, 690; II, 1254, 1283-1311.

[34] *Ibid.,* I, 273-82, 319-20; II, 1316-27, 1889-92.

[35] *Ibid.,* I, 885-89, 895-99, 913-21, 977-79; Acts of the Choctaw Nation, October 3, 1906.

[36] *Ibid.,* I, 906-13; II, 1160-73.

Cherokee and Chickasaw ancestry—one-fourth Cherokee and one-eighth Chickasaw by blood—but he was a Chickasaw citizen and had been educated in the excellent Chickasaw tribal schools. At the time of the Senatorial visit, he was a fire insurance salesman at Ardmore. He believed that the restrictions should be removed from the entire allotments of whites and Negroes and from the surplus of mixed-blood Indians; but that only the surplus of fullbloods should be alienable after a hearing before a Federal or state court.[37]

Of all the tribes the Creeks made the most careful attempt to formulate a definite policy and present it officially to the Senators. The matter was thoroughly discussed in the Council, and a delegation was appointed, consisting of the Chief, the President and two other members of the House of Kings, and the Speaker and two other members of the House of Warriors. A Negro member of the Council was appointed so that his race would not go unrepresented. The delegates expressed not only the judgment of the Council, but the opinion of their constituents, for at least part of them took the trouble to consult as many of their people as possible to learn their sentiments. Unofficial witnesses who appeared before the Senators also expressed a private belief that was in harmony with the position taken by the delegation.[38]

Most of the delegates were fullbloods, and spoke through an interpreter. They were more given to eloquence than to clear-cut thinking, and were somewhat confused by the leading questions which the Senators used to trap them into declarations in favor of the removal of restrictions; but there is no doubt of their essential position. They regarded the McCumber Amendment as the fulfilment of the pledge made by the Dawes Commission to induce them to consent to allotment, and they desired similar legislation to protect the mixed-bloods also. They were in favor of the sale of inherited land, and the division of the proceeds among the heirs.[39] As an example of unin-

---

[37] *Ibid.*, II, 1175-77.
[38] *Ibid.*, I, 425-40; Indian Territory Division Files, Special File 39c, 24026/06.
[39] *Select Committee*, 425-40, 622-23, 672-82; II, 1312-16, 1957.

fluenced Indian opinion some of these expressions deserve to be quoted. George Cosa, fullblood member of the House of Kings, spoke through an interpreter as follows: ". . . The full-blood Creek people have heard that the Congress of the United States has enacted a law whereby the full-blood Indian is prohibited from the sale of any of his land for twenty-five years, and also is not to be taxed for that length of time. If this has actually occurred, then it is true, gentlemen of the committee, that the large majority of the full-blood people are satisfied with that piece of legislation. Some of our people are disposed to think that this is only a make-believe, and that even if you have enacted such a law you probably do not intend to carry it out fully as written, but for myself and quite a large proportion of our people, the full bloods, we are disposed to believe that so intelligent and great a people as you are would not do a thing of that sort simply to make them feel good when you did not mean to do what your law seems to intend.

"The reason that they are satisfied with that legislation arises from the fact that they believe that they are not competent to cope with the intelligence of the white man and that ways and means will be devised, if the bars are all thrown down, whereby the lands of the full-blood Indians will be taken away from them by the white people, and that would be very bad for our people. They say that this legislation of Congress seems, however, to be in keeping with the spirit of the first overtures that were made by the officials of the Government, whereby the Indians were told: If you will consent I will come in and sectionalize your country and individualize your country, and when so individualized you will be able to hold and enjoy the benefits of your lands."[40]

M. L. Mott also appeared before the committee and urged the Creeks' position with great ability and earnestness.[41] This action aroused angry opposition, and many slurs were cast upon his motives; he was accused of advocating protection to the Indians in order that he might continue to draw a salary

[40] *Select Committee*, I, 426-27.                    [41] *Ibid.*, II, 1263-83.

as their protector, and of prompting the Creeks in their position. There is no doubt, however, that the opinion expressed by the Creek delegation was voluntary and that it was supported almost unanimously by the tribe.

The Creek delegation also described the disastrous effects of the law of 1904 removing restrictions from the surplus of adult freedmen. They protested that the action of Congress was an injustice to that class of citizens and had been done without their consent. They requested that the restrictions should remain as they were on the homesteads, and that the minors should be protected by a provision similar to the McCumber Amendment.[42]

Negro societies throughout the Territory also presented resolutions and memorials. The Choctaw and Chickasaw freedmen, whose small allotments were classed as homesteads and were therefore inalienable, expressed opposition to any removal of restrictions except possibly upon personal proof of competency. The Inter-Territorial Negro Protective League endorsed the restrictions upon the homestead allotments of Choctaw-Chickasaw Negroes, but favored the removal from the surplus of all Five Tribes allottees.[43] Attorneys for the Choctaw-Chickasaw freedmen advanced the usual arguments for transferring their clients to the Indian rolls or selling them additional land "at the appraised valuation."[44]

The Four Mothers Society also sent delegates to present the views of the irreconcilables who were still refusing to take allotments. They expressed no opinion regarding restrictions, for they refused to accept allotment as an accomplished fact. They spoke at length, in most cases through interpreters, reciting again and again their adherence to the ancient treaties and their desperate confidence that the United States would never break its pledges. Brief extracts from these many pages will serve to illustrate the workings of the fullblood mind—its dogged persistence, its refusal to make adjustments, its strong

[42] *Ibid.*, I, 440-41, 620-21.
[43] *Ibid.*, I, 963-66; *Seminole Capital*, September 27, 1906.
[44] *Select Committee*, II, 1139-46.

religious trust, and, in spite of all evidence to the contrary, its ultimate dependence upon the good faith of the American Government.

Eufaula Harjo, fullblood Creek, declared: ". . . We full-blooded Indian people used to live east of the Mississippi River and we made a treaty with the white man. That treaty was made in 1832, on March 24. Our Great Ruler was a witness to this treaty that we had.

"Q. Whom do you refer to as the 'Great Ruler'?—A. I mean God—God looked upon us all and he always looks on us and sees us and rules us all.

"Q. Well, go ahead?—A. The Government of the United States made a treaty and this land was given to us forever, as long as grass should grow and water run. It was given to us and the Government of the United States has divided the land up without the consent of the Indian people. The Indian people did not know anything about it until the land was cut up, and it was done without their consent.

"SENATOR LONG. Have you taken your allotment?—A. No, sir.

"By the CHAIRMAN:

"Q. Well, what do you mean or want?—A. I love my treaty, and I want my old treaty back. That is what I am asking for—the original treaty—I want it back.

"Q. Well can't you understand that the great majority of the Indian people having supplemented that treaty by other agreements, and having taken their land in severalty and in some instances this land has been transferred—can't you understand that the Congress of the United States can not at this time nor at any other time give you any inducement to hope that what has been done will be undone or that the other acts of Congress that have been passed with reference to this land, and its division among the Indians, can not be repealed? Now you understand what I mean, don't you—the action that has been taken in that regard with reference to the division and allotment of this land is irrevocable and something that can't be undone?—A. I can not take the allotment. . . .

"Q. That is all?—A. Well, I am not through yet. I am here asking for the treaty, and the treaty that I am asking for—I will never stop asking for this treaty, the old treaty that our fathers made with the Government which gave us this land forever, as long as the grass grew and the water ran. I will keep on asking for it, for my old fathers and your old fathers made that treaty with us away back there on the other side of the Mississippi, and they said that this land out here was to be ours as a nation for ever, and that is the treaty I want, for we are to have it as long as the grass grows, water runs, and the sun rises, we should have this land, and we are still asking for this land just as the treaty says. . . ."[45]

Redbird Smith, Cherokee fullblood, showed the Senators a photograph of the original patent to his tribe, and presented an eagle feather that had been given to his great-grandfather at the negotiation of the Removal Treaty. He spoke as follows: ". . . I say that I never will change; before our God, I won't. It extends to heaven, the great treaty that has been made with the Government of the United States. Our treaty wherever it extends is respected by the Creator, God. Our nations and governments all look to our God.

"THE CHAIRMAN. Tell him that Congress in order to protect him in his farm and the possession of it forever has provided a way for him to make a permanent home as the result of his work; that we all hope he will agree to the after treaties that were made and thus preserve what he now has.—A. I can't stand and live and breathe if I take this allotment. Under the allotment rules I would see all around me—I see now all around me and all the Indians—people who are ready to grab from under us my living and my home. If I would accept such a plan I would be going in starvation. To take and put the Indians on the land in severalty would be just the same as burying them, for they could not live."[46]

Willis F. Toby, Choctaw fullblood, testified: ". . . They took all our children from their father and mother and made a guardian for them in the United States court, and we don't want

45 *Select Committee*, I, 89-93.                    46 *Ibid.*, I, 97-100.

it that way. I am still faithful to the Great Father of the United States, who made this treaty with the Indians, and I am faithful to that treaty, and the Almighty God that rules the world, I trust in him, and he will stand as the guardian of my people. . . ."[47]

Osway Porter, Chickasaw fullblood, stated his views: ". . . I am a full blood and I know what the full bloods want, and I know that I have not ever wanted our country to be divided, and I know that none of the fullbloods have ever wanted it divided. I have been loving my own mother, and I love this country as I love my mother, for it is my mother. I love it as I love my own father. I love its hills and mountains, and its valleys and trees and rivers, and everything that is in this country. I am here before you my father, humbly asking for your help, and humbly asking you to protect me and my people. We are poor and ignorant, but we know that we love our country, and have confidence in our father's protection. I am faithful and my people are faithful, and we trust that our old original rights will be restored."[48]

The Senators showed their impatience with most of these speakers, but they became impressed in spite of themselves by the eloquence and sincerity of Chitto Harjo. The hearings were held that day in the new oil town of Tulsa where the strongest forces on all that harsh frontier surged into a harmony of growth. Into this alien atmosphere, where young, active, pushing men came to present the cause of the future—the cities they would build, the rich land they would turn into productive fields, the institutions they would establish—the old man came quietly with his interpreter to plead the cause of the past. He began: "I am telling you now about what was done since 1492.

"THE CHAIRMAN:

"All this is unintelligible, and we can not spend all afternoon in this way. We want you to condense everything. We can not commence back with the time of the discovery of America. . . . Please translate that to him.

---

[47] *Select Committee,* I, 100.        [48] *Ibid.,* I, 104-7.

7. Chitto Harjo, or Crazy Snake. "I am telling you now about what was done since 1492."

"MR. JONES:[49] I am going to make a foundation for what I have to say, for, of course, a thing has to have a root before it can grow; and so I am going to talk about 1832 and that treaty."

With his usual habit of personification he went on then to present the history of the two races—". . . I have always lived back yonder in what is now the State of Alabama. . . . We had our troubles back there, and we had no one to defend us. At that time when I had these troubles it was to take my country away from me. I had no other troubles. The troubles were always about taking my country away from me. I could live in peace with all else, but they wanted my country and I was in trouble defending it. It was no use. . . . Then it was the overtures of the Government to my people to leave their land, the home of their fathers, the land that they loved. . . . He said, 'You look away off to the West, . . . and there you will see a great river called the Mississippi River, and away over beyond that is another river called the Arkansas River'; and he said, 'You go away out there and you will find a land that is fair to look upon and is fertile, and you go there with your people and I will give that country to you and your people forever.' . . . That was the agreement and the treaty, and I and my people came out here and we settled on this land, and I carried out these agreements and treaties in all points and violated none."

He produced a copy of the Treaty of 1832, and insisted that in view of its guarantees, the Creek Agreement did not provide, could not possibly have provided, for allotment—"I think the treaty of 1901 is a twin brother of the one of 1832." He had gone to Washington the preceding winter and had told Senator Long that he would ask the President, and that if the President told him the Agreement provided for allotment he would believe it. Long had arranged the interview, and now he asked what had transpired. The old man answered that the President had not even mentioned the treaty—"he just shook hands with me, and that was all."

[49] Chitto Harjo sometimes went by the English name of Wilson Jones.

The exasperation of the Senators changed to sympathy as they observed the Indian's despairing earnestness. They inquired of the Federal officials if he had "a place to rest his head," and were reassured by the answer that like other Snakes he had an allotment somewhere if only he could be persuaded to accept it.

A few minutes later Chitto Harjo came back and asked the Senators for an expression of their opinion. They told him kindly and courteously that the Treaty of 1832 had been modified by subsequent agreements, and that any attempt to resist was hopeless. He seemed to realize then that his desperate appeal had failed, and that there was no hope of redress from the American Government; but his undefeated spirit flared up in a wild plan to refer the interpretation of the treaties to international arbitration: "After I think it over a minute or two I shall desire to say something. [A pause.] I was a member of the Creek national council when that treaty was ratified that you refer to, and I want to say a word about it.

"THE CHAIRMAN. Very well; proceed.

"MR. JONES. In the agreement made between me and my government and the Government of the United States there was a misunderstanding, and there was and is no other alternative that I can look to, for I think I have the privilege of appealing to the other tribes and notifying them in response to the disagreement between you and me in reference to the allotments.

"THE CHAIRMAN. Do you mean the other four tribes?

"MR. JONES. I do not mean the other four civilized tribes, but I can call on the Spanish Government and the British Government and the French Government—I can call on four of the civilized Governments across the mother of waters to come in and see that this is right. That is all I have to say."[50]

All through the hearings the committee showed their personal bias by their encouragement to the "booster" element and their attempts to lead all witnesses to their way of thinking. They overlooked no opportunity to cast slurs at Secretary Hitchcock, to the great delight of their audience. About the Indian, Chairman Clark expressed the characteristic view, "So long as he owns the face of the earth there is no particular inducement for him to work." They were frank to say that their committee had not recommended the McCumber Amendment, and that they considered it unconstitutional, and they constantly reminded the witnesses that it would be impossible to establish a state government with non-taxable land. They expressed the utmost readiness to turn the entire Indian problem over to local control. When Senator Teller said, "I am sure that . . . you are going to govern yourselves right, and with that faith I am ready to put everything in your hands that can possibly be placed in them, and I know that you will not abuse the trust," the hall rang with applause. They constantly assumed that the new status had been established at the request of the Indians and for their benefit. Senator Clark of Montana asked the naïve question, "Governor Porter, did I understand you to say that the Indians down here in the Creek Nation would have preferred to remain under the tribal form of government?" and when he was answered in the affirmative, Senator Brandegee wanted to know, "Well, if that was the case, why did you not remain under the old government?"[51]

They reported to Congress that the McCumber Amendment was "unwise, injurious to the Indians, and of no validity," and by encouraging speculative purchases based upon a belief in its unconstitutionality it would be a "fruitful source of dishonest transactions." They recommended the removal of all restrictions from whites and Negroes and from the surplus of adult Indians.[52]

Bills to that effect were introduced, but the short session of Congress adjourned without taking action.[53] The people of the

[51] *Ibid.*, I, 6, 90, 96, 99, 101, 171, 320, 395, 549, 646, 994; II, 1183, 1322-24, 1413-14, 1432.

[52] *Ibid.*, I, v-vi; *Congressional Record*, XLI, 1195.

[53] *Congressional Record*, XLI, 322, 372, 1246, 1308, 2340-61, 3258; *Muskogee Phoenix*, January 25, 1907.

Indian Territory did not work so actively for legislation as they had in former times. They probably reflected that the next year would see their own delegation in the halls of Congress, and that as a strong and confident people they would take their destiny into their own hands.

# CHAPTER VI

# The Price of Statehood

ALTHOUGH statehood has represented the most ardent aspirations of every new American community, it is doubtful if any other people ever longed for that magic goal with the intensity of the white inhabitants of the Indian Territory. A white population very much larger than that of any state at the time of its admission to the Union had been living under conditions of political dependence never experienced before by a frontier settlement. The tribal leaders had felt a profound sadness when they surrendered the political independence that was rooted in countless generations of unrecorded history, but they began to enter with pride into the larger opportunities of a greater citizenship; but the more conservative Indians withdrew in passive disapproval from a movement in which they felt they had no part, and the new government was established without their participation. The vigorous young commonwealth that came so lustily into the Union soon realized its ambition of dealing with its own problems of Indian administration.

The various agreements with the Indians had contemplated the continuance of the tribal and Federal administration during the entire period of dividing the communal property. When the date had been fixed at March 4, 1906, for the termination of the tribal governments, it was believed that the liquidation of the tribal estates would be completely effected by that date and that statehood would follow immediately. But the white inhabitants were not willing to wait. The new settlers especially discovered the inconveniences of their environment as soon as they arrived, and began to clamor for the creation of a territorial government or for immediate statehood on any terms.

The most expeditious method of securing statehood seemed to lie in union with Oklahoma; for that territory from the standpoint of population and political and economic advancement had for a long time been more deserving of statehood than any state ever admitted to the Union. As early as 1900, when only three of the tribes had consented to surrender their autonomy, the white residents of the Indian Territory began to assemble in conventions and to lobby in Washington to secure territorial government or statehood with Oklahoma.

The Indians opposed both these plans. They desired that the Interior Department and the Dawes Commission should administer and divide their property unhampered by the demands of local white settlers, and that as long as any communal interest remained undivided the tribal governments should continue to have a voice in its control. Moreover, they objected strongly to the open saloons that carried on such a thriving business in Oklahoma Territory; realizing their susceptibility to the white man's fire water, they had passed "prohibition" laws long before such a policy had been adopted by any American state, and although their enforcement had been greatly complicated in recent years by the extraterritorial status of the white residents, they preferred the system to the arrogance with which the liquor traffic dominated the life of Oklahoma.[1]

These principles were formulated at an intertribal conference called by Green McCurtain at McAlester in 1896, immediately after his induction into office as the first tribal executive to be elected upon a platform of surrender to the Dawes Commission. When the promoters of territorial government began to hold conventions and adopt petitions, another intertribal conference held at Eufaula, in the Creek Nation, November 28, 1902, adopted resolutions condemning both plans of the white enthusiasts as premature.[2]

---

[1] Acts of the Choctaw Nation, December 12, 1902; Debo, *op. cit.*, pp. 48, 52, 65-66, 169, 187-91.

[2] *Indian Citizen*, November 12, 19, 1896; Acts of the Choctaw Nation, December 12, 1902, text of resolutions.

Another meeting was held at Eufaula the following May, and the Five Civilized Tribes Executive Committee was created. Resolutions were adopted reciting the guarantees in the various removal treaties that no territorial or state government would ever be placed over the Indians without their consent. Each Council was advised to petition Congress for separate statehood to go into effect March 4, 1906, and to address a memorial to various religious and temperance organizations throughout the United States for assistance in combating the union with Oklahoma and the legalization of the liquor traffic. It was recommended that an election be held in each tribe upon the question of calling a constitutional convention to meet not later than February 1, 1904; and the Executive Committee was authorized to carry on an active educational campaign to acquaint the citizens of the various tribes with the importance of the election. Non-citizens were invited to call a convention to approve the constitution or to propose amendments, and it was recommended that conference committees should be appointed to settle any difference of opinion. Each convention was then to appoint a delegation to proceed to Washington and lobby for the passage of an enabling act providing for a popular referendum on the proposed constitution and the election of state officers.[3]

At least part of the tribes adopted the petitions and memorials recommended at this meeting and forwarded them to the Executive Committee,[4] and at least one legislature, the Choctaw, directed the Chief to call an election, and made an appropriation for its share of the printing of the educational circulars. But elections were not held in all the tribes, and although some of the tribes appointed delegates, the proposed constitutional convention was never held.[5] In the meantime, Congress ignored the protests of the Indians and proceeded with a joint statehood project.

[3] Indian Territory Division Files, Special File 39c, 458/04, text of resolution.
[4] *Ibid.*, Special File 39c, 458/04, 462/04, 83156/03.
[5] *Ibid.*, Special File 39c, 458/04; Acts of the Choctaw Nation, October 23, 1903.

When the Councils met in the fall of 1904, they passed further resolutions against the proposed union with Oklahoma. They also directed a letter to the President, written in the informal style that the Indians always seemed to affect when addressing Theodore Roosevelt. This letter quoted the guarantees of the Cherokee treaties of 1828 and 1835, the Choctaw treaty of 1830, and the Creek and Seminole treaty of 1856. It pointed out that "As a people we have kept our faith with the United States government," but "as the time approaches for the consummation of the sacred pledge made to us," Congress was preparing to violate it in spite of the most solemn protests from the tribes. Therefore, "Knowing your intense honesty, your hatred of shams, . . . we turn to you, Mr. President, feeling that you will understand us better than Congress. . . . you know the West—you know our hopes and our ambitions; and we appeal again to your sense of justice and fair dealing."[6] This appeal also was disregarded.

In 1905 occurred the most notable attempt ever made by the Indians to create a state government of their own choosing. The initiative seems to have been taken by James A. Norman, a mixed-blood Cherokee living at Muskogee, who issued a pamphlet in the fall of 1904 suggesting the creation of a separate state to be named Sequoyah. In July 1905, Norman and Chiefs Rogers and McCurtain issued a call for a constitutional convention. They were joined by Chiefs Porter and Brown, but Governor Johnston, who was said to favor joint statehood with Oklahoma, refused to participate. Each Federal recording district was to hold a local convention for the selection of seven delegates and seven alternates to the constitutional convention. Each Chief appointed a chairman for each district in his nation to arouse interest and encourage attendance at the local convention as well as to preside. The local conventions were held August 7. They seem to have aroused considerable interest except in the Chickasaw Nation, where the call was generally ignored. The constitutional convention met August 21 at Mus-

<hr />

[6] Indian Territory Division Files, Special File 39c, 12124/04; Acts of the Choctaw Nation, November 1, 1904.

kogee. Committees were appointed, especially a committee of fifty to draft the constitution, and it adjourned after two days' session. It reconvened September 5, adopted the constitution, and adjourned September 8.

The whole movement was a most impressive demonstration of the political vitality that still existed in the Indian citizenship. The white residents had been invited to participate, but they took little interest, and the press and public sentiment seemed to be generally hostile. The account of any of the local conventions with its tribal leaders in attendance, its debates in English and the local Indian language, and its smoothly running parliamentary procedure is strongly reminiscent of the great days of tribal politics. The constitutional convention was characterized even by a hostile newspaper as the most representative body of Indians ever assembled in the United States. Pleasant Porter was elected president, and the list of delegates reads like a roll call of the great names in recent tribal history. John R. Goat, a fullblood Creek, addressed the chair in his native language asking to have the proceedings interpreted to his delegation. His speech was interpreted to the convention by Pleasant Porter, and his request was granted. Robert L. Owen read a memorial from the Kee-too-wahs expressing their desire for separate statehood. The committee of fifty appointed to draft the constitution was said to have forty Indian citizens in its membership. Only the Chickasaws were not fully represented; but Johnston had sent William H. Murray, a recently intermarried citizen, who had been serving as his private secretary, and a few delegates were present from Pauls Valley. Two non-citizens, A. Grant Evans and Charles N. Haskell, took a very prominent part in the proceedings.[7]

The constitution of the proposed "State of Sequoyah" was submitted to the people November 7. It received a light vote if the total population of the Territory is taken into consideration, but the vote cast was overwhelmingly in its favor.[8] A copy of

[7] *Muskogee Phoenix*, July 6, 14, 19, 22, 23, 30, August 8, 16, 19, 22, 23, September 6, 7, 9, 1905.

[8] *Ibid.*, November 10, 1905.

the constitution was sent to Congress, but it was not considered. There was never the slightest chance that Congress would consent to the admission of two Western, radical, and probably Democratic, states in the place on the map that could be occupied by one.

The white residents of the Territory thought of statehood largely in terms of securing a Congressional delegation to work for the removal of restrictions. They were impatient to assume all problems of Indian administration, and they expected to settle them quickly. J. W. Orr, a banker of Vinita, expressed this aim laconically to the Senatorial committee in 1906—"As to that, I will say that when they come into statehood they will give the boys their land."[9]

Besides the abstract and impersonal desire to "develop the country" and the individual desire to develop a portion of it for their private interest, the citizens of the embryo commonwealth were confronted with a serious tax problem. The Indians had never paid taxes except in a limited sense, and they had consented to accept their lands in severalty only upon the condition that the allotments should be non-taxable for a certain period. Moreover, this exemption was in line with the general allotment policy of the Federal Government—a policy designed to accustom the Indians gradually to the responsibilities of citizenship. The Choctaws and Chickasaws had secured tax exemption for all their land for twenty-one years so long as the title should remain in the original allottee; the Cherokee Agreement exempted the homestead as long as it should be held by the original allottee; and in the other tribes the tax exemption was coincident with the restricted period. Very little of the land, therefore, would be subject to taxation under the agreements until the expiration of the restrictions on the Creek surplus in 1907. This would be followed by the Cherokee surplus and by whatever Choctaw-Chickasaw surplus should pass out of the hands of the original allottees.[10]

---

[9] *Muskogee Phoenix*, November 1, 1905; *Select Committee*, I, 193; II, 1493-94, 1984.    [10] Kappler, *Laws and Treaties*, I, 664, 764, 772, 788.

In a political society accustomed to rely almost exclusively for its revenue on the general property tax, this problem seemed insurmountable. The more progressive Indians admitted its seriousness, and were willing to make concessions to the needs of the new state. When the Senatorial committee questioned them in 1906 most of them favored the removal of the restrictions and tax exempt privileges from non-Indian allottees and possibly from all Indian land except the homestead. Several had secured the removal of their own restrictions through the Department with no intention of selling their land; they were willing to pay taxes, and preferred to hold their property under the same tenure as their white neighbors.[11]

The Department officials were sympathetic toward the future state in its predicament, and almost as soon as the agreements were made they advised Congress to abrogate them. A bill was drafted by Bixby in the fall of 1905 to make all land taxable except the homesteads, and to limit the exemption of Seminole homesteads to twenty-one years. His recommendations received the approval of the Indian Office,[12] and Congress adopted the same policy of arbitrary legislation without regard for the vested rights that the Indians had acquired under the agreements with the Federal Government.

Although it seemed impossible to create a state government without taxation, the Indian Territory "boosters" were not willing to wait until most of the land would become taxable; they wished to secure statehood immediately, even before the date set for the expiration of the tribal governments, and then obtain the premature removal of the restrictions to deliver them from their difficulties. But statehood was not secured until after the date set in the agreements. The same session of Congress that passed the Five Tribes Act also passed the Enabling Act for the admission of Oklahoma Territory and Indian Territory as the State of Oklahoma. It became a law, June 16, 1906.

Congress recognized the fact that the Federal Government had many unfulfilled obligations to the Indians. The Enabling

[11] *Select Committee*, I, 287, 303, 313, 337-39, 977-79; II, 1176-77.
[12] Indian Territory Division Files, 16716/05, Enclosures No. 19, 21, 23.

Act required the state to prohibit the liquor traffic for twenty-one years in the area formerly constituting the Indian Territory. The state constitution was further limited by the following clause: "*Provided,* That nothing contained in the said constitution shall be construed to limit or impair the rights of person or property pertaining to the Indians of said Territories (so long as such rights shall remain unextinguished) or to limit or affect the authority of the Government of the United States to make any law or regulation respecting such Indians, their lands, property, or other rights by treaties, agreement, law, or otherwise, which it would have been competent to make if this Act had never been passed."[13]

The election of delegates to the Constitutional Convention took place in November 1906. Mixed-blood Indians and intermarried whites entered very prominently into the campaign. Trained in the difficult school of tribal politics, they demonstrated at this first election the political ability that has given them ever since an influence far out of proportion to their numbers in the government of the state. But there is overwhelming evidence that the fullbloods, who had entered so actively into the government of their tiny republics, took little interest in the election.

It was apparent in the very beginning of the work of the Dawes Commission that the Indians would not be able to exercise their new citizenship as fully and as satisfactorily as they had exercised the old. When the Cherokees began their first negotiations, they asked in behalf of the fullblood group the privilege of jury service. The Dawes Commissioners explained that such a concession would be impossible unless they understood the English language, that it was the universal practice in United States courts to use only English-speaking jurors. The Cherokees argued very earnestly for this privilege; it was the custom in tribal courts to use an interpreter, their citizens understood jury service and were competent, and to deprive them of this right would take away

---

[13] *Statutes at Large,* XXXIV, 268-69.

their feeling of participation in the government and would place them under a humiliating sense of disability.[14]

Now the first general election in the Indian Territory demonstrated that the fullbloods could not participate in public affairs. Very few of them voted at all; they were bewildered by the unfamiliar issues, and distrustful of the whole proceeding. In one tribe, the Creek, several Indians did announce themselves as candidates, but every one was defeated in the election. The Indians who sat in the Constitutional Convention were educated mixed-bloods. A few days after the election, Pleasant Porter expressed the opinion that the real Indian would have no part in the new state, would never sit on a jury or hold office. "The white element and the element that it can control is in the saddle, and in the ordering of things the Indian has neither place nor part." Jacob B. Jackson expressed the same distrust. "Now here is a state going to be organized, the State of Oklahoma. When that comes everything is going to be changed. After that the United States Congress will have no power and everything will have to be settled here. The State government will have to regulate everything about the land. If that is to be the condition, we are not pleased with the movement."[15]

The Constitutional Convention met at Guthrie soon after the election. It was generally recognized throughout the proceedings that the state would take action for the removal of restrictions and the placing of Indian administration under local control. As the result of the political alliances that he had formed at the Sequoyah convention William H. Murray was elected president. When he was escorted to the platform he made an opening speech in which the removal of restrictions was taken for granted. At the close he approached a grandiloquent climax; he wished he could say to England, "Hands off the Irish!" to Russia, "Hands off the Jew!" and "to Hitchcock

---

[14] Cherokee Papers, Joint Session United States Commission and Cherokee Commission.

[15] Select Committee, I, 639, 681, 687, 823, 911, 956-60.

and other grafters: 'Hands off the Indian and his property.' (Great applause)"[16]

Later in its sessions the convention unanimously adopted a resolution memorializing Congress to remove the restrictions on sale and leasing from all land except the homesteads of full-bloods, "without delay, as a necessary means to the development of our State and the development and welfare of our citizens of Indian blood." The memorial was presented to the Senate by Clark of Wyoming, but it will be remembered that no action was taken on the matter during the session of 1906-1907.[17]

The year 1907 was the campaign year for ratification of the proposed constitution and the election of state officers. Both political parties were in perfect agreement with regard to the removal of restrictions, but the Democrats naturally expressed more opposition to the "carpetbag" government.

The Democratic platform adopted at Oklahoma City, June 18, contained the following paragraphs:

"We believe the people of this sovereign state should have the full measure of liberty enjoyed by citizens of other sovereign states.

"We believe that the various federal bureaus established in this state should be immediately terminated and that the basis of this bureau government, the restrictions on the sale and lease of land of our citizens should be removed summarily, except as to homesteads of full-bloods; and we favor the immediate settlement of all tribal affairs and the immediate distribution of all tribal funds.

"We believe that the estates of those mentally incompetent, of whatsoever race, should be protected by our state courts. We will take care of our own defectives of whatever race or color, and will not rely upon the federal government to discharge this proper function of our own state."

The Republican platform was adopted at Tulsa, August 2. It ran as follows: "We demand the removal of all restrictions

---

[16] Johnson, *Oklahoma History South of the Canadian*, I, 310-18.
[17] *Select Committee*, II, 1859; *Congressional Record*, XLI, 1193.

upon the alienation of lands belonging to Indians. We favor the enactment of such laws by congress as will give to each member of the Indian tribes in this state, all the rights and privileges of other American citizens, including the right to control, sell, lease, mortgage, or devise the lands allotted to him, the same as white persons under similar conditions: except that the homestead of full bloods shall be inalienable, as now provided by law, and we request our members in congress to urge such immediate legislation."[18]

Many people thought these platforms did not go far enough. The influential Republican *Muskogee Phoenix*, of which Tams Bixby now owned the controlling interest, expressed its dissatisfaction with the stand taken by its party. "The plea that the fullblood will be reduced to beggary by the removal of restrictions is not valid. Society is under no obligation to feed him who will not work. The Indian who has sold his land and spent the money ought to stand just where any other citizen of the state stands—there will be work for him to do even if he be a profligate, and if he will not do it, organized society cannot be made, by any conceivable argument, to be his pension giver."[19]

The election was held September 17. The proposed constitution was accepted by a large majority, and a separate provision extending prohibition of the liquor traffic over the entire state was also adopted. The new state proved to be overwhelmingly Democratic. Charles N. Haskell was elected Governor. The Democratic primary had chosen candidates for Senator, who would be elected as a matter of routine as soon as the legislature should convene. The old territorial divisions had been recognized in these nominations; according to a tacit understanding Robert L. Owen was chosen from the "East Side," and Thomas P. Gore from the "West Side." The Enabling Act had granted the state five Representatives, and had created the Congressional districts. Charles D. Carter, Chicka-

---

[18] Seth K. Corden and W. B. Richards, *The Oklahoma Red Book* (Oklahoma City, 1912), II, 356, 363.

[19] *Muskogee Phoenix*, August 17, 1907.

saw citizen, and James S. Davenport, who had recently married a Cherokee citizen, were chosen from the East Side. Bird S. McGuire, former territorial delegate from Oklahoma and the only Republican, Elmer L. Fulton of Oklahoma City, and Scott Ferris of Lawton, whose district included some Chickasaw territory, represented the West Side. The entire delegation in Congress was solidly committed to the removal of the restrictions.

In general the Indians seem to have acquiesced in this policy. They were even more hopelessly outnumbered by the union of the two territories than they had been before; the new state had a population of 1,414,177, and the Indians, including those tribes settled in the West Side, constituted only 5.3 per cent.[20] The conservative element had no voice in the new order, and most of the progressive leaders had come to believe that at least a modification of the restrictions was necessary to the welfare of the state.

Only the Creeks set themselves against the rising tide of public opinion. It will be remembered that the restrictions on their surplus expired that summer, except that the McCumber Amendment had halted the process in the case of fullbloods. Just before this date Chief Porter called a special session of the Council to secure an expression of opinion regarding the McCumber Amendment, believing that the influence of this law would be strengthened by the endorsement of the Council. The Snake members surprised observers by voting almost solidly for it, and it was approved by a vote of 22 to 7 in the House of Kings, and 55 to 21 in the House of Warriors.[21]

Porter died suddenly, September 3. According to the Creek constitution he would have been succeeded by the Second Chief, Moty Tiger; therefore President Roosevelt appointed Tiger, to make the succession legal. The new Chief was a fullblood about sixty-five years old, intelligent but conservative. When the Council convened soon after his appointment, he informed the legislators of the efforts that would be made to influence

20 *Population of Oklahoma and Indian Territory 1907*, pp. 8-9.
21 *Muskogee Phoenix*, July 30, August 3, 1907.

the coming session of Congress to remove further restrictions, and he advised them to pass a resolution against the change. He also recommended that they endeavor to impress upon the fullbloods the fact that they could legally sell only their inherited land, and that sales could be conducted only through the Agency, and to warn them that the signing of deeds "away from the Agency is but one of the ways the spiders have of pulling them into their webs."[22]

Meanwhile, the new state government was inaugurated at Guthrie, the temporary capital, November 16. It was a time of almost universal rejoicing. A part of the inaugural ceremony was a symbolic marriage signifying the union of the two territories. A young Indian woman wearing the graceful costume of her ancestors represented the Indian Territory, and a young white man in cowboy dress took the part of Oklahoma. The large number of Indian citizens elected to important positions in the new state indicated that a real union of the two races had been effected. Nobody remarked that there was an unassimilated Indian element in the population, helpless and utterly hopeless.

Less than two weeks after the inauguration of the state government an event occurred that brought this fact into dramatic notice. The Trans-Mississippi Commercial Congress met at Muskogee in the midst of the general rejoicing. It was the most important gathering ever held in the area now constituting the state, and the strong young city thrilled to its opportunity. Governor Haskell and "Senator" Owen returned to their home town, which they had left as private citizens so short a time before, to extend an official welcome to the visitors. The preceding political campaign had been marked by bitter personalities, but these were all forgotten in the great and generous pride of welcome which the city gave to its two distinguished sons. "Senator" Gore was also present and received an ovation that was almost overwhelming. The Governors of Kansas, Arkansas, New Mexico, and Hawaii, John W. Noble

22 *Ibid.*, September 4, 5, October 1, 1907.

of St. Louis, former Secretary of Agriculture, and D. R. Francis and other former Secretaries of the Interior appeared upon the program. They were hospitably and even enthusiastically received, but a perfect storm of emotion swept the hall whenever one of the new state officers appeared.

Moty Tiger, as Chief of the Creeks, had been invited to give an address of welcome. He spoke quietly in the deep gutturals of his native language, but his words struck a strange note in the general triumph. Speaking of his people, he said: "As a part of the new state into which we shall merge, there lies a path new and full of uncertainties upon which, however, we enter with a hope that the burden which we shall share with our white brother shall not be too heavy for our untrained shoulders. We have been admonished to look with hope upon this inevitable destiny and I assure you that whatever sorrows and trials it may bring, will be borne with resignation and unflinching fortitude."

He said that the question of the removal of restrictions would probably come before the meeting, and he earnestly requested that no declaration of policy be made, that the question be left with the Indians and the Government. Owen sat on the platform immediately behind him in the full glory of his triumphant career, handsome, dominating, one of the ablest men ever produced by the state of Oklahoma. The audience understood that the Chief referred directly to him when he said: "The polished and educated man with the Indian blood in his veins who advocates the removal of restrictions from the lands of my ignorant people, apart from governmental regulations, is only reaching for gold to ease his itching palms, and our posterity will remember him only for his avarice and his treachery." He said that many fullbloods were incompetent, and as for the removal of restrictions, "It is a fight between greed and conscience with this great government as arbiter, and upon the decision rests for generations, the fate of these untutored children of nature."

Owen for once lost the poise that made him such a master of argument. When his turn came on the program, he discarded his set speech and defended himself in fiery language that made a great impression upon his sympathetic audience. At a later session he introduced a resolution by which the meeting would commit itself in favor of the removal of restrictions and would ask the Senators and Representatives from the participating states to carry out the program. Of Tiger's speech he said, "It is the federal official drawing a salray [sic] that puts the words in the mouths of the men in this territory," and cited the Shakespearean reference to the "itching palms" as proof that it did not originate in the mind of the untutored fullblood. He read a draft statute, which he said he had drawn up with the approval of Governor Haskell, for protection of the Indians by the state courts. The state of Oklahoma, he said, had no desire to exploit the fullbloods, for if they were reduced to pauperism who would take care of them?—"Will it be the interior department [or] will it be the generous hearted sons of Oklahoma who will take care of their own defectives? They are our children and we want to take care of our own children and we don't want any stepmother."[23]

The stars in their courses fought for the brilliant Cherokee and the meeting unanimously adopted his resolution. But some impression was made upon the visitors by the Indian's speech, for the *Kansas City Star-Times* carried a strong editorial comment. The *Muskogee Phoenix* reminded this critic that the development of Oklahoma was of great financial importance to Kansas City. It hoped it would not be necessary for the business interests of Oklahoma to bring the editorial independence of the *Star-Times* to the attention of Kansas City wholesale dealers, and to warn them that the St. Louis newspapers were friendly to the progress of the state and that the St. Louis wholesalers would be glad to secure the Oklahoma trade. As for the pathetic speeches of Indians, they were all composed by Federal officials anyhow.[24]

It must be admitted that Tiger's speech was hardly in his usual style, but there is no doubt that it expressed his sentiments. It was easy to influence Indians to sign deeds or other

[23] *Muskogee Phoenix*, November 20, 22, 1907.
[24] *Ibid.*, November 23, December 7, 1907.

papers that they did not understand; but the continued refusal of the Snakes to accept the fact of allotment illustrates the tenacity with which they held to their convictions, and certainly it was seldom necessary for any Indian to delegate the pleasant responsibility of making a speech.

According to the plan which Owen presented to the Trans-Mississippi Congress, the Governor would appoint three philanthropic citizens in each county containing allotted land, to serve without pay. It would be their duty to nominate a curator of fullblood Indian estates to be appointed by the district judge. The curator would be placed under bond and would be authorized to assist the fullblood allottee to develop his land and secure fair compensation in leasing it. A forty-acre homestead would be inalienable.[25]

Owen expressed himself more fully to the state Senate, which he addressed December 12. He said that the Oklahoma delegation would work as a unit in compelling the Interior Department to give up jurisdiction over all Indian lands in Oklahoma. If the state should exempt Indian homesteads from taxation, it should take over all the tribal school buildings as compensation. He recommended that the Indians of each county should elect a curator to assist the county judge to pass on all Indian land matters. He had drawn up a bill to present to Congress for the removal of all restrictions except on an eighty-acre homestead, and for the right of parents to represent their children without bond in the management of the alienable land. It was his ultimate purpose, he said, to secure the removal of all restrictions; and he promised that if the Federal Government should insist upon retaining them, he would compel it to reimburse the state for the loss in taxes. As for the McCumber Amendment, he believed it to be unconstitutional and would prove his contention in the courts.[26]

Owen developed a logical theory of the position of Five Tribes allottees and presented it with great impressiveness upon many occasions during the entire period of Federal admin-

[25] *Muskogee Phoenix,* November 22, 1907.    [26] *Ibid.,* December 13, 1907.

istration. He claimed that it was he who had secured the enactment of the citizenship law of 1901, and that its sole purpose
was the termination of the supervisory power of the Department. After the passage of this law an Indian's freedom of
action could not be restricted by discriminatory legislation
not applying to other United States citizens. Under the agreements no transfer of property could take place during the
restricted period, but the allottee could not be prevented from
selling his equity and giving a valid deed to go into effect at
the expiration of the restrictions. As to the non-taxable provisions, they were not binding upon the state of Oklahoma; for
the Indians were citizens of the state and completely under its
jurisdiction. The McCumber Amendment, by extending the
restrictions, had impaired the value of contracts or sale made
subject to the early expiration of the restricted period; it was
therefore an *ex post facto* law, and clearly unconstitutional.

He became very sarcastic in discussing the need of the
restrictions. He pointed to the absurdity of a policy that would
protect *him* against exploitation. He supposed he could secure
the removal of his own restrictions if he would consent to
humiliate himself and prove his competence to some underpaid
clerk in the Interior Department. There were, of course, some
Indians who were incompetent just as there were unthrifty
individuals in any society; but he could not conceive of protecting people simply "because they are not good traders, because they are not learned in values, and not experienced in
the ways of the world." And why should the white settlers of
the Territory be regarded with such distrust? The census of
1900 showed that thirty-odd thousand had been born in Hitchcock's own state of Missouri. Had they all become thieves as
soon as they crossed the border? The only possible purpose
of the continued guardianship of a race that did not need it
was to provide salaried positions for Government employees.[27]

[27] *Select Committee*, I, 392-409; II, 1920-26; Indian Office Files, 53683/08
Cherokee 311; *Proceedings of the Third Annual Meeting of the Oklahoma and
Indian Territory Bar Association* (Oklahoma City, 1906), pp. 132-39; *Congressional
Record*, XLII, 2584-96.

It has been customary for oversentimental defenders of the Indians to place the whole responsibility for the legislation enacted during the session of 1907-1908 upon the Oklahoma delegation in Congress. There is no doubt, however, that the policy embodied in this legislation was, like the allotment policy itself, advocated by the President, the Interior Department, the Indian Office, and the Union agent, and supported by public sentiment throughout the country. The members of Congress from Oklahoma, of course, were influential; Owen, Carter, and McGuire all received appointments on the Indian Affairs Committees of their respective Houses, and every member of the delegation introduced a bill during the session to secure the modification of the restrictions.[28]

In their enthusiasm the Oklahomans made many irresponsible statements during the course of the debate. Carter said that 100 per cent of the Chickasaws were literate. Davenport asserted that among the Cherokees not a man or woman over fifteen was unable to read and write; and he estimated that not 10 per cent of the people between the ages of eighteen and thirty had failed to receive a high school education, and that 40 per cent had received a college education.[29]

While the legislation was taking form, James R. Garfield, who had succeeded Hitchcock as Secretary of the Interior, reported to the Senate Committee on Indian Affairs that more than 1,300 tracts of Seminole land constituting about half the area of the Nation had been illegally conveyed; that about 467 tracts belonging to Cherokee fullbloods and not less than 1,200 belonging to Creeks, mostly fullbloods, were known to have clouded titles; and that although no investigation had been made of conditions in the other two tribes, the number of illegal conveyances was believed to be "far in excess" of these figures. He stated on the authority of Wright that speculators who had purchased restricted land in violation of law had instituted suits in the state courts upon the advent of statehood

---

[28] *Congressional Record*, XLII, 383, 427, 673-74, 835, 899-900, 1314, 1315, 1714, 1958, 4960.

[29] *Ibid.*, XLII, 5079, appendix, 427.

for the purpose of quieting title, and that the Indians, not understanding legal procedure, had allowed the suits to go by default. He therefore drafted a bill authorizing the Attorney-General to bring suit in the Federal courts for the cancellation of fraudulent conveyances made prior to the removal of restrictions. His bill provided that the expense of the litigation should be borne by the tribe or by the individual allottee.[30]

Owen, in pursuance of his theory that any allottee could sell his equity in restricted land regardless of laws to the contrary, had been insisting that the purchasers should be protected. Early in the session he was quoted as follows: "One thing should be conserved that appears to have been overlooked and that is the equity of would-be purchasers who have a clouded title. In protecting a full blood Indian he should be required to do equity toward those from whom he has received money. The law which prevents a fraud on an Indian should also prevent a fraud by an Indian." Now when Garfield made his proposal for the clearing of clouded titles in the Federal courts, Owen was reported as saying that he would surrender the entire program of removing the restrictions if it were joined with such a policy.[31]

The law as finally adopted was a Department measure; it was drafted by the solicitor of the Interior Department after a conference between the Secretary and the Oklahoma delegation. President Roosevelt had been willing that Congress should go much further; he told a delegation of Tulsans who had chartered a "booster" train and were visiting the Eastern cities that he had gone over the question with the Oklahoma members of Congress and had concluded that justice to Indian and white demanded the removal of all restrictions except from a forty-acre homestead.[32]

The bill was introduced by Bird McGuire as the only Republican from Oklahoma, and was supported according to

[30] *Muskogee Phoenix*, February 27, 1908.

[31] *Ibid.*, December 24, 1907; February 27, 1908.

[32] *Ibid.*, January 18, 21, 30; April 18, 1908; *Congressional Record*, XLII, 3931-34; LXV, 4462-63; Department of the Interior, *Annual Report*, 1908, II, 101-2.

agreement by every member of the delegation, although some of them believed it to be too conservative. The only amendment which it received in Congress was a provision granting the same protection to three-quarters blood Indians that was given to fullbloods. It was generally accepted that any removal of restrictions should also repeal the tax exemption. With the exception of some of the allottees, the Indian Rights Association seems to have made the only protest that such imposition of taxes in violation of the agreements would be a breach of faith on the part of the United States.[33]

While the legislation was pending, a number of Indians or their representatives appeared before a sub-committee of the House Committee on Indian Affairs to present tribal or individual points of view. These expressions indicate that the mixed-bloods had accepted the viewpoint of the white settlers and the Federal officials with regard to the need for taxation and the desirability of developing the country. The fullbloods, on the other hand, and the Creek government, which was under fullblood dominance, desired no modification of the restrictions. As Chief Tiger expressed it through his interpreter, "if you should remove that protection, there are persons here in this city who will touch the wires all over this town, and the information will be down there in our country in a moment's time, and the people who are down there ready to rob our people, as it may be said, of their lands, would have the lands already signed away to them in a few hours."[34]

Apparently none of the Federal officials took the trouble to inquire as to what provision the state of Oklahoma had made to discharge the obligation it was so eager to assume. Owen's recommendation to the legislature that curators should be chosen for the Indian counties had not been carried out, and two special messages by Governor Haskell later in the session had met the same fate. When the Federal Government willingly abdicated its tremendous responsibility, the First Legislature

[33] *Congressional Record*, XLII, 1314, 3338-43, 3931-34, 5075-80, 5425, 6598-99, 6780-83, appendix, 406-62.

[34] *Ibid.*, XLII, appendix, 407-23, 432-33, 445-46.

had already adjourned without making the slightest attempt to protect even the minor allottees.[35]

The law was enacted May 27, 1908. Its provisions are important for they remained in force for twenty years. It divided the allottees into three classes: whites, freedmen, and mixed-bloods of less than one-half Indian blood were released from all restrictions; mixed-bloods of one-half or more and less than three-fourths Indian blood were free to sell their surplus, but their homesteads remained inalienable; and Indians of three-fourths or more Indian blood were restricted in all their holdings. All these restrictions were to remain in effect until April 26, 1931, unless they should be removed by the Secretary under such regulations as he might prescribe concerning terms of sale and disposal of the proceeds for the benefit of the allottee. All unrestricted land was declared subject to taxation and all other civil burdens, except that it was not liable for any claim against the allottee arising prior to the removal of restrictions. Any attempted alienation or incumbrance by deed, mortgage, contract to sell, power of attorney, or other instrument made before the removal of restrictions was expressly invalidated; and $50,000 was appropriated to defray the expense of suits to be brought at the request of the Secretary to set aside such illegal conveyances. Restricted allottees might give agricultural leases of their surplus land for five years, and their homesteads for one year without supervision; but agricultural leases for longer periods and all mineral leases were subject to the approval of the Secretary.

The person and property of minor allottees were made subject to the probate courts of Oklahoma; but the Secretary was empowered to appoint local representatives to investigate the conduct of guardians and curators, and report any neglect of duty to the proper probate court, and to prosecute any necessary remedy, either civil or criminal, to protect the minors. These local representatives were further authorized to advise all allot-

---

[35] *Journal of the Proceedings of the Senate of the First Legislature of the State of Oklahoma* (Muskogee, 1909), appendix, pp. 42, 50.

tees, either adult or minor, having restricted lands and to bring suits to annul any illegal conveyance.

All restrictions were removed upon the death of any allottee except in the following cases: the conveyance of any interest of a fullblood heir was subject to the approval of the probate court; and the homesteads of restricted Indians who should die leaving issue born too late to receive allotments, would be held for the benefit of such issue until April 26, 1931. Restricted Indians were expressly empowered to make valid wills, except that no will of a fullblood disinheriting parent, spouse, or child would be valid unless acknowledged before and approved by a Federal or county judge.[36]

Although this law fell far short of the aims expressed by both political parties in Oklahoma, it made 12,002,897 acres of land immediately subject to taxation and sale,[37] it restored the leasing system that the Five Tribes Act had endeavored to correct, and it gave the probate courts almost complete control of Indian administration. It offered no comfort to the holders of illegal titles, but they still hoped that the courts would uphold them. It was received with almost universal rejoicing as a charter of opportunity to the state. Muskogee as the metropolis of the East Side planned a whole week's celebration, with special entertainment to excursionists from all parts of the United States, and speeches by Governor Haskell and members of the Oklahoma delegation in Congress.[38]

For several years the people of Indian Territory had groaned under bureaucratic control, and had defiantly asserted that they could take all local problems into their strong young hands. The Indian had suffered great material and greater spiritual damage under Federal administration. What would be his fate under the new régime?

36 Kappler, Laws and Treaties, III, 178, 351-54.

37 Superintendent, Files, Report of A. M. Landman, 1935, p. 47.

38 Muskogee Phoenix, May 30, 1908; Muskogee Times-Democrat, July 20-25, 1908.

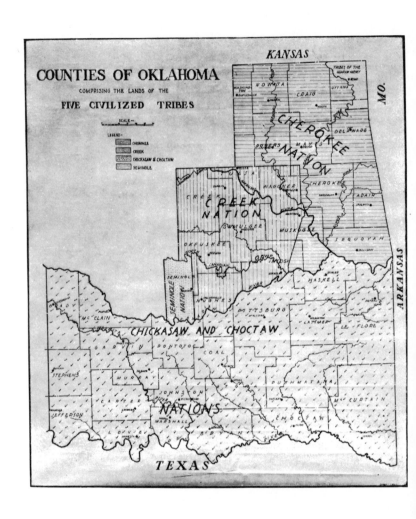

# CHAPTER VII

# Protection by the State

T HE immediate effect of the law of 1908 was a new orgy of buying land from allottees too innocent or too thriftless to protect themselves against their new freedom. But the most significant result was the enormous increase in opportunities for exploitation through the courts. Moreover the fact that much of the land was now legally alienable created a stronger inducement to secure it; and a speculator who had obtained temporary control of large areas through legal or almost legal leases might now resort to forgery, kidnaping, or even murder to acquire permanent possession. An enormous inducement to crime arose from the increasing value of oil property. The exploitation of those Indians who remained under restriction by the law of 1908 continued under the comparatively mild forms of swindling developed during the Federal period.

The law went into effect July 27. The sale of land belonging to minors was delayed slightly by the necessity of guardianship formalities, and the land buyers concentrated their efforts upon Negro and mixed-blood adults. Picturesque scenes were enacted in the county seats of the forty counties into which the old Indian Territory had been divided. The object of the land buyers was to bring as many allottees as possible to town, entertain them royally, and secure deeds and record them before a rival dealer could record a similar instrument. The dealers in Seminole County, which almost exactly coincided with the old Seminole Nation, established camps in the woods and hills, stocked them with generous quantities of food and intoxicants, and attempted to herd the allottees there until midnight. Others made up excursion trains and carried their guests to various places in Oklahoma and neighboring states to keep them away from adverse influences until the law should go into effect. In other cases the deeds had been secured and post-dated as soon as the act was passed, and the only remaining formality was the race to the recorder's office. In these hurried transactions, as a cynical Wewoka newspaper expressed it, "many errors very naturally occurred"; some buyers "had neglected to deposit the money in the bank before they drew their checks," while others had "carelessly" made out their checks for $3.50 instead of $350.[1]

But apparently the allottees were learning a certain amount of caution, for reports of disappointingly light sales came from all over the Five Tribes area. Most of them, however, disposed of their land eventually. Warren K. Moorehead, of the Board of Indian Commissioners, who made an especially earnest attempt to call attention to the exploitation of Five Tribes allottees, visited twenty or thirty Negro cabins on the rich land around Muskogee about 1913. He found only two persons of this group who had retained their land. Most of them were tenants, but in some cases the white purchaser had permitted them to remain in their old homes. They lived in flimsy and rudely furnished but clean cabins, worked industriously in the fields, and seemed unresentful over their loss. Grant Foreman, the historian, who was then a prominent Muskogee attorney and certainly a remarkably accurate observer, estimated at about the same time that not one in ten of the mixed-blood Indians had retained any considerable portion of their land.[2]

More serious than the losses of adult allottees was the legalized robbery of the children through the probate courts. The Enabling Act had provided that all except Federal cases pending in the United States courts for Indian Territory should be transferred to the state courts and that the laws of Oklahoma Territory should be extended over the entire state. The state constitution gave to the county court original jurisdiction in

---

[1] *Muskogee Times-Democrat*, July 25, 27, 1908; *Seminole Capital*, July 30, 1908.

[2] Warren K. Moorehead, *Our National Problem* (Privately printed about 1913), pp. 5-6.

all probate matters.[3] The probate code and probate machinery established by these two fundamental laws were sufficient for normal probate administration, but they were entirely inadequate for the unprecedented needs of the Five Tribes area.

Approximately sixty thousand minors with land valued at $130,000,000, besides an oil valuation of $25,000,000, were placed under the jurisdiction of forty county judges. For various reasons the allotments of minors had not been evenly distributed; two counties had about thirty-five hundred minors each, and a considerable number had between two thousand and three thousand. In addition the judge who had thousands of minors on his hands had the usual civil and criminal jurisdiction entrusted to the county judge of the West Side, who possibly did not have half a dozen children's estates in the entire county.[4]

Upon the whole the county judges seem to have been a little more conscientious in their probate administration than their predecessors, but they found it impossible to check and organize the great masses of neglected cases dumped upon them by the Federal courts. The extortionate scale of fees for guardians and attorneys that had developed under Federal administration continued as a matter of course, and even in the counties where probate matters were the most carefully supervised, something always seemed to happen to the income from the estate before it reached the child. And just as Northern politicians had paid their debts by Indian Territory spoils, county judges began to reward their supporters by guardianship appointments. When the act of 1908 removed the restrictions from 70 per cent of the minors who were direct allottees in addition to the land which they inherited from deceased allottees,[5] the condition was enormously complicated. Corrupt guardians and thriftless or even unprincipled parents began to sell the children's land and squander the proceeds.

[3] *Statutes at Large*, XXXIV, 275-77; Constitution of Oklahoma, Article VII, Sections 12, 13, 16; Henry G. Snyder, *The Compiled Laws of Oklahoma* (Kansas City, 1909), pp. 1156-1218.

[4] Department of the Interior, *Annual Report*, 1909, II, 419; 1912, II, 486-87.

[5] *Ibid.*, 1912, II, 475-76.

The only serious attempt upon the part of the state to correct the situation came through the efforts of a remarkable woman, Miss Kate Barnard of Oklahoma City. In territorial days she had been active in philanthropic organizations, and had become convinced that the state should take greater responsibility for the protection of various dependent and delinquent classes. Largely through her efforts and the efforts of women's organizations that had come under her influence, the office of Commissioner of Charities and Corrections had been created by the Constitutional Convention, and at the first state election she herself had been elected to the position by an overwhelming majority.[6] She had a certain emotional instability, but through her sincerity and her sensitiveness to human needs she achieved a greater insight than the most critical thinker among her contemporaries. A frail, diminutive person with a sweet voice, who was not above political tricks and was even more ready to trade upon her femininity, she had a power over an audience that is seldom equalled.[7]

The Constitutional Convention seems to have created the office as a gallant gesture that might please the women and would do no particular harm. The salary was placed far below that of other executive officers, and the duties were confined to the inspection of public institutions of charity and correction and the submission of annual reports to the legislature.[8] But the First Legislature authorized the Commissioner to appear before the probate court as "next friend" for all minor orphans, dependents, and delinquents who were inmates of any public institution, and to appoint an Assistant Commissioner.[9]

Like other state officials elected from the West Side, Miss Barnard was at first entirely ignorant of conditions in the Five Tribes area. She said afterward that the hideous exploitation

[6] *Democratic Nominees for State Office* (Campaign Document, 1910, Phillips Collection, University of Oklahoma); *Muskogee Times-Democrat*, February 24, 1930.

[7] See, for example, speech at Lake Mohonk, October, 1914 (Lake Mohonk Conference, *Report*, 1914, pp. 16-26).

[8] Article VI, Sections 27-29; Schedule, Section 15.

[9] Snyder, *Compiled Laws*, pp. 1738-41.

of children was brought to her attention soon after her induction into office by a report of three "wild" children living near one of the East Side cities. She found three small Indians sleeping in the hollow of an old tree, drinking from a stream, and securing food from neighboring farmhouses. No one knew to whom they belonged and it was six weeks before her assistant was able to locate their guardian. She found then that their parents were dead, that they owned valuable oil land, and that the guardian had been collecting their royalties and charging them exorbitant prices for their education and support. He had fifty-one other children under his protection.[10]

In her inspection of state institutions Miss Barnard soon discovered that scores of Indian orphan children supported by the taxpayers had valuable property from which they received no income. She reported these conditions in the fall of 1909, and requested authority to intervene in the courts as next friend of all minors. She did not secure this power, but early in 1910 another assistant to be known as Inspector was added to her department, all orphans in the Oklahoma State Home were placed under the guardianship of the Board of Control, and private institutions were authorized to nominate guardians for their inmates, who should take precedence over all other nominees.[11]

But although more than two years had elapsed since the state government was inaugurated, no machinery had been created to protect the thousands of children who were entirely at the mercy of professional guardians throughout the Five Tribes area. Very little public sentiment was aroused against this gigantic evil. The first election of state officers since the admission of Oklahoma to the Union took place in 1910. The

[10] Lake Mohonk Conference, *Report*, 1914, p. 18; *Muskogee Times-Democrat*, December 11, 1909. Miss Barnard was never accurate in matters of detail; she said the children were Cherokees and that they owned Glenn Pool allotments—an obvious impossibility. But there is no doubt of the essential truth of her statements; cutting the matted hair from the heads of the neglected children made a more vivid impression upon her feelings than the location of their allotments made upon her mind.

[11] *Muskogee Times-Democrat*, December 11, 1909; State of Oklahoma, *Session Laws of 1910*, pp. 175-78; see also *ibid.*, pp. 37-38, 114-21; Commissioner of Charities and Corrections, *Report*, 1910, p. 68.

Republican platform ignored the matter entirely. The Democrats expressed great indignation over "the deplorable condition resulting from misgovernment" of Indian affairs in Oklahoma by the Republican national administration, and requested the Federal Government to put honest men in control; but as to the local and immediate problem that was in their own hands, they expressed only a pious wish for the protection of minor Indians from "all classes of dishonest and unscrupulous grafters." Only the Socialists took a definite stand; their platform demanded the "enactment of a law abolishing 'professional' guardianship, for the purpose of cutting our court expenses and lawyer fees, which are now gobbling up practically all the income from small estates, especially that of Indians in the eastern half of the state."[12]

The probate question was hardly mentioned in the campaign. Miss Barnard's energy in other departments of her work had created a favorable impression throughout the state, and she was reelected by an overwhelming majority. Lee Cruce, an intermarried citizen of the Chickasaw Nation, succeeded Haskell as Governor.

Miss Barnard submitted her second report in the fall of 1910. She had chosen an attorney, Dr. J. H. Stolper, as Inspector, and her department therefore had the benefit of legal service; but she pointed out that her authority was limited to the small number of orphans in state institutions, and in private institutions that requested her intervention, and she asked for the right to protect the estates of all minor Indians.[13]

When the legislature convened in January[14] under the new administration, she made a determined fight to secure this legislation; but her bill was amended before its passage to restrict her intervention to orphans. She then drafted another bill creating the office of Public Defender, an attorney in her depart-

---

[12] Corden and Richards, *Oklahoma Red Book*, II, 369-79.

[13] Commissioner of Charities and Corrections, *Report*, 1910, pp. 5, 40, 68-70.

[14] For action of the special session in the fall of 1910, see *Journal of the Senate of the Extraordinary Session of the Third Legislature of the State of Oklahoma*, 1910, pp. 19-20; *ibid.*, House of Representatives, pp. 26, 72-74, 77-78, 85, 91; State of Oklahoma, *Session Laws*, 1910-11, p. 4.

ment who should intervene for the protection of all minors. This bill finally passed after a bitter legislative battle, but it was vetoed by Governor Cruce. She managed, however, as she expressed it, "to slip a joker" into the appropriation bill, giving her a liberal allowance for court costs.[15] Now, for the first time, she had real authority to go into the forty counties of the East Side and attempt to clean up conditions.

The law authorizing her to protect all orphans did not go into effect until June 9. Although she had failed to secure her Public Defender, Stolper, the only attorney in her department, worked so actively that by October 1 he was able to report that he had intervened in 207 cases in 25 counties, had won all of them, and had recovered $187,991.94 for orphan minors who had been defrauded. Many heartbreaking cases were uncovered of wrongs done to orphan children, cases that were only isolated examples of a practice so general as to be almost universal. Stolper was not exaggerating when he said that it had been the general policy of the guardians to sell everything the ward possessed and dissipate the proceeds in court costs, and that a very large proportion of the bonds were worthless.[16]

Stolper received the most cordial cooperation from many of the county judges, who were genuinely distressed at the wholesale robbery which they had been unable to prevent. At the beginning of 1912 a few of them adopted the policy of sending duplicate copies of all guardians' reports to the office of the Commissioner of Charities and Corrections. Some, however, refused to cooperate, and since obviously Stolper had many times as much work as he could manage, he made no attempt to extend his assistance where it was not welcomed. He also adopted the policy of prosecuting only those cases where com-

---

[15] Commissioner of Charities and Corrections, Office Files, Letter from Kate Barnard to M. L. Alexander, February 24, 1911; State of Oklahoma, *Session Laws,* 1910-11, pp. 45-46, 371-72; Commissioner of Charities and Corrections, *Report,* 1911, pp. 12-13; *Daily Oklahoman,* January 1, 1911; Lake Mohonk Conference, *Report,* 1914, p. 18.

[16] Commissioner of Charities and Corrections, *Report,* 1911, pp. 86, 88-103, 106-12, 153-98, 200; 1912, p. 138. The amounts recovered were listed in statistical tables with the names of the children, and the items upon which recovery was made.

plete proof was furnished by the minor or a volunteer informant.[17]

It is apparent, moreover, that although Miss Barnard had the utmost confidence in Stolper, his selection had been unfortunate. Many discerning people of the time gave him great credit for his energy and fearlessness, but his published reports and, to an even greater extent, his official correspondence, do not attest to his sincerity. He paid the most fulsome compliments to all public officials, but most of all he filled his reports with grandiloquent accounts of his own achievements.[18] It was a time when "reform" was a popular word throughout the nation, and there is some indication that he expected, as champion of the orphans, to be politically rewarded by a grateful people. He accomplished a great deal, but the wrongs he righted were so notorious that failure would have been almost impossible. The swindlers whose business he disturbed hated him with all the unrestrained ferocity of a crude young society; but he also alienated Miss Barnard's own supporters by the indifference with which he dismissed appeals for aid.

One example chosen almost at random will show how the usefulness of his office was limited by this attitude. The correspondence began with the following appeal: "Miss Kate I would like to ask you for a favor. I would like for you to come to wagoner if you posibely can. I have a case that i would like to get closed if you can help me i can not do it by my self. i am a miner and my land has ben sold through fraud and i want the land back or the value of it. I heard you was hear last summer but I was not hear now i will stay hear and wait for answer from this letter so please wright me at once in full I am a miner and an orphant and I ask for pertection."

Stolper replied in a tone so formal and impersonal as to be hardly courteous, asking for a sworn statement, and pointing out the absurdity of Miss Barnard's making a trip to Wagoner —"you must realize that we have over 18,000 cases on our

---

[17] Commissioner of Charities and Corrections, *Report*, 1911, pp. 154-55, 194-95, 201; 1912, pp. 74-81, 137; Commissioner of Charities and Corrections, Office Files.
[18] Commissioner of Charities and Corrections, *Report*, 1911, 1912.

hands." The boy then went to a notary and secured assistance in making out the affidavit. He said that he had been away from Wagoner, and when he returned he found that his land had been sold for about one-third of its value. He had been told that his guardian was holding $700 for him which he would receive when he would reach his majority. Stolper answered this letter:

"DEAR SIR:

"Your letter of Feb. 14, 1912 addressed to Miss Kate Barnard has been received. In reply, I wish to say to you that as you are of age this office has no power to interfere over you. We can only help minor orphan children.

"As a matter of advice, I wish to inform you that a guardian has a right to sell land of his ward by confirmation of the court without having to consult his ward in the premises.

"I would suggest to you to consult any good lawyer, state your case to him and he may help you in the premises."

With this unwarranted assumption that the boy was not a minor Stolper closed the incident.

Stolper seemed to feel contempt for the ignorance of such applicants—to one helpless, illiterate appeal he answered, "Your letter of no date and no beginning has been received"— but when intelligent people wrote to give specific instances that had come under their notice he antagonized them by his demand for affidavits. One M. L. Alexander, who was in the most cordial sympathy with Miss Barnard during her legislative fight in 1911, when the Senator from his county was leading the opposition, became so incensed at Stolper's failure to investigate cases he had called to his attention that in the fall of 1912 he wrote an angry letter to Governor Cruce expressing the hope that the Governor would recommend to the incoming legislature radical changes in Miss Barnard's department or its complete abolition. He stated, moreover, that he intended to send a copy of the letter to every member of the legislature.[19]

[19] Commissioner of Charities and Corrections, Office Files; Commissioner of Charities and Corrections, *Monthly Bulletin*, I (November 15, 1912).

It was probably true that Stolper could not investigate these cases, but the vast amount of work he was forced to leave undone contrasted unfavorably with his boastful pretensions. It had been Miss Barnard's practice to answer such appeals with sympathetic concern, frankly stating the financial and legal difficulties under which she worked, but she had ceased to be familiar with the details of her office; her frail health had been so badly shattered by her public fight in behalf of various groups of unfortunates that she entrusted all routine work to her assistants.[20]

But in spite of the limited character of his work, Stolper accomplished a great deal during 1912. His report of that year listed 1,361 orphans in whose behalf he had intervened and a total recovery of $949,390.70. His salary and expenses had cost the state less than $10,000, and his intervention had saved the children the 10 per cent attorneys' fees that it had become customary for the courts to allow in suits to recover property lost through the mismanagement of guardians.[21]

Early in 1912 Miss Barnard decided that the act creating the Public Defender in her department had become a law through a technical error in the Governor's veto. But she was extremely anxious not to antagonize Cruce, and Stolper addressed a most ingratiating communication to him requesting that he issue a proclamation declaring the act in force. He enclosed an appeal which had come to him for intervention in a case where a family of children whose parents were living were going hungry and unclothed while their guardian devoured their estate, and explained that if he could serve as Public Defender at the same salary that he was then receiving he could intervene in that class of cases. But the Governor failed to respond and Stolper for a time assumed the title, although the legality of the act was not passed upon by the courts.[22]

---

[20] Commissioner of Charities and Corrections, *Report,* 1912, p. 281; *Sapulpa Evening Democrat,* March 5, 1912.

[21] Commissioner of Charities and Corrections, *Report,* 1912, pp. 139-55, 282.

[22] *Ibid.,* 1912, pp. 124-27; Commissioner of Charities and Corrections, Office Files, copy of letter dated March 23, 1912.

Stolper believed that a Public Administrator should be added to the department. This officer would appoint deputies in the various counties to act as public guardians, and no private guardians would be accepted. The Public Defender would represent these deputies free of charge, thus destroying a business that had become very profitable to a certain class of attorneys.[23] But this legislation was never enacted. The authority exercised by Miss Barnard's department in 1912 represented the strongest attempt ever made by the state to create machinery for the exercise of its supervision over minor allottees.

But Miss Barnard's earnestness and Stolper's reputation for fearlessness had attracted some attention, and Congressmen from Oklahoma were fond of pointing with pride to their work as an example of the vigilance with which the state was carrying out its trust. Carter, in a characteristic speech, expressed his confidence in the protection furnished by "that fearless defender of the weak and helpless—Miss Kate Barnard," and her "equally capable and enthusiastic" assistant, Dr. Stolper; and he said he "would like to see the color of the grafter's eye that puts any shady deal across the plate when these two crusaders are on watch."[24]

Congressmen from Oklahoma can hardly be blamed for these assertions, for at the same time that Stolper was refusing to consider orphan cases except where the opportunity for intervention was the most favorable and was pointing out to the Governor the pitiable condition of non-orphans, he was boasting to Congress that the state was adequately protecting the Indian children and would be glad to take over the adults. He wished to show the country at large "that while Oklahoma has inherited from Federal Territorial rule the chaotic conditions existing among Indians that the State of Oklahoma, through its legislature and the State officials, is doing all within our power to protect the Indians as well as all citizens of Okla-

---

[23] Commissioner of Charities and Corrections, *Report,* 1911, pp. 197-99; 1912, pp. 138-39.

[24] *Congressional Record,* XLVIII, 4446-47, 11410-14.

homa, and be it said to the honor of Oklahoma that in all cases we uniformly are succeeding."[25]

H. Huson, the Assistant Commissioner, who was in charge of Miss Barnard's office during her illness in 1912, wrote more frankly to a member of Congress. He said that some success had been achieved in decreasing the sale of orphans' land through the probate courts—the department had prevented the sale of 115,000 acres since it had secured the authority to intervene, most of the judges were giving careful attention to sale petitions, and the number of petitions had decreased—and that several of the judges who had been unable to compel guardians to make reports had invited assistance; but he made no effort to conceal the fact that only orphan children came under the department's supervision, and he admitted that the office was so handicapped by insufficient personnel that it confined its efforts to the most notorious cases.[26]

The greatest of all abuses by the county courts was not even touched by Miss Barnard's office; that is, the approval required by the law of 1908 for conveyances of inherited land by full-blood heirs. The procedure was not specified, and there was no provision for appeal. The tendency was to require no publicity, make no investigation, and rely completely upon the statements made by the purchaser and his witnesses. The consent of the Indian was often taken as the sole reason for approval. Many deeds were approved privately in chambers, and the only record in the case was the signature of the judge upon the instrument itself. The higher courts decided that mortgages and oil and gas leases were conveyances and subject to the same rule, and the same principles of perfunctory approval were observed.[27]

The Interior Department had no control over this matter, but in general it retained supervision over Five Tribes allottees. The law of 1908 had appropriated $90,000 for the "local representatives" of the Secretary, and had defined their duties

---

[25] *Congressional Record*, XLVIII, 11414-15, letter to Carter, April 13, 1912.

[26] *Ibid.*, XLVIII, 11402, Huson to Charles H. Burke, August 20, 1912.

[27] *Ibid.*, LXXIV, 3957; Indian Office Files, 135712/13 Creek 311.

in sufficiently comprehensive manner.[28] The area was divided into fifteen districts with two or three counties in each, and the employees selected under these provisions were known as "district agents." This force consisted of two supervising district agents working under Wright's direction, and one supervisor, fifteen agents, fifteen office assistants, two Indian assistants, three special agents qualified for probate matters, and one assistant for general relief work, all assigned to Kelsey's office. Only the three supervisors seem to have been attorneys.[29]

Since the law creating this force had no merit provision, Oklahoma Republicans welcomed the first opportunity they had ever had to participate in the spoils of the Five Tribes service. Bird McGuire said, "We had a right under the bill to make these places political," but he found Wright so lukewarm that he had to appeal directly to President Roosevelt to secure any appointments. Politicians were disappointed because a number of the positions were filled by men who were already in the Dawes office or the Agency. Before the end of the year it began to be rumored that the state Republican organization would demand the removal of both Wright and Kelsey for their indifference to the welfare of the party.[30]

It would seem that in this large district agency force the Federal Government had effective machinery to accomplish what the state was neglecting in probate supervision; but the district agents devoted only a minor part of their time to this work. Oklahomans have always been quick to repeat the slur that Indian service officials sought to supervise and control the allottees in order to multiply positions; but for almost a generation after the negotiation of the agreements with the Five Tribes the Department was only a trifle less willing to relinquish its supervision than were the Oklahomans to see it withdrawn. The law creating the district agents was plainly worded, and its undoubted purpose was the protection of minor allot-

[28] Kappler, *Laws and Treaties*, III, 352-53.
[29] Department of the Interior, *Annual Report*, 1908, II, 104; 1909, II, 406, 418-19.
[30] *Congressional Record*, LI, 3504, 12835-36; *Muskogee Times-Democrat*, October 5, 1908; *Muskogee Phoenix*, June 10, 24, December 13, 1908.

tees in probate matters and of restricted adults against illegal conveyances; but for the first six months they devoted almost their entire attention to passing upon applications for the removal of restrictions. Secretary Garfield adopted the policy of advising the fullbloods to sell a portion of their land under Departmental supervision and use the proceeds to improve their homesteads; and the district agents were directed to make investigations and recommendations in each individual case, supervise the sale of the land, and assist the allottee in constructing his improvements or in purchasing livestock and farm machinery.[31]

This phase of their work was the most popular with the citizens of Oklahoma. It was very common for members of the delegation in Congress to request the Agency to hurry a certain application for the removal of restrictions.[32] These requests were made as a matter of course and without investigation as a favor to any constituent who desired to purchase a certain tract of land. Since the agents were political appointees, this interference must have subjected them to a certain amount of pressure. At the same time, it does not seem that a single request was ever made that a guardianship abuse should be investigated.

The district agents did, however, devote a portion of their time to the specific purposes for which they had been appointed. They investigated agricultural leases upon the request of restricted allottees, sometimes securing a modification of the contracts and carrying cases of evident fraud to the courts; and they endeavored with slight success to persuade the Indians to accept the longer-term leases that came under Department supervision.[33] They also attempted to check the probate administration.

Although the law of 1908 had certainly entrusted them with the responsibility of protecting all minor allottees, it was de-

[31] *Muskogee Phoenix*, June 24, 1908; *Muskogee Times-Democrat*, July 1, 1908; Department of the Interior, *Annual Report*, 1909, II, 419.

[32] Indian Office Files, 15521/08, 51849/08, 53083/08, 12002/09, 36106/09.

[33] Department of the Interior, *Annual Report*, 1909, II, 424; 1910, II, 217; 1911, II, 431, 433, 451-52.

cided at the very beginning to limit such protection to restricted children. It was, of course, the unrestricted children of Negro, mixed Indian and white, or mixed Indian blood who were subject to the greatest exploitation, but the Department officials believed it wiser to concentrate upon the "real Indians"; as Kelsey said in 1910, with reference to some especially shocking pillaging of unrestricted children, "in my judgment the only remedy . . . is for the general citizenship of the State of Oklahoma to awake to the fact that the less intelligent residents of the community are being robbed by the connivance of grafters and dishonest officials, and that sooner or later these people who have been robbed will become public charges, and to avoid this ultimate condition public sentiment with respect to getting what the allottee has must change and the citizens must elect honest officers who will protect the minors, whether they be white, red, or black."[34]

But although the district agents' work was limited by such administrative decisions, there was so much need for reform that like Stolper they accomplished a great deal. During the last six months of the first year of their employment they recovered about $300,000 for minor allottees, and during the fiscal year 1911-1912 they saved $548,306.78.[35]

The efficiency of this work depended largely upon the cooperation of the county judges, and that was not always given. The new state officials, rejoicing in their deliverance from "carpetbag" domination, showed a tendency at first to regard them as interlopers. Kelsey handled the matter with extreme tact, and some of the judges entered into the most active cooperation. They invited appraisements of inherited land sold through their courts, requested the presence of the agents when guardians' reports were presented, disallowed charges that had been successfully challenged by the agents, and requested in-

[34] *House Reports*, 61 Cong., 2 Sess., No. 2273, Vol. II, appendix, 1322-23.

[35] Department of the Interior, *Annual Report,* 1912, II, 486; Indian Office Files, 72545/08 Five Tribes 311. Each agent made a monthly report showing the exact sums that he recovered in specific cases, and these amounts were added to form the totals.

formation through the agency service regarding property located in counties far distant from the domicile of the ward. At the end of two years of the district agency work Kelsey reported that 27 judges were cooperating fully, and 3 partially, and that 10 resented the appearance of the agents on behalf of the minors. Several of the judges even refused to allow the agents to appear in their courts.[36]

Federal protection to minor allottees was therefore limited to restricted children living in counties where the judges invited cooperation, just as the state's protection was limited to orphans. And in neither case did the remedy more than touch the surface of the evil; the district agents had many more duties than probate supervision, and the Department of Charities and Corrections had only one man to protect the orphans in forty counties.

In addition the Choctaws continued to employ McCurtain and Hill. These attorneys represented the tribe in other matters also, and they were not able to accomplish much for the thousands of minors distributed through the eleven counties comprising the old Choctaw Nation; but they reported at the end of the first year after its creation that the district agency service had greatly relieved the situation. The agents constantly reported cases that they had uncovered, and called upon the firm for legal service. The attorneys reported that year that they had defeated the scheme of one man who was about to secure the guardianship of 350 children from one county court and the approval of the sale of timber from the whole 350 allotments; and that they had prevented another man from securing the guardianship of 140 children in order to sell inherited land scattered throughout the Choctaw and Chickasaw nations.[37]

But in spite of the partial protection offered by the county judges, the Department of Charities and Corrections, the district agents, and one firm of tribal attorneys, the entire Five

---

[36] Indian Office Files, 72545/08 Five Tribes 311; Department of the Interior, *Annual Report*, 1910, II, 194; 1913, II, 477; *Congressional Record*, LII, 1205-6.

[37] *House Reports*, 61 Cong., 2 Sess., No. 2273, Vol. II, appendix, 1272.

Tribes area was dominated by a vast criminal conspiracy to wrest a great and rich domain from its owners. In the process of leasing the restricted land or purchasing the unrestricted from ignorant adults or ignorant or corrupt guardians the allottee was overreached by every possible sharp practice or criminal action.

In cases where the speculators were unable, because of the vigilance of the county judge or the honesty or rival schemes of the guardian, to secure minors' land through guardian sales, they began to take advantage of a state law that conferred majority upon married minors. An unprincipled man or woman would be employed to win the confidence of the young Negro or Indian; the marriage would take place in the real estate office and the deed would be signed immediately after; and the charmer would walk out of the office, never to be seen again by the allottee. In 1910 Governor Haskell informed the legislature that the law conferring majority by marriage was "frequently abused, particularly among minors holding Indian Allotments," but the legislature took no action to correct the evil. Another method that seems to have been resorted to less frequently was the conferring of majority by court action.[38]

Both these practices were declared illegal by the Oklahoma Supreme Court in 1910, and by the United States Supreme Court in 1915. When the act of 1908 placed minor allottees under the state probate courts, it fixed the age of majority at twenty-one years for males and eighteen years for females; and the courts ruled that the general statute of Oklahoma could not change this delegation of authority. These decisions ruined an extensive and highly profitable industry.[39]

Many young allottees were virtually kidnaped just before they reached their majority. They were put on the train, spirited from place to place, kept in hotels under constant surveillance, and induced to sign deeds at midnight on the morn-

[38] *Muskogee Times-Democrat,* September 28, 29, 1909; *Muskogee Phoenix,* June 14, 1911; May 8, 1913; April 22, 1915; *Daily Oklahoman,* January 1, 1911; *Senate Journal,* 1910, pp. 155-56; *Supreme Court Reports,* LIX, 549-52.

[39] *Pacific Reporter,* CX, 755-59; *Supreme Court Reports,* LIX, 549-52.

ing they became of age. A woman who secured an oil lease in this way boasted that she had travelled over three thousand miles with her young prospect, evading his brother, the county judge, and Federal secret service men, who were hot on her trail. One young Creek who owned land near Jenks supposed to be valuable for oil was under the guardianship of his father. Five months before he became of age he disappeared. His parents became almost frantic. They sought help from the Masonic Lodge, of which his father was a member, and from the Interior Department. After five months he was located in England by a Federal secret service man, and returned to his home with his property intact. But most young allottees were not so fortunate; and this form of kidnaping became a recognized branch of the swindling profession.[40]

Forgery was a more convenient and scarcely more dangerous method of securing deeds and oil leases. An incident reported from Holdenville in 1909 illustrates the boldness of this class of criminals. An eighteen-year-old girl, whose father was dead, came with her mother to the office of District Agent William A. Baker. The girl was a fullblood Indian unable to speak English; but her surplus land was legally alienable for she was the daughter of a Creek mother and a Seminole father. Baker said that this land was one of the most valuable tracts in Hughes County, and was easily worth $2,500. According to the story she told, a white man with two Creek assistants had tried to persuade her to sell but she had steadfastly refused. They were all standing in the yard with a wire fence between them. Suddenly the white man thrust his pencil through the fence and touched her hand. They handed her a piece of paper and left. The women immediately told their story to another Indian, and he came with them to see Baker. They brought along the piece of paper, which proved to be a check for four hundred dollars. Baker went at once to the register's office and found that the deed had been recorded. He prepared an affidavit for the girl

[40] *Muskogee Phoenix*, March 28, 1911; March 7, 1912; January 11, 21, June 13, 1913; January 14, 1914; Moorehead, *Our National Problem*, pp. 21-22; Department of the Interior, *Annual Report*, 1913, II, 476.

declaring the deed to be a forgery, and placed it on record so that the land could not be bought by an innocent purchaser. As soon as he took this action to protect the girl, he found that the men were making repeated efforts to induce the two women to sign various papers, but they were not successful. Baker was then arrested upon charges of subornation of perjury and criminal libel, in writing and recording the affidavit, and the most prominent law firms in Holdenville actively assisted the county attorney in the prosecution. The trial aroused intense excitement, but he was acquitted of the perjury charge, and the other charge against him was dismissed.[41]

Forgeries were usually carried on by organized gangs with one or two Indian or Negro members to impersonate the allottees of their race.[42] A very few forgers were sent to the penitentiary, but convictions were not frequent enough to discourage the practice. The Indians feared and distrusted the courts and made notoriously poor witnesses; and the forgers were usually intrenched in public favor. Those who practised their crimes against the freedmen profited from the reluctance of white jurors to convict members of their own race upon the testimony of Negro witnesses.[43] Very little of the land lost through forged deeds was ever recovered by the allottees.

Some of the allottees, especially the freedmen, were not averse to carrying on swindling operations of their own. A young Creek Negro established a record in illegal sales. He owned an allotment in Tulsa County worth four or five thousand dollars for agriculture, but with a much higher speculative oil value; and he was under the guardianship of his mother, who had steadfastly held to her own allotment. He was married twice, taken on many trips, and wined and dined by oil men for four years before he became of age. It is said that he gave forty-three deeds during his minority; whenever

[41] *Muskogee Phoenix*, May 20, 28, 1909; Indian Office Files, 38818/09 Union 175.
[42] *Sapulpa Evening Democrat*, February 7, 17, April 26, 1913.
[43] *Muskogee Phoenix*, January 2, 17, 18, 24, 29, 30, 31, February 22, 23, 27, March 5, 6, 8, 9, 14, 18, 19, April 27, November 9, 1913; *Muskogee Times-Democrat*, February 27, 1913; October 3, 10, 1914.

he needed money he signed away his allotment at any price ranging from fifty cents to $1,100. When he approached his majority, land dealers spirited him away to Colorado, in order to secure a legal deed upon the instant. In the meantime his mother, apparently for his protection, sold his land, and the county judge of Muskogee County approved the sale the day before he became of age. An automobile was waiting in front of the courthouse, and the purchaser made a wild race to Tulsa to record the deed before the register's office should close, knowing that the young owner would sign a deed at midnight. When the young man returned from Colorado, he sued to have the guardian's deed set aside, and protracted litigation followed between the rival purchasers.[44]

In this confused atmosphere of guardian frauds, forgery, and the great speculative value of uncertain titles, murder became very common. Some spectacular crimes occurred, such as the dynamiting of two Negro children as they slept, in order that the conspirators might secure title to their Glenn Pool property by forged deeds;[45] and many sinister stories were told of Indians who died under suspicious circumstances after bequeathing their property to white men. An epidemic of such deaths broke out among aged Choctaws in McCurtain and Choctaw counties, and the Federal officials became convinced of an organized plot whereby the Indian made out a will to the land dealers in return for a ten-dollar monthly pension for the remainder of his life. A suspicious fatality followed the making of such wills, and in several cases carbolic acid or ground glass was found on the premises. Several prominent real estate dealers were arrested, but the mystery of the Choctaw murders was never solved.[46]

[44] *Muskogee Times-Democrat*, September 1, 1911; *Muskogee Phoenix*, September 12, 1911; *Sapulpa Herald*, May 15, 1915; *Sapulpa Evening Democrat*, January 12, 1914.

[45] *Muskogee Phoenix*, March 24, April 4, 18, 19, 1911; January 7, 1912; May 20, 25, 1916; Indian Office Files, 33268/11 Union 175.

[46] Indian Office Files, 13712/13 Creek 311, 141675/13 Union 175; *Muskogee Phoenix*, May 1-7, 1913; *Nowata Star*, May 2, 1913; *Congressional Record*, LI, 3501.

This traffic in wills could have been prevented if it had not been legalized by the law of 1908; for, as it has already been pointed out, the state and Federal courts both ruled that the restrictions in the agreements extended also to the making of wills.[47] Federal officials constantly urged the repeal of this law, but it remained on the statute books to encourage this class of crime. It was almost impossible to prevent such practices, for the existence of the wills could not be known until they were offered for probate. Many were set aside by the courts because of their obvious fraud, but swindlers continued to secure them on the chance that they might be upheld. The making of Indian wills remained as a menace to the lives of the allottees and of litigation and financial loss to their heirs.[48]

In the midst of all this sharp practice and fraud and crime the Federal employees were, of course, not entirely untouched. More of them could be censured for lack of imagination and initiative, and for general inertia and indifference, than for downright dishonesty; but examples of the latter also occurred, and Agency employees were occasionally dropped from the service for corrupt agreements with guardians and land speculators.[49] After their dismissal they gravitated naturally to the grafting profession, for which their inside knowledge of Indian matters especially fitted them. In running over the names of conspicuous swindlers of Five Tribes allottees, it is astounding to observe how many had served for a time with one of the Federal agencies. This fact is, of course, no index to the general character of the Government employees; but it does indicate that the large number who afterwards turned out to be exploiters of Indians could hardly have been vigilant in protecting them while in the Government service.

But faulty as Federal protection may have been, the ones who desired the Indians' property were invariably the loudest

---

[47] *Supreme Court Reports,* LIX, 121-23; Kappler, *Laws and Treaties,* III, 178, 354. See also State of Oklahoma, *Session Laws of 1909,* p. 641.
[48] *Muskogee Times-Democrat,* September 13, 1909; February 23, 1917; *Sapulpa Evening News,* March 3, 1914; Superintendent, Office Files, Report of Victor Locke, 1922, p. 77.
[49] *Congressional Record,* XLIX, 609.

in their demand that the Government should cease its oppressive control of free American citizens. The Four Mothers Society, with its membership of Snakes and Nighthawks, was certainly not subservient to Agency influence; but the winter after the passage of the act of 1908, and again the following winter, it sent delegates to Washington to petition Congress and the President that the Federal Government should continue as the guardian of the Indians and that United States citizenship be withheld.[50]

The Federal officials managed to recover a large amount of property that had been lost to the Indians. The suits undertaken by the Federal Government or prosecuted by the state officials on behalf of allottees dominated the legal history of the East Side for several years after statehood. Because of the widespread attention that they attracted and their influence upon the history of the state, as well as their effect upon the lives of the Indians, some of these cases are deserving of special notice.

[50] *Muskogee Phoenix,* January 9, 1910.

# CHAPTER VIII

# A Tangle of Litigation

T HE most extensive of all the litigation involving East Side land titles was undertaken by the Federal Government to clear up the condition that had been permitted to develop before statehood; part of the townsite frauds were prosecuted, and an attempt was made to clear the allotted land of the illegal conveyances that took place during the Federal period. These suits were brought in the Federal courts. Other litigation involved the transactions of certain county judges under the law of 1908, and was brought in the state courts.

Early in 1907 in accordance with resolutions of the Creek Council, M. L. Mott brought suit against most of the large property owners of Muskogee and the Frisco Oil and Gas Company of Tulsa, to recover for the town lot frauds. Although Chief Porter was one of the defendants, he acquiesced in this action; but it brought a storm of protest from the business interests of Muskogee.[1] President Roosevelt used the fact that Governor Haskell was one of the defendants to good political advantage in the national campaign of 1908. His logic is not exactly clear, for his own administration was responsible for the frauds; but Haskell had been made treasurer of the Democratic National Committee, and Roosevelt attacked him so bitterly for this and other matters that he resigned to avoid embarrassing the party.[2]

[1] Indian Office Files, Correspondence Land Division, Letter Book, CMXXVII, 297; *Muskogee Phoenix,* January 12, February 2, July 10, 20, 30, 1907; *Muskogee Times-Democrat,* April 10, 11, 24, 25, May 9, 18, 25, June 25, 1907.

[2] *Muskogee Phoenix,* December 9, 10, 11, 1908; January 10, 1909; *Muskogee Times-Democrat,* September 1, October 1, November 3, 1908; Department of the Interior, *Annual Report,* 1908, II, 113-14.

Early in 1909 the Government instituted a criminal prosecution, and Governor Haskell, Clarence W. Turner, Walter R. Eaton, William T. Hutchings, Albert Z. English, Frederick B. Severs, and Jesse Hill,[3] all prominent citizens of Muskogee, were indicted for conspiracy to defraud the Creek Nation. The defendants made no attempt to assert their innocence, but they pointed to the undoubted fact that the system of false scheduling had been promulgated by the Federal officials. Public sentiment was overwhelmingly in their favor. Every possible slur was cast upon Mott's motives, and scurrilous tales of his past life were freely circulated. The two Oklahoma Senators and several of the Representatives used all their influence to persuade President Taft to drop the prosecution, and "Jake" Hamon, prominent Republican politician of Ardmore, made a trip to Washington for the same purpose. Every possible technicality was invoked, but the cases finally came to trial at McAlester in the fall of 1910. Judge John A. Marshall of Utah, who was presiding, ruled that the statute of limitations began to operate in 1901 when the Creeks parted with the title. It was impossible to make out a case under this ruling, and the trial came to an abrupt end with a wild demonstration in a courtroom packed to suffocation.[4]

Mott continued his prosecution of the civil suits, but in 1909 the defendants began to settle out of court. The Creeks received $40,000 and 110 lots in the settlement with Severs and English; and smaller amounts were recovered from the Porter estate, from the Presbyterian Mission Board for the campus of Henry Kendall College, from Tams Bixby, and others. The remaining lots were recovered by suit—twenty-seven lots in Tulsa from the Frisco Oil and Gas Company in 1913, and twenty-two in Muskogee from Haskell and Turner in 1921. The recovered lots in Muskogee sold slowly, for by this time the city had halted in the rapid growth that had once made it

[3] It will be remembered that Porter had died in 1907.

[4] *Muskogee Phoenix*, January-May, 1909; May 3, 4, 15, June 25, August 6, 24, 28, 1910; *Muskogee Times-Democrat*, November 3, 1908; August 16, October 13, 16, 18, 29, November 3, 5, December 9, 1909; September 15-29, 1910.

the metropolis of the East Side; in 1939 the tribe had received about $100,000 from cash settlements and the resale of lots, and owned fifty-five lots, for which the prospects of sale were exceedingly remote. The recovery in Tulsa was more profitable; eleven lots sold during 1923 and 1925 brought $85,960, and the others probably brought similar prices. Only two remained unsold in 1939. The suits cost the Creeks $100,995.95. They profited only slightly, therefore, from their victory. No attempt was ever made to right the wrong done the Indians in the other towns of the Nation.[5]

An even more complicated and prolonged litigation than the prosecution of the townsite frauds was the so-called Thirty Thousand Land Suits instituted by the Department of Justice under the act of 1908. The Federal employees worked with such haste because of the fear that as soon as the law went into effect it would automatically validate illegal conveyances of all land from which it removed the restrictions, that some cases were overlooked and a large number of lawful sales were included; but 301 suits, involving 27,517 conveyances, 12,500 tracts of land comprising 3,842,553.2 acres, and approximately 16,000 defendants, were brought in the United States Court for the Eastern District of Oklahoma.[6]

Public sentiment in the state was at first inclined to favor the suits. Some indignation was expressed against the "land sharks" for clouding titles to the detriment of the bona fide purchaser, and some confidence was felt that the clearing of these titles would aid the development of the country. But there was a tendency to accept the cynical view of the *McAlester Daily News* that it would be about as practicable to attempt to recover Manhattan Island and the state of Pennsylvania for

5 *Muskogee Phoenix,* April 15, 1910; Indian Office Files, 91106/07 Creek 175.2; Federal Court Records, Eastern District of Oklahoma, Equity Nos. 261, 522, 1132; Superintendent, Office Files, Muskogee Townsite Record; *ibid.,* Report of Shade Wallen, 1923, p. 18; 1925, p. 21; Report of A. M. Landman, 1935, p. 60; *Court of Claims Reports,* LXXVIII, 491-93.

6 Kappler, *Laws and Treaties,* III, 353; *Congressional Record,* XLVIII, 8262; *Senate Docs.,* 61 Cong., 1 Sess., No. 89; Department of the Interior, *Annual Report,* 1908, II, 104-5; 1909, II, 389-90; Lake Mohonk Conference, *Report,* 1914, pp. 29-30; Attorney-General, *Annual Report,* 1919, pp. 97-98.

the benefit of the Indians that had been overreached by their bargains with William Penn and the thrifty Hollanders.[7]

Senator Owen seems to have worked more actively than anyone else at this time to prevent the bringing of the suits. He took the position that all purchasers of restricted land who had not sought to impose upon the allottee by inadequate consideration should be reimbursed for all they had expended on contracts and improvements. Apparently he had ended his own connection with the Indian Land and Trust Company about 1904,[8] but the ownership of his great ranch near Bartlesville rested upon deeds given by restricted Cherokees and he was determined that all such transactions should be recognized. Before the act of 1908 was passed, he was reported to have had a conference with Secretary Garfield explaining his holdings and stating frankly that he was depending upon the unconstitutionality of the McCumber Amendment. After the passage of the law, he insisted that the suits should be confined to cases brought at the request of the allottee, and should be tried in the state courts. As soon as it went into effect, he made the strongest efforts to secure validation of his contracts through Departmental approval.

He wrote a peremptory letter to Secretary Garfield the next day after the act became operative. He said that he had attempted that morning to secure the removal of restrictions from a "very fair red-headed woman" enrolled as three-fourths Cherokee, in order that she might give clear title to a tract "of land in my Caney farm, which I had previously bought from her"; but when he sent his secretary to present her application to the Agency, he was astonished to learn of the circumlocution and the waste of two or three months' time required to refer

---

[7] *Muskogee Phoenix*, May 30, June 4, 1908; *Muskogee Times-Democrat*, July 14, 15, 1908; *McAlester Daily News*, June 3, 1908.

[8] He is reported to have stated to an audience July 12, 1912, in a campaign speech that he had closed out his interest nine years before at a loss of ten thousand dollars. This date is not exact, for he was connected with the company at the time of the Bonaparte investigation; but there is no reason to doubt that he withdrew soon after. See *Muskogee Phoenix*, July 13, 1912; September 21, 1915; November 27, 1919.

such cases to the Secretary's office, when he had supposed that they were to be settled "on the spot and without any delays whatever." He demanded immediate action so that the woman could carry out her contract with him. A few days later he wrote again asking that his contracts with fullbloods be investigated at once, and validated if found as represented.

The Agency recommended the removal of this woman's restrictions, but when the matter was referred to Washington C. F. Larrabee, acting Commissioner of Indian Affairs, withheld his approval. He pointed out that in her application she was asking to dispose of her surplus in order to improve her homestead, while at the same time she was requesting the removal of restrictions from her homestead. Also, said Larrabee, it was apparent from Owen's letter that he had made an illegal contract with her. He admonished the Agency to be more careful in its future recommendations. It was eventually decided that a portion of the woman's surplus should be sold under sealed bids by the Agency, and that the money should be expended under Departmental direction for improving her homestead. Secretary Garfield afterwards advised Federal employees that restrictions should not be removed from land when a suit was pending to remove clouds on the title.[9]

At the next session of Congress Owen introduced the following amendment to the Indian Appropriation Bill: "The Attorney-General is hereby authorized and directed to immediately dismiss the suits brought by the United States to set aside land titles in the eastern district of Oklahoma where the consideration was not inequitable and where there is no actual fraud involved." It was adopted by the Senate, but failed to become a law.[10]

But as soon as the first suits were filed, the Department of Justice began to make compromise settlements. At the end of the first year 3,076 cases had been dismissed—1,756 because

[9] *Ibid.*, January 3, 1908; February 21, 1909; *Wewoka Democrat,* May 19, 1911; *Seminole Capital,* August 20, 1908; Indian Office Files 53683/08 Cherokee 311, 72545/08 Five Tribes 311.

[10] *Congressional Record,* XLIV, 2780, 2790-91.

of quitclaim deeds given to the allottees, 1,161 because of error, and 159 by adjustment. Similarly, 1,543 cases were dismissed during 1909-1910, 822 in 1910-1911, and 783 in 1911-1912. Before the defendant was allowed to quitclaim, a district agent was consulted regarding the occupancy of the land, the improvements, and the disposition of rents and profits. Adjustments were made in those cases where the land had become unrestricted by the act of 1908; the land was appraised by the district agent, and if it was found that the purchaser had paid a fair price, or if he was willing to make an additional payment and the allottee was still willing to sell, the deed was validated.[11]

The main legal points involved were decided by the Supreme Court in 1912. In the meantime, while the ownership of one-fifth the area of eastern Oklahoma was in question, the initial desire to see the matter settled by Federal action changed to exasperation over the prolonged business disturbance. Illogically, but naturally, public sentiment blamed the Government for its interference rather than the land speculators for their obstructive tactics. Representatives in Congress, especially Charles E. Creager of Muskogee, Charles D. Carter, and their sympathetic neighbor, John H. Stephens of Texas, commonly blamed the suits for the uncertain titles in eastern Oklahoma and referred to them as the greatest imaginable wrong to the Indians and the white people of the state.[12]

In 1911 the Supreme Court passed upon the constitutionality of the McCumber Amendment. The case involved the interpretation of the obscure legislation relating to the sale of inherited land.

Marchie Tiger was a fullblood Creek who had sold the surplus of an inherited allotment. According to the Creek Supple-

[11] *Senate Docs.*, 61 Cong., 1 Sess., No. 89; Department of the Interior, *Annual Report*, 1909, II, 389-90; 1910, II, 183; 1911, II, 416, 432; 1912, II, 433-34; *Muskogee Phoenix*, March 17, 1909; Indian Office Files, 5642/09 Five Tribes 013, Commissioner Valentine to R. A. Ballinger, November 11, 1910.

[12] *Muskogee Phoenix*, June 11, 1910; *Congressional Record*, XLV, 2222-23; XLVIII, 4447, 8260-61, 8265; Indian Office Files, 29520/09 Five Tribes 175.2.

mental Agreement, restrictions on surplus expired August 8, 1907; but the Five Tribes Act of 1906 had provided that land should become alienable upon the death of allottees except that conveyances by fullblood heirs were subject to Departmental approval. Land dealers had contended that the Secretary's approval was not required in the sale of inherited surplus after the expiration of the restrictions in 1907, and in 1908 the state Supreme Court upheld this interpretation. The case illustrates the real difficulty which the land dealer experienced in view of the confused and conflicting laws, and the element of chance that entered into many of his investments. One land dealer in Muskogee, for example, boasted that he had gained $40,000 by this decision, and it was reported that the value of another's estate was increased by $25,000.[13]

But Creek Attorney Mott appealed the case to the United States Supreme Court. He had considerable trouble with his client, for the land company immediately prepared a new deed for approval by the county court under the law of 1908. According to a facetious newspaper account Mott had to take Tiger to his own home and guard him not only from the land dealers but from his wife, who had been promised a commission if she could secure her husband's signature.[14]

The United States Supreme Court gave its decision May 15, 1911. It reversed the state court's ruling with regard to the Secretary's approval of inherited land, and it went very fully into the whole question of the power of Congress to impose additional restrictions—"our conclusions are that Congress has had at all times, and now has, the right to pass legislation in the interest of the Indians as a dependent people; that there is nothing in citizenship incompatible with this guardianship over the Indians['] lands inherited from allottees, as shown in this case; . . . that it rests with Congress to determine when its guardianship shall cease; and while it still continues, it has the right to vary its restrictions upon alienation of Indian

[13] *Muskogee Phoenix,* June 28, 1908.
[14] *Muskogee Times-Democrat,* July 29, 1908.

lands in the promotion of what it deems the best interest of the Indian."[15] An Oklahoma newspaper sorrowfully commented upon this decision, "Three centuries of civilization have not brought the fullblood Indian to the point where his rights equal those of a white man."[16]

The questions involved in the Thirty Thousand Land Suits were decided a year later in accordance with this ruling. The constitutionality of the restrictions and the right of the Government to sue for the allottees were uniformly upheld, but the United States lost several decisions with regard to the interpretation of various statutes.

The Heckman and Owen case was decided April 1. It had been chosen as typical of forty-six suits to cancel 3,715 Cherokee fullblood conveyances. Following the Marchie Tiger decision the court ruled that the sales were void, and that the purchasers were entitled to no return of their purchase price, for the restrictions had been matters of common knowledge. This settled the illegality of all sales made in deliberate violation of law.[17]

The Mullen and Jansen case was decided April 15. It will be remembered that the Choctaw-Chickasaw Supplemental Agreement had provided for progressive expiration of the restrictions on the surplus and the inalienability of the homestead for twenty-one years during the lifetime of the allottee. According to these badly drafted provisions, the death of the allottee therefore removed the restrictions from the homestead without affecting the surplus. The question arose as to whether the surplus inherited from a citizen who died before receiving his allotment was subject to the same restriction.[18] The court decided that there was no reason to designate part of the allotment as homestead and part as surplus if the allottee was already dead, and the entire allotment therefore became alienable

15 *Supreme Court Reports,* LV, 738-50. 16 *Sapulpa Evening Light,* May 16, 1911.
17 *Supreme Court Reports,* LVI, 820-34.
18 Kappler, *Laws and Treaties,* I, 772; Bledsoe, *Indian Land Laws,* pp. 42-51; *Supreme Court Reports,* LXI, 622-26.

by the heirs. The same reasoning applied to the Creek Supplemental Agreement.[19]

These decisions, of course, applied only to conveyances made under the agreements, before Congress specifically removed the restrictions from inherited land. But the Choctaw-Chickasaw ruling validated titles to an immense amount of property in the best part of the Chickasaw Nation, for the purchasers of "dead claims" had made their selections wisely. The *Ardmore Statesman* estimated that the decision had released assets of from one to two million dollars in Carter County alone; for hundreds of purchasers whose title had been doubtful would now be able to secure a fair loan or sell their land for its actual value. It would also lighten the tax burden, for the purchasers had failed to pay taxes while the title to the property was in doubt.[20]

The court handed down its decisions in the Goat case and the Deming Investment Company case April 29. These decisions involved the alienability of Seminole land before the patents were issued. The Seminole Agreement had provided that allotment deeds should be executed at the close of the tribal government and that no land should be alienable prior to the date of patent. The tribal government, however, had been extended by the Five Tribes Act; and Seminole allottees had been so notoriously overreached by land dealers that the Federal authorities had withheld all patents, thinking thus to invalidate these transactions. But the land dealers contended that they had the right to purchase under the act of 1904 releasing the surplus of adult Seminole freedmen, and the Oklahoma Supreme Court had decided in their favor. Now the United States Supreme Court also ruled that the Department's failure to issue the patents did not prevent the alienability of the land through act of Congress. The day after this decision a celebration was held at the county court house in Wewoka. The local band fur-

---

[19] *Supreme Court Reports,* LVI, 834-41; Kappler, *Laws and Treaties,* I, 764.
[20] *Ardmore Statesman,* April 20, 1912.

nished music, and several leading citizens made speeches commemorating the victory.[21]

As soon as the legal questions were settled by these decisions, the Department of the Interior attempted to bargain with the state of Oklahoma. Assistant Secretary Samuel Adams and the Indian Office went into the matter very fully. They had called the attention of Congress many times to the need of additional legislation to protect the Indians, but their requests had been refused and appropriations to administer existing laws had been denied. It was apparent that Congress would never restore authority it had once taken away; there was instead a constant demand that the Department take its hands off Indian affairs. But about twenty-four thousand suits were still pending to be disposed of in accordance with the recent Supreme Court decisions, and Congress and the people in general were extremely anxious for the end of the litigation; hence the opportunity for a trade. They decided to give up the prosecution in exchange for (1) control of agricultural leasing, (2) the right to purchase land for an Indian and place it under a restricted tax-exempt title, and (3) a penalty for placing clouds on the title of restricted land.

A bill embodying these provisions was accordingly drafted. It authorized the Secretary to validate, at his discretion, sales made prior to 1912, where no fraud was shown and the Indian had received full value, or should be paid an additional compensation satisfactory to the Secretary; it empowered the Secretary to purchase land for Indians who had failed to receive allotments, or to reinvest the proceeds from land sales in land, to be held under the same restrictions as the original allotment; it provided that no lease of restricted land and no timber sales from restricted land should be valid without the approval of the Department; and it prescribed fine or imprisonment for one who should cloud the title of restricted land. The Senate Committee on Indian Affairs approved the bill unanimously, after eliminating the provision prohibiting unrestricted timber sales. It was introduced by Senator Owen, but it failed to pass. At the same time Carter in the House vainly tried to eliminate the appropriation for further prosecution of the suits. [22]

Owen was nominated for a second term by the Democratic primary in 1912. When the legislature went through the formality of electing him, he advised the enactment of a law making it a penal offense to cloud the title of a fullblood homestead, and the legislature carried out this recommendation. His own position was greatly strengthened by the national Democratic victory of that year, but he encountered some active opposition. J. H. Godfrey, intermarried Chickasaw citizen, who had vainly fought Owen in the campaign, worked tirelessly to defeat any attempt to dispose of the land suits through the Interior Department rather than the courts. He wrote in April to President Wilson, Secretary Lane, and each member of the Senate and House Indian Affairs Committees, recounting the details of Owen's real estate dealings, pointing out the oil possibilities of the Caney ranch, and warning them that Owen would secure the appointment of his close friend, J. Haden Linebaugh, as the representative of the Interior Department to adjust the land transactions.[23]

Godfrey's charges made little impression. A few days after his letters were written Owen introduced a bill authorizing an Interior Department settlement and carrying none of the compensating features that the Indian Office was still supporting as its share of the compromise; but it received the approval of the Indian Affairs Committee and apparently was not opposed by Secretary Lane. It failed of passage, however, and the Department of Justice continued to handle the land suits.[24]

During the fiscal year 1912-1913 the Attorney-General reported 3,390 cases dismissed, of which 1,942 were Seminole freedman and Choctaw-Chickasaw "dead claims" cases lost by

[22] Indian Office Files, 24634/12 Five Tribes 013; *Congressional Record,* XLVIII, 4965-66, 8259-61; Kappler, *Laws and Treaties,* III, 527-28.
[23] Indian Office Files, 53683/08 Cherokee 311; State of Oklahoma, *Session Laws of 1913,* pp. 124-25.
[24] Indian Office Files, 24634/12 Five Tribes 013; *Congressional Record,* L, 2042. The bill was introduced May 1, 1913.

the Goat and Mullen-Jansen decisions. On one day in February, 1913, four of the largest defendants filed 372 quitclaim deeds affecting 734 cases and 42,935 acres of land. They told A. N. Frost, who was in charge of the prosecution, that they valued this land at more than a million dollars for its agricultural and oil resources.[25]

In the summer of 1913 Linebaugh was appointed as United States Attorney for the Eastern District. Frost continued to prosecute the land suits until about August 1, 1914, when his services were discontinued, and this work was placed under Linebaugh's office.[26]

Linebaugh had never favored the Government's prosecution of cases involving unrestricted adult allottees. He said that inasmuch as the law of 1908 had made them competent to sell, they were also competent to sue; and that moreover, since four-fifths of them had sold their land again subsequent to 1908, any clearing of the title would benefit the purchaser rather than the allottee. He did not advise, however, that the Government should drop the suits involving unrestricted minors. He made a careful tabulation and found 6,177 cases of unrestricted adults: 3,012 freedmen; 475 intermarried whites; 1,661 mixed-blood Indians of less than one-half Indian blood; 685 mixed-blood Indians of one-half and less than three-fourths, entitled to sell their surplus; and 371 whose restrictions had been removed by the Secretary. He had a conference in the fall of 1914 with Kelsey, the five tribal executives, and the three tribal attorneys, and they agreed to recommend the dismissal of all these cases. The Interior officials accepted this proposal, stipulating only that the names of the mixed-bloods should be referred to them for final approval. This reference proved to be merely nominal, however, for the Interior officials approved the lists as a matter of routine as soon as they were presented.[27]

[25] Indian Office Files, 29520/09 Five Tribes 175.2; Attorney-General, *Annual Report*, 1913, p. 43.

[26] *Sapulpa Evening Democrat*, May 5, 1913; *Muskogee Times-Democrat*, March 6, 1917.

[27] Indian Office Files, 111840/14 Five Tribes 175.2; *Muskogee Phoenix*, September 7, 1915.

It is apparent from these names that a majority of the mixed-bloods were of such a slight degree of Indian blood as to be virtually white, but it is also apparent that a serious wrong was done to a number of fullblood Indians enrolled as mixed-blood Seminoles. Of this latter group, those listed as half-bloods lost their surplus and those listed as quarter-bloods lost their entire allotment, because they had been enrolled according to the citizenship of their mothers or their maternal grandmothers. They could, of course, institute suits in the state courts to recover their property, but this was a remedy that this primitive people could not possibly understand.

Linebaugh prosecuted the remaining suits vigorously, and only 2,946 remained on the docket in 1918. Most of the deeds were canceled or the suits were dismissed because the purchaser had given a quitclaim deed or made a settlement satisfactory to the Agency, or because the allottee had died in the course of the prolonged litigation and the heirs had sold the land through the county court. Among the heavy losers were: several dealers in the Seminole country who had secured title to fullblood land; a ranching company that operated in the Choctaw country; a man in Missouri who had been an extensive buyer of Cherokee land; the Kansas speculators who had obtained powers of attorney from the Choctaw fullbloods; and several land companies of Muskogee which had made large scale purchases of Creek land.[28]

Because of his high standing with the Wilson administration, Eastern philanthropic friends of the Indians were very apprehensive that Senator Owen might escape his share of these losses. He himself said in 1913 that all but one of the mixed-blood allottees whose restrictions were removed in 1908 gave deeds validating their previous contracts, and Frost said in 1914 that Owen had secured 154 such deeds. Of the fullblood land, he secured a portion by a settlement through the Agency; the Indian's restrictions were removed, and Owen pur-

[28] Federal Court Records, Eastern District of Oklahoma, Land Suits; Attorney-General, *Annual Report*, 1915-18.

chased the land at a price satisfactory to the Department. In other cases the allottee died, and the land was sold by his heirs. The remaining deeds, about twenty-five, were canceled by the District Court.[29]

After 1918 the suits were disposed of more slowly. In 1925 twenty still remained on the docket. In most cases the defendant was dead and the heirs were unknown or unwilling to quitclaim; the Government, therefore, dismissed these suits without prejudice, trusting to a separate suit in equity if it should ever become necessary to quiet title. This ended the most extensive Indian litigation in the history of Oklahoma.[30]

It is impossible to determine accurately the results of the Thirty Thousand Land Suits. The Government was completely vindicated in its claim to the guardianship of Indians and its right to restrict their land, and millions of dollars' worth of restricted land was restored to the allottees by voluntary quitclaim and by the cancellation of illegal deeds. In cases where the suits were dismissed because of inheritance sales or Agency settlements it is impossible to discover to what extent the speculator was able to benefit from his original purchase. With regard to the allottees from whom restrictions were removed by the act of 1908, there is no means of knowing the proportion who validated the previous sale. Frost believed that deeds taken in pursuance of illegal contracts were void, but the Department of Justice never authorized him to test this contention in the Federal courts. A few such cases came into the state courts, and the Oklahoma Supreme Court ruled that the second sale was legal, that the fact that the allottee was honest enough to remember and recognize the first consideration did not impose restrictions upon his power to alienate under the act of 1908.[31]

[29] Lake Mohonk Conference, *Report*, 1914, pp. 29-36; J. H. Godfrey, "Suggestions for an Oklahoma Investigation," *Quarterly Journal of the Society of American Indians*, I (1913); Indian Office Files, 54683/08 Cherokee 311; Federal Court Records, Eastern District of Oklahoma, Land Suits, Journals L, LI, LXIV.

[30] Indian Office Files, 111840/14 Five Tribes 175.2; *Muskogee Times-Democrat*, June 19, 1925.

[31] Lake Mohonk Conference, *Report*, 1914, p. 33; *Pacific Reporter*, CCXXIV, 645-47.

The Attorney-General's published reports are not entirely frank in their statements of the amount of land recovered. Apparently they include the land involved in the 6,177 unrestricted cases dismissed in 1915 and 1916 in their statistics of recovery, probably upon the theory that the unrestricted allottee was technically free to make a second sale or to sue in the state courts. They also claim credit for the land sold by full-blood heirs through the county courts.[32] It is obvious in both these cases that the land was sold by the allottee under a clouded title, and that the speculator had a monopoly of the purchase.

Another important litigation, which in some of its aspects constituted a branch of the Thirty Thousand Land Suits, arose from transactions in Seminole County. This county comprised the Seminole Nation and a small strip of Creek territory. The special census of 1907 showed a population of 10,678 white, 2,759 Negro, and 1,250 Indian inhabitants.[33] It was a crude and fierce society of clashing racial hatreds, personal and business feuds, and frequent crimes of violence.[34] The Indians were nearly all fullbloods of the most conservative type, and the Negro allottees were equally primitive.

Speculators operated by wholesale in the Seminole country during 1906 and 1907, buying land without restraint from all classes of allottees. At least twenty-five persons were engaged in these transactions on a large scale,[35] and so widespread was the practice that almost the entire white citizenship of the county energetically resisted all efforts at restitution and applauded and even elected to high office those under attack. When it is remembered that the Government denied the legality of all sales of Seminole land except the Wewoka townsite, the temper of these settlers can be readily imagined.

[32] Attorney-General, *Annual Report*, 1916, p. 50; 1917, pp. 46-47; 1919, p. 97.
[33] *Population of Oklahoma and Indian Territory 1907*, p. 11.
[34] This is apparent in any issue of a Seminole County newspaper. See, for instance, *Seminole Capital*, December 1, 1910 with three murders for the week, and the statement that there had been forty-five murders since statehood.
[35] Federal Court Records, Eastern District of Oklahoma, Land Suits, Journals XXX, XXXV, LII, LXVII, LXVIII.

The state government, as has been pointed out, was inaugurated November 16, 1907. Before the end of the year, notices by guardians for the sale of real estate began to appear in the *Wewoka Democrat*, and by March such notices were so numerous as almost to fill the paper. In most, if not all, of these cases the land sold by the guardians consisted of inherited land which had been released from restrictions by the Five Tribes Act of 1906.[36] When the law of 1908 released 255,246 additional acres, the saturnalia of sales by adult allottees was matched only by the notices that filled the newspapers as guardians hastened to unload the land of Negro and mixed-blood children through the county court. It was also reported that speculators flocked to the premises when an Indian was known to be dying, and crowded the church and cemetery during his funeral until it was difficult to conduct the services; and that several Seminole freedmen who had been tricked into giving deeds under the impression that they were signing other instruments had helplessly remained in their old homes and had been arrested and placed in jail for trespass.[37]

The act of 1908 gave the Government its first opportunity through the district agents and the land suits to clear up conditions in Seminole County; and in July Federal court writs were served on all purchasers of Seminole allotments. The land dealers then formed the Seminole County Protective Association to employ counsel in defense of the transactions; while on the other hand it was reported that some two hundred citizens of the county had sent petitions to the Federal officials, to Governor Haskell, and to Attorney-General Charles West, charging that several county officers were participating in the probate sales, and asking an investigation.[38]

36 *Wewoka Democrat*, December 20, 1907-March 13, 1908.

37 *Ibid.*, January 17, April 2, 1908; Indian Office Files, 2996/08 Seminole 314, 25992/08 Seminole 352. For guardians' sales see, for example, *Seminole Capital*, January 4, 1909; *Wewoka Democrat*, May 27, 1908.

38 *Wewoka Democrat*, July 29, 1908; *Muskogee Phoenix*, November 17, 1908; *Daily Oklahoman*, May 26, 1911; *House Reports*, 61 Cong., 2 Sess., No. 2273, Vol. II, appendix, pp. 1340-42.

These disturbances were echoed in several small newspapers of Seminole County. These publications changed their management and policy with bewildering frequency, but to a considerable extent they were owned by land dealers, and they were greatly influenced by their desire to secure the public printing, which consisted largely of probate notices.

The *Seminole Capital* of Wewoka and the *Seminole County News* of the rival town of Seminole violently defended the land transactions by such expressions of editorial policy as the following:

"Sympathy and sentiment never stand in the way of the onward march of empire.

"The days of the Indian who values the domain only in its wild natural state, and the good-for-nothing lazy criminal nigger, are numbered in Seminole County.

"They are on the level with all humanity and like water, they will seek their own level. If they don't learn the value of property and how to adjust themselves to surroundings, they will be 'grafted' out of it—that is one of the unchangeable laws of God and the constitution of man.

. . . . . . . . .

"The 'grafter' has come to stay and onward the power of empires take their way."[39]

But the *Wewoka Democrat,* under the editorship of Don Lawhead, began early in 1908 to comment upon the land transactions with a mild disapproval, which soon reached the fervor of a crusade. Lawhead and his two opponents then fought each other with an unrestrained coarseness that makes strange reading in a more conventional society. "Ex-convict," "buzzard," "skunk," and "nigger-lover" were among the more printable of the epithets that they hurled at each other.

Early in 1909 Attorney-General West, acting on advice from Secretary Garfield, and using evidence obtained by the district agents, attempted to oust one of the county officials. The turbulent spirit of the citizens was strongly apparent dur-

[39] *Seminole County News,* April 17, 1908.

ing the investigation. One grand jury was dismissed after it had been in session two days when it was charged that an attempt had been made to bribe two members. Another was called, but suddenly the newspapers omitted all mention of its activities. The *Wewoka Democrat*, which had condemned the land transactions in such virulent language, came out under the editorship of a custodian, with a strong defense of the officials who were under investigation. The whole county seemed to be approaching open rebellion as its citizens defiantly asserted their ability to maintain local self-government without the interference of Federal "carpet-baggers." Mass meetings were held in Wewoka, Seminole, Konawa, and Little, and ringing resolutions were adopted.[40]

Enough news filtered through to indicate what had happened to the *Wewoka Democrat*. One of the land dealers who held a note against Lawhead brought suit for $819.32 and costs. Lawhead made fruitless efforts to obtain the money, and the plant was attached by the sheriff. Other stray references show that Lawhead was convicted of criminal libel, but apparently the matter was dropped in the general confusion without the enforcement of the sentence. Perhaps it was felt to be enough when the only critic of the land transactions was so dramatically silenced.[41]

It is impossible now to discover what happened to the indictments said to have been returned by the grand jury. A charge of false acknowledgment seems to have been dismissed by a special county judge for want of jurisdiction. A special district judge seems to have dismissed a forgery charge for want of prosecution, despite the protest of the prosecutor, who had been forced into the trial when he was not prepared. At-

---

[40] *Seminole County News*, March 12, 1909; *Wewoka Democrat*, February-March, 1909; *Seminole Capital*, July 23, 1908; February-March, 1909; *Muskogee Phoenix*, February 7, 1909; *Daily Oklahoman*, May 26, 1911.

[41] *Wewoka Democrat*, August 18, October 20, 1909; *Seminole Capital*, February 20, April 29, May 27, 1909; *Muskogee Times-Democrat*, October 19, 1909. Apparently Lawhead did not suffer seriously in his personal fortunes from this prosecution, for the next year he was employed as press agent by Lee Cruce in his campaign for Governor—see *Seminole Capital*, June 16, 1910.

torney-General West then attempted to persuade the state Supreme Court to assume original jurisdiction, but the Supreme Court ruled that such action would require a jury trial and there was no constitutional method by which it could summon a jury.[42]

The guardians' petitions published in the newspapers show that the sale of minors' land through the courts was not checked in the slightest degree by the attempted prosecution in 1909. In 1910 John Cordell, district agent at Holdenville, reported that "forgery in securing deeds is now the rule instead of the exception"; and he mentioned another grand jury investigation where "specific cases" he had presented were "ignored." He made a desperate appeal for help, telling of the local government paralyzed, swindlers victorious and unhindered, and homeless allottees constantly besieging him for redress. Congress then made a special appropriation of Seminole funds, and James E. Gresham, who had been assisting Frost in the Thirty Thousand Land Suits, was sent to Wewoka as tribal attorney.[43]

The press and the public continued to uphold the land buyers. In the election of 1910 two of the most active were elected to the legislature, where they and a Representative from Atoka County introduced a memorial to Congress complaining of the land litigation that was hindering the progress of the state and the prosperity of the Indians—"These people have long since established their right, and vindicated their claim to manage their own affairs in their own way without having thrown around them those restrictions imposed by law upon infants, idiots, and other legal incompetents."[44]

[42] *Muskogee Phoenix*, February 24, 1909; *Seminole Capital*, April 29, July 1, 8, 15, 1909; *Wewoka Democrat*, April 21, 1909; January 12, 1910; *Daily Oklahoman*, May 28, 1911; Indian Office Files, 15317/09 Seminole 175.2; *Pacific Reporter*, CIV, 361-65.

[43] Indian Office Files, 62989/10 Seminole 174; *Muskogee Phoenix*, June 3, July 29, 1910; Department of the Interior, *Annual Report*, 1910, II, 210; *Statutes at Large*, XXXVI, 703-4; XXXVII, 417, 464. McKennon's employment with the Seminoles had terminated, and the tribe had been without an attorney for some time.

[44] *Wewoka Democrat*, June 10, August 5, December 23, 1910; *Seminole Capital*, November 10, 1910.

Soon after, an event occurred that brought Seminole County matters indirectly into the courts through one of the most celebrated libel suits in the history of Oklahoma. Early in 1911 when Miss Barnard was making her fight in the legislature for authority to protect Indian minors, the *Daily Oklahoman* in an attempt to influence legislation, published an article with regard to probate conditions in general, and quoted excerpts from the brief West had filed with the Supreme Court in his attempted ouster proceedings.[45] T. S. Cobb, who had been judge of the Seminole County court and the center of much of the controversy in the county, immediately sued the paper for libel. The trial judge admitted the entire brief in evidence to prove that the published excerpts had been representative. He also admitted other records of proceedings in estates of minor Seminoles to substantiate the truth of the general statements made by the newspaper, and allowed Judge Cobb to be cross-examined regarding his land transactions. Cobb lost his suit and appealed to the Supreme Court; and the Supreme Court ruled that West's brief was a privileged publication, and that the admission of testimony regarding general probate conditions in Seminole County was permissible, for it furnished the best evidence as to whether the article in the *Oklahoman* was true or false.[46]

One of the judge's own purchases of freedman land eventually came to the Supreme Court, which set aside the deed and delivered a scathing opinion against Cobb, against the educated Creek Negro—designated as "his Man Friday"—who had assisted him in the transaction, and against the general land practices in Seminole County. The court expressed "undivided sympathy" for the "helpless Indians and freedmen . . . for, with an intelligent and scheming white man, they have an unequal chance even at the best; but when to this unequal chance is added the dishonesty of public officials, on whom these simple people have a right to rely implicitly for

---

45 *Daily Oklahoman*, January 1, 1911.
46 *Ibid.*, May 26-30, 1911; *Pacific Reporter*, CXL, 1079-84.

fair dealing and protection, and the duplicity and treachery of their own kith and kin, it is next to impossible to prevent them from being most shamefully mistreated and robbed."[47]

Gresham could have endorsed this sentiment, for he found his untutored clients very difficult to protect. The money appropriated by Congress for the Thirty Thousand Land Suits was available only for suits in the Federal courts to set aside conveyances made prior to 1908. The small special appropriation from Seminole funds paid Gresham's salary and a few other expenses, but the suits were carried on in the state courts at the expense of the allottee. Gresham found many cases of outright forgery, but the Indian in his poverty could hardly be induced to provide the money for the suit, and it was even more difficult to persuade him to go into a strange court and testify; he reasoned that he had signed nothing, the land rightfully belonged to him, and he withdrew in fear and disapproval from the whole proceeding.

The Federal officials labored under a nerve-racking strain, in an atmosphere charged with hostility and threats of violence. But in spite of local sympathy for the land dealers and the uncertain character of the witnesses against them, when Gresham's work ended in 1914, thirteen men who had formerly operated in Seminole County, including several prominent citizens and their Negro assistants, had been sent to prison for forgery. Others, by their advertising of land to which they held a forged title, had been sent to the Federal penitentiary for using the mails to defraud. Apparently all the convictions were secured outside Seminole County, and it is fairly evident that many criminals escaped.[48]

With the success of these criminal prosecutions, other land dealers abandoned their defiant attitude. Holders of illegal

---

[47] *Pacific Reporter*, CXXXI, 165-69.

[48] Indian Office Files, 25992/08 Seminole 352, 62898/10 Seminole 174, 101931/09 Union 175; *Muskogee Times-Democrat*, December 21, 1911; *Muskogee Phoenix*, January 22, 30, 1910; June 8, December 21, 1911; August 3, 5, 7, 15, 1913; February 22, 1914; *Hugo Husonian*, August 8, 21, 1913; *Wewoka Democrat*, March 10, 1911; Attorney-General, *Annual Report*, 1913, p. 43; 1914, pp. 41-42.

deeds began to quitclaim, and many forged deeds were canceled by District Judge Tom D. McKeown. Allottees arraigned for trespass and other trumped-up charges were defended and vindicated. Some guardians' sales were prevented, but the newspaper notices continued with little diminution during the entire time that Gresham was in Wewoka. The children whose land had already been sold, of course, did not recover it, for all legal formalities had been observed. A large amount of property lost through forgery also was never recovered.[49]

All these transactions involved inherited land or the unrestricted allotments of freedmen or mixed-bloods. The illegal deeds to restricted land secured in 1906 and 1907 were canceled in due course by the Thirty Thousand Land Suits.[50] It is safe to assume, however, that none of the unrestricted cases dropped by the Department of Justice in 1915 and 1916 was ever prosecuted by the allottee.

The forgery convictions and the clearing of Indian titles changed public sentiment in Seminole County. The land speculators lost their political supremacy in the election of 1912.[51] The Supreme Court decisions of the same year settled several disputed questions, and the people now understood what land was legally alienable. The county had, indeed, carried a heavy burden while the title to every foot of Seminole land was in question, but the citizens had added to their difficulties by their defiant championship of a condition that encouraged forgery, murder, the dispossession of helpless people, and the robbery of little children.

Although the Seminole County frauds attracted more attention than any others, a controversy only a little less serious developed in McCurtain County. Nearly all the allottees were fullblood Choctaws, but a great deal of timber and inherited land was subject to sale.

[49] Indian Office Files, 62989/10 Seminole 174, 29520/09 Five Tribes 175.2; *Wewoka Democrat*, 1911-14; *Pacific Reporter,* Second Series, II, 1030-31.

[50] Federal Court Records, Eastern District of Oklahoma, Land Suits, Journals XXX, XXXV, XLII, LXVII, LXVIII.

[51] *Wewoka Democrat,* February 9, July 25, August 2, 15, 1912.

In 1910 the district agents began to report bad guardianship conditions, but the matter was not pressed because the official believed to be responsible was a candidate for reelection. Oklahomans so frequently and angrily asserted that the district agents were exercising undue political influence that Kelsey was making every effort to avoid criticism. He did call the matter to Miss Barnard's attention, and was informed that she had no authority to intervene but hoped to obtain it at the next session of the legislature.[52]

It will be recalled that Miss Barnard did receive a limited measure of authority in 1911; and, as probate conditions remained unchanged after the election, Kelsey presented his evidence to her office and to Governor Cruce. Stolper was accordingly sent to Idabel to clear up the situation. Kelsey was extremely anxious to avoid all appearance of conflict between the Federal and county officials, and he hoped that if a state department could receive favorable publicity for correcting abuses, the people of Oklahoma would develop a feeling of local pride in protecting the Indians. Stolper, therefore, was placed in complete charge, and the Agency force worked so quietly in the background that state newspapers hostile to Federal supervision praised Miss Barnard's department for "getting results where the federal government has failed."[53]

The county attorney advised Stolper that in view of local sympathy with the land dealers it would be extremely difficult to secure convictions for any crime against Indian property. Stolper, therefore, decided—according to his own published reports—that restitution was more important than punishment, and he promised immunity from prosecution to those who would make a voluntary settlement. During the summer of 1911 the county judge resigned, 4,133.48 acres of land was quitclaimed through the office of the district agent, about $30,-

---

[52] Indian Office Files, 81967/10; Commissioner of Charities and Corrections, *Report*, 1911, pp. 118-24.

[53] Indian Office Files, 81967/10; Commissioner of Charities and Corrections, *Report*, 1911, pp. 113-17, 124-29; Commissioner of Charities and Corrections, Office Files.

000 in cash belonging to minors was recovered, and three of the largest purchasers of land and timber signed agreements to refer all their titles to arbitration boards.[54]

These settlements were achieved in an atmosphere tense with hostility. The lives of the investigators were threatened, and one of the employees of the district agent's office was arrested and another was assaulted on the streets of Idabel. The local press heaped abuse upon the Federal and state officials, and soon after the judge's resignation the McCurtain County Bar Association presented him with a gold-headed cane.[55]

Stolper and the Agency force worked in perfect harmony, but friction soon developed between Stolper and the tribal attorneys, McCurtain and Hill. According to Stolper, it arose from the determination of McCurtain and Hill to present the accumulated evidence to a grand jury. The district agents were very careful to avoid taking sides in the controversy, but they, too, believed that if no criminal prosecutions were undertaken the public would have no faith in the sincerity of the investigation.[56]

The county attorney, greatly to Stolper's chagrin, decided to prosecute, and the state Attorney-General appointed McCurtain to assist him. Several prominent McCurtain County citizens were indicted for forgery and other crimes, but some of them were acquitted and about one hundred indictments were set aside by the district judge on technical errors.[57] The district agents had also secured evidence that they believed would revoke the commissions of twenty-two notaries charged with acknowledging blank deeds to be filled out later according to the plans of the purchaser. The Governor cited them to appear,

[54] Indian Office Files, 81967/10, 80681/11; Commissioner of Charities and Corrections, *Report*, 1911, pp. 127-53; Commissioner of Charities and Corrections, Office Files; *Congressional Record*, XLVIII, 11155, 11405-6.

[55] Indian Office Files, 80681/11; *McCurtain Gazette*, July 1, 22, August 9, 1911; *Idabel Democrat-Record*, August 10, September 7, November 9, 30, December 7, 21, 1911.

[56] Commissioner of Charities and Corrections, *Report*, 1911, pp. 139-50; 1912, pp. 259-63, 265; Indian Office Files, 80681/11.

[57] *McCurtain Gazette*, October, 1911; *Idabel Democrat-Record*, December 7, 1911; February 29, 1912.

but none responded, and Stolper then recommended that no further action be taken, in view of the failure of the criminal prosecution.[58]

Meanwhile an arbitration board met to pass upon about seventy titles submitted by one of the land dealers. It consisted of three members: Kelsey, representing the Secretary of the Interior, acted as chairman; and the other members were Stolper, chosen by Miss Barnard, and Thomas C. Humphrey, former judge of the Indian Territory court, selected by the land dealer whose titles were under examination. McCurtain represented the interests of the allottees before this tribunal.

It is impossible now to discover what actually happened after the first day's proceedings. In 1911 Kelsey and Stolper described the creation of the board as a great victory for Indian minors; but both were completely silent in their reports of the following year as to what it accomplished, and no record of its sessions is to be found in the office of the Commissioner of Charities and Corrections, the Agency at Muskogee, or the Indian Office. Apparently the silence that descended upon the entire matter after the loud announcements of the previous year was intended to cover a humiliating failure. It was stated in the press, however, that all the titles were confirmed, and the files of Miss Barnard's office contain a long list of land that apparently was passed upon and approved. It is probable that the arbitration under the other two agreements never took place.[59]

But even though the McCurtain County investigation fell far short of the expectations of the state and Federal officials, a situation developed in Adair County that was corrected largely by local sentiment. Deed forgery and guardianship frauds were reported to be very common in this Cherokee

[58] Commissioner of Charities and Corrections, *Report*, 1911, pp. 152-53; 1912, pp. 55-60; *Congressional Record*, XLVIII, 11405-7.

[59] Commissioner of Charities and Corrections, *Report*, 1911, pp. 139-50; 1912, pp. 262-63; Commissioner of Charities and Corrections, Office Files; Department of the Interior, *Annual Report*, 1911, II, 422-23; *Congressional Record*, XLVIII, 11405-7; *Idabel Democrat-Record*, November 30, 1911; June 27, 1912; *McAlester News*, October 5, 1912; *McCurtain Gazette*, November 29, 1911.

county. The matter came to a head just at the close of 1912 when W. W. Hastings, Cherokee tribal attorney, brought charges against several leading citizens of Stilwell for mal-administration of an estate. The county commissioners at once petitioned for the judge's removal, and a grand jury returned a number of indictments for forgery, perjury, bribery, and conspiracy; but a compromise settlement was made whereby the judge resigned and the indictments were dismissed.[60]

After the resignation of the judge the county commissioners appointed John A. Goodall to finish his unexpired term. Goodall immediately effected a revolution in probate practice, citing guardians to appear, checking shortages, and securing high prices for oil leases by extensive advertising and competitive bidding. Many large sums of money were recovered from delinquent guardians. Bonding companies began to sue the defaulters and to put pressure on all their guardians to file reports. Several of the more active land speculators were soon in difficulty on various criminal charges, and a number were sent to the penitentiary for forgery of deeds and embezzlement of minors' estates.[61]

There is no evidence that public sentiment in Adair County supported guardianship frauds. The *Adair County Republican*, of which one of the men under indictment was editor, based its defense upon assertions of his innocence rather than upon a justification of Indian exploitation. The *Standard-Sentinel* supported the guardianship investigation, declaring "we are frank to say that we do not believe in robbing the full blood Indian and the minors of this county." It is also ap-

[60] *Standard-Sentinel,* December 19, 1912; January 2-April 17, July 24, October 9, 1913; June 4, 1914; *Cherokee County Democrat,* January 2, 1912; Indian Office Files, 7383/13 Cherokee 173.1.

[61] *Standard-Sentinel,* March 23, November 23, December 14, 1911; February-March, November 14, December 5, 1912; March 13, May 15, August 7, September 13-December 11, 1913; June 18, July 2, November 12, 1914; March 4, 11, 25, October 14, 1915; *Adair County Republican,* December 12, 1913; January 23, October 16, November 14, December 12, 1914; *Congressional Record,* XLVIII, 11155, 11410.

parent that the land speculators had a wholesome fear of District Judge Pitchford.[62]

Before the end of 1913 Goodall had established a precedent that attracted a great deal of attention throughout eastern Oklahoma. A guardian had sold one child's land for $225 when it was worth $2,000 for agriculture and was producing oil, and had sold the land of another and delivered the deed before any consideration was paid. He had accounted for nearly all the funds he had handled, but Goodall ruled that he and his bondsmen were liable for the money lost through his mismanagement of the sales.[63]

The probate conditions in Seminole, McCurtain, and Adair counties are fairly typical of those existing throughout the Five Tribes area. They attracted more attention only because a stronger effort was made to bring the guardians to accountability. But in spite of all the wrongs that were left unrighted, the activity of the district agents, the tribal attorneys, and the state Department of Charities and Corrections; the many financial losses sustained by speculators through adverse court decisions; and the few criminal convictions began to check the unrestrained plunder that had been ushered in by the law of 1908. Kelsey stated in 1912 that "there is no question but that the appalling criminal practices are not as frequent as heretofore."[64] But the criminals and their respectable allies formed the same conclusion as did the Indian agent, and 1912 marked the beginning of their most relentless efforts to destroy all the forces that stood in the way of their avarice.

[62] *Standard-Sentinel,* June 5, 1913; *Adair County Republican,* June-July, 1914.
[63] *Standard-Sentinel,* December 25, 1913; *Muskogee Phoenix,* December 23, 1913.
[64] Department of the Interior, *Annual Report,* 1912, II, 484.

## CHAPTER IX

# The Fight Between Despoilers
# and Defenders

FOR about three years a bitter fight raged between those who were determined to sweep away every vestige of protection given to the Five Tribes allottees and those who were trying to defend them. The issues were complicated by the personal ambitions and rivalries of the principals and the appetite of politicians for the spoils of office. The battle was waged in Congress and the state legislature and in the smallest political subdivision in Oklahoma, and Eastern philanthropists entered the lists before it ended. Some of the most active agencies and some of the most fearless individuals that had been working to protect the Indians were destroyed; but some improvement was made in legislation and administrative policy and in a better working agreement between state and Federal agencies.

The admission of Oklahoma to statehood did not entirely eliminate the influence of Northern Republican politicians in the Five Tribes spoils. The Indian Office files contain hundreds of letters written from 1907 to 1913 by Joseph G. Cannon, Boies Penrose, Charles Curtis, and others recommending appointees or requesting promotions as a special favor. Naturally this practice was deeply resented by the intensely self-conscious citizenship of the new state. Although an additional Republican had been elected to the House of Representatives in 1910, Oklahoma was still overwhelmingly Democratic, and its delegation in Congress was therefore out of political harmony with the Indian Office.

In response to this sentiment of local pride, resentment over the spoils situation, and the violent demands of the land sharks, the Democratic Representatives from Oklahoma made a determined fight during the session of 1911-1912 against the appropriation for the district agents. Ferris, Davenport, and Carter asserted that the state government was adequately protecting the Indians and that Oklahoma resented being placed under surveillance; and they charged that the service had been created solely to provide for the henchmen of politicians from other states and to strengthen the local Republican organization. Carter asserted that he had received hundreds of communications from his constituents condemning these Federal employees; and he read a letter from W. B. M. Mitchell, the county judge of Garvin County, "who it must be admitted has had abundant opportunity to view the action of the district agents at close range," and whose judgment might be regarded "as a sample of the opinions held by many good citizens of Oklahoma along this line." In this letter the judge made a violent attack upon the integrity of the district agents; he characterized the effort to dispense with them as "the greatest move that has been made since Oklahoma was admitted to the Union"; and he urged Carter, "If you can't abolish the office, for God's sake cut off the appropriation." Carter also read the letter previously mentioned from Stolper expressing the competence of Miss Barnard's department to assume supervision over all the Indians in the state.

Charles S. Burke of South Dakota led the fight for the appropriation. He taunted the Oklahomans as subject to pressure from a grafter constituency, and predicted that the state would soon pauperize the Indians and then come to Congress for their support. The debate indicates that there was no basis for the charge that the position of district agent had been created solely to increase the number of Republican appointees; for the members of Congress that had been most active in using the spoils of the Oklahoma Indian service showed the greatest unconcern.

Cannon, for instance, savagely insisted that the Indians must learn to "root hog or die."[1]

The Oklahomans were successful, and the district agents were eliminated. Other Agency employees were thereupon designated as "field clerks" and detailed to such administrative duties as lease supervision, the removal of restrictions, and general advice to restricted allottees; but they gave no attention to probate matters. The Interior Department attempted to carry on the probate work through attorneys employed by the tribes under contracts approved by the President in accordance with the Five Tribes Act. McCurtain and Hill, and their successors, Thomas B. Latham and W. M. F. Semple, continued their probate work for the Choctaws. A supplemental contract was made with Creek Attorney Mott, September 5, 1912, by which he was authorized to serve in a probate capacity. A similar contract was made with W. W. Hastings for the Cherokees. It was under this authority that Hastings had intervened in the Adair County case, and after the appointment of Goodall as judge he was very active in the prosecution of delinquent guardians. William A. Baker, former district agent at Holdenville, was employed as assistant tribal attorney, to take charge of probate matters for the Chickasaws. James E. Gresham continued until 1914 to serve the Seminoles under special authorization by Congress. All these attorneys were paid from tribal funds, and were supposed to protect both restricted and unrestricted allottees.[2]

The most famous incident in the history of Oklahoma Indian administration grew out of this policy. Mott took his new duties very seriously. With his additional appropriation he employed fifteen men to investigate and compile all the data from the guardianship records of the eight counties comprising the old Creek Nation. He found 6,900 cases involving a much

[1] *Congressional Record*, XLVIII, 4429-52, 8280, 11155-60, 11233-39, 11400-20, 11690-93; Department of Charities and Corrections, *Monthly Bulletin*, I (May 15, 1912).

[2] Indian Office Files, 77012/13 Union 175, 135712/13 Creek 311; Department of the Interior, *Annual Report*, 1913, II, 446-47, 462.

larger number of minors, but in only 2,300 were the records complete. In 3,057 cases he was able to determine the status of the minors—203 white guardianship cases, 2,320 of Indian minors under professional guardians, and 534 of Indian minors under competent natural guardians—and he grouped his statistics under these three heads. His findings, whether examined case by case in the eight great volumes of exhibits, separately by counties, or under his statistical groupings, are shocking almost beyond belief. The totals, which give a fair summary of the condition revealed in the separate reports, are as follows:

|  | INDIAN | | WHITE |
|  | Professional | Natural |  |
|---|---|---|---|
| Funds handled | $3,896,693.06 | $1,346,523.07 | $328,536.00 |
| Attorneys' fees | 346,095.39 | 21,762.41 | 3,117.94 |
| Court costs | 138,205.46 | 11,295.92 | 2,625.51 |
| Guardians' fees | 279,483.34 | 19,972.58 | 2,021.40 |
| TOTAL COST | 763,483.34 | 53,030.91 | 7,775.85 |

The cost of administration by professional guardians of Indian children was therefore 19.3 per cent of the amount handled, while the cost to Indian children under natural guardians was only 3.1 per cent, and the cost of white guardianships was 2.3 per cent. Mott also secured partial statistics from thirty states, and found that guardianship costs averaged about 3 per cent—a figure very close to that of the natural Indian and white guardianships in the Creek counties.[3]

Mott's report showed only the receipts and expenditures actually reported to the courts. It failed to show the disposition of the property where the guardian felt no sense of accountability whatever; and it disregarded the immeasurably greater waste that took place through selling the minors' land at a prearranged price to a favored buyer, and investing minors' money in unsecured loans or worthless property. But even these

[3] Secretary of the Interior, Office Files (Department of the Interior, Washington), File 5-127, original report with eight volumes of exhibits; *Congressional Record,* XLIX, 498-99, published summary of the report.

incomplete figures bear eloquent witness to the vast profits of the guardianship business, and the corrupting influence which it was able to exert upon the life of Oklahoma.

The report was dated November 27, 1912. The Department made copies of the summary, and one copy was sent to Stephens of Texas, who had been chairman of the House Committee on Indian Affairs since the Democratic victory in the off-year election of 1910, and who was usually in active sympathy with Oklahoma aspirations. Stephens ignored the communication, although he afterwards admitted that he had received it. Other copies were supposed to have been sent to the Senate Indian Affairs Committee, to the two Oklahoma Senators, and to Carter and Ferris. Carter and Ferris later denied that they had ever seen the document; it is possible that their copies had really been withheld for strategic reasons, or that they had lain on their desks with other papers and escaped notice. But Burke had been furnished with a copy, and he and James R. Mann of Illinois prepared a dialogue to introduce the report effectively; Burke was to make a general charge about the dishonesty of probate administration in Oklahoma, Mann was to spring to the defense of the state and demand proof, and Burke was to answer by statistical information from the report.

The stratagem worked perfectly. On December 13 the House in Committee of the Whole was considering the Indian Appropriation Bill, which was so drawn as completely to eliminate the field workers at the end of the fiscal year. Suddenly Burke and Mann sprung their trap. Davenport, Ferris, and Carter were thrown into angry confusion; they took refuge in emphatic denial and in furious condemnation of Mott and the Indian Office in general. They denounced the whole report as a trick to perpetuate Republican appointees, whose tenure would soon be terminated by the incoming Wilson administration.[4]

The Oklahoma delegation, however, mailed a copy of the summarized report to Governor Cruce, requesting him to in-

[4] *Congressional Record,* XLIX, 596-610; LI, 3486-3500.

vestigate and inform them whether the charges were true. Carter wrote again to the Governor, December 30, saying he was receiving letters from leading citizens of Oklahoma confirming some of Mott's statements. He implied that only a searching investigation by the state could forestall a Congressional investigation after the Christmas recess.[5]

Mott was extremely anxious for the state to correct the probate situation. He advised that the Governor be furnished with a copy of the Wagoner County exhibits, since the cost of administration was highest there; and he said that if necessary his office would bear all the expense of copying. The copy was accordingly transmitted to the Governor, and L. E. Cahill was detailed by the State Examiner and Inspector to go to Wagoner County and investigate. Mott's published report had summarized the entire cost of guardianships since the beginning, and had therefore included the Federal period. In seven of the eight counties most of the guardians had filed reports recently or at least since statehood; but in Wagoner County an overwhelming majority had never reported since the county was established. The statistics from that county, therefore, dealt almost exclusively with the Federal period, and about the only fact that could be determined of the county administration was that there had been no supervision at all. But the fact that Mott had suggested the selection of Wagoner County for special investigation indicates that he had no desire to conceal the laxity of the Federal courts.[6]

The Governor submitted Cahill's report to the legislature February 17. He characterized probate costs as "extravagant beyond defense." In view of the record of the Federal courts he did not believe a return to Federal control was the remedy; but he earnestly advised the legislature to enact a schedule of maximum fees, and in other ways to correct probate abuses.[7]

---

[5] *Ibid.*, LI, 3490.
[6] Secretary of the Interior, Office Files, File 5-127; Indian Office Files, 135712/13 Creek 311.
[7] Indian Office Files, 135712/13 Creek 311.

Senator Owen also made a speech to the legislators warning them plainly that if they should fail to protect the Indian children, Congress would "never take its hands off the eastern side of the state." During the entire session of the legislature and a special session that immediately followed it, the Oklahoma delegation sent urgent letters and telegrams to the Governor, to the presiding officers of both Houses, and to the chairmen of committees, exhorting them to take action. One may search vainly through these insistent communications for some expression of condemnation or concern over the exploitation of the children. A telegram signed by both Senators and the eight Representatives to which Oklahoma had become entitled since the census of 1910, is characteristic. It read: "The numerous investigations of these matters by federal employees report appalling conditions. These reports have been exploited in both chambers of congress. An investigation by our state authorities confirms such reports and finds the derogatory accusations of the Mott report substantially correct. Your delegation is sure to be confronted with these charges and this admission when attempts are made to get legislation. Unless something is done toward outlining a procedure which will regulate and reduce to a minimum the cost of administering these estates, which will give to the incompetent proper representation in the sale of his property and disposition of the proceeds thereof, which will provide hearings in open court after due notice on important matters affecting these estates, and which will generally tighten up our probate procedure along safe and honest lines, your delegation in congress will be unable to get congressional legislation necessary for the development of our state, and it may be extremely difficult to retain such probate jurisdiction as we now have."[8]

The response of the legislature was disappointing. Mott and E. P. Hill of McCurtain and Hill, who was chairman of the Judiciary Committee of the House, worked together in drafting legislation to correct the procedure in the guardianship of mi-

[8] *Congressional Record*, LI, 3490-91; *Muskogee Phoenix*, April 29, 1913.

nors and the approval of sales of inherited property by fullbloods, and to establish the accountability of the guardian who
wasted his ward's property through mismanagement of sales
and investments. Hill succeeded in passing these bills through
the House at both the regular and special sessions, but the Senate Committee on Probate Procedure, of which J. T. McIntosh
of Durant was chairman, blocked the legislation in spite of all
the efforts of the Governor and the Congressional delegation.[9]

Two feeble attempts were made to correct a situation that
had become a national scandal. The law recommended by
Owen prescribing a penalty for recording a deed against a restricted homestead was enacted at this time. Another law limited professional guardians to five wards each; but in the
absence of any improvement in probate procedure, this attempt
to distribute the children more equitably among the despoilers
scarcely benefited the despoiled.[10]

On the other hand, the legislature destroyed the only agency
of the state that had any right to intervene to protect some of
the children from the rapacity of their guardians. This action
may have been taken partly through personal distrust of Dr.
Stolper—M. L. Alexander had probably carried out his threat
to send each member of the legislature a copy of his letter condemning the department for its failure to act upon his charges,
and E. P. Hill may have been honestly convinced that Stolper
had pursued a temporizing policy in the recent McCurtain
County investigation—but there is little doubt that the attack
was inspired in the main by the rage of the guardians who had
been brought to account by the Department of Charities and
Corrections.

Early in the session a House investigating committee, of
which Speaker J. H. Maxey of Muskogee and E. P. Hill were
members, considered charges against Stolper. The Lieutenant-
Governor had pardoned two men who were serving peniten-

[9] Indian Office Files, 135712/13 Creek 311; *Congressional Record*, LI, 3490-91;
*Muskogee Phoenix*, April 29, 1913.

[10] State of Oklahoma, *Session Laws of 1913*, pp. 124-25, 391. See also pp. 59,
103-4.

tiary sentences for selling liquor; and evidence was introduced to show that Stolper had received a fee for presenting their case in his official capacity as Inspector in the Department of Charities and Corrections. The committee adopted a report calling the matter to the attention of the county attorney of Pittsburg County, and condemning Stolper for trips he had made to Washington and other cities [apparently to attend national meetings of friends of the Indians] as "the practice of running and galloping all over the state and part of the continent on every little pretext of official duty." Stolper resigned his position as the result of these charges.[11]

At the same time a House Committee on Efficiency censured Miss Barnard and Huson and Stolper for attending "some national convention" at Boston in 1911, and concluded "that the office of commissioner of charities could be dispersed [sic] with in its entirety and the duties devolving upon it, discharged more economically by county authorities than at present." The committee regretfully admitted, however, that the legislature could not abolish an office created by the constitution, and that it commanded a great deal of popular support.[12]

But Miss Barnard's work could be curtailed by cutting off her appropriation and eliminating her assistants. She herself said that Hill, Maxey, and J. E. Wyand, another member of the legislature from Muskogee, offered to abandon the fight on her department if she would appoint Frank L. Montgomery, also of Muskogee, to fill the vacancy caused by Stolper's resignation. The men denied that they had suggested a "trade" although they had unquestionably recommended Montgomery; but she refused to appoint him, and the legislature destroyed her department by cutting off all the appropriation except her salary.[13]

The Oklahoma delegation had a great deal to explain when Congress convened the following year. Their Republican op-

[11] Muskogee Phoenix, February 14, 20, 26, 1913; Tulsa Daily World, February 26, 1913.

[12] Muskogee Phoenix, March 7, 1913.

[13] Ibid., May 8, 9, 1913; Lake Mohonk Conference, Report, 1914, pp. 21-22.

ponents took pleasure in forcing Ferris, Carter, and Davenport to admit that the Governor had confirmed the truth of the charges they had denied so violently. The Oklahomans were then questioned concerning the action taken by their state to correct the evils that Burke had brought to their attention, and were forced to the humiliating confession that the legislature had done nothing at all. Carter, more candid than his colleagues, admitted that a certain element in the state was attempting to defeat probate legislation; but Joseph B. Thompson, a new Representative from Pauls Valley, failing to profit by the delegation's tactical error of the previous year, insisted that probate conditions in Oklahoma were no worse than in Mann's own state of Illinois.[14]

Oklahoma also had to suffer general condemnation from Eastern friends of the Indians. George Vaux, Jr., chairman of the Board of Indian Commissioners, spent some time in the state in 1912, and he was followed the next year by Warren K. Moorehead, also of the Board, and J. Weston Allen of the Boston Indian Citizenship Committee. Moorehead's report gave specific instances of the exploitation of minors' estates, citing names of men high in public life, and showing how local sentiment was influenced by the magnitude of the plunder. The Department officials decided that since these statements would cause resentment in Oklahoma they had better be suppressed; and the published report, therefore, contained only a general mention of the evil and a pious wish that it might be corrected. Moorehead then published the pamphlet at his own expense. He was aided by the able pen of Grant Foreman, who was deeply concerned lest Congress should yield to pressure and "tear down the pitiful remnant of protection that remains." Moorehead's publication attracted some attention, although it provoked sarcastic local comment about his "short Pullman car trip through eastern Oklahoma."[15]

[14] *Congressional Record,* LI, 3294, 3489-3500. See also LII, 1205.
[15] Moorehead, *Our National Problem;* Moorehead, *The American Indian,* pp. 147, 149; Board of Indian Commissioners, *Annual Report,* 1912-13, pp. 11-12; Lake Mohonk Conference, *Report,* 1913, pp. 56, 61-62; *Nowata Star,* June 20, 1913.

Apparently it was largely the result of Moorehead's influence that the Lake Mohonk Conference in 1913 and 1914 took a decided stand against the wrongs suffered by Oklahoma Indians. Kate Barnard made a remarkable speech in 1914. A perfect storm of emotion swept her audience as, with considerable inaccuracy of detail but deep sincerity of feeling, she told of the destruction of her work and her personal struggle with disillusionment and a sense of futility. She appealed to her hearers to see that her story was told; the local press, she said, profited largely from the unholy traffic she was fighting, and therefore remained silent. John M. Oskison, brilliant Cherokee writer, at that time connected with *Collier's,* said he had talked the Oklahoma situation over with the editors of national magazines and found that "muck-raking" articles and the correction of wrongs were no longer popular; as to the silence of the Oklahoma newspapers, he warned his audience that if Miss Barnard had told her whole story it would have involved "names of some whom even you would not like to have mentioned." As a result of this agitation, both the Lake Mohonk Conference and the Board of Indian Commissioners began to work for increased Federal protection for the Five Tribes Indians.[16]

Although the action of the state legislature in 1913 was a disappointment of all friends of the Indians, there were unseen forces at work that were to effect an improvement. A strong factor in the situation was the greater harmony between the Oklahoma delegation in Congress and the Indian Office after the inauguration of Woodrow Wilson in 1913; but the good effect of this cooperation would have been lost if the national administration had yielded fully to the local hunger for spoils.

Senator Owen had hoped to place an Oklahoman as Secretary of the Interior, but Franklin K. Lane received the appointment. There was some hope that Thomas P. Smith of Muskogee, who had worked so actively in territorial days to defeat the restrictions, would be chosen as Commissioner of Indian Affairs, but the choice fell upon Cato Sells, a Democratic poli-

[16] Lake Mohonk Conference, *Report,* 1913, 1914.

tician of Texas.[17] Like most of his predecessors, Sells had had
no experience in the Indian service and no particular interest
in Indians, but he became deeply and sincerely concerned over
the situation in Oklahoma. He had a flair for publicity that
caused him to fill his reports and the public press with boastful accounts of his achievements; but he was an able executive
and he managed to carry out an independent policy and at the
same time to conciliate local politicians. His administration
marks the period of greatest harmony between the Indian
Bureau and the state.

In the special session of Congress called immediately after
Wilson's inauguration, the Oklahoma Democrats, now controlling the patronage, reversed their policy with regard to
Federal appointees; and the Indian Appropriation Act carried
a generous grant for the Five Tribes work and authorized the
Secretary to expend a portion of the funds for the employment
of probate attorneys. Apparently this item had not been recommended by the Department, and represented the reaction of
Congress to Mott's sensational exposé of the previous year.

Kelsey, with his usual reluctance to interfere with the state
courts, recommended the expenditure of the main part of the
appropriation for the regular field service; applications for the
removal of restrictions and the approval of oil and gas leases
were coming in at the rate of five or six hundred a month, and
"If all of this administrative work is not handled expedi-
tiously, the Department is immediately flooded with complaints
and severely criticized." Wright, on the other hand, recommended that all such activities should be suspended for a time
to let the field force devote all its efforts to probate work. The
Department decided to employ eight probate attorneys, but the
appointments were not made until the beginning of 1914. In
the meantime, the probate work inaugurated in 1912 through
the expenditure of tribal funds under special contract made by

---

[17] *Congressional Record*, L, 2035-38; *Muskogee Phoenix*, February 26, July 20,
1913.

the President, was greatly extended; and ten additional attorneys were employed to assist the regular tribal attorneys.[18]

Mott's administration of this work for the Creek Nation is significant, because more than any other man who served in the Five Tribes area he attempted to analyze the legal defects of the system and to fill the gaps by legislation. During 1913 he prepared a series of masterly reports, each dealing with a separate kind of probate abuse not touched in his famous report of 1912. He had hoped at first that the legislature would correct the evil; but when this plan failed, he tried to induce the Department to work for Congressional legislation to prevent the abuses that lay within the sphere of Federal authority. In the meantime he believed that probate supervision by the tribes was a temporary expedient that might serve as a precedent for a permanent reform.

Six of the eight county judges who had been in office at the time of the report of 1912 had retired at the beginning of 1913. Seven of the eight incumbents were now willing to cooperate with Mott's attorneys, and four referred all guardians' reports to his office for investigation. Citations were issued to delinquent guardians, and as the reports came in, Mott's attorneys checked the expenditures, and in many cases secured the disallowance of the claims by the county judge. One of Hill's ill-fated bills had set a scale of attorneys' fees in the sale of minors' land; and Mott regularly sent a copy of this schedule to each guardian advertising to sell land, with a notification that if the guardian could not secure an attorney at that price his office would do the work without charge. But although he reported a great decrease in the number of sales, he was unable to reduce the extravagant cost; for the guardians preferred to pay exorbitant fees to favored attorneys rather than to avail themselves of the free services furnished by the Creek Nation.[19]

When one considers the immense value of the minors' estates in any Five Tribes county, and the vast amount of plunder that

[18] Indian Office Files, 13520/09 Creek 174.1, 135712/13 Creek 311; Department of the Interior, *Annual Report,* 1914, II, 253.
[19] Indian Office Files, 135712/13 Creek 311.

was passing into the hands of guardians and their attorneys, and into various business channels to influence the press and the pulpit and educational and philanthropic agencies, it is easy to understand why reform was difficult. In Creek County, where the value of the estates had been increased by oil discoveries, it was estimated in 1912 that of the 1,691 probate cases fourteen minors owned estates worth more than $100,000 each, and more than two hundred each owned property valued at over $25,000.[20] But in spite of this corrupting influence, the malodorous publicity that the state had received through the Mott report had put at least part of the citizenship in a frame of mind that Commissioner Sells resolved to utilize.

In October 1913, Kelsey, who had approached the probate evil with such hesitation, recommended a specific appropriation of $50,000 for probate attorneys, and Sells raised the estimate to $75,000. In December the State Bar Association adopted a unanimous resolution favoring "radical reform in the probate procedure of this state."[21] Apparently this was the first expression of disapproval on the part of any influential local group of the robbery of Five Tribes allottees that had been generally and systematically carried on since 1900.[22]

Sells visited Oklahoma early in January. When he arrived at Muskogee, the town presented the appearance of a political convention, with Democrats from all over the state crowding the hotel lobbies and forming in knots to exchange patronage agreements with each other. In the evening he attended a Democratic dinner. The speeches were largely political, entirely frank, and to the effect that undeserving Republicans should be removed from tribal and Federal positions for the benefit of the "right" Democrats. Davenport was quoted as saying that

[20] For notorious Creek County cases see, for example, *Sapulpa Evening Democrat,* March 4, 1912; *Sapulpa Herald,* September 10, 11, 16, 1915; *Congressional Record,* XLVIII, 11404, 11407-10.

[21] Indian Office Files, 135712/13 Creek 311; Department of the Interior, *Annual Report,* 1913, II, 8; *Congressional Record,* LI, 3496.

[22] *House Reports,* 68 Cong., 2 Sess., No. 1527, p. 9. The declaration of the Socialist platform in 1910 is not an exception to this statement, for the Socialists did not represent the influential and prominent classes.

"It was not good principle to take politics out of government. . . . Don't talk to me about republicans holding office during a democratic administration." But Sells showed a disappointing indifference to the welfare of the party. He had spent the day at the Agency in conferences over probate matters, and when he spoke at dinner he failed to mention the real purpose of the meeting, and confined himself to an emphatic exposition of the probate situation.[23]

These events took place on Saturday. On Monday he called a meeting attended by most of the district and county judges of the Creek, Cherokee, and Seminole counties, several county attorneys, and the whole Agency staff; and the county judges adopted rules of procedure following very closely the bills that Hill had introduced in the legislature the year before, and drew up a strong resolution pledging support to Sells, and stating that they would "gladly welcome the assistance of his department and his attorneys." Sells also found time during the day to take lunch with the ministerial alliance, and in the evening he attended a reception given by Muskogee business men.[24]

The next day the tireless Sells spent at McAlester, greatly banqueted by that hospitable town; and the judges of the Choctaw counties also adopted his probate rules. He spent the next day at Ardmore; but he snatched time meanwhile to see Cruce at Oklahoma City, and the Governor issued a public statement of unqualified approval. At Ardmore he was banqueted again, and the probate rules were adopted by the judges of the Chickasaw counties. He returned the next day to Oklahoma City, where the state officials and the leaders of the capital turned out to do him honor. The next day he returned to Muskogee, still refusing to discuss anything but probate reform.[25]

Every stage of Sells' truly appalling itinerary was a triumphal procession. He found the unorganized and inarticulate disapproval with which some lonely individuals had watched

23 *Muskogee Phoenix,* January 3, 4, 1914.     24 *Ibid.,* January 6, 1914.
25 *Ibid.,* January 7, 8, 10, 1914.

the swindling, the humiliation which a self-conscious citizenship had suffered under the weight of national censure, the joyous local pride and hospitality of a new community; and he was able to sweep it all into the swelling tide of his reform.

The rules required guardians to file complete annual or semi-annual reports covering receipts and disbursements, the condition of the bond, and the domicile, schooling, etc., of the ward; and any failure to report constituted grounds for removal. Certain court days were to be set aside for public hearings of guardians' reports, and notice was to be given the Interior Department or the probate attorney. Certain days were also to be set aside for the sale of land, and a scale of fees was established. Oil and gas leases were to be sold to the highest bidder in open court. Safeguards were provided for the investment of funds and the expenditure of income. Upon the final accounting, the ward was to be brought into court, and stenographic notes of the proceedings were to be taken and filed with the papers in the case. Land inherited by fullbloods was to be sold only after advertisement, notification to the probate attorney, appraisement, and testimony by the heirs in open court. No will of a restricted Indian covering land was to be admitted to probate without notice to the Department or the tribal attorney. At first the observance of these rules was voluntary; but on June 11, the Supreme Court formally adopted them under its constitutional authority to prescribe procedure for inferior courts.[26]

The importance of these rules can be appreciated by contrasting them with a report made by the State Examiner and Inspector the same month they were formulated. The report stated that one county judge was accustomed to telephone to favored individuals when minors' oil leases or land was to be sold, take them into his office and lock the doors, and sell to the highest bidder present. An instance was given of three allotments of minors of which the oil leases had recently been sold by the lessee to another oil company for $100,000; and

[26] Department of the Interior, *Annual Report*, 1914, II, 271-74.

the county judge approved the sale of the entire allotments for $5,200.[27] When Sells' probate rules were put into effect, this procedure became impossible.

Obviously the success of this reform depended largely upon the character of the probate attorneys. It is apparent that the Indian Office under Sells' administration tried to make good appointments. The examination of one typical application in detail is an enlightening experience, for it presents almost a complete cross-section of contemporary conditions, and motives, and procedures.

It will be remembered that in 1912 Representative Carter read a letter to Congress from Judge Mitchell of Garvin County condemning the district agents. Mitchell was elected to the legislature that year, and became one of the active leaders in the opposition to Miss Barnard's department. He was succeeded as county judge by W. R. Wallace, who immediately invited the cooperation of the Federal officials.

Garvin County was one of the rich agricultural counties of the old Chickasaw Nation. William A. Baker, as Chickasaw probate attorney, and a man from Kelsey's office assisted in checking the guardians' reports. They found that a large number of the children's allotments had been sold. In a majority of the cases they listed, it was a white or mixed-blood father rather than a professional guardian who had managed the estate; but each guardian usually had several children, and the amount realized from the sales often ran from $15,000 to $20,000 and in one case reached $56,775. They charged the guardians with squandering this money, and a number of criminal prosecutions were instituted. By November 1913 one father had been convicted in the district court and sentenced to the penitentiary for five years, and fourteen other guardians were facing charges involving misappropriation of amounts totaling $170,000. At that time Wallace made an almost desperate appeal to Kelsey for an attorney to assist him permanently. He said that it was customary to appoint an attorney

27 *Muskogee Phoenix*, January 31, 1914.

to act as guardian *ad litem* in contested cases; but it was difficult to find one who would act, because of local pressure and because it was more profitable to serve as attorney for the guardian. He believed an attorney employed by the Government to be the only solution, and was extremely anxious for the probate attorneys authorized by the recent appropriation to be appointed.[28]

In the fall of 1913, at the very time that the investigation was at its height, Mitchell applied for a position as probate attorney. He collected a sheaf of recommendations, and Representative Thompson presented them to the Indian Office. These letters usually stated that Mitchell was an intermarried Choctaw, that he had lived twenty-three years in the Chickasaw Nation, that he had served as county judge, and that he was a member of the legislature, all of which facts were relevant; but they stressed such qualifications as "loyal party worker," "life-long Democrat," "an avowed fighter for the Democratic Party in season and out of season," and "The night was never too dark for him to get up to go help a friend or to help the Democratic party." These recommendations form a file literally a half-inch thick, and were written by such prominent Oklahomans as: Attorney-General West and three of his assistants; J. H. Maxey, Speaker of the House, and a number of Representatives; Senator J. T. McIntosh; the three judges of the Criminal Court of Appeals; Robert L. Williams, justice of the Oklahoma Supreme Court; William H. Murray, J. B. Thompson, and Claude Weaver, of the Oklahoma delegation in Congress; the Secretary of State, the State Treasurer, the president of the State Board of Agriculture, and the State Superintendent of Public Instruction; the president of one of the largest state colleges; Governor Douglas H. Johnston, of the Chickasaw Nation; the state president of the Anti-Horse Thief Association; the mayor, the Methodist and Presbyterian pastors, officials of three banks, real estate dealers, a large number

[28] Indian Office Files, 77012/13 Union 175, 4236/14 Five Tribes 350, 4854/14 Union 175.3; *Pauls Valley Free Lance*, June 16-20, 1913; January 12, 15, 1914; *Daily Oklahoman*, June 17, 1913; *Nowata Star*, January 16, 1914.

of attorneys, and the editors of two newspapers of Pauls Valley; the county treasurer, the county superintendent of schools, and several other officials of Garvin County; and long lists of business men from the small towns of the vicinity. Only one of these writers expressed any degree of caution; Murray stated that Mitchell stood high in the state, but that he personally was entirely unfamiliar with his record as county judge and that he believed the Department should investigate it before making the appointment.

Two lonely protests went up to combat this overwhelming endorsement. Kate Barnard sent a telegram, and Judge Wallace reminded the Bureau officials of the letter Carter had read in the House and of the recent records in their own files of guardianship conditions in Garvin County. One of Wallace's letters was signed by County Attorney Stanley, a few other city and county officials, and the editor of the *Pauls Valley Free Lance,* the one newspaper that in the face of overwhelming opposition had defended the guardianship prosecutions. An office memorandum for Commissioner Sells enumerated the imposing list of recommendations, but advised that in view of the protests of Miss Barnard and Judge Wallace the appointment had better not be made.[29]

In protesting against another applicant, who was eminently qualified for the position because he had worked for Woodrow Wilson *before* the national convention, Miss Barnard wrote an earnest but dignified letter explaining that her own work in behalf of Indian minors had been cut off, and requesting an opportunity to present the facts regarding the past record of every applicant before he should receive an appointment. Her protest in this case was successful, but her request for consultation was not granted, and she was deeply chagrined when Frank L. Montgomery received one of the appointments in the Creek counties.[30]

[29] Indian Office Files, 146702/13 Five Tribes 162.
[30] *Ibid.,* 120070/13 Five Tribes 162; Lake Mohonk Conference, *Report,* 1914, pp. 24-25.

The eight probate attorneys were selected early in 1914. Congress, with the Oklahoma delegation in active leadership, made a more specific appropriation for the next fiscal year, and twenty were appointed. The tribal contracts expired June 30, 1914, and the work was financed entirely by the Federal appropriation. Technically the probate attorneys worked directly under the Commissioner of Indian Affairs, but at first each tribal attorney formulated the policy and assumed the active direction of those who worked within his territory.[31]

Unlike the district agents, the probate attorneys worked for both restricted and unrestricted allottees, and they had no other duties. Whether their work is examined in the detailed reports or the statistical summaries, it presents an imposing accomplishment. During the first six months of 1915 they instituted 213 civil actions involving $1,525,377, and 37 criminal actions; secured the removal of 602 guardians and the filing of 713 new bonds covering $687,500; saved to minors and others $462,111; represented allottees in 415 sales of inherited land and 151 sales of minors' allotments; and obtained 43 quitclaim deeds. There were at that time 52,045 probate cases pending in the Five Tribes area.[32]

There was, of course, the possibility that minors' estates might be plundered by collusion between the probate attorney and the county judge, but they were protected as far as it was humanly possible to protect them. Kelsey reported in June 1914 that only three judges were disregarding the probate rules. But unfortunately 1914 was an election year, and in a number of counties judges who had adopted the rules and been conscientious in enforcing them were facing defeat by opponents who openly advocated a return to the old conditions. Sells was genuinely distressed when he learned of this complication,

---

[31] Department of the Interior, *Annual Report*, 1915, II, 387, 413; *Congressional Record*, LI, 3294; Indian Office Files, 43333/14 Five Tribes 352; *Sapulpa Evening News*, February 18, 1914; *Standard-Sentinel*, February 19, 1914.

[32] Indian Office Files, 43333/14 Five Tribes 351; Department of the Interior, *Annual Report*, 1915, II, 33-34.

but he warned the Federal employees that it was essential for them to remain neutral in local politics.[33]

Most of these attacks were unsuccessful, but H. Tom Kight of Rogers County, who had bitterly assailed County Judge Walter W. Shaw for his adoption of the probate rules, was triumphantly elected. As soon as he went into office he set the rules aside and denied the right of the probate attorney to appear in any matter involving the fifteen hundred Cherokee cases pending before his court. Owen Owen, the probate attorney, appealed, and the Oklahoma Supreme Court upheld its own authority to adopt probate rules and the right of the probate attorney to represent the Indian wards of the United States. The state Attorney-General's office sent a letter of congratulation to Owen, and offered the fullest cooperation of the department in securing honest administration of Indian estates.[34]

There is no doubt that this reform in probate procedure grew directly out of the Mott report, but Mott himself was sacrificed to popular clamor. Sells refused to commit himself when he visited Muskogee in 1914, but within a few days it was apparent that Mott could not stand against the enmity he had created. He had interfered with the exploitation of Creek allotments in eight counties representing an oil wealth running into staggering figures; he had held up the Oklahoma probate courts to the execration of the nation; he had humiliated the members of Congress from Oklahoma in a way that their Republican opponents would never let them forget; and he had initiated a prosecution that forced the Governor of the state and the former chairman of the Dawes Commission to relinquish some of their profits in Creek townsites.

He was engaged at the time in the prosecution of Wagoner County guardians. As a result of the Mott report of 1912 and the investigation ordered by the Governor early in 1913, a grand jury had returned indictments against a number of

---

[33] Indian Office Files, 49983/14 Five Tribes 350.

[34] *Ibid.*, 69135/14 Five Tribes 160.3, 4236/14 Five Tribes 350; *Pacific Reporter*, CLII, 362-65, decision of October 12, 1915; *Nowata Star*, October 15, 1915.

guardians in August, and in November and the first few days
of December thirty more were indicted. The Wagoner County
investigation followed a pattern too familiar for repetition: the
condemnation of guardian frauds by District Judge R. C.
Allen; the prominence of the men who were indicted; the activity in their behalf by the local bar; the indignation of the local
press over the "persecution" of "our best and most prominent
citizens," and the unqualified rejoicing when the court fund
was exhausted and "There being no money available for juries
very little harm was done the community"; and the final ac-
quittal of nearly all the defendants. Some of the trials were in
progress during January 1914 when Mott's contract as Creek
attorney expired, and this circumstance did not contribute to
his popularity.[35]

Moty Tiger made every effort to save his attorney, and
although the voice of Mott may be heard in these letters, the
hand is the hand of Tiger, and there is no doubt that they
express the old Chief's sentiments. Warren K. Moorehead also
intervened in Mott's behalf. The Secretary finally sent for
Mott to come to Washington for a hearing, and for six days he
defended himself against the united attacks of the Oklahoma
delegation.[36]

At the same time Inspector Trowbridge was sent to Oklahoma to investigate Mott's standing there. Mott's closest friend
could not have testified more eloquently of the essential loneli-
ness of his position than did his enemies in their accusations
against him. One judge declared that in all the years Mott had
lived in Muskogee he had never attended a lodge, a civic meeting, or a social function, that he had never helped to build a
park or found a church. Another judge stated that he was
*persona non grata* to nine-tenths of the men, women, and children of Muskogee, and for that reason was unsuccessful before

[35] *Wagoner County Courier*, August 14, 1913; *Wagoner County Record*, November
27, December 4, 18, 25, 1913; February 5, 12, 19, 26, March 19, 1914; *Muskogee
Times-Democrat*, November 26, December 1, 5, 1913; *Muskogee Phoenix*, November 21, 25, 26, December 6, 1913; January 10, 11, 1914; Indian Office Files,
135712/13 Creek 311, 43333/14 Five Tribes 352.
[36] Indian Office Files, 13520/09 Creek 174.1.

any judge or jury. The local Democratic organization was unanimous in demanding his removal.[37] A slur constantly cast at Mott was that he was a "carpetbagger," that he owned not one foot of land in Oklahoma—a strange charge in view of the tendency shown by even the best of Federal appointees to enrich themselves by speculating in Indian land.

Secretary Lane decided to yield to these considerations. At the end of the investigation he wrote to the disappointed Chief, characterizing Mott as "a brave man, a conscientious man, and an able man," giving him full credit for the exposure of the guardian frauds and the aroused public sentiment that had culminated in the adoption of the probate rules, but stating his decision that another attorney could secure better cooperation from the courts and the people of the state. In the letter notifying Mott that he had decided against the approval of his contract Lane said, "I shall always take pleasure in contemplating the manner in which you conducted yourself during the inquiry here. That you have been honest under difficulties and fearless at all times in doing your duty, seems to be admitted even by those to whom you have been most antipathetic."[38]

Mott remained in Oklahoma, where he exerted a strong unofficial influence upon the policy of the Indian Office during this and the succeeding administration. This influence was not always wholesome—his own point of view may have been warped somewhat by personal bitterness—but for the ten years that he served the Creeks his name is written large upon their history.

Judge R. C. Allen, mainly upon the basis of Mott's recommendation, was appointed as his successor.[39] Allen, both individually and through the Coweta Realty Company, had been extensively engaged in land transactions. Apparently most of his purchases had been made after the expiration of the Creek restrictions in 1907 under the contention that the McCumber Amendment was unconstitutional; the Marchie Tiger case, in

[37] *Muskogee Phoenix*, February 4, 5, 12, 1914.
[38] *Congressional Record*, LI, 10928-30; Indian Office Files, 13520/09 Creek 174.1.
[39] *Muskogee Phoenix*, January 4, 6, February 13, 1914.

fact, was a Coweta Realty Company case. He was said to be a defendant in seventy-three cases of the Thirty Thousand Land Suits, forty-six of which were still pending at the time of his appointment as Creek attorney. The impropriety of this connection may be realized from the fact that he was consulted in his official capacity by Linebaugh with regard to dropping the suits of unrestricted allottees.

Moty Tiger had consented to Allen's appointment, but in 1915 he and other Creek leaders opposed the renewal of his contract. Brosius of the Indian Rights Association went to Oklahoma to investigate, and protested to Lane against his employment as Creek attorney while the Federal Government was suing him on behalf of the Creeks. In 1916 and 1917 James S. Davenport tried to remove him by fighting the appropriation for his office, and he supported his arguments in Congress by documents to show specific details of Allen's real estate dealings. Strong opposition to Allen developed throughout the Creek counties.[40] The records of his office indicate, however, that he rendered the Creeks some good service in probate matters. His usefulness was impaired by his own land transactions, but it is apparent that part of the opposition to his continuance in office came from those whose exploitations he was attempting to curb.[41]

Except for the removal of Mott, Sells made few concessions to local politicians. He even followed a somewhat independent policy with regard to the Agency.

It had been apparent for some time that the maintenance of separate offices for Wright and Kelsey caused useless duplication, and as early as 1910 the Indian Office had recommended a consolidation. After the Democratic victory of 1912 the Oklahoma Congressmen seized upon this plan to increase their

[40] *Ibid.*, June 4, 25, July 1, 1915; *Supreme Court Reports,* LV, 738-50; Indian Office Files, 111840/14 Five Tribes 175.2; *Congressional Record,* LIV, 229-32, appendix, 488-93; Federal Court Records, Eastern District of Oklahoma, Journal XXI, 304; LXVI, 247-48; LXVII, 512.

[41] *Congressional Record,* LIV, 232; Indian Office Files, 43333/14 Five Tribes 352; *Sapulpa Evening Democrat,* February 18, 21, March 14, 1914; *Sapulpa Herald,* July 1, September 10, 11, 1915.

patronage; and in 1914 they secured the abolition of the two positions and the creation of a Superintendent for the Five Civilized Tribes who should be a spoils appointee.[42]

Wright was transferred to another branch of the Indian Service, and Kelsey received an excellent position with the Prairie Oil and Gas Company, which was glad to use his comprehensive knowledge of Indian land matters. Thirty politicians applied for the new position, but the members of the Oklahoma delegation could not agree upon a candidate, and Sells made a personal selection. The choice fell upon Gabe E. Parker, a mixed-blood Choctaw, who had been a member of the Constitutional Convention, and was at that time Register of the Treasury. As soon as he took charge of the office he was besieged by a horde of hungry applicants for positions, but most of the work was under civil service regulations. Fifty-nine employees including sixteen field clerks, were dropped from the force because of the saving effected by the consolidation. If proper care was exercised to place the names of undeserving Republicans on this list, the politicians may have found some comfort; for the new probate attorneys, of course, were all Democrats.[43]

From the standpoint of appointment by merit there was little difference between the Republican employees, who had obtained their positions through the favor of Northern politicians and had received their civil service status by executive order, and the probate attorneys, who owed their appointment to the endorsement of local Democrats. But Miss Barnard, ill and disillusioned, regarded the probate attorneys with profound distrust; she saw only that a civil service group had been legislated out of office to make way for spoils appointees.

---

[42] Department of the Interior, *Annual Report*, 1912, II, 425; Indian Office Files, 5642/09 Five Tribes 013; *Congressional Record*, XLVIII, 4436-37; L, 2097; LI, 3294, 3678-80, 3719-20, 10924-32, 12832-35; Kappler, *Laws and Treaties*, IV, 23-24; *Nowata Star*, March 14, 1913; *Standard-Sentinel*, February 5, 1914.

[43] *Nowata Star*, December 25, 1914; *Sapulpa Herald*, January 8, 11, 1915; *Muskogee Phoenix*, January 3, April 3, June 22, 1915; *Muskogee Times-Democrat*, March 29, May 16, 1916; *Congressional Record*, LI, 3487-88, 10925-27, 12832-35; LIII, 8418.

Miss Barnard's own work had not entirely stopped when the legislature cut off her appropriation. Eastern friends of the Indians made voluntary contributions for the necessary running expenses of her office, but after the elimination of her attorney she seems to have dropped the legal work and to have confined her efforts mainly to agitation. She refused to be a candidate for reelection in 1914; but she began to organize what she called a "people's lobby" to work with the legislature for probate laws, child labor laws, and the support of the Department of Charities and Corrections.[44]

She attempted to organize the state by counties to defeat hostile candidates in the election of 1914. She came to Muskogee to fight Wyand, who was a candidate for mayor, and Maxey, who was seeking election to Congress. Both men were defeated, although Wyand did serve a few years later as mayor of Muskogee. In October and November she spoke throughout the state to packed and wildly cheering audiences. At the close of these meetings men, apparently working men, crowded up to sign an agreement to go to Oklahoma City during the next session of the legislature and fight personally for the maintenance of the department and the restoration of its legal work. She secured from her audiences a large number of twenty-five- and fifty-cent contributions to employ an attorney and a stenographer for her "people's lobby," and to maintain a mailing list to inform constituents of the actions of their legislators.[45]

When the legislature convened in 1915, Miss Barnard, whose term had just expired, was actively on hand as the representative of the "people's lobby." In February she distributed a circular to the members charging that thirteen bills to "rob Indians" were pending before the legislature. At one time she was granted the privilege of the Senate floor, and spoke for ten minutes pleading for the protection of Indian minors and condemning prominent members for their legislative record. A hostile newspaper—and most of the newspapers were hostile to

[44] Lake Mohonk Conference, *Report,* 1914, pp. 23-26.
[45] *Ibid.,* 1914, p. 25; *Sapulpa Herald,* November 18, 1914; *Muskogee Phoenix,* March 17, May 9, 1914.

Miss Barnard at this time—reported that she even lobbied on the floor during a roll call, going from one Senator to another and urging them to vote in favor of a bill to enact the probate rules into a statute.[46]

It was hoped by others than Miss Barnard that the legislature would give legal sanction to the probate rules. The county judges of the state had formed an organization, and had elected W. R. Wallace as president. This group met in Oklahoma City and drafted a number of bills. Allen took an active part in this work; and he also held conferences with legislators and with Governor Robert L. Williams, who had just succeeded Cruce. He brought two of his probate attorneys, one the son of a prominent legislator, and the other a close friend of the Governor, to the capital to assist in the passage of the bills. There is little doubt that Sells had authorized Allen to take this course, but when Allen reported his activities, an employee of the Indian Office initialed on the margin, "This is not advisable." Sells then telegraphed Allen not to call the probate attorneys away from their posts of duty again without consulting him.[47]

A prolonged battle over probate legislation raged throughout the entire session, and again as in 1913 the state failed to take the hoped-for action. The House defeated a Senate bill providing attorneys in the Department of Charities and Corrections to protect Indian minors, and only one section of the probate procedure—the section dealing with fullblood conveyances of inherited land—was enacted into law. Even this law was a step backward, for it eliminated most of the safeguards adopted by the former rules; it dropped the compulsory advertising, notification to the probate attorney, and testimony by the heirs in open court, and left most matters to the discretion of the county judge. It did attempt to abolish one unpleasant feature of Indian land transactions by the provision

[46] *Sapulpa Herald*, March 11, 1915; *Muskogee Phoenix*, February 28, March 13, 1915.
[47] *Sapulpa Herald*, January 14, 1915; Indian Office Files, 43333/14 Five Tribes 352.

that no deed should be approved within thirty days of the death of the decedent.[48]

It was disappointment over the action of the legislature that caused the Indian Office to appeal the Kight case to test the validity of the Supreme Court adoption of the probate rules.[49] This decision established the binding force of the rules as fully as though they had been enacted into law, except that the portion relating to fullblood conveyances had been superseded by statute and was no longer effective.

Miss Barnard had said that if she failed to secure legislation through her "people's lobby" she would carry the fight to Washington and demand that the Federal Government resume its jurisdiction over the Indians; but probably because of her illness she dropped out of active life after her efforts with the 1915 legislature. The Board of Indian Commissioners, completely hopeless of any reform by the state, strongly urged this action in its report for 1915; but the Congressional appropriation for the probate attorneys and Sells' work in securing the adoption of the probate rules ended the contribution of the Federal Government to probate protection.[50]

The United States, however, exercised jurisdiction over a large field in which it had never relinquished control. The administration of the undivided tribal property and the supervision of individual restricted allottees will be the subject of the next chapter.

[48] *Senate Journal*, 1915, *passim*; *House Journal*, 1915, *passim*; Indian Office Files, 28028/15 Five Tribes 013; State of Oklahoma, *Session Laws of 1915*, pp. 330-31; *Muskogee Phoenix*, March 18, 1915.

[49] Lake Mohonk Conference, *Report*, 1915, p. 64.

[50] Department of the Interior, *Annual Report*, 1915, II, 434-35; Board of Indian Commissioners, *Annual Report*, 1915, pp. 8-9.

CHAPTER X

# Federal Administration Within the State

ALTHOUGH it had been expected when the agreements
were made with the Five Tribes that the work of the
Dawes Commission would be entirely completed by
1906, a vast amount of unfinished work remained to be carried
out after statehood. The Federal Government showed a tendency to prolong the process of closing the tribal estates and to
expend tribal funds extravagantly for the supposed benefit of
the Indians; but the members of Congress from Oklahoma
carried out the desires of both their Indian and white constituents by forcing a stricter accountability than had been observed during the Federal period. At the same time that Federal
administration of tribal affairs gradually decreased, the successive removal of restrictions decreased the number of Indians
whose individual affairs were under the supervision of the
Union Agency. In 1914 both branches of the work were consolidated under the Union Superintendency.

The tribal governments gradually declined in importance or
passed entirely out of existence. Pleasant Porter died in 1907,
Green McCurtain in 1910, and W. C. Rogers in 1917; the
Seminole tribal officers were asked to resign in 1915; but
Douglas H. Johnston lived on until 1939 as the only executive
elected during the days of the tribal governments. With the
death of the elective Chiefs a shadowy executive was continued
irregularly through Presidential appointment, but the office
eventually lapsed in all tribes except the Choctaw and the
Chickasaw. These appointments were frankly regarded as
spoils by Oklahoma politicians.[1]

[1] Department of the Interior, *Annual Report,* 1916, II, 55; 1918, II, 438; Superintendent, Office Files, Report of A. G. McMillan, 1928; *Muskogee Times-Democrat,*

Tribal attorneys were employed under contract with the President upon recommendation of the Chief. The Seminole position was discontinued before statehood, with the exception of Gresham's special work in clearing up fraudulent land transactions. The appointments for the other tribes roughly approximated the continuance of the tribal executive. For a short period beginning with Mott's supplemental contract in 1912 these attorneys were very active in probate matters; but Sells notified them in 1915 that the probate attorneys as Federal rather than tribal employees were under his own supervision. The tribal attorneys were then limited to tribal instead of individual matters, and they usually devoted part of their time to private practice.[2]

The Choctaw Council, which continued to meet longer than any other, held its last session in 1911.[3] But the Indians, with their genius for group action, continued to hold conventions and to maintain voluntary organizations. The Seminoles never ceased to maintain their fourteen band organizations with a chief and two councilmen from each, and these forty-two officers met once a month to discuss tribal affairs, appoint committees, and adopt resolutions. The Kee-too-wahs and Nighthawks continued to flourish among the Cherokees. The Choctaws and Chickasaws met in frequent conventions to petition for the sale of their tribal property and to resist the raids on their rolls to which they were exposed by their vast undivided wealth.[4]

After the Indians had once consented to a division of their property, they had a natural desire to secure their individual

June 4, July 4, 30, 1923; October 20, November 23, 1925; December 28, 1928; August 16, October 25, 1929.

[2] Indian Office Files, 43333/14 Five Tribes 352; Kappler, *Laws and Treaties*, IV, 431, 489, 928.

[3] Department of the Interior, *Annual Report*, 1911, II, 454; Kappler, *Laws and Treaties*, III, 542.

[4] Senate Committee on Indian Affairs, *Survey of Conditions of the Indians in the United States* (Washington, 1931), XIV, 5754, 5756, 5831; *Congressional Record*, LII, appendix, 930-32; LIII, 125-26; *Sapulpa Evening Light*, June 24, 1911; *Muskogee Times-Democrat*, November 1, 1911; *Muskogee Phoenix*, October 29, 1914.

shares as soon as possible. They were supported in their demands by their white neighbors; prospective purchasers were eager to acquire and develop the land that was lying unproductive, and the distribution of millions of dollars of tribal funds would stimulate business throughout the Five Tribes area. As soon as Oklahoma was represented in Congress its delegation worked uniformly for this object.

The Indian Appropriation Act of 1908 authorized the Department to sell the public buildings of the tribes. The most important ones were acquired by the towns or counties where they were located or by the state government, and are still in use as public buildings. These unromantic business transactions were fraught with significance, marking as they did the passing of a great era; and the buildings are still regarded by the Indians with melancholy interest as memorials of their lost citizenship.[5]

The amount of unallotted land subject to sale was approximately as follows: Choctaw-Chickasaw, 3,053,816 acres; Cherokee, 50,985 acres; Creek, 65,965 acres; and Seminole, 4,223 acres. Wright began to sell this land in the fall of 1910, and most of it was disposed of within the next three years. The Choctaw-Chickasaw freedmen under a provision of the Five Tribes Act were allowed to purchase 21,134.95 acres "at the appraised valuation" in spite of the indignant protests of the Indians, and the rest of the land was sold at auction to the highest bidder at prices usually running slightly above $6.00 an acre.[6]

These sales did not include the Choctaw-Chickasaw timber land that had been so arbitrarily set aside by the Department. Most of this land was sold during 1914-16, but the sale of the remainder dragged on for many years. During the period that

[5] Kappler, *Laws and Treaties*, III, 319; Department of the Interior, *Annual Report*, 1909, II, 414, 452, 454; 1910, II, 197-98; 1912, II, 445; 1913, II, 452-53; 1919, II, 349; *Nowata Star*, June 20, 1913; *Standard-Sentinel*, July 2, 1914.

[6] Department of the Interior, *Annual Report*, 1910, II, 201-2; 1911, II, 385-402; 1912, II, 434, 437; 1913, II, 417-23, 452-57; 1914, II, 219; Kappler, *Laws and Treaties*, III, 175-76; *House Reports*, 61 Cong., 3 Sess., No. 2273, Vol. I, p. 519; Acts of the Choctaw Nation, October 6, 1910.

it was in Departmental hands millions of feet of pine were stolen by lumber companies.[7]

The Choctaws and Chickasaws were very impatient over the delay in disposing of their unallotted land, but they were almost desperate over the failure of the Government to carry out the Supplemental Agreement for the sale of their coal and asphalt. At first they hoped that they might sell to the state. In the statehood election the Democratic platform declared for the purchase, and when the first legislature convened, a committee appointed by the Constitutional Convention to investigate the matter made a favorable report. The legislature then memorialized Congress for authority to negotiate with the tribes. Gore presented the memorial to the Senate, and Carter actively supported the plan in the House, but no action was taken.[8] The Indians had been forbidden to sell to a private purchaser; their suggestion that the United States should acquire the land had been rejected with scorn; and now they were not permitted to sell to the state. The first plan may have been vetoed through fear of monopoly, but the rejection of the last two looks suspiciously like a favor to the lessees.

In the meantime in spite of the competition of oil as a fuel the royalties from 1909 to 1920 ran from $200,000 to $250,000 a year. The investigation and appraisement authorized by the Five Tribes Act was completed in 1909, and the total valuation was placed at $18,913,969—a figure surprisingly close to the unofficial offer of $15,000,000 reported by Green McCurtain in 1905.[9]

But even after the appraisement was made, the Indian Office was unwilling to sell. Finally the Oklahoma delegation in Congress decided to compromise, and in 1912 they secured legisla-

[7] Department of the Interior, *Annual Report,* 1907, II, 345; 1909, II, 388-89; 1912, II, 52, 440-41; 1914, II, 225-40; 1915, II, 31, 336-37; 1916, II, 56; 1917, II, 49, 52; Superintendent, Office Files, Report of C. L. Ellis, 1926, p. 15; Acts of the Choctaw Nation, October 26, 1905.

[8] *Select Committee,* II, 1639-41, 1752-53; Corden and Richards, *Oklahoma Red Book,* II, 355; *Congressional Record,* XLII, 5049; *Muskogee Times-Democrat,* August 13, 1908.

[9] Department of the Interior, *Annual Report,* 1908, II, 223; 1909, II, 400, 411; 1910, II, 51, 219; 1917, II, 180; 1919, II, 369.

tion for the sale of the surface, subject to the mining rights. The sales began in 1914, and most of the work was completed during the next three years. In 1919 it was reported that the unallotted, timber, and segregated mineral land sold for the Choctaws and Chickasaws since 1910 had brought the staggering total of $19,775,436.08.[10]

The Oklahoma delegation continued to work for the sale of the minerals. It had long been apparent that the development of the oil industry had destroyed the Indians' market, but when the United States entered the World War it was believed that conditions were once more favorable for the sale. Carter finally managed to secure the passage of a law in 1918 providing that the minerals should be sold at auction subject to the rights of the lessees; and during the next two years a small amount was sold for $2,338,432.94. Another attempt at sale was made in 1925, but it was largely unsuccessful.[11]

The royalties declined sharply after 1920. The income that year in spite of the sales that had been made was $236,075.51, but it had dropped to $88,843.81 by 1928. The administration of the mines became very lax during the 1920's. The operators were allowed to become delinquent in paying the royalties on coal actually mined and sold, and an unknown amount in deferred payments due on the 1918-1925 sales remained uncollected.[12]

Nothing illustrates more strongly the discouragement of the Indians regarding the procrastination of the Government than the celebrated incident of the McMurray contracts. It will be

[10] Indian Office Files, 5642/09 Five Tribes 013; State of Oklahoma, *Session Laws of 1910-11*, pp. 387-88; *Congressional Record*, XLVI, 883, 1040, 2608; XLVII, 560, 2307, 2753, 3668; XLVIII, 867-79, 4168, 4791-93; Kappler, *Laws and Treaties*, III, 513-16; *Muskogee Phoenix*, August 15, 1914; Department of the Interior, *Annual Report*, 1919, II, 345, 349.

[11] *Congressional Record*, LIV, 272-73; LVI, 39-45, 189-212; Kappler, *Laws and Treaties*, IV, 143-45, 215, 287; Department of the Interior, *Annual Report*, 1918, II, 434; 1919, II, 341, 350-53; 1920, II, 14-16; Superintendent, Office Files, Report of Shade Wallen, 1923, p. 16.

[12] Department of the Interior, *Annual Report*, 1920, II, 55; *Congressional Record*, LXVI, 4100-1; LXX, 2723-24; *Survey of Indians in the United States*, XIV, 5502-4, 6570-76.

remembered that in 1905 they were facing the complete extinction of their governments and that there was not the slightest disposition on the part of the United States to observe the terms of the agreements and close their estate, and they were deeply concerned at the prospect that their vast property would pass completely under Federal control. They decided, therefore, to sacrifice one-tenth of their possessions to secure the remainder.

In the fall of 1905 the executives of both tribes acting under authority conferred by the Councils signed contracts with Mansfield, McMurray, and Cornish and with Cecil A. Lyon of Sherman, Texas, to effect the sale of the mineral land upon a contingent fee of 10 per cent. They had included Lyon for his political influence; he was Republican National Committeeman and State Chairman, and they had been given the impression that he was influential with President Roosevelt. These contracts were not binding, for they had not been submitted to the President; they had been adopted, in fact, to thwart the policy of Secretary Hitchcock, and it was necessary that they be kept secret.

It was at this time that McCurtain informed the Council of the offer he had received for the mineral land, and it is entirely possible that it had come through the attorneys. The attorneys and tribal officials continued to work actively but fruitlessly for the sale. Finally, in 1908, McCurtain submitted the contract to Wright, explained the whole transaction with the utmost frankness, and requested that it be disapproved. Governor Johnston, however, still supported the Chickasaw contract.

By this time Mansfield, McMurray, and Cornish were no longer in active partnership, and in 1909 the firm was dissolved and all its interests were assigned to McMurray. McMurray never attempted to claim under the unapproved tribal contracts, but in the fall of 1908 he began to send out agents and secured contracts with a large number of individual allottees. By these instruments he was to prosecute in court all unsettled claims against the United States and procure the sale of all undivided tribal property and its per caput distribution; and he was to receive as compensation 10 per cent of all claims collected and 10 per cent of the common property. The contracts were to run for five years.

Governor Johnston advised his people to sign these agreements. McCurtain on the other hand worked actively to defeat them. He protested to Secretary Ballinger, he sent out a letter to his people warning them that the contracts were illegal because no individual had the authority to convey the property of the tribes, and he influenced the Council to petition the Federal Government for protection against these commitments.[13]

Early in 1910 McMurray attempted to secure approval of the contracts by President Taft, but Father William Henry Ketcham of the Board of Indian Commissioners, S. M. Brosius, and the Oklahoma delegation in Congress made vigorous protests to the President and he was not successful. He almost succeeded in securing Congressional approval, but was defeated through the vigilance of Senator Gore and Representative Carter. Gore and Representative Creager then charged that Jake Hamon, who was in Washington in the interest of Governor Haskell in the town lot prosecution, had approached them and offered them a bribe if they would withdraw their opposition. The House accordingly voted an investigation.[14]

The investigating committee came to Oklahoma, and took an immense mass of testimony, which is eloquent of the general weariness of the Indians over the unsettled condition of their affairs. It was also discovered that many of the Indian leaders were financially interested in the approval; Green McCurtain, in fact, testified that a prominent tribal official had offered him a 25 per cent interest in the contracts if he would withdraw his opposition. It was, of course, impossible to determine the relatively unimportant question as to whether Hamon had attempted to bribe members of Congress or whether he had been

[13] *Congressional Record,* XLV, appendix, 496-507; *Court of Claims Reports,* LXII, 460-61; *Muskogee Phoenix,* August 17, 1910; Acts of the Choctaw Nation, October 12, 1909; *House Reports,* 61 Cong., 3 Sess., No. 2273, I, 43-53, 548 ff.

[14] *Congressional Record,* XLV, 8620, 8878-80, 8903-4, 8963, 8969, 9109-13, appendix, 489, 508; *House Reports,* 61 Cong., 3 Sess., No. 2273, I, 7, 8, 209, 233 ff.; II, 714.

authorized by McMurray; the committee decided that Hamon had made the offer, but exonerated McMurray from any proved connection with the affair.[15]

McMurray continued to work for the approval of the contracts, but Gore finally secured legislation providing that no contracts for the Five Tribes would be valid unless the consent of the United States had been previously given. In 1918 Congress provided that the many claims for services rendered by Mansfield, McMurray, and Cornish should be audited by the Court of Claims; but the next year the law was amended to exclude claims relating to the sale of the segregated or unallotted land.[16] This ended a sinister influence in tribal and Federal politics that grew directly out of the failure of the United States to carry out its pledges to the Indians.

The anxiety of the Indians to dispose of their property arose from their old dissatisfaction with the Federal administration of their finances. In 1912 the Oklahoma delegation managed to secure legislation forbidding the expenditure of tribal funds without specific appropriation; but the principle observed by Congress was the same as that followed by the Indian Office during the period of its irresponsible control, and the Indians continued to bear the expense of dividing the tribal estates.[17] At the same time, according to several impartial studies made between 1915 and 1928, the Indian Office practised such chaotic accounting methods that it was impossible to differentiate between tribal funds and gratuities from the Government.[18]

[15] Lake Mohonk Conference, *Report,* 1913, pp. 30-31; *House Reports,* 61 Cong., 3 Sess., No. 2273, I, xix-xxx, 38, 62-119, 142-46, 162-69, 251, 280-96, 336 ff.

[16] Lake Mohonk Conference, *Report,* 1913, pp. 30-31; *Congressional Record,* L, 2042-47; LI, 10722; *Sapulpa Evening Democrat,* May 12, 1913; *Muskogee Phoenix,* May 25, 28, 1913; Parker La Moore, *Pat Hurley* (New York, 1932), pp. 61-64; Kappler, *Laws and Treaties,* IV, 169, 230.

[17] Department of the Interior, *Annual Report,* 1912, II, 317-21, 458, 475; *Congressional Record,* XLV, 2222; LXVIII, 4380-86, 4431-48, 4452, 11403; Kappler, *Laws and Treaties,* III, 506, 542; IV, 78, 914; Lake Mohonk Conference, *Report,* 1913, p. 39.

[18] Laura Cornelius Kellog, *Our Democracy and the American Indian* (Kansas City, 1920), appendix, pp. 134-46; Laurence F. Schmeckebier, *The Office of Indian*

It seemed to be easier to get the tribal funds out of the United States treasury for every other purpose than the division among the citizens according to the agreements made with the Dawes Commission; but by 1912 the litigation that had delayed allotment had been settled, the property was in process of sale, and the Department was anxious to complete the distribution.

The Cherokee estate was settled first. This populous tribe had expended so much of its funds to compensate those citizens who had failed to receive allotments that the per caput distribution was very small. A payment of $15 was made in 1912, $12 in 1915, and $3.30 the next year; and the estate was closed in 1920. The Cherokees still owned a few pieces of unsalable land, and they hoped to secure the adjudication of several claims against the United States.[19]

The Seminoles were not rich in land, but their population was so small that they received large per caput shares when the trust funds were distributed. Each Seminole received $734— $20 in 1909, $50 in 1911, $20 in 1912, $200 in 1913, $300 in 1916, $34 in 1917, and $100 in 1918. So far as it was possible the estate was closed in 1920, but oil was subsequently discovered on the ground of one of their boarding schools, and in 1934 they received a $35 payment from this unexpected source.[20] It seems unfortunate that these Indians who had so much money to their credit were in such dire poverty in 1910 that many of them lost their land because it was virtually impossible for them to advance the small amounts required by Gresham to clear it of forged deeds. There was no reason for the delay of the Seminole distribution except general inertia.

The Choctaws and Chickasaws received $40 in 1904, $35 in 1906, and $20 in 1908 from their townsite sales, and $50 in

*Affairs* (Baltimore, 1927), pp. 509-13, 527-28; *Senate Docs.*, 70 Cong., 2 Sess., No. 263, pp. 39-40, 109, 115-16.

[19] Department of the Interior, *Annual Report*, 1912, II, 502; 1915, II, 378-81; 1920, II, 8; Kappler, *Laws and Treaties*, III, 510-11; IV, 26-27, 168.

[20] Department of the Interior, *Annual Report*, 1912, II, 502; 1913, II, 493; 1914, II, 295; 1918, II, 67; Superintendent, Office Files, Report of A. M. Landman, 1932, p. 4; 1935, pp. 3, 6, 17-18; *Wewoka Democrat*, October 6, 20, 27, 1909; Kappler, *Laws and Treaties*, III, 579; IV, 76-77, 121-22, 215; *Statutes at Large*, XLVIII, 146; *Congressional Record*, LVI, 6632.

1911 from their trust funds, but the division of the proceeds from their land and timber sales encountered almost unsurmountable obstacles. Senator Jeff Davis of Arkansas and Representative Stephens of Texas were especially zealous in behalf of the "court citizens" and freedmen—Stephens said in 1908 that fully ten thousand of these two classes were entitled to enrolment[21]—but the strongest effort was made in the interest of the Mississippi Choctaws by the legislature and Congressional delegation of Mississippi.

The Department for a time seemed unopposed to the reopening of the rolls. One special investigator reported without any attempt at satire that such a policy "would prove an easy and quick method of disposing of the surplus, and might possibly hasten rather than retard the final disposition of the land problem." But the Indian Office finally prepared a list of 312 persons apparently entitled to citizenship in the five tribes, and in 1914 Congress with the consent of the tribal attorneys added their names to the rolls.[22] By this time the Department had taken a firm stand against further opening of the rolls, but it is almost certain that the Choctaws and Chickasaws would have lost all their undivided property if it had not been for the vigilance of the Oklahoma delegation in thwarting a conspiracy that was almost nationwide in its ramifications.

The fight began to assume a serious aspect in the 1912-1913 session of Congress. The two tribes had at that time a cash balance of over five and a half million dollars, deferred payments on their land sales of five and a quarter million more, and unsold property valued at nineteen and a half million.[23] The members of Congress from Mississippi began to introduce bills for the enrolment of the Mississippi Choctaws without any removal requirement and with the right to share in all per caput distributions and to receive a cash payment in lieu of allotment; and for several years they succeeded in blocking all

21 *Congressional Record*, XLII, 1849-69, 6190-92; XLV, appendix, 24; L, 2084.
22 *Ibid.*, LI, 7603, 10669-70, 10726, 10756-67; LII, 1245-46, 5149; *Senate Docs.*, 62 Cong., 3 Sess., No. 1139.
23 *Congressional Record*, L, 208, statement by J. George Wright, February 8, 1913.

appropriations for per caput payments to the enrolled members of the tribes. Ostensibly their efforts were on behalf of the exploited fullbloods, but the bills they introduced were so worded as to enroll every white or Negro in the United States who could prove remote descent from a Choctaw ancestor. The Mississippi legislature also memorialized Congress to the same effect.[24]

Byron P. Harrison began the fight in the House of Representatives. He supported his measure in a speech that for its many misrepresentations, its maudlin sentimentality, and its unsound conclusions is almost a masterpiece of chicanery. He spoke grandiloquently of the constant friendship which the Choctaws had shown to the white man and the wrongs that they had suffered at the hands of the United States and the state of Mississippi—for those who had emigrated to the West, the bitterness of exile, and for those who chose to remain, the faithlessness and cruelty of the Federal agent who had refused to allot them and the degraded condition to which they had been reduced by the exploitation of Mississippi whites. Dramatically he asked how the United States could refuse to right so great a wrong to these faithful people when not one cent would come out of the Federal treasury, but the entire cost would be borne by the tribe. He used almost pure invention in building up a fantastic story to the effect that the Choctaws in the West had monopolized the property that belonged to their brothers in Mississippi, and had reached the climax of their selfishness by paying a firm of attorneys to keep these deserving people from the rolls. John Sharp Williams, who was now in the Senate, and James K. Vardaman, his colleague, used the same arguments in the other House—arguments that were to become familiar to the point of nausea during the weary years that followed.[25]

[24] *Congressional Record,* LI, 2089, 3717, 8729, 10672-73, 10713-28, 10765-68, 10947-51, 11013-18; 11468-69, 11719-49, 11938, 12942-44; LII, 997-98, 1194, 1211-73, 1295-1303, 5074-75, 5143-62, 5361-5407, 5445, 5524-27, appendix, 928-30.

[25] *Ibid.,* XLIX, 556-60, 955; L, 955, 1286, 2083-93.

Patrick J. Hurley, the Choctaw tribal attorney, and Major James McLaughlin, an inspector of the Indian Office, made a quiet investigation and unearthed some illuminating material, which was presented to Congress by the Oklahoma delegation. During 1910 and 1911 speculators had secured thousands of contracts carrying a 30 to 35 per cent contingent fee, from citizenship claimants in all parts of the United States. One firm had even been capitalized for $100,000 and a large number of shares had already been sold. A letter was read in Congress from this company to a prospective investor urging him to purchase twenty of these contracts for twenty-five dollars each: Choctaw citizenship was worth $8,000, and the 30 per cent contingent fee would be divided equally between the attorneys and the investor; hence the investor would realize a profit of $23,500 upon his $500. Another letter was produced from a firm of Ardmore attorneys that specialized in freedman contracts. These men claimed to possess 13,000 contracts, of which they were willing to assign a share; and the lucky purchaser was certain to receive $120 for every dollar invested. Still another speculator had collected contracts from the Glenn-Tucker family. This numerous group was descended from a woman born in 1760, said to be half Choctaw, who had left the Choctaw Nation in her infancy. They were scattered all over the United States and had never been recognized as members of the tribe. The Choctaw government had spent thousands of dollars and years of litigation in defeating their claims long before the Dawes Commission was created.[26]

Another inspector in the Indian Office reported that affidavits to prove the case of the Negro claimants had been secured through professional Negro witnesses who received fifty cents to $2.50 for every thumb print they placed on the record. The enterprising Hurley then went to the state penitentiary and secured the photographs of the witnesses wearing the convict numbers which they had borne while serving time for various

[26] *Ibid.*, LI, 10720-22, 11729-36; Debo, *op. cit.*, p. 183.

crimes; and Ferris displayed them to the House of Representatives.[27]

Gore, Owen, Carter, and Ferris also presented historical and legal arguments that were irrefutable, but the interests of the speculators and the claimants were so widely distributed that several members of Congress were subject to pressure from their constituents. On the other hand it is apparent that many of the legislators were genuinely perplexed as to the merits of the controversy, and wished to take no action that would make the United States liable for damages in case the claim should later prove to be a just one. The history of the Choctaws and of their relations with the Federal Government was not available in any published form, and the average member of Congress could hardly be expected to undertake the research necessary to expose the falsity of the statements made by the Mississippi delegation.

In the Indian Appropriation Act of 1914 the Mississippians permitted a per caput payment of one hundred dollars to the Chickasaws, apparently not understanding the joint property interests of the two tribes; but the Choctaw case seemed as hopeless as ever. The Indians became greatly aroused over the situation. Delegates from fourteen of the seventeen extinct counties of the old Nation assembled at McAlester and selected the prominent Choctaws, W. A. Durant, who had long served as Speaker of the Oklahoma House of Representatives, and D. C. McCurtain, to go to Washington and assist the Oklahoma members of Congress. They also instructed Hurley to institute mandamus proceedings to compel the Secretary to distribute the tribal funds under existing law.[28]

Finally in 1916 the Mississippians failed in their efforts to block the legislation, and the Indian Appropriation Act carried a per caput payment of three hundred dollars for the Choctaws and two hundred for the Chickasaws.[29] The Missis-

---

[27] *Congressional Record*, LIII, 2174.

[28] *Ibid.*, LII, appendix, 930-33; Kappler, *Laws and Treaties*, IV, 26-27; *Sapulpa Herald*, October 2, 29, 1914; March 6, 1915.

[29] *Congressional Record*, LIII, 1925-28, 2158-75, 2180, 4922-30; *Muskogee Times-Democrat*, February 8, 1916; Kappler, *Laws and Treaties*, IV, 76-77.

sippians then began to work for a Federal appropriation for educational and social work among their neglected fullbloods. In 1918 they secured $75,000 for this purpose, although they had to listen to some sharp condemnation of the treatment of this defenseless people by the citizens of their state.[30] There is no doubt that these Indians had been greatly wronged by the Federal Government and the state of Mississippi, and it was their fate to be used as helpless puppets by those who wished to seize the possessions of their brethren in the West.

Subsequent distribution of the tribal funds was secured with little difficulty as balances accumulated in the treasury. The Choctaws received $300 in 1916, $100 in 1917, $200 in 1918, $140 in 1919, $100 in 1920, $50 in 1921, $25 in 1924, and $10 in 1929—a total, with previous payments, of $1,070. The Chickasaws received a total of $1,075 through a somewhat different series of payments.[31] The difference in the per caput shares of the two tribes is due to the fact that their trust funds and governmental expenditures had always been separate.

The appropriation act usually authorized the Department to supervise the expenditure of the shares of restricted Indians. When the largest per caput distribution ever made was authorized by the law of 1916 providing $300 to the Seminoles, $300 to the Choctaws, and $200 to the Chickasaws, the Indian Office prepared elaborate regulations. The checks were mailed to unrestricted adults, and the shares of unrestricted minors and adults under legal disability were paid to their guardians upon proof of satisfactory bond and good standing. Payment to restricted Indians might be withheld and expended by the Agency for their benefit; or it might be paid directly to adults and to the guardians of minors, but the guardians in this case were required to secure the approval of the probate attorney. The shares of deceased members were not turned over to the administrators, but were paid to the heirs under the same regu-

[30] *Congressional Record,* LIV, 228-29; LVI, 1136-43, 5113, 6687; LIX, 1239-41, 1452.

[31] *Ibid.,* LXIX, 8730-31; Kappler, *Laws and Treaties,* IV, 121-22, 353, 389, 431; Superintendent, Office Files, Report of A. M. Landman, 1932, p. 4.

lations as the shares of original allottees. No powers of attorney were recognized.[32]

When it is realized that this one payment totaled nine million dollars, its importance to the state may be understood. During the three years preceding 1918 the total distribution, including Creek equalization, was more than nineteen million dollars. Of course it was not a gratuity from the Federal Government to the state as some Eastern members of Congress professed to believe. A small portion of the money came from trust funds that the Federal Government had held for many years; but the bulk came from the sale of property in Oklahoma, and simply represented a business transaction between citizens of the state. The money derived from the latter source had been deposited in local banks ever since the Oklahoma delegation in Congress secured a law to that effect in 1911.[33]

Ironically enough the importance of these payments created a mighty zeal for clean government and law enforcement. In Seminole County, which was entitled to almost a million dollars in the 1916 distribution, the business men and county officers delivered an ultimatum to the liquor dealers, and that turbulent community became a model of sobriety and good order. In Choctaw, Pushmataha, and McCurtain counties, which were entitled to even larger shares, Superintendent Parker suspended the payments because of crime and unsatisfactory probate conditions. The righteous indignation which this act produced changed almost immediately to a moral revival, with mass meetings of citizens, armies of special police and deputies, and suppliant delegations to Muskogee. In McCurtain County alone at the end of the two months and a half that it remained under this interdict twenty-four persons had been convicted in the district court for every imaginable crime and were already in the penitentiary serving sentences ranging from one to ninety-nine years.[34]

[32] *Congressional Record*, LIII, 1300-1.

[33] *Ibid.*, XLVI, 341; LIII, 4922; LVI, 6632; Department of the Interior, *Annual Report*, 1912, II, 438-39; 1917, II, 22; Kappler, *Laws and Treaties*, III, 499.

[34] *Muskogee Times-Democrat*, July 18, 21, 26, August 14, 18, October 27, Novem-

But the Indian still ran a financial hazard from more legitimate business men, who were glad, no doubt, that their chief rivals had been eliminated. As soon as he emerged from the postoffice with his check he was forced to run a gauntlet of creditors, salesmen, and promoters of various schemes. As one old Choctaw expressed it, "Choctaw, he gets $300, Chickasaw, he gets $200. White man, he gets $500." Parker reported, however, that many Indians showed considerable sales resistance and deposited their money in banks to be used for their actual needs.[35] But it is apparent that whether the Indians used the money thriftily for living expenses or extravagantly for luxuries it contributed in no constructive way to their permanent economic advancement.

Since the tribal funds of the Creeks were insufficient to equalize their allotments, these Indians received no per caput payments. In 1913 the Federal Government began suits in their behalf that it was hoped would increase their wealth enormously, but the attempt was largely unsuccessful.

Because of the errors that had occurred in making out the Creek rolls several citizens received two allotments under different names, or allotments were made to the heirs of those who had died too early to be entitled to enrolment. Some of these mistakes were corrected with little difficulty, but this group, of course, had received arbitrary allotments of undesirable land, and in 1913 the value of some of this land soared to fantastic heights by the discovery of the great Cushing oil pool in Creek County. If the United States could have succeeded in canceling even one or two allotments in this section, the equalization matter would have been settled with probable per caput payments besides. But the oil companies holding leases from various individuals claiming to be the original allottee or from

ber 16, 1916; April 3, 1918; *Idabel Democrat-Record*, July 20, August 10, 17, 24, October 11, December 14, 1916; *Sapulpa Herald*, July 25, 26, 28, 1916; Department of the Interior, *Annual Report*, 1917, II, 22-23; 1918, II, 77-78.

[35] *Sapulpa Herald*, August 19, 1916; Department of the Interior, *Annual Report*, 1917, II, 23.

rival groups claiming to be heirs fought with each other and the Federal Government for possession of the leases.

Among the allotments involved were: the Barney Thlocco, where the Federal Government claimed that the Indian had died shortly before the rolls were opened; the Tommy Atkins, where it was doubtful if such person had ever existed; the Emma Coker, said to be a duplicate for Hettie Lena; and about a dozen others. Before some of these cases were settled the accumulated royalties aside from the value of the land itself ran into millions of dollars. In 1917 the United States Supreme Court decided in the Barney Thlocco case that the Dawes Commission had exercised great care in making the rolls, and that in absence of proof of fraud or gross error the cancellation would reopen so many questions and disturb so many titles that the Dawes rolls should stand. This settled the question so far as recovery by the Creek Nation was concerned, but litigation between rival groups of heirs continued for many years and swallowed up most of the estate.[36] The Creek Nation lost the Tommy Atkins case through a similar ruling, but the ensuing litigation between oil companies and their protégés was even more complicated than the Barney Thlocco litigation. Five living "Tommys" and three "mothers" of deceased "Tommys" appeared at one time, each sponsored by an oil company holding a lease, and supported by an army of witnesses. The allotment finally went to one Minnie Folk, who managed to prove that she had given birth to an illegitimate son named Tommy Atkins, and the lease went to Charles Page, well known oil millionaire and philanthropist of Sand Springs, who had discovered Minnie and developed the allotment under the lease she had given him.[37] The Creek Nation also lost the Emma

[36] *Muskogee Phoenix*, May 7, 8, 1915; May 11, 1919; March 26, 1922; *Muskogee Times-Democrat*, February 18, 25, 1924; *Federal Reporter*, CCLXXIII, 113-19; *Supreme Court Reports*, LXI, 1024-36.

[37] *Muskogee Times-Democrat*, September 12, 1916; May 1-30, June 6, 7, 1917; May 13, June 21, 1918; February 13, November 13, 1920; June 6, November 20, 1930; February 11, 1932; *Muskogee Phoenix*, January 19, February 26, 27, March 4, 5, 9, 20, 1915; July 15, 28, 29, August 23, September 10, 1921; March 19, 1922; *Sapulpa Herald*, March 6, 1916.

Coker case before the Circuit Court of Appeals upon the same principle of the integrity of the Dawes rolls, but the man who secured title to the land compromised for $75,000. One other compromise settlement was made for $50,000.[38] These two settlements represent virtually all the gains which the Creek Nation made from the suits.

At the same time the United States tried to recover for the tribe the portion of the Cimarron River bed that lay in the Cushing pool. This claim was contested by the state of Oklahoma and by the Creek allottees that were the riparian owners and the oil companies that held leases from them. Royalties amounting to millions of dollars were impounded under receiverships, until the case was finally decided in favor of the riparian owners.[39]

In 1915 when highest hopes were entertained for the cancellation of the allotments and the recovery of the river bed for the Creek Nation, attorneys became interested in four or five Creek minors who had not yet received allotments because they had filed on contested land and had lost the contest. Ironically enough M. L. Mott, recently dismissed from the service of the Creek Nation for guarding its interests too vigilantly, was the most active of these attorneys. The prospect of selecting allotments for these Negro children—all but one were Creek freedmen—in the heart of one of the richest oil fields in the world opened up dazzling possibilities. The Department recommended legislation withdrawing from allotment any land that should be recovered, and it was supported by the Oklahoma delegation; but several members of Congress whose constituents held contingent contracts expended as much lachrymose eloquence in behalf of these humble Creeks as the Mississippians were devoting to their Choctaws. They managed to block the legislation, but President Wilson, acting upon a

[38] Attorney-General, *Annual Report,* 1921, pp. 91-92; Indian Office Files, 43333/14 Five Tribes 352.

[39] *Muskogee Times-Democrat,* May 1, 1923; January 24, 1924; December 24, 31, 1925; January 30, May 5, 1926; February 2, 1928; *McAlester News-Capital,* February 26, 1926; Department of the Interior, *Annual Report,* 1913, II, 449-50.

recent Supreme Court decision in a California case, withdrew the land by executive order. When the Federal Government failed to recover the oil land for the tribe, the children received a money payment in lieu of allotment; but the incident illustrates a technique painfully familiar to students of Indian legislation.[40]

As the tribal revenues shrank or stopped entirely through equalization and per caput distributions, and as the tribal property was disposed of by successive sales, the number of tribal schools progressively declined. But the hope that the Indian children would fit easily into a state school system was seen to be illusive; consequently as the tribal support of schools diminished, it was supplemented by Federal appropriations.

The Cherokee tribal school system came to an end in 1913 when the Federal Government purchased the one remaining plant and began to operate it for the education of restricted orphans of the Five Tribes. Two schools were maintained from Creek funds until 1928, when the United States assumed their support. Unlike the other tribes the Seminoles desired the continuance of their boarding schools; but the permanent school fund set aside by their agreements was distributed without their consent in per caput payments and their last school was closed in 1930. The Agency officials on the other hand tried to persuade the Choctaws and Chickasaws to set aside a permanent endowment for their schools, but the Indians continued to request that the schools be abolished. Finally in 1932 the one school remaining to the Chickasaws and the two remaining to the Choctaws were placed on Federal funds.[41]

[40] *Sapulpa Herald,* March 16, April 9, July 7, September 22, 1915; July 1, 1916; *Congressional Record,* LII, 5419-30, appendix, 717-19; House of Representatives, Committee on Indian Affairs, *Withholding Certain Lands from Allotment in the Creek Nation* (Washington, 1915); Kappler, *Laws and Treaties,* IV, 124.

[41] *Survey of Indians in the United States,* XIV, 5295, 5719-23, 5730-31, 5736, 5741, 5753, 5847-54; Department of the Interior, *Annual Report,* 1917, II, 60; 1918, II, 436; Kappler, *Laws and Treaties,* III, 579; Subcommittee of House Committee on Appropriations, *Interior Department Appropriation Bill for 1931,* pp. 136-37, 523-24; *Statutes at Large,* XLVII, 106; Superintendent, Office Files, Report of Victor Locke, 1921, p. 83; 1922, pp. 75, 78.

In the educational reorganization that took place in 1910 the Government began to send Five Tribes Indians to the non-reservation boarding schools of Chilocco on the West Side and Haskell in Kansas. Additional boarding school facilities were provided, especially for the Choctaws, by the payment of tribal money for tuition to denominational schools that received Indian children under contract.[42]

The public schools which the Indians attended in the remote fullblood settlements were very poor. Funds were insufficient; often half the land was non-taxable, and although the Federal Government continued to pay tuition for the Indian children the amount averaged only ten or twelve cents for a day's attendance. Bad roads, poverty, and indifference to education on the part of both Indians and whites contributed to the bad situation. The state had a compulsory attendance law, but little attempt was made to enforce it in the rural districts. The Federal census of 1910 showed that more than one-third of the Indian scholastic population was not enrolled in school, and there is no reason to believe that there was any subsequent improvement.[43]

This same census of 1910 was the only statistical survey ever made of the educational situation. At that time the Interior Department had been operating the schools for ten years, but all except the younger group had grown up under the tribal régime; hence these statistics are significant as an indication of the achievements of the tribal schools and of the task awaiting the Federal Government and the state in completing the work the tribes had begun. It should be pointed out that the high illiteracy among the Choctaws was partially due to the recent immigration from Mississippi. Only persons of appreciable

---

[42] Department of the Interior, *Annual Report*, 1914, II, 258.

[43] Bureau of the Census, *Indian Population in the United States and Alaska* (Washington, 1915), pp. 206-7; Lewis Meriam and others, *The Problem of Indian Administration* (Baltimore, 1928), p. 417; *Interior Department Appropriation Bill for 1931*, pp. 540-44; Department of the Interior, *Education of Indians in Oklahoma* (Washington, 1922).

Indian blood were included in the enumeration. The statistics are as follows:[44]

| | Total pop. 10 years and older | Number of illiterates by age | | | | | | Unable to speak Eng. | |
|---|---|---|---|---|---|---|---|---|---|
| | | 10-14 | 15-19 | 20-29 | 30-39 | 40 up | Total | 10-19 | 20 up |
| Cherokees | 18,827 | 383 | 432 | 826 | 585 | 1256 | 3487 | 506 | 1515 |
| Choctaws | 9,265 | 210 | 207 | 510 | 413 | 1063 | 2445 | 387 | 1516 |
| Chickasaws | 2,551 | 32 | 34 | 58 | 70 | 176 | 376 | 24 | 136 |
| Creeks | 4,503 | 151 | 176 | 462 | 414 | 666 | 1889 | 237 | 1053 |
| Seminoles | 1,044 | 55 | 89 | 120 | 124 | 193 | 583 | 133 | 386 |

The census of 1920 showed that Indian illiteracy in the full-blood sections of the Five Tribes ran from 25 to 37.4 per cent.[45]

It is difficult to evaluate the general effect of the Federal educational policy; but it may be safely said that after a generation of this training the conservative fullbloods were no more fitted to cope with a competitive economic society than they were when they were first thrown upon the white man's mercy in 1900. Social work for the adult Indians was even more ineffective, probably because it was never undertaken upon a sufficiently important scale to accomplish results.

In 1910 six "expert farmers" were assigned to Kelsey's office, and the number was soon increased to twelve. High hopes were expressed of the influence which these workers would exert in showing the Indians how to develop their own farms instead of leasing them and living in dire poverty upon the inadequate rental. Obviously six or twelve men could not exert any revolutionary influence upon thousands of allottees, but they were men entirely without the agricultural and sociological training that is now expected of a farm demonstration agent. They soon fitted into the field clerks' offices as appraisers and

---

[44] *Indian Population in the United States and Alaska*, pp. 220-21, 238-39. The totals include illiterates of unknown age and therefore run slightly in excess of the numbers given in the age columns.

[45] Bureau of the Census, *Fourteenth Census of the United States* (Washington, 1922), III, 815, 829-30.

handy men, and the Agency and the Commissioner continued to publish glowing reports of the agricultural progress of the Indians, while the Indians themselves gradually forgot even the simple farming methods that had been sufficient for their needs in a more primitive society.[46]

The health work also proved to be abortive. It is not known when the Five Tribes Indians became infected with tuberculosis, but it is certain that in tribal days it had been a serious menace to health among the Choctaws, and it probably existed to the same extent in some of the other tribes. From 1912 on the Agency began to point out the prevalence of the disease but no systematic health work was authorized by Congress or the central office. The last session of the Choctaw Council requested that a tract of tribal land be set aside at Talihina and that $50,000 in tribal funds be appropriated to erect a tubercular sanitorium there, with the understanding that its subsequent maintenance be provided by the United States. Congress accordingly made the appropriation of Choctaw-Chickasaw money, and the institution was opened for the citizens of the two tribes in 1916. It was an excellent sanitorium, but it never became popular with the Indians, and had very little influence in checking the ravages of the disease. Almost as serious to the general well-being if not the lives of the Five Tribes Indians was trachoma. It was first reported by Linnen in his sensational exposé of boarding school conditions in 1909; it was then said to exist to an alarming extent in some of the schools and to be spreading rapidly among the children because of the insanitary conditions that prevailed. There is no indication that the boarding schools ever again became centers of infection, but Kelsey reported in 1913 that the disease was serious throughout the Five Tribes area, and it was constantly mentioned from this time on in official reports. Superintendent

[46] Department of the Interior, *Annual Report*, 1910, II, 222; 1911, II, 434-35; 1912, II, 505; 1913, II, 497; 1918, II, 442-43; 1924, p. 25; 1926, p. 25; Superintendent, Office Files, Report of Shade Wallen, 1924, p. 4; *Survey of Indians in the United States*, XIV, 6639.

Wallen reported in 1923 that both tuberculosis and trachoma still seemed to be on the increase.[47]

The failure of the Federal Government to undertake definite medical and social work among the Five Tribes was due to their previous independent history. They had prospered under tribal institutions with no help from the United States, and it was believed that they had reached a stage of development where they required no guidance. Kelsey constantly called attention to the necessity for social work, and Parker urged it as the greatest need of the Five Tribes, but it must be admitted that the Agency did not make the most of the limited opportunities that Congress provided. During the whole period the field workers tended to become office workers; adding columns of figures and making reports seemed a more tangible employment than assisting a hopeless people to enter with zest into a new form of living. From the Superintendent down, all the workers were untrained. If they had had specialized training in social case work, agriculture, domestic science, or public health nursing, and if they had possessed some knowledge of anthropology, ethnology, and related social subjects, their vague intentions might have crystallized into definite action.

Kelsey, Parker, and their successors blamed the system of agricultural leasing that existed under the law of 1908 for the failure of the Indians to make a proper agricultural effort. As long as the allottee could legally surrender his surplus for five years and dispossess himself of his homestead for one year the speculator continued to monopolize his land. Few fullbloods knew even the location of their surplus and for many years thousands of Snakes refused even to claim their allotments; hence the "lease grafter" easily possessed their property through unconscionable contracts, forgery, or no lease at all. Kelsey estimated that about a million dollars was lost to unrestricted allottees every year through inadequate rentals, but

[47] Department of the Interior, *Annual Report*, 1912, II, 504; 1913, II, 487-97; 1917, II, 60, 352-60; 1918, II, 349-51; 1919, II, 335-37; 1920, II, 14; Superintendent, Office Files, Report of Shade Wallen, 1923, pp. 12-14, 78-80; Debo, *Choctaw Republic*, p. 233; Indian Office Files, 2272/10 Indian Territory Schools 150.

very few could be persuaded to seek assistance in drawing up the long term leases over which the Department exercised control.[48]

Although the Department officials desired to supervise the leasing of restricted land, they took active steps to relinquish control over Indians believed to be competent. In this matter they proceeded arbitrarily, with no recognition of the fact that the tribes had surrendered to the United States in return for valuable considerations specified in the agreements, including restriction against alienation and exemption from taxation.

When the district agents were first appointed in 1908 Secretary Garfield directed them to urge all competent persons to apply for the removal of restrictions, and if they encountered refusal to report all such cases to him. "The law undoubtedly gives the Secretary peremptory power to remove restrictions without application but such authority will not be exercised until after full opportunity has been given to the Indian to show why his restrictions should not be removed." In 1910 Commissioner Valentine began creating competency commissions to examine individual Indians throughout the United States and remove restrictions from all who appeared capable of managing their own affairs. He believed such a policy would "so relieve all proper land-hunger in the regions round about, that the pressure to open reservations should lose some of its momentum." Secretary Lane and Commissioner Sells were more energetic in pushing this policy, which Sells hailed as "the dawn of a new era" and "the beginning of the end of the Indian problem"; and more Indians were released from restrictions by Departmental action during the Wilson era than in any other period.[49]

[48] Lake Mohonk Conference, *Report*, 1915, pp. 178-81; Department of the Interior, *Annual Report*, 1913, II, 487; 1914, II, 284-86; 1915, II, 364-65; Superintendent, Office Files, Report of Victor Locke, 1921, pp. 29-30; Report of Shade Wallen, 1923, p. 81; Report of C. L. Ellis, 1928, p. 6.

[49] Indian Office Files, 72545/08 Five Tribes 311; Robert G. Valentine, "Making Good Indians," *Sunset Magazine*, XXIV (1910), 601-8; *Muskogee Phoenix*, July 16, 1913; Department of the Interior, *Annual Report*, 1917, II, 3-5, 12-13, 41.

Competency commissions began working in the Five Tribes in 1916. They were composed of one or two general Indian service officials and the field clerk of the district. They began under the general authority of the Indian Office; but Charles D. Carter, who was an ardent supporter of the policy, secured a specific appropriation of $15,000 in 1918. The amount eventually dropped to $5,000, but the appropriation was continued until 1928.[50]

In 1920 John R. Wise, who had been working for three years in Oklahoma and other states, and had removed the restrictions from 931 Five Tribes Indians, explained his methods to a committee of the House of Representatives. The commission made a house-to-house canvass and interviewed every restricted Indian. It required from fifteen minutes to half an hour to examine each case. In passing upon competency Wise considered education desirable but not a final test; he declared that some of the best cases he had passed were fullbloods who had no education whatever.

Wise was asked what became of the Indian after he had been declared competent. He said that it was difficult to answer; the Indian Office dropped such individuals immediately and had no more contact with them. He himself had had little opportunity to check results, for in all but one region he had gone over the ground only once; but he *had* made two surveys about a year apart in three Choctaw counties, and had received the impression from his second visit "that the percentage of failures was not any greater than we could expect," and that perhaps 50 per cent of the released Indians "still own a portion of their allotment."[51]

During the fiscal year 1917-1918 restrictions were removed from 652 Five Tribes Indians by the competency commission, and from 162 by recommendation of Superintendent Parker; and other years showed similar activity. After 1920 an increas-

[50] *Muskogee Times-Democrat*, June 2, 1916; Kappler, *Laws and Treaties*, IV, 152 ff.; *Congressional Record*, LVI, 1063; LIX, 1193-96, 1540-58.

[51] House of Representatives, *Indians of the United States*, III (*Investigation of the Field Service*), 58-74.

ing proportion of the removals were made upon recommendation of the Agency, and in 1926 in spite of the Congressional
appropriation the competency commission was not employed.
In 1919 a blanket order from Sells removed the restrictions
from the 1,309 adult half-bloods, who it will be remembered
were restricted only as to homesteads by the law of 1908. The
next year an additional ninety-two, apparently young people
who had just attained their majority, came under this order,
but the practice was discontinued in 1921 at the close of the
Wilson administration.[52]

Some of the Indians objected to this unsolicited grant of
competency. Parker testified before the House committee in
1920 that an increasing number of Seminole, Creek, and Choctaw fullbloods individually or in small delegations claiming to
speak for groups had come to him to protest that they were unable to compete with the white man's commercial system. At the
same time John Burgess, an influential Seminole fullblood, and
a number of his fullblood neighbors secured the services of a
compatriot who was able to write broken English, and addressed a number of earnest letters and petitions to the Commissioner of Indian Affairs and later to President Harding.
They said that the only Indians who favored the grant of competency were in the pay of the land dealers or were thriftless
and desired to squander their children's heritage; and that they
would lose their property, and their children born after the allotment period would be paupers.[53]

Wise testified that most of the Indians he examined desired
competency. He had no compunction about forcing the status
upon an unwilling recipient in other parts of the United States,
but with the Five Tribes he "hesitated" to take such action because of the pledge the Government had made in the agreements. The committee warned him that the only way the Indian

[52] Department of the Interior, *Annual Report,* 1918, II, 444-45; 1920, II, 21;
Superintendent, Office Files, Report of Victor Locke, 1921, pp. 28-29; 1922, p. 3;
Report of Shade Wallen, 1923, p. 3; 1924, p. 4; 1925, p. 5; Report of C. L. Ellis,
1926, p. 30.

[53] *Indians of the United States,* III, 28; Indian Office Files, 32108/19 Seminole
306.

Office could refute the frequent charge that it was keeping competent people under tutelage in order to keep the service in operation indefinitely was to "cooperate" with Congress in the removal of restrictions; and he hastened to explain that his "hesitation" was only temporary and did not affect the result.[54]

If the newly emancipated allottees did not sell their land at once, the delay was not due to lack of opportunity. As soon as the first commission began its work, the Agency and the Indian Office were swamped with inquiries from real estate and farm loan dealers asking for a list of competents. In 1928 the Department officials for the first time exhibited some curiosity regarding those allottees whose names they had so summarily erased from their rolls, and they directed a questionnaire to the field clerks regarding the welfare of unrestricted Indians. The answers varied widely, for the field clerks had no official contact with this class, but most of them stated that an overwhelming majority were entirely destitute and were living with relatives who still retained their allotments.[55] Another widely advertised effort to elevate the Indians by external means had come to a sorry end.

The Department also continued to cut the size of the Indians' holdings by conditional removal of restrictions—advertising and sale of the land by the Agency, and investment of the proceeds in the improvement of the homestead and the purchase of livestock and farm machinery. In his first instructions to the district agents in 1908 Secretary Garfield urged that such sales "should be made as soon as possible without sacrificing the Indian's real welfare," and Commissioner Valentine advocated the same policy. Kelsey and Wright stated that the purpose was two-fold: to help the Indian by exchanging his unwieldy holdings for a small improved piece of property that he could use effectively; and to develop the state and increase its taxable area. When the new administration came in, Com-

[54] *Indians of the United States*, III, 58-74.

[55] *Survey of Indians in the United States*, XIV, 5403, 5415, 5660, 5882, 5968, 5982, 5994-95, 6327, 6350.

missioner Sells and Superintendent Parker announced an even more liberal policy with regard to the sale of Indian land.[56]

This process of attrition went on constantly for twenty years after the passage of the law of 1908. During the greater part of the period the amount of money expended for the Indians' benefit from these sales ran above a million dollars annually.[57] Unfortunately the Indians did not automatically become successful farmers by the simple process of selling part of their land; they turned over their new houses to tenants, ate or sold their livestock, mortgaged and lost their farm machinery, and soon became as destitute as before. But they were so rich at first that the shrinkage of their holdings did not seem a serious matter; it was not until about 1930 that the Department officials began to realize that they had gradually consumed most of their land and all of their per caput shares for living expenses, that they were approaching the end of their supply, and that they were not fitted for any productive means of livelihood.

The statistics furnished by the Agency show that removal of restrictions began immediately under the law of 1908; that it increased under the Lane régime and reached almost a quarter of a million acres during the year 1919-1920; and that it declined sharply after 1921, but continued to be important until the close of the decade. During the past few years it has virtually ceased. The total acreage from which restrictions were removed by the Department, and the amount received from conditional removals are shown at the top of the next page.[58]

But if the Department did not succeed in developing the Indians' business judgment to the point where they were able to use their land constructively, it was much more successful in such tangible matters as the development of their oil resources.

[56] Indian Office Files, 72545/08 Five Tribes 311; Valentine, "Making Good Indians," p. 601; Department of the Interior, *Annual Report,* 1911, II, 430, 458; 1912, II, 6-7, 483-84; 1917, II, 4-5; *Indians of the United States,* III, 12-13; Lake Mohonk Conference, *Report,* 1913, pp. 50-51.

[57] Department of the Interior, *Annual Report,* 1913, II, 463; 1914, II, 280; 1915, II, 358; 1924, pp. 24-25; Superintendent, Office Files, Report of Superintendent, 1930, pp. 87-88.

[58] Superintendent, Office Files, Report of A. M. Landman, 1935, pp. 46-49.

| | unconditional | | conditional | | SCHOOL SITES | AMOUNT RECD. FROM CONDIT. |
|---|---|---|---|---|---|---|
| | CASES | ACREAGE | CASES | ACREAGE | | |
| Cherokee | 4043 | 186,795.62 | 4284 | 190,377.38 | 68.62 | $2,259,190.16 |
| Choctaw | 3238 | 397,980.97 | 5312 | 420,610.81 | 134.57 | 3,902,577.80 |
| Chickasaw | 1453 | 161,705.29 | 1079 | 62,528.66 | 45.22 | 836,755.40 |
| Creek | 1367 | 74,164.35 | 1863 | 78,541.91 | 76. | 3,925,389.46 |
| Seminole | 219 | 10,202.98 | 372 | 12,318.27 | 21.17 | 659,978.93 |
| TOTAL | 10,320 | 830,849.21 | 12,910 | 764,377.03 | 345.58 | $11,583,891.75 |

The dramatic oil discoveries of eastern Oklahoma continued to add a lurid color to the lives of Five Tribes allottees.

The Glenn Pool reached its peak in 1907. It was far surpassed by the Cushing Pool, which began phenomenal production in 1913 and soon became the most prolific high-grade producing territory of its size in the world. Many of the Snakes who had received arbitrary allotments in that supposedly worthless region soon began to receive royalties of five hundred dollars a day. The great Healdton field near Ardmore was discovered in 1913, and although the oil from this area brought a comparatively low price, the production was great enough to bring enormous wealth to several Choctaws and Chickasaws fortunate enough to own allotments there. Other discoveries of only slightly less importance took place throughout the Cherokee, Creek, and Chickasaw nations. No important development occurred in the Seminole country until the great Seminole Pool was discovered in 1926.[59]

The removal of restrictions by the law of 1908 and by Departmental action and the death of allottees removed a large proportion of Five Tribes leases from Agency supervision. It was estimated in 1915 that one-seventh of the Healdton field and two-fifths of the Cushing were held under Departmental leases. Probably the proportion of one-seventh was about the average throughout the Five Tribes area; the higher proportion in the Cushing field was due to the fact that it was a full-

[59] Department of the Interior, *Annual Report*, 1913, II, 486; 1914, II, 282-94; 1915, II, 367-72, 392-412; 1919, II, 425-26; *Daily Oklahoman*, July 17, 1936.

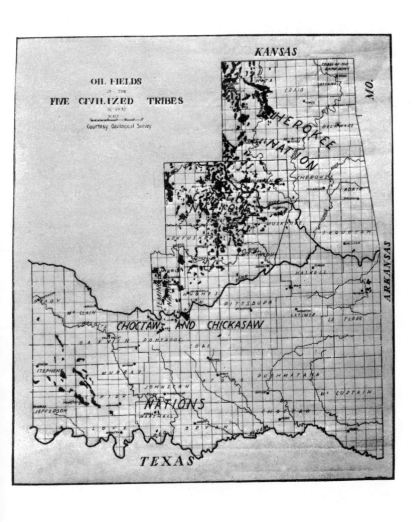

OIL FIELDS
OF THE
FIVE CIVILIZED TRIBES
1912
SCALE
Courtesy Geological Survey

blood settlement.[60] In most cases the remaining land had passed into the possession of white purchasers.

In spite of the fact that the restricted area was constantly shrinking, and that it constituted only a small fraction of the original landed wealth of the Five Tribes, the amount of royalty collected by the Department ran into imposing figures. The receipts rose to over a million and a half dollars during the year 1907-1908, and continued over the million mark in spite of the removal of restrictions from millions of acres that year; they reached two millions in 1913-1914, four millions in 1915-1916, five millions in 1919-1920, and reached the peak of production during 1929-1930 with more than six million dollars; and they remained at a considerable figure even during the depression of the Thirties. The entire receipts collected by the Agency for Five Tribes allottees from the thirteen $100-leases of 1903-1904 to the $883,212.10 collected during 1938-1939 reached the stupendous total of $101,075,553.12.[61]

Only a small proportion of the Indians received the grotesque incomes represented by this oil development; but the acquisition of immense wealth by these simple people, who had no conception of the use of money, constituted a problem for the Agency that seemed insoluble. At first the royalties were paid directly to adults and to the guardians of minors; but it soon became apparent that the guardians were applying the money to their own purposes, and that the adult Indians were constantly overreached and were becoming debauched. The Agency therefore began about 1911 to supervise the Indians' expenditure through the district agents and to withhold the payments to those guardians whose mismanagement was notorious. A system soon developed by which the Indian was required to secure advance approval from the Agency for the purchases he desired to make. The amount of individual money

[60] Department of the Interior, *Annual Report*, 1911, II, 453-57; 1915, II, 410-12; Superintendent, Office Files, Report of C. L. Ellis, 1926, p. 3.

[61] Superintendent, Office Files, Report of A. M. Landman, 1935, p. 42; 1936, p. 52; 1937, p. 49; 1938, p. 43; 1939, p. 279.

expended in this way upon the advice of the field clerks during 1926-1927 amounted to over four million dollars.[62]

This surveillance was only a little less damaging to the Indian's self-respect than unsupervised expenditure would have been to his property and his morals; but it is difficult to see how a better system could have been devised. The development of attitudes that would have enabled a primitive people to use such vast unearned wealth to advantage would have required educational disciplines beyond the power of the Indian Office to impart in one generation. At the same time it was an unfortunate condition; a survey of the Agency made by the General Accounting Office in 1928 showed that "by far the larger part" of the activities of the field employees was concentrated on protecting the property of a wealthy group of Indians constituting about 2 per cent of the population of the tribes.[63] In the main the oil property was honestly and efficiently administered by the Agency, but it served no good purpose to the ones who owned it, and the remaining 98 per cent of the Indians were deprived of the social and educational counsel that they needed so sorely.

The problem of investment remained; for although the Indians were greatly gifted in using up automobiles and houses and clothes in the shortest possible period, there was an obvious limit to their powers of consumption. The money was at first deposited in bonded national banks, but in 1915, when almost three million dollars had accumulated, with an additional two millions in the Federal treasury, a constructive use of the money became a real problem. The World War offered a temporary solution, and about eleven million dollars was invested in liberty bonds and war savings stamps; but by 1920 an additional six million dollars had accumulated and was deposited in

[62] Department of the Interior, *Annual Report*, 1911, II, 431; 1912, II, 489; 1922, p. 21; 1927, p. 67; *Survey of Indians in the United States*, XIV, 6605-6; *Sapulpa Herald*, April 20, 1915.

[63] *Senate Docs.*, 70 Cong., 2 Sess., No. 263, pp. 78, 90-91.

Oklahoma banks to collect about a quarter of a million more every year in interest.[64]

No attempt was made to develop the business capacity of the Indians by any system of accounting. If they inquired, they were informed as to the amount of their balance, but no statements were ever furnished them.[65] The confusion that existed in their minds regarding their financial affairs is illustrated by a letter received by the Agency in 1930 from a fullblood whose oil wells had shut down during the dull times:

"I will write to beg advice. I want to know all about my royalty and I will find soon how my oil wells are producing or find out all about the runs.

"There is something wrong somewhere or else crooks might have cause of it. I hope you fellows will look into it and find out please. I suppose to know all about my place, my own land, and here I don't even try to know. . . .

"I believe there is crook somewhere, I can't locate him, so I beg you agents with all my heart to help please. You know can not trust a thief, a liar, not even a robber or outlaw, but I can trust my own kind, the good people. I need little money.

"I wish I could get my money soon when I really need it. . . .

"You guys want to hurry up a little and whip up and send that money please. I want you all to mail my checks every first of each month or send it every second. All of you men must do what I say.

"I work mighty hard for my own money every day. I work until I have all kinds of boils and carbuncles are sores of every kind, but I get money by working, but I do not get enough money from the government. . . .

"I love you men just same as I love my own country and all my people. I love you all same as I love the stars and stripes. I love all America with all myself. I cannot love or serve my

[64] Department of the Interior, *Annual Report*, 1909, II, 107; 1915, II, 376-77; 1919, II, 48; 1920, pp. 28-29; *Senate Docs.*, 70 Cong., 2 Sess., No. 263, pp. 78, 90-91.
[65] *Survey of Indians in the United States*, XIV, 6300-4, 6321-22, 6602-3.

America and salute my flag enough. I am the true American on all the earth. . . .

"Whatsoever I asked you men must be sure and do it soon. If you fellows serve Uncle Sam you must be sure and serve me next please. You agents could treat me just good by serving me with my own ways. If you fellows take my way I will join in with you. Well I hope you all would send all my money please and I want you to keep track of my land and my oil wells too, all about my farm and all about my royalties.

"I ought to be a rich Indian right now. I got good land. I got everything. I also need a brand new house on my homestead, so when I got married I can take my wife to my own house. You fellows look into it. Well I will close. I am yours for everlasting with great loves and wishes."[66]

 Such were the second-hand ideals that one young Indian had pieced together out of "Americanization" influences, dependence upon the Agency, and complete bewilderment with the economic situation. He was a product of the new order just as Chitto Harjo and his followers were products of the old.

[66] *Muskogee Times-Democrat,* November 21, 1930.

# CHAPTER XI

# The Indian's Place in Oklahoma

PRECEDING chapters have shown the stormy conflicts that attended the creation of a state in which a considerable number of citizens and an immense amount of property were under a special status. These controversies were in a manner settled and a working basis was reached during the first few years of statehood. The white people soon accepted the unusual situation as a permanent feature of Oklahoma life; the adjustments involved the spiritual and cultural acceptance of a strongly marked minority race, the handicap placed upon economic development by the special status of Indian land, and the constant litigation growing out of the desire to prey upon Indian property or uncertainty as to its legal status. For the Indians the adjustment meant the acceptance of an alien economic system and a political and social order in which they were greatly outnumbered. The cultural amalgamation of the two races was the most successful. Probably more than any other state in the Union Oklahoma has accepted the cultural heritage of the Indian, and has used it as the background of its own traditions; on the other hand even the most conservative Indians have adopted the clothing and habits and religion and to a certain extent even the language of their white neighbors.

The spiritual union of the two races was accepted from the beginning. The name of the state itself is a Choctaw expression meaning "Red People," and was first suggested by an able and cultured Choctaw Chief during the treaty negotiations of 1866. The Great Seal of the State, designed by young Gabe E. Parker, in the Constitutional Convention, and Dr. A. Grant Evans, is a five-pointed star with the seal of Oklahoma Territory in the center and the seal of one of the Civilized Tribes in each of the rays. The Oklahoma Territory seal itself showed a frontiersman and an Indian clasping hands, with an industrial and a hunting scene as their respective backgrounds, and a figure of justice with her scales poised between. If this ideal was not entirely realized, the fact was due to the individual greed of the white man and the individual ineptitude of the red rather than to any general racial discrimination. The constitution, which expressly legalized the segregation of the colored race, defined the term "colored" to apply only to persons of African descent and "white race" to include all other persons.[1] The union of the two races was portrayed in the allegorical wedding of the statehood ceremonies, and Governor Haskell in his inaugural address glorified Oklahoma as a state where the original owners of the soil had not been conquered, but had joined with their white neighbors in forming a new commonwealth, and he found in the red and white stripes of the American flag a new symbolism of the red man and the white united under the azure sky.[2]

Before a year had elapsed—as soon, in fact, as the educational officers could select textbooks and arrange a course of study—the young sons and daughters of frontiersmen in every prairie schoolhouse of the West Side and the children of the recently arrived settlers in the Five Tribes area were learning a personal pride in the achievements of the five Indian republics as their own historic past.[3] They accepted Sequoyah and Pushmataha as their ancestral heroes, and the "Trail of Tears" of the Removal exiles rather than the voyage of Columbus became their odyssey. Historical investigators and college professors and newspaper and magazine writers began to recreate and popularize the vanished past of the Five Tribes; and within a generation their efforts had received national recognition as a distinctive Oklahoma contribution to literature and

[1] Article VI, Section 35; Article XXIII, Section 11.

[2] Charles Evans and Clinton Orrin Bunn, *Oklahoma Civil Government* (Ardmore, Oklahoma, 1908), p. 88.

[3] *Ibid.*, pp. 72-88; Joseph B. Thoburn and Isaac M. Holcomb, *A History of Oklahoma* (San Francisco, 1918), pp. 35-102.

scholarship.[4] When the great and gifted Cherokee, Will Rogers, remarked that his ancestors had not come on the Mayflower, that they had been waiting to receive the Mayflower immigrants when they arrived, he was expressing a profound truth. And if there were people in Oklahoma racially prejudiced against Indians, their influence was more than offset by those who idealized them and regretted their own exclusively European descent, or those blond individuals who proudly proclaimed themselves as Indians because of 1/64 or 1/256 quantum of Indian blood.

Those Indians, whether mixed-bloods or fullbloods, who were able to assert themselves in the new society became leaders in the state. Usually they had more property and better educational training than the newly arrived white man who was trying to establish himself in a frontier community. Certainly they had more poise, more of the instinctive grace and assurance of a natural aristocracy developed through many generations of leadership in a small and closely integrated society. Whether from racial heritage or from an environment that stimulated individual development, their intellectual capacity was very high. The physical amalgamation of these Indians with their white neighbors is plainly apparent. The young grandchildren of the great fullblood families of tribal days, who proudly assume a natural leadership on college campuses, are usually half-bloods or quarter-bloods; and many descendants of the mixed-blood families are no longer appreciably Indian. This dilution of blood, that naturally results from the Indians' numerical inferiority, is not necessarily a disappearance of the Indian strain, but only a widening of its influence; Indian tradition is strong with many of these apparently white people, and Indian traits survive to add richness to their char-

---

[4] This intellectual predilection of Oklahomans may be seen in any grade school or high school text book in Oklahoma history, the feature articles in any Sunday newspaper, any college course in state history, and the publications of the University of Oklahoma Press.

acter—a mystical appreciation of beauty, strength and depth of feeling, creative artistry.[5]

In sharp contrast to these self-reliant individuals were the bewildered fullbloods and freedmen snatched from the obscurity of their primitive lives by the discovery of oil on their allotments. The fantastic doings of about a dozen of these undisciplined children of nature filled the newspapers throughout the country and created the impression that all Oklahoma Indians were rich and irresponsible. The most famous were Creeks with Glenn Pool or Cushing allotments. The lurid escapades of Katie Fixico; the financial and matrimonial troubles of Eastman Richards, a lieutenant of Chitto Harjo, who built and managed a town for his amusement and was unable to resist a woman; the wrongs suffered by gentle Lucinda Pitman; the spectacle of simple, kindly Jackson Barnett roaming the woods about his hut while the oil broke from a wild gusher on his allotment and flowed down the creek; and the legal battles waged for the guardianship of Edith Durant, Luther Manuel, Sarah Rector, and other young Creek Negroes created headlines for many years.[6]

The average Oklahoman with his personal acquaintance with many capable persons of Indian descent and his amused observation of the unwieldy wealth of a few oil beneficiaries scarcely knew of the remote fullblood settlements with the conservatism and destitution and the physical and moral deterioration that presented such a tragic contrast to the self-reliant society of tribal days. In these inaccessible regions a whole generation of children born subsequent to 1906 was growing up in illiteracy and squalor with no land and no tribal relations

[5] The Federal census taken in 1910 shows the wide vocational diversification of Indians in the Five Tribes, especially of the Cherokees and Choctaws (*Indian Population of the United States and Alaska*, pp. 267-70).

[6] For example, *Muskogee Times-Democrat*, February 9, 1916; March 31, August 14, September 28, October 2, 1917; *Sapulpa Herald*, March 13, 19, 25, 27, 1915; February 8, 1917; September 11, 1918; *Muskogee Phoenix*, October 20, 1911; July 5, 1919.

and no hope for the future. Even their names were unknown to the Agency.[7]

In the main these Indians expressed their disapproval by passive resistance, and only once did any conflict occur with the state authorities. In 1909 a constable of the township attempted to search the tents of a group of Negroes who were living at the Old Hickory Stomp Ground, for goods stolen from the surrounding country. They denied him admittance, and he organized a posse and captured forty Negroes, one half-blood Indian, and one white man. No Snake had any connection with the affair, but the authorities of McIntosh County attempted for no particular reason to arrest Chitto Harjo. Five deputies proceeded to his house, where seven Indians were assembled. A fight ensued and two deputies were killed and Chitto Harjo and one of his followers were wounded. The Indians escaped and were never captured, but four counties were thrown into turmoil by this "Snake Uprising." The state militia was rushed to the affected locality, and quiet, which had never been endangered except by the deputies, was restored. This ended the affair so far as the Indians were concerned, but Chitto Harjo's fame reached international proportions in headlines that increased in virulence with the distance from the scene of the disturbance.[8]

The Snakes and Nighthawks continued an underground organization that eluded the Agency officials and was almost unknown to the general citizenship of the state. As late as 1923 a Cherokee convention met at Fort Gibson to work for the restoration of the old order—"just like we were before statehood, a common title to all Indians." In 1924 about sixty Creek Snake families were said to be living the year round in little

---

[7] Moorehead, *Our National Problem*, pp. 34-35; Department of the Interior, *Annual Report*, 1912, II, 474; 1915, II, 365; 1916, II, 359-63; 1918, II, 363-66; 1919, II, 334-35; Lake Mohonk Conference, *Report*, 1915, p. 178.

[8] Department of the Interior, *Annual Report*, 1909, II, 390-91; *Muskogee Phoenix*, March 26, April 2, 1909. An American who was in England at the time has informed the writer that the newspapers there were so filled with accounts of this latest "Indian Uprising" that he was unable to learn until he received a local newspaper what had really happened in Oklahoma.

cabins at the Old Hickory Stomp Ground with some semblance of the old tribal communal life. At least as late as 1930 these groups continued to send delegations to Washington, and for many years they secured the perfunctory introduction of bills in Congress to erase the vigorous growing state of Oklahoma from the map and restore the untroubled tribal life that had gone forever.[9] A letter written from Okemah, "Indian Territory," in 1912 by a Creek Snake shows the still undefeated spirit of these conservatives:

Okemah (Oklah)<br>I.T.<br>June 29, 1912<br>Secretary of Indior

DEAR STEPFATHER

I request you a few reasonable words. to do tell me something about. Wilson Jones and John Jonas was sent to Washingto as delagates for Creek Nation and they word tell sun down and had the Bill Pass two houses. Bill was an old treaty of 1832 treaty. If the Bill was Pass the houses. Please send me the copy of it. Well you the man was looking over Poor Indians What have you fined out about and what you gone to about it. Are you look after them, or you wont do it Are Have you don Report on it If you did. in this matter do write me about it. I am welcome to yours works. If you have take care the Poors. I am respecting was this. Yours all had said the home of the Indians be west of Arkansas River. This is what your all have said In the treaty your have syned in the year of 1832. June 9. This treaty will be life as long as the sun rise and go down. and as long as grass grew. And as long as the sky dont fell to the earth. As long as the water runs. The home of Indians will be there for ever. The big flat bottom land of West bas of Arkansas River. To-day the sky is still in the air yet. and grass grew yet. and water run yet. In regard. this matter. In mistaking write. But you the man know all this matter. So fill out what I want and answer. I remain hoping to hear in earliest date. Yours ever

Respect.

---

P.S. Answer this letter and tell all about what I ask. I'll be much suprized. like to hear before 10the of July. 1912.[10]

[9] *Muskogee Times-Democrat,* May 15, 1923; May 3, June 20, 1924; *Muskogee Phoenix,* March 5, 1930.

[10] Indian Office Files, 82904/10 Union 302.

The persistence and vitality of this movement is an indication of the strong traits of Indian character that had been deprived of their natural outlet by the breaking of tribal relations. At the same time because of the secrecy with which it was guarded it exposed the Indians to the schemes of swindlers. In 1915 through a Choctaw who finally told his story, a field clerk learned for the first time of the regularity with which for twenty years they had made pitiable payments out of their poverty for their lost cause. Their delegations and officers were no doubt sincere, but an unknown number of sharpers traded upon their desperation and ignorance. A letter written to Commissioner Sells in 1914 apparently by a Choctaw gives an intelligent Indian's opinion of one man's activities:

"I am very glad that you have found the Atty. that was doing this very trick. He is the man because I read his letters which he wrote to the members of the society, which they call tham selves Foure-Mothers.

"Now Mr. Sells some of these members are very hard headed and their Atty. told tham that every thing is ready now the bill is now before the congress that they will pass the thing through Some time in May. Many Dollars they have spent over this thing. Some of these members have very good sensible but the believe it so much.

. . .          . . .          . . .

"I read his letters his Treaty and who's was the President the time when the made their Treaty with the white people, so on. I am very glad that you have locate the Gentlemen. I hope that you will do some thing with the Gentlemen for he has been robbing many Dollars away from my tribe."[11]

The pathetic feature of the whole situation is summed up in this man's broken English—"the believe it so much."

It might not have been so easy for swindlers to collect money for such visionary projects if the Indians had not had so many enforceable claims arising from unfulfilled commitments by the Federal Government. J. M. McMurray secured thousands

[11] *Loc. cit.*

of ten dollar contracts for which he engaged to defeat the laws by which Congress in removing restrictions had made the land subject to taxation in violation of the Choctaw-Chickasaw agreements; and the Treaty Rights Association was formed, and Governor Johnston was made permanent chairman. M. L. Mott secured authorization from the Creek Council to institute a similar suit for that tribe.[12]

The United States Supreme Court decided in 1912 that tax exemption was a vested right and that the attempt of Congress to abrogate it was a violation of the Fifth Amendment to the Constitution.[13] The status of unrestricted land therefore was exactly as it had been under the agreements. As long as it was held by the original allottee the Cherokee, Creek, and Seminole homestead and the entire Choctaw and Chickasaw allotment remained tax exempt for periods varying from twenty-one years to "in perpetuity" in spite of the removal of the restrictions by act of Congress. On the other hand by extending some restrictions to 1931 Congress had extended the tax exemption of a large acreage of surplus land that would have become taxable under the agreements about the time of statehood.

The news of this decision brought consternation throughout the state, and bonds for $2,907,000 were issued to meet the emergency. When the allottees began to sue for the return of taxes already paid under protest, some of the counties were forced to borrow hundreds of thousands of dollars to make the restitution.[14] The Oklahoma delegation in Congress tried to secure legislation to compensate the state for the handicap it suffered by reason of Federal commitments; but they succeeded only in raising the appropriation for the tuition of Indian children in the public schools, which had been lowered after 1908,

[12] *House Reports,* 61 Cong., 3 Sess., No. 2273, Vol. I, 340, 1165; *Survey of Indians in the United States,* XIV, 5354-55; Moorehead, *The American Indian,* pp. 141-42.

[13] *Supreme Court Reports,* LVI, 665-79, 949-52.

[14] *Ibid.,* LXIV, 759-60; *Muskogee Phoenix,* May 14, 1912; *Sapulpa Evening Democrat,* May 14, 22, 28, 1912; *Standard-Sentinel,* May 23, 1912; *Nowata Star,* April 11, 1913; January 9, February 20, May 8, August 14, 1914; A. L. Beckett, *Know Your Oklahoma* (Oklahoma City, 1930), pp. 104-5; C. C. Childers, *How Oklahoma Collects Taxes* (Compiled for the legislature, 1925), p. 7.

to its former figure of $300,000,[15] where it remained until about 1920. This appropriation did not nearly compensate the state in the one field of educational costs. A survey made by the United States Commissioner of Education in 1922 showed an annual loss of nearly half a million dollars from this source.[16]

The question also arose as to the taxability of Indian land after the death of the allottee. The courts decided that two classes of inherited land were restricted—land in the possession of fullblood heirs was restricted by the requirement that it could be sold only with the approval of the county judge, and land held for the use of issue born too late for enrolment was restricted by that provision—and that in such cases it was non-taxable.[17]

The special status of Indian land carried an additional tax exemption that could not have been foreseen when the agreements were made. In 1908 and 1909 the state placed a gross production tax on the mining of coal. The companies operating on the segregated land refused to pay. In 1914 the United States Supreme Court ruled that since the mining company was the instrumentality through which the Government carried out its agreement with the Indians to lease their land, the law placed a tax upon a Federal agency and was therefore unconstitutional. It was estimated at the time that the state lost half a million dollars in uncollected revenue by this decision.[18] A more serious loss occurred when the court ruled that oil companies holding Departmental leases were also Federal instrumentalities, for the decision placed a considerable portion of the great oil industry beyond the reach of any income or production tax.[19]

The income which the allottee received from his tax exempt land was also tax exempt. When the state Supreme Court made

[15] *Congressional Record*, LI, 3680; *Sapulpa Evening Democrat*, June 6, 1912; *Standard-Sentinel*, May 30, 1912; March 12, 1914.

[16] *Education of Indians in Oklahoma*, pp. 12-13.

[17] *Federal Reporter*, CLXXXVII, 870-74; *Pacific Reporter*, CXLIV, 611-14.

[18] *Supreme Court Reports*, LIX, 234-38; *Sapulpa Evening Democrat*, April 29, 1914.

[19] *Supreme Court Reports*, LXVI, 338-42; *Congressional Record*, LXIX, 8729-30.

this ruling in 1920, it was estimated that the annual loss to the state through its inability to collect income taxes from Five Tribes allottees and other Indians amounted to $100,000. The Federal income tax was paid by the Agency without question from the Indians' funds until 1921, when the Attorney-General ruled that the tax was illegal and the money was refunded with interest.[20]

Restricted Indians like other citizens paid taxes upon personal property, income from unrestricted property, and even land purchased for them by the Agency and held under a restricted deed. In spite of the court decision upholding the tax exemption of land from which the restrictions were removed, most of it soon became subject to taxation because it passed from the hands of the original allottee. But the loss was serious enough to arouse considerable ill feeling against intermarried whites and well-to-do mixed-blood Indians, who were felt to occupy a privileged position; and a number of them, especially candidates for public office, avoided this unpopularity by the voluntary payment of taxes.

The intricate legal questions involved in the tax decisions were characteristic of the general uncertainty with regard to the status of land throughout eastern Oklahoma. The first Supreme Court decisions in the Thirty Thousand Land Suits settled the broader questions regarding the authority of the Federal Government over Five Tribes allottees, but complicated questions of interpretation remained to unsettle titles for many years.

There was for example the question as to whether the Government could reimpose restrictions after they had expired. The Creek restrictions on the surplus expired in 1907 except that the McCumber Amendment in 1906 extended the restrictions of fullbloods. The Act of 1908 placed allottees of three-fourths or more Indian blood under the same restrictions as fullbloods. Would this act reimpose the restrictions upon a

[20] Department of the Interior, *Annual Report*, 1914, I, 287; 1919, II, 367; *Congressional Record*, LV, 4472; LXXVI, 3547-48, 3591-92, 4380.

three-fourths blood Creek, whose surplus had become unrestricted in 1907? A Creek of this classification attempted to sell his surplus in 1912, and the United States Supreme Court decided that the law of 1908 was not retroactive and that the sale was valid. What then of the three-fourths blood minor who became of age between August 8, 1907, and May 27, 1908, or the one who became of age after May 27, 1908? The courts decided that the surplus of the former was released, but that of the latter was restricted.[21] The same ruling would apply to the small amount of Choctaw-Chickasaw land that had become unrestricted under the agreements.

A still more tangled question involved the determination of the system of law governing inheritance. Choctaw and Chickasaw cases were comparatively simple; tribal law was in effect until 1904, Arkansas law administered by the Federal courts from 1904 to 1907, and Oklahoma Territory law upon the advent of statehood. Cherokee cases were similar, except that the Arkansas law went into effect in 1898. Seminole inheritance was complicated by the provision of the Supplemental Agreement that citizens of the tribe should inherit to the exclusion of non-citizens. The Creek Supplemental Agreement contained a similar provision, and the question was almost hopelessly tangled by the stipulation of the first Creek Agreement that the tribal law of descent should govern, and the provision of the Supplemental Agreement that substituted the Arkansas statutes. The uncertainty involved in the interpretation of these questions was serious because of the frequency of intermarriage between citizens of different tribes and the magnitude of the interests involved in oil estates. Should the Creek wife and Creek (by enrolment) daughters of a Seminole be disinherited in the interest of distant Seminole relatives? The United States Supreme Court decided in the affirmative, that the Indians' tribal interests were paramount to family interests. Would this principle apply not only to the heirs of the original allottee but to all descendants and distributees? The state Supreme Court

---

[21] *Federal Reporter,* CCXXXV, 95-98; *Supreme Court Reports,* LIX, 137-39,

decided that it applied only to the first succession, but the United States Supreme Court reversed the decision. What law was in force if the Indian died after the Arkansas statutes were placed in effect throughout the Territory in 1904, or the Oklahoma laws in 1907? The courts uniformly decided that the specific preference to citizen heirs was not repealed by the general Arkansas statute, but it was generally accepted that it ended with statehood. These are only a few of the least complicated questions that made the purchase of East Side land one of the most hazardous of investments.[22]

An eloquent commentary upon the situation was the decision of the Federal Land Bank of Wichita, Kansas, to refuse all loans upon inherited Five Tribes land. It was stated in 1919 that although this bank had loaned six million dollars to Kansas farmers it had loaned less than half of that amount in Oklahoma, mainly because of the uncertainty over titles. Compilations of land laws and syllabi of cases were prepared for the guidance of the legal profession, and even at the present time a course in "Indian Land Titles," dealing exclusively with complications growing out of the Five Tribes allotment is among the most difficult courses offered to law students at the state university.[23]

An attempt was made to remove one cause of the inheritance muddle by the partition law passed by Congress in 1918. The legislation was sponsored by Carter, and by the Cherokee, W. W. Hastings, who entered Congress in 1915 and became very active in Indian affairs; it was urged by W. P. Z. German, general attorney of the Federal Land Bank at Wichita; and apparently it was approved by the Indian Office.

[22] Kappler, *Laws and Treaties*, I, 88, 109; *Pacific Reporter*, CLV, 602-3, 852; CLXXV, 737; CXCVIII, 309-17; CCIV, 439-42; *Supreme Court Reports*, LIX, 198-200, 295-99, 308-12; LXII, 1117-23; LXIII, 192-98; LXIX, 652-56; *Muskogee Times-Democrat*, April 20, 1920; July 26, 1924; April 6, 1927; *Muskogee Phoenix*, December 22, 1914; *Sapulpa Herald*, January 20, 1915; *Sapulpa Evening Democrat*, June 10, 1912.

[23] *Pacific Reporter*, CLXXXIV, 113-25; Bledsoe, *Indian Land Laws*; Henry P. Langworthy, *Indian Land Titles* (Tulsa, Oklahoma, 1914), pp. 123 ff. The law course in "Indian Land Titles" is taught by Dr. John Begg Cheadle.

No partition proceedings had been possible before this time if one of the heirs was a fullblood; the state Supreme Court had decided that the state laws conferring authority upon the district court could not apply, because partition was a form of alienation, and it had also ruled that the county court had no authority, because the act of 1908 had provided only one method of fullblood conveyance—a voluntary conveyance approved by the county judge. There was also no method under the existing law by which the county court could determine heirship; when it approved a fullblood conveyance, it simply vested in the grantee whatever interest the Indian had, if any, but the rights of the other claimants remained unsettled. The district court had the right to determine the heirship between parties to a suit in any case that came before it, but no general authority. The title to land therefore remained uncertain as long as any claimant remained whose rights had not been adjudicated; and after the land had been sold through the county court, many suits arose in behalf of other heirs.[24]

The act authorized the county courts to determine the heirs of deceased allottees who had left restricted heirs, with the right of appeal as in general probate matters. It also authorized the district courts to partition the estates inherited by fullbloods according to the general state law. Land allotted in such partition proceedings to a fullblood heir was made subject to the same restrictions regarding alienation and taxation that it had before, but in case of sale it was released from restrictions.[25]

But although this law brought an improvement with regard to titles, its effect was unfortunate so far as the fullblood heirs were concerned. It was almost always possible to persuade one heir to sell his interest. The courts then in a suspicious number of cases found it impossible to partition the land, found for example that a 220-acre tract could not be divided between two

---

[24] *Pacific Reporter,* CLXII, 786; CLXXIII, 1136-37; CLXXIV, 498; CLXXXIV, 113-25; CLXXXIX, 537; CXC, 263.

[25] Kappler, *Laws and Treaties,* IV, 179; *Pacific Reporter,* CCXIX, 392-402; CCXXXII, 797-800; *Muskogee Times-Democrat,* June 13, 1924.

heirs, and that a child's two-thirds interest in 120 acres shown by the appraisement records to be of uniform value could not be separated from that of the other heir. A forced sale almost invariably resulted, in which the other heirs were helpless because they had no money to purchase the interest of the heirs who wished to sell. The Agency had no opportunity to protect the Indians in these proceedings, for there was no obligation to serve notice to the probate attorney. As an example of the manner in which heirs were overreached in these forced sales the Agency furnished a number of instances in 1924 where the purchaser had immediately borrowed money on the land far in excess of the purchase price which he had paid. The law proved to be another method by which the state courts could deprive Indians of their land with no possibility of redress by the Federal Government.[26]

Another question of fullblood inheritance was decided by the United States Supreme Court in the Eastman Richards case in 1919. In this and other cases involving fullblood heirs the administrators appointed by the county had attempted to force the Agency to turn accumulated royalties over to them; but the court ruled that the death of the allottee removed restrictions only to the extent of providing a method for the land to be sold, and that so long as it remained unsold it was still restricted. The Department therefore had authority to control oil leasing of land inherited by fullbloods and to supervise the use of the royalties. The property of Eastman Richards, whose great wealth was derived from a deceased son's allotment in the Cushing field, was thus placed under Agency control. The Department now assumed jurisdiction over the leasing of such land for oil and gas, but it approved leases made in good faith through the county courts before the ruling was made.[27]

[26] Department of the Interior, *Annual Report,* 1919, II, 382-83; House of Representatives, *Investigation of the Administration of Indian Affairs in Oklahoma* (Washington, 1924), pp. 192-93, 213-16, 278-82, 295-302.

[27] *Supreme Court Reports,* LXIII, 954-57; *Muskogee Times-Democrat,* September 15, 1916; October 31, 1917; Department of the Interior, *Annual Report,* 1920, II, 32.

The courts also settled the disposition of royalty from land inherited partially by heirs born too late to receive allotments and entitled, therefore, to the exclusive use of the land until 1931. The United States Supreme Court decided that the royalty should be held during the restricted period, and that such special heirs were exclusively entitled to the interest or other income from its use until 1931, when the accumulated royalties should be divided among all the heirs the same as the allotments.[28]

All these decisions were important in the economic development of the state, but the most important legal matter so far as the allottees themselves were concerned was the continued control over their estates by the county court. The feeling that had been aroused in 1914 against probate abuses soon died out, and the protection given to allottees was steadily undermined by the legislature and the Oklahoma delegation in Congress.

A neglected field of exploitation was opened up by the discovery that Indian adults also needed guardians. It had always been recognized that mentally defective Indians like other defective adults could be placed under guardianship, but it was not until about 1913 that it began to be apparent that all Indians and freedmen who owned oil property were mentally defective. Like other vicious practices this custom seems to have originated in a real need of the allottee for protection. Not all guardians and probate courts had conspired to sell the land of unrestricted minors, and in some cases when these untutored children approached their majority they were hounded by real estate speculators who hoped to secure their property the instant they could execute a valid deed. To prevent this practice they were brought into court, declared incompetent, and continued under guardianship. Young people who had been virtually kidnaped by speculators were rescued and placed beyond the reach of their despoilers in this way, sometimes upon the initiative of the probate attorneys.[29]

---

[28] *Supreme Court Reports*, LXIII, 847-50.
[29] Indian Office Files, 43333/14 Five Tribes 352.

But it was only a short time until county judges began to build political machines by apportioning these profitable guardianships among their supporters, and rival claimants and their attorneys fought each other in the courts for the privilege of plundering rich estates. Even those Indians whose wealth came from restricted allotments and who were therefore adequately protected by the Government were declared incompetent, and a horde of guardians and attorneys were richly compensated for services consisting mainly of cashing royalty checks from the Agency. Young allottees approaching their majority began to hide or to seek refuge in distant states to avoid being brought into court and declared incompetent.[30]

The Mannie Lewis case illustrates the rapidity with which guardians and attorneys fastened themselves upon Indian estates. John Lewis, a Creek fullblood of excellent character, was killed in an automobile accident August 1, 1924. He and his family had been living quietly and frugally in an Indian settlement in Okfuskee County, but great oil production had recently begun on his Creek County allotment and at the time of his death his income was $24,000 a month. This money was, of course, under Agency supervision, and he had gone to Muskogee to arrange for the education of a minor child at the time of the fatal accident. He left as heirs his wife, Mannie Lewis, to whom he had been married for more than thirty years, and two adult and two minor children and grandchildren. All the heirs were fullbloods.

As County Judge Seawell expressed it, as soon as the family came into this inheritance "They had more lawyers following them around than a $10,000,000 corporation." Five days after Lewis' death a petition was filed in the county court to declare the three adult heirs incompetent. At the same time a firm of Okemah attorneys secured a contract carrying a 50 per cent contingent fee with a Creek woman who claimed she had lived

---

[30] *Muskogee Times-Democrat,* February 8, 1916; February 16, March 31, May 5, August 14, 21, 22, 1917; August 12, 1920; April 5, 26, 1923; *Muskogee Phoenix,* March 17, 26, 1915; April 23, May 15, 1919; *Sapulpa Herald,* March 25, 27, September 14, 1915.

with Lewis before his marriage to Mrs. Lewis and was therefore his legal wife; and this contract was approved August 8 by the county judge. Apparently she had no case, for she was still living with the man who had been enrolled by the Dawes Commission as her husband, and two children had been placed on the Dawes rolls as the issue of this marriage; but the Lewis heirs became alarmed at the prospect of litigation and employed an Okmulgee attorney upon a 25 per cent contingent contract to defend them. Judge Seawell approved this contract September 19, although the incompetency petition had already been presented, and obviously if the Indians should be declared incompetent they would not be competent to employ attorneys. He held the competency hearings October 6, declared the three adults incompetent, and appointed two guardians for each. Each of the minors also had a guardian; hence there were eight guardians for the family. If each of the guardians followed the usual custom of employing an attorney, there were sixteen people authorized by the court to draw fees from the estate, besides the attorney also authorized by the court to carry out the 25 per cent contract to quiet title. Still another attorney had been employed by the family to rid them of the guardians, first by opposing the incompetency proceedings, and later by contesting the court's jurisdiction. There was also the prospect of endless litigation, with the guardians' attorneys attempting to annul the 25 per cent contract upon the ground of the Indians' incompetency; one of the Lewis' attorneys attempting to establish the competency of his clients before a higher court and incidentally to save his contract, and the other admitting their incompetency but trying to move the case to another county; and the attorneys of the other "wife" trying to secure a favorable settlement for their client and incidentally for themselves.[31]

The legal difficulties of the Lewis family continued for several years,[32] but it would serve no good purpose to carry the case through its tedious ramifications. The allotment had been

---

[31] *Indian Affairs in Oklahoma*, pp. 34, 180, 219-44, 464-70.
[32] *Survey of Indians in the United States*, XIV, 6543-44.

absolutely clear when sturdy, upright John Lewis went to arrange for his son's schooling, and his royalties had been safely accumulating at the Agency; and the developments that took place within two months and five days after the estate came under the jurisdiction of the courts is fairly typical of the general practice.

After the legislative rebuff administered to Miss Barnard the Commissioner of Charities and Corrections made no general attempt to assist the county court in Indian guardianship matters. Miss Barnard's successor, William D. Matthews, was less aggressive in his methods before the public and his published reports are more restrained, but an examination of his files indicates that he worked earnestly and efficiently in protecting the estates of those Indians who were maintained in state institutions. He had only one assistant, but like Miss Barnard he had chosen an attorney for this position and several cases were vigorously prosecuted. Matthews' successor, Mrs. Mabel Bassett, apparently did not continue his guardianship work even in this restricted field, although in 1924 she characterized the crimes committed against Indian minors as "a shame and disgrace to the state," which would create a pauper class to be supported by future taxpayers.[33] The Department of Charities and Corrections was no doubt a valuable state department but so far as the protection of Indian minors was concerned the legislature had succeeded in making it innocuous.

The limited number of cases that came under Matthews' observation show an exploitation of childhood so serious and so general that it seemed impossible for any estate to survive. One instance taken at random will illustrate a condition that appeared universal. The mother of the two children involved was dead and their father was in the penitentiary. The guardianship was in Craig County, but the children were said to be in Bryan County, on the other side of the state. The guardian first gave his brother-in-law a five-year agricultural lease on

33 Commissioner of Charities and Corrections, *Report,* 1915-16, pp. 6-7, 37; 1924, p. 213.

the two allotments in order to destroy the sale, and an oil and gas lease to be in effect until the children's majority. The same year he sold the property to the brother-in-law for $1,125 and loaned the money to him immediately, taking a mortgage on the land, so that no cash exchanged hands during the "sale." Fearing that this transaction would not stand they then allowed the taxes to become delinquent, and the brother-in-law's wife purchased the tax title. The guardian charged the children ninety dollars in commission for his services in selling their land, and padded his report with such items as $202.50 to each child for a team of horses. The brother-in-law also sold an oil lease for a comfortable amount, which, considering he had paid nothing for the land, was clear profit. The guardianship ran on in this way for eight years, and many people in the neighborhood of Vinita doubted that such children existed. When Matthews took up the case, it was said that one of the minors, who was still a mere child, had married and died in McIntosh County. A man claiming to be her husband appeared and was appointed administrator of her estate, and made a settlement with the guardian. The other child, a boy, was said to have gone to Kentucky, but he was never found. The guardian's final report was approved by the county judge over the protest of Matthews' assistant and the Federal probate attorney. The property was gone, and the fate of the children themselves was undetermined.

A more drastic method was employed in Rogers County, when the county judge placed a boy in the reform school and his mother in the state institution for the feeble minded while the guardian sold the child's land for $2,000 and squandered the proceeds within nine months. In commenting upon this case Matthews wrote to the head of the reform school, "It looks to me as though a great majority of those orphan indians over on the east side have been about cleaned up." There is unconscious irony in the report made by Matthews' assistant of a girl in the state industrial home. One guardian, who apparently had mismanaged the estate, had been removed and it had proved difficult to secure another because the land was of little value; "however," said the Assistant Commissioner, "the estate will remain in tact and can-not be wasted by any one until a guardian is appointed." The cases in Matthews' files in 1916 and 1917 certainly do not indicate that any revolutionary change had been effected in guardianship matters by the probate reforms that had been undertaken with such enthusiasm in 1914.[34]

One of the reform measures, however, was effective for several years—the recognition given the probate attorneys by the courts. Before their appointment it had been purely a voluntary matter with the county judge as to whether he would invite the assistance of the Agency employees or the representative of Miss Barnard's office. Now in a number of cases the probate attorneys appealed to the district court in opposition to a decree of the county judge, and the state Supreme Court uniformly upheld their right to represent the interest of the ward in opposition to the guardian.[35]

But the protection given unrestricted minors by the probate attorneys lasted only four years. It was withdrawn at the instance of Senator Owen and Representative Hastings by the simple expedient of inserting the word "restricted" in the appropriation bill. From this time on, the probate attorneys not only ceased their work for unrestricted allottees, but they were not permitted by the courts to appear for restricted Indians in matters involving unrestricted property.[36]

The attempt to regulate the approval of fullblood conveyances did not last much longer. It will be remembered that that portion of Sells' rules had been supplanted by a statute enacted at the next session of the legislature. The state Supreme Court decided that this law was unconstitutional; since the power had been conferred by Congress in the act of 1908, the county court was acting as a Federal rather than a state agency, and

[34] Commissioner of Charities and Corrections, Office Files.

[35] *Pacific Reporter,* CLXVI, 736-40; CLXXXII, 233-37.

[36] *Ibid.,* CCVII, 293-96; *Muskogee Times-Democrat,* June 24, 1918; *Congressional Record,* LVI, 6635; Kappler, *Laws and Treaties,* IV, 166.

the state therefore had no right to legislate in the matter. The question next arose as to the validity of the much more stringent rule that this law had attempted to supplant. The court decided that the rule also was not binding. The county court in approving fullblood conveyances exercised a ministerial rather than a judicial function, and it was a Federal agency with no appeal from its decisions; and the Supreme Court held that its own authority to make rules for inferior courts was limited to their judicial functions, and to those cases that could be appealed to the Supreme Court. These decisions placed the responsibility squarely up to the Federal Government, but Congress took no action to fill the legislative gap. It was not necessary that any consideration be paid, or that the judge even see the deed, or that the fullblood grantor be notified or be present, and the approval could be given on the street or at the judge's home. The judges easily fell into the habit of giving their approval as a matter of routine to every conveyance that was presented.[37]

The remaining probate rules were specifically abrogated by the legislature in 1919, and each local court was directed to formulate its own procedure. The judge was required to name two days a week for hearing the affairs of restricted Indians, and to serve notice of these hearings upon the probate attorney and to furnish him a copy of his private rules, but no other safeguard was provided. The act also stipulated that "No court within the State of Oklahoma, other than the County Courts of said State shall be authorized to make rules governing the County Court of the State of Oklahoma." It was believed that this act was in violation of the provision of the state constitution giving the Supreme Court "general superintending control" over all inferior courts and Sells said that steps would be taken to test it, but apparently nothing was done.[38]

[37] *Indian Affairs in Oklahoma*, pp. 58-85, 147-49, 172-85, 197-207, 257, 357, 477-81; *Pacific Reporter*, CXLIV, 613; CXCII, 197-99; CXCIV, 1077-80; CXCV, 484-86; CCXVIII, 813-16; CCXXIII, 141-42; CCXXIV, 990-91.

[38] State of Oklahoma, *Session Laws of 1919*, p. 288; *Constitution*, Article VII, Section 2; Department of the Interior, *Annual Report*, 1919, II, 50.

The truth seems to be that there was no one to take hold of the matter with Mott's unswerving logic or Miss Barnard's emotional fervor; upon the whole it was easier for Sells and pleasanter for the Oklahoma delegation in Congress and the citizenship in general to assume that the probate reform of 1914 had been permanent. In 1920 when virtually every one of his temporary accomplishments had been swept away, Sells published a boastful article showing in detail how the bad conditions that had existed upon his induction into office had been corrected by his reforms.[39]

Forgery, embezzlement, criminal conspiracy, misuse of notary's seals, and other crimes against Indian property continued with monotonous regularity, but these grosser and slightly more dangerous forms of swindling were not as common as the more respectable methods of investing Indian money in worthless real estate, padding guardians' accounts, and allowing excessive fees to guardians and attorneys. It was almost impossible to secure a conviction for outright crime, and the many legal methods of overcharging minors and incompetents passed almost without notice.

The courts were hopelessly congested. In Creek County, where guardianship frauds were especially notorious and were rarely corrected, a newspaper reported in 1916 that there were 219 civil cases on the district court docket, involving oil property worth fifteen to twenty million dollars. Some of these cases had been pending ever since the discovery of oil in the county, but for the preceding two years they had been piling up enormously because of the uncertainty over Indian titles and the sudden value of Creek County land since the discovery of the Cushing Pool. There was no prospect that one out of twenty of these cases would be disposed of during the few days that the court would be in session—it was estimated that continuous sessions for two years would not clear the docket—and about the only recourse open to litigants was settlement out of court. As to criminal prosecutions, the same newspaper stated, "The

[39] Department of the Interior, *Annual Report,* 1920, II, 39.

dismissal of these cases makes a record for the attorney general's office in Creek county that is perfect so far as acquittals are concerned." Under such circumstances it is not strange that frauds against Indians usually went unpunished.[40]

A few criminal convictions were obtained, but only after prolonged legal battles that almost bankrupted the counties and exhausted the patience of the citizens. The many trials of one Muskogee attorney are fairly typical. He had been one of the leading members of the local bar association, and had been very prominent in social and civic life. His first indictment grew out of the abortive Wagoner County grand jury investigation in 1913. Several embezzlement charges were next brought against him in Muskogee County involving estates in which he had served as attorney for the guardian. The first trial resulted in a hung jury; in the second trial, involving a different estate, he was convicted and upon the recommendation of the jury received a sentence of twenty-four hours in prison. At the third trial, involving still another estate he received a three years' penitentiary sentence, which was subsequently confirmed by the criminal court of appeals; and after more than five years' delay he went to prison. Prominent bankers, lawyers, and judges of Muskogee and Tulsa, the publishers of two newspapers, and one of the United States Senators signed a petition for his pardon and after he had served three months his wife secured his release from Governor Robertson.[41]

Few attempts were ever made to disbar attorneys for unprofessional conduct. In 1917 the conduct of six Muskogee attorneys was investigated with regard to the guardianship of wealthy Negro minors. The newspaper report of the testimony of one of the accused attorneys before the Supreme Court referee is significant. According to this account he admitted that he had received fees from the owners of land which was purchased for a rich Negro minor while he was attorney for the guardian. It was customary, he said, for an attorney rep-

[40] *Sapulpa Herald,* April 4, October 2, 1916.

[41] *Muskogee Phoenix,* May 8, 1914; April 9, November 10, 13, 1915; April 30, 1918; May 10, 1919.

resenting an estate to receive besides his regular fees for legal services, additional fees from persons who secured loans from the estate. The custom had been extended to oil and gas leasing, and the lessee regularly paid the attorney a fee when he secured the lease. This practice was a matter of common knowledge, and often the court itself included these fees in the cost of administration. So far as he knew, he was the first attorney who had represented the guardian in purchasing real estate for the ward, and he had applied this general principle to a slightly different transaction. Two of the six attorneys were eventually suspended for six months and one was disbarred.[42]

In the case of restricted Indians, whose oil royalties, per caput shares, and equalization money were under control of the Agency, funds were sometimes not turned over to the guardians if conditions were believed unsatisfactory. Kelsey began in 1913 to withhold these payments from guardians whose wards were not in school, and in 1914 he withheld payments from Tulsa County because of unsatisfactory probate conditions there.[43] Parker's refusal to make the per caput payments in some of the counties in 1916 was due as much to unsatisfactory guardianship conditions as to the illicit liquor traffic. Although this weapon was not used to any great extent, it gave the Agency some check upon the guardians of restricted Indians. In spite of all the shortcomings of the Indian service it is unquestionably true that the property of the restricted Indian was much safer under Agency protection than that of the unrestricted minors and incompetents under the probate courts.

Under these circumstances the clamor for the removal of additional restrictions continued. In the campaign of 1912 especially, the telegraph and telephone poles and the trees were generally placarded with promises of Congressional candidates to secure such legislation, and for the next few years

[42] *Muskogee Phoenix,* July 30, 1922; *Muskogee Times-Democrat,* August 7-10, 1918; August 31, 1920.

[43] Lake Mohonk Conference, *Report,* 1913, pp. 20-21; Indian Office Files, 43333/14 Five Tribes 352.

many bills to that effect were introduced in Congress.[44] But the pressure was less insistent as Oklahomans gradually came to accept the restricted status of Indian land as a necessary evil, and by 1920 efforts to change the situation had virtually ceased.

The Oklahoma delegation worked constantly for legislation investing the Superintendent with final authority; and in 1918 they managed to place all matters but oil and gas leasing under control of the Agency. The Department showed a hidebound rigidity in its requirement that every minute transaction should be referred to the Secretary; obviously the Secretary could not give his personal attention to such details, and since it was acted upon by a minor clerk at Washington it could have been settled more rapidly and efficiently by a more responsible official at Muskogee. On the other hand the Superintendent was a political appointee subject to the influence of local patronage and there was a strong element of danger in the insistence of Oklahomans that final authority in all matters should be conferred upon such an official.[45]

The Oklahoma delegation always had an important influence upon Indian legislation. For a considerable portion of the time three of the Representatives and both Senators served as members of the Indian Affairs committees of their respective houses. Moreover, the conspicuous ability of the three Indians who represented Oklahoma in Congress, Owen, Carter, and Hastings, gave weight to their opinions about Indian matters. Their influence was especially noticeable during the frequent Congressional investigations.

[44] Moorehead, *The American Indian,* p. 145; Lake Mohonk Conference, *Report,* 1913, pp. 35-40, 44-45; *Standard-Sentinel,* February 15, May 23, 1912; *Congressional Record,* XLVIII, 4168, 8233; LIV, 1317; LVI, 1033-34; LVII, 1940, 2011-12; LVIII, 180-81, 262; LIX, 903, 6104; LX, 1433.

[45] *Congressional Record,* LIII, 3308-9, 10995-97; LIV, 1437; LVI, 5114, 5239-40, 6625-35, 6679, 6687; LVII, 2205-9, 4592-93, 4999; LVIII, 263-64; LIX, 1279-80, 3729; *Muskogee Times-Democrat,* January 5, 29, March 21, 28, April 8, 1916; March 21, 1917; *Idabel Democrat-Record,* March 29, 1917; *Muskogee Phoenix,* November 23, 1915, January 8, 1921; State of Oklahoma, *Session Laws of 1916,* p. 154; Kappler, *Laws and Treaties,* IV, 165, 212, 254.

With so large a field of financial and social administration under Federal guardianship, Oklahomans became accustomed to frequent visits by Congressional committees. A few of these committees made a sincere attempt to discover the wishes of the white population, one made a thorough inquiry into Indian contracts, but not even one from the creation of the Dawes Commission down to 1930 tried to learn of the welfare of the people in whose behalf the whole Indian policy of the Federal Government was supposed to have been undertaken.

Most of the investigations were too superficial to benefit anybody. An account of a typical visit made by a subcommittee of the House Indian Affairs Committee in 1920 was given by a Muskogee paper with no attempt at conscious irony. Its purpose was stated as an "extended investigation" into Indian affairs throughout the United States as a guide to legislation. Hastings and Carter served as two of its five members. They were to arrive on Sunday and hospitable Muskogee made plans for their entertainment: first they would be conducted over the city and to old Fort Gibson, and places of historic interest would be pointed out; next they would be taken to the country club for a tea, "which will incidentally open the club's social season," and those who desired would have an opportunity to try the golf course; and at dinner they would be guests of the local business men at the Severs Hotel. Monday morning the committee would meet at Parker's office, and it was expected that it would "satisfy itself as to the exact conditions that obtain for Indians in Oklahoma." At an open meeting in the afternoon Agency officials, citizens, and Indians would be given an opportunity to be heard; and at 5:10 the committee would leave to spend one day at the Osage Agency before going on to New Mexico.[46] A community of fullbloods living in the most abject destitution and ignorance was located in the hills of Muskogee County only a few miles from the city, but obviously this place of "historic" as well as immediate interest was not included in the itinerary.

46 *Muskogee Times-Democrat*, May 8, 1920.

It may be said in summing up, that the presence of its Indian population had a profound effect upon the development of Oklahoma: upon the credit side was the cultural gain of a historic past different from that of any other American commonwealth, and of a strong and able racial element that made an important contribution to its society; upon the debit side was an unassimilated group that was becoming increasingly impoverished and degraded, a widespread opportunity for plunder that corrupted government and church and press and public opinion, an uncertainty regarding land titles and other business transactions that hindered legitimate development, and an unequal tax burden that handicapped the schools and stopped the courts in their functions and thus limited the very agencies of which the Indians were most in need. But outward friction had largely ceased, and both whites and Indians had to a certain extent accepted the conditions, when the election of 1920 upset the precarious balance that had been established between the state and Federal governments.

# CHAPTER XII

# The Battle for Spoils

THE election of 1920 ushered in a stormy period with various Republican factions fighting for the spoils of the Indian service. A sinister influence behind the political factions, so far as they affected Indian administration, was the fierce competition between rival oil companies to secure the leases of rich allotments. This motive complicated the guardianship system; the contests between rival applicants and their attorneys for the opportunity of plundering the estates of wealthy Indians were entangled with the efforts of the oil companies to secure the appointment of guardians favorable to their interests. Control of the Agency with its supervision of oil leasing and its discretionary power over the guardians of restricted Indians became the goal of these rival groups, just as the important patronage that it offered continued to be the spoil of rival politicians. While these dark forces worked in the background to control the Agency, the Indians became helpless pawns in the game. At the same time, while this specialized form of greed increased in menace to Indian welfare, the humbler and more widespread varieties of swindling declined in importance; the exploitation of Indian land continued through uncontrolled agricultural leasing and inheritance sales, but the plundering of children through guardianships almost ceased through natural limitation. Because of the sordid influences controlling appointments to the Indian service the protection offered by the Federal Government probably reached its lowest level during this period.

In 1920 Oklahoma for the first time joined the Republican ranks. It gave its electoral vote to Warren G. Harding; chose a Republican, John W. Harreld of Oklahoma City, to take the place of Senator Gore; and elected Republicans for five of the eight seats in the House of Representatives. The Republicans also gained control of the lower house of the state legislature. This sweeping victory was part of the general Republican "landslide" of 1920, but in a more specific sense it was brought about through an alliance between Jake Hamon, oil man of Ardmore, who became National Committeeman, and his friend, Harry M. Daugherty. Hamon and Daugherty had worked before the national convention for Harding's nomination, and it was partly due to this effective combination of politics and oil that Oklahoma joined the Republican column.[1]

When Harding became President, and Daugherty became chief patronage dispenser and Attorney-General, and Oklahoma became a Republican state, a harmonious era similar to that which followed the Wilson election should have been ushered in. But Oklahoma Republicans were hopelessly divided and the distribution of spoils increased the bitterness of their feuds. Hamon was shot to death by his mistress a few days after the election, but upon his deathbed he drew up a list of his henchmen to be rewarded with appointments, and for years his influence remained as a force in Oklahoma politics. James A. Harris of Wagoner succeeded to Hamon's office in the party, but his control was challenged by J. J. McGraw, Tulsa banker, brother of the president of the Gypsy Oil Company, and former National Committeeman. A three-cornered patronage fight ensued among Harris and McGraw and Senator Harreld, who naturally felt that *he* ought to control the spoils. The struggle was further complicated by the influence of Mrs. Hamon, who lived in Chicago, but who took an active part in the Oklahoma patronage fight in behalf of the Hamon interests. Frank Ketch, the administrator of the Hamon estate, was also recognized because of that fact as a power in Republican politics, although he was himself a Democrat. The Republican representatives sometimes joined these factional leaders and sometimes fought independently for their share of the patronage; and one of

[1] *Muskogee Phoenix,* April 16, 1921, for example.

them, Miss Alice Robertson of Muskogee, who had succeeded W. W. Hastings, attempted to further her appointments through a strong personal friendship with Mrs. Harding. Mrs. Hamon was also said to be a relative of the Hardings, and E. C. Motter, a Muskogee politician, was a close friend of Harding, and had been very useful in handling the crowds and performing similar services during Harding's "front porch" campaign. Various alliances and counter-alliances were formed by these political and financial rivals only to break up and re-form with dizzying instability.[2]

The Oklahomans apparently would have been permitted to select a local man as Commissioner of Indian Affairs, but the leaders fought so bitterly with each other over three rival candidates that Charles H. Burke received the appointment.[3] Representatives of the various factions then gathered in Washington and attempted to draw up a "slate." Department of Justice appointments entered largely into their considerations, but the Five Tribes Superintendency was also an important office. Miss Robertson fought for L. G. Disney of Muskogee, her campaign manager; T. A. Chandler, Republican member of Congress from Vinita, was supporting Shade Wallen, a Hamon lieutenant, also of Vinita; and seventeen of the nineteen Republican state senators held a caucus and endorsed E. M. Frye, Cherokee member of the state Senate. The appointment finally went to Victor M. Locke, who had been one of the unsuccessful candidates for the position of Commissioner of Indian Affairs. He seems to have owed his victory to the favor of Daugherty and E. C. Motter and to the personal selection of Secretary Fall; and apparently the Oklahoma factions accepted him as a compromise candidate.[4]

Locke assumed office June 1. A mixed-blood Choctaw, he was the son of an intermarried white man who had figured prominently in the most serious factional disturbance of the

[2] *Muskogee Phoenix,* March 1, April 3, 16, 21, May 7, 23, 1921; May 16, 19, 1922; February 14, 1923; *Muskogee Times-Democrat,* May 3, 1928.

[3] *Muskogee Phoenix,* March 16, 24, 25, 27, April 1, 1921.

[4] *Ibid.,* April 3, 15, 16, 24-28, May 1, 7, 12-18, June 1, 1921.

tribal period, and he himself had strong friends and bitter enemies within the tribe. He had held office several years as appointive Principal Chief of the Choctaws, had been a member of the state legislature, and had served with distinction in the World War. He was, as he once expressed it, a "poor politician," and attempted to administer the Agency with an independence that soon brought him into serious disfavor with the spoilsmen.[5]

The names of the probate attorneys were made public July 1. The number had been gradually diminished and it was now cut to eight. The appointment of the Creek and Chickasaw tribal attorneys was announced at the same time. The political considerations that had dictated these selections were frankly recognized throughout eastern Oklahoma, and the newspapers glibly recounted the trades that had taken place. There was an ominous note of disharmony in the report that Locke had been opposed to most of the nominations.[6]

More serious was the break between Locke and Motter. Motter had been appointed assistant attorney-general, a new Oklahoma position with a generous salary, and it was generally believed that he was the chief patronage dispenser in the state. At first he spent a great deal of time at the Agency, but just before the end of the year an open break occurred between him and Locke. He suddenly resigned his own position the following May, but the break continued. At the same time it was apparent that the political alliances in eastern Oklahoma were shifting to form new combinations.[7]

Locke apparently made no effort to align himself with a faction, and adopted a policy devoted to the interest of the Indians. But probably no local man who owed his office to the considerations that had dictated this appointment could have satisfied a sufficient number of the rivals who sought favors

5 *Ibid.*, June 18-25, 30, July 1, November 13, 1921.

6 *Ibid.*, June 5, July 1, 1921; *Indian Affairs in Oklahoma*, pp. 55, 146, 171, 247-48, 251-52, 256, 264.

7 *Muskogee Phoenix*, May 22, June 19, December 30, 1921; May 19, 1922; February 14, 1923.

from the Agency, to retain his position. He was surrounded by politicians hungering for the spoils of office, oil companies fighting each other for leases, guardians demanding the privilege of squandering the vast accumulated funds of restricted Indians, and automobile salesmen, furniture dealers, and even undertakers quarrelling for the opportunity of selling their wares.

Before he had been in office a year, it was apparent that underground forces were working for his removal. Rumors of his resignation, investigations of his conduct, and official denials filled the air. In April 1923, Dr. Hubert Work, who had recently succeeded Fall as Secretary of the Interior, came to Oklahoma with Burke. The politicians were waiting on the platform when the train pulled into Muskogee. Harris outsprinted his rivals, but Work managed to break away from his fervid custody and proceeded to his real business of inspecting the Agency. Work and the Commissioner gave the impression that they had no intention of sacrificing Locke to appease local politicians.[8]

But events soon began to move rapidly. There were direct appeals to President Harding; an atmosphere of feverish expectancy in Muskogee with Federal secret service men investigating Locke, while crowds of politicians from all over the state jammed the halls and held sessions behind closed doors at the Agency; rumors of a complete patronage "shake-up" with a hurried conference of Republican leaders at Oklahoma City, where a new "slate" was prepared; and frenzied trips to Washington to settle the new appointments before the President's departure for his fatal Alaskan trip. Locke steadfastly refused to resign, but with a prophetic insight that indicated inside knowledge the newspapers announced Shade Wallen as his successor. Apparently the investigators were unable to uncover any irregularity in Locke's official conduct; but Wallen was summoned to Washington to take the oath of office, and

[8] *Muskogee Phoenix,* November 23, December 12, 1922; March 27, 28, 1923; *Muskogee Times-Democrat,* April 3, 4, 1923; *Okmulgee Daily Times,* June 24, 1923.

apparently as an afterthought Locke was removed for participating in drinking parties at his home. It was said that with Wallen's appointment the last of Jake Hamon's dying behests had been carried out. He owed his position to the continued insistence of T. A. Chandler, who had not been returned to Congress in the election of 1922, but who was still a power in Republican politics, and to an amicable agreement among Harris, McGraw, and Harreld.[9]

Within a few days after Locke's removal it was reported that thousands of applications had already been received from persons desiring employment with the Agency. Most of the positions were under civil service, but several dismissals and consolidations took place in the interest of "economy," and the resulting new positions should have yielded some consolation to politicians. New appointments were made to some of the tribal offices after political fights as complicated as the one that led to Locke's dismissal.[10]

Strangely enough, while Republican politicians were fighting each other for control of the Muskogee office, there was at first no serious antagonism between Burke and the Congressional delegation. The Democratic party resumed its normal ascendency in state affairs in 1922, and elected seven of the eight representatives, but the old feud between a Democratic state and a Republican administration of Indian affairs did not at once break out. With regard to general Indian policy Hastings—who had defeated Miss Robertson in 1922—and Carter earnestly argued for Departmental protection and supervision, and warned Congress of the danger of placing the property of minors and incompetents under state courts; and they even attempted to secure legislation to check the unholy power of the Osage guardians, which had created a situation in that small and wealthy tribe even more scandalous than

[9] *Muskogee Phoenix*, June 10-25, 1923; *Muskogee Times-Democrat*, June 12-26, 1923; *Okmulgee Daily Times*, June 15-29, 1923; *Survey of Indians in the United States*, XIV, 5324-25.

[10] *Muskogee Times-Democrat*, June 26-29, July 3, 20, 31, August 1, September 13, 14, 1923; January 1, March 20, April 7, October 16, December 6, 1924; *Muskogee Phoenix*, June 30, 1923.

existed in the Five Tribes area. It is doubtful if Carter or Hastings could have retained their seats in Congress if they had supported the same policy for the Five Tribes, but their position with regard to Indians outside the state or outside their districts indicates their general harmony with the Indian Office.[11]

The Osage bill was opposed by Everette B. Howard of Tulsa, a Democrat who alternated several times with Chandler according to the shifting tides of politics,[12] and whose district included the Osage region. Howard soon became actively hostile to the Indian Office, and he began to present specific charges of incompetent or corrupt administration of Indian affairs and of an understanding between Chandler and Shade Wallen.[13]

But the Indian Office found its most relentless enemy when Oklahoma elected a second Republican Senator in 1924. Owen retired at that time, and W. B. Pine, a millionaire oil man of Okmulgee, won the election through a combination of Ku Klux Klan influence and a defective primary law that gave the Democratic nomination to an unacceptable candidate.[14] Pine's desire to control the Agency spoils brought him into conflict with the Indian Office; moreover the Indian Office had come to a definite break with the county judge and guardians of Okmulgee County regarding the accumulated funds of restricted Indians, and Pine became the champion of the guardians.

The battle for the control of fat guardianships had become one of the major factors in East Side politics. A newspaper story chosen almost at random will show the connection that existed in the popular mind. Briefly, the account was as follows:

[11] *Congressional Record*, LXII, 2421; LXIV, 4689-92; LXV, 859-61, 4471-73, 5759-66, 9675; LVIII, 1440-41.

[12] Chandler, 1917-19; Howard, 1919-21; Chandler, 1921-23; Howard, 1923-25. Howard was an unsuccessful candidate for the Senate in 1924, but served again in the House, 1927-29.

[13] *Congressional Record*, LVI, 197, 329-36, 4570-71.

[14] *Muskogee Times-Democrat*, August 19, November 6, 1924.

How a Muskogee attorney and political henchman of Big Jim Harris entered a guardianship contest in Wagoner County and emerged with $70,000 is being told in Muskogee today. He sold to a Negro minor through his guardian 700 acres of farm land just west of Muskogee at nearly $100 an acre. How he put the deal over will remain a mystery as the guardianship machinery of Wagoner County is supposed to be strongly anti-Harris. The attorney for the guardian is the sworn enemy of Harris, and is credited with furnishing the machinery that elected the county judge.[15]

In the early 1920's the newspapers were filled with accounts of legal battles between rival guardianship-and-attorney combinations, dizzying charges and counter-charges of mismanagement, "recoveries" bringing hundreds of thousands of dollars to successful attorneys, and desperate attempts on the part of young Creek freedmen to break away from the jurisdiction of the Oklahoma courts. Some great estates were completely dissipated by the process; others were based on oil wealth so vast that it seemed impossible to exhaust it.[16]

Other hands began to clutch at the property of oil-rich Indians. Bacone College was still maintained at Muskogee by the American Baptist Home Mission Society, and students from many Indian tribes were enrolled there. There is no question of the value of its work, or of the philanthropic motives that prompted it. About 1920 it became apparent to the administrators of this school that wealthy Indians might be induced to create a great endowment for the education of their own race. The Indians responded willingly; they still practised the instinctive and uncalculating generosity that had made them the prey of the white man, they believed in education and religion, and they were glad to devote a portion of their wealth to uplifting their own people. Some of them believed that their property would be placed beyond the grasp of predatory interests if they were to create a trust that would yield them an income during their life and would revert to the college after their death or the

<hr />

[15] *Ibid.*, December 17, 1923.  [16] See especially *ibid.*, 1923-25.

death of their heirs. Superintendent Parker, who had grown up in the tribal schools and had a great respect for the old system of higher education for Indians, was entirely sympathetic toward such considerations; and after the change in administration, Commissioner Burke, who apparently thought Indian money might as well be diverted from its usual channels of waste and spoliation and used for a good purpose, gave the policy his enthusiastic support. The school began to receive large contributions in 1920, and within the next four years nearly a million dollars had been secured either in cash or in trust funds. A few contributions were made to Presbyterian schools during the same period.[17]

But there was something demoralizing about soliciting money from a people too naïve to resist a religious appeal, and the prospect of the vast wealth that might be secured in this way was enough to turn the head of almost any church executive. The Baptists began to solicit contributions too eagerly, and rivalry soon appeared between the Northern and Southern branches of the denomination.[18] There was another dangerous element in the situation. It is very improbable that Commissioner Burke was deliberately purchasing Baptist support by approving these gifts to Bacone; but there was at least a possibility that an Indian Office-Baptist alliance might eventually develop. In his annual report of 1923 Burke answered recent critics by publishing a resolution by the Board of Managers of the American Baptist Home Mission Society expressing "its continued and growing confidence" in the Commissioner.[19] Unquestionably part of the hostile criticism of the Indian Office was based upon selfish considerations, but this unqualified Baptist endorsement was open to the same suspicion of interested motives and was even more menacing to the efficiency of the service.

[17] *Muskogee Times-Democrat,* December 22, 1923; June 20, 1924; February 28, 1925; January 13, 14, 1931; *Muskogee Phoenix,* February 11, May 22, June 17, 1921; *Senate Docs.,* 70 Cong., 2 Sess., No. 263, pp. 107-8.

[18] *Survey of Indians in the United States,* IV, 1647-51; *Muskogee Times-Democrat,* January 12, 1929.

[19] Commissioner of Indian Affairs, *Annual Report,* 1923, pp. 21-22.

Burke had believed ever since the sensational Mott exposé of 1912 that the solution of the whole Five Tribes problem lay in removing the Indians from the control of the probate courts. In the fall of 1923 he began to take active steps to accomplish this purpose. Following the Mott precedent he ordered a statistical study of probate conditions. At the same time Matthew K. Sniffen of the Indian Rights Association, Gertrude Bonnin, research agent of the Indian Welfare Committee of the General Federation of Women's Clubs, and Charles H. Fabens, attorney for the American Indian Defense Association, came to conduct a private investigation.[20]

Edward Merrick, chief of the law division of the Muskogee office, prepared a study of fullblood inheritance sales through the county courts from 1912 to 1922 in order to discover the adequacy of the price received by the Indians. Disregarding the sale price recorded in subsequent deeds, because this price was sometimes inflated and did not always represent the actual consideration, he confined his statistics to the unmistakable evidence of loans subsequently secured upon the property from conservative companies, the same day, the following day, or possibly three months from the date of purchase. He found many instances where the amount of this loan was far above, in one case more than three times as great, as the purchase price paid to the Indian.[21] Obviously in such sales the land had cost the purchaser nothing at all.

The investigation of the cost of guardianship covered six counties: Creek, Okmulgee, Okfuskee, and Muskogee, in the oil belt; McCurtain with its fullblood allottees, several of whom owned oil land in Carter County; and Stephens, an agricultural county. There were 14,229 guardianship cases in the six counties, but 9,042 had to be disregarded because the records were incomplete or entirely missing. Of the remaining cases, 2,821 were unmistakably those of Five Tribes allottees, and these were made the object of statistical analysis. The total

20 Indian Office Files, 86053/23 Five Tribes 350; *Muskogee Times-Democrat*, February 6, 1924.
21 *Indian Affairs in Oklahoma*, pp. 208-13.

income from these estates was $14,750,043.94, and the total cost of administration was $2,002,385.37, an average of 13.57 per cent of the receipts. Apparently some of the estates were economically administered in the interest of the wards, hence the average cost gives no indication of the excessive fees charged in many instances. An analysis of the cases according to the cost of administration is as follows:[22]

| NUMBER OF CASES | COST OF ADMINISTRATION |
|---|---|
| 431 | less than 5 per cent |
| 490 | 5 to 10 per cent |
| 832 | 10 to 20 per cent |
| 485 | 20 to 30 per cent |
| 260 | 30 to 40 per cent |
| 116 | 40 to 50 per cent |
| 252 | more than 50 per cent |

Individual cases are even more revealing than the statistical summary. In a large number the entries are all of recent date, showing that the bad conditions that existed before statehood or even before the reforms of 1914 could not be cited as an explanation of the excessive costs. The items charged against the wards themselves are also indicative of padding or extravagant expenditure. The case of one young Negro is fairly typical. He was nearly seventeen years old when a big oil strike was made on his allotment in 1920. His two guardians, each of whom received a salary of nine hundred dollars a month for cashing his royalty checks and investing the proceeds, reported during the next two years that they purchased six automobiles for their ward at a total cost of $18,250.58.[23]

These data were submitted to the Commissioner by Wallen, December 31, 1923. Copies of the statistical summary were furnished the Indian Affairs Committees of both houses, and a strong attempt was made by Burke upon the basis of this evidence to secure legislation during that session of Congress to

[22] *Indian Affairs in Oklahoma*, pp. 408-9, 471.
[23] Indian Office Files, 86953/23 Five Tribes 350; *Muskogee Times-Democrat*, May 27, 1920; *Muskogee Phoenix*, March 4, 1923.

remove all affairs of restricted Indians from the probate courts.[24]

At the same time Burke received assistance from an unexpected source. Three days before the submission of the Wallen report the State Bar Association in its annual meeting adopted a resolution not specifically mentioning Indian cases, but condemning general probate administration as follows:

"The dissipation of estates by the appointment of one or more guardians or administrators without business experience and wholly incapable of handling business affairs, many of them graduates of the bankruptcy court, or a committee woman who has rendered valiant service to the successful candidate, and the appointment 'by the court' of two or more attorneys on fat salaries to aid these guardians and administrators in the 'faithful, efficient performance of their duties' and to keep their clients at large while the widows, orphans, and wards go hungry and poorly clad, cause one to wonder why he should die and leave an estate in Oklahoma. . . .

"The probate business is regarded as so essentially 'political' that the better class of lawyers are seldom found connected with it except in contested cases, or in winding up the estates of former clients so controlled by will or otherwise."[25]

Few people took the trouble to read these resolutions, or the arid statistics of the Wallen report, but sensational interest was aroused over the appearance in February of a pamphlet entitled *Oklahoma's Poor Rich Indians*. It had been written by Sniffen, Fabens, and Gertrude Bonnin as the report of their investigations, and it described and condemned the probate situation in vigorous terms and recommended that so far as was constitutionally possible all control over Indian property

---

[24] Commissioner of Indian Affairs, *Annual Report,* 1924, p. 26; Indian Office Files, 86943/23 Five Tribes 350; *Muskogee Times-Democrat,* February 8, 1924; *Congressional Record,* LXV, 23333.

[25] *Indian Affairs in Oklahoma,* p. 397; M. L. Mott, *A National Blunder* (Probably published at Washington, 1924), p. 2.

should be taken from the Oklahoma courts and restored to the Department.[26]

The members of Congress from Oklahoma had improved in technique since the unexpected presentation of the Mott report. They held a hasty meeting and agreed to insist upon a Congressional investigation, and they finally secured a resolution authorizing an inquiry by the House Indian Affairs Committee. They telegraphed to the Governor, and the Governor and the Attorney-General notified Burke of their readiness to institute ouster proceedings against any county judge guilty of corrupt probate administration if Burke would furnish them with specific proof.[27]

At the same time the Oklahomans worked as a unit to defeat Burke's bill restoring control to the Department. They characterized the charges in the Sniffen pamphlet as exaggerated and untrue, and accused Burke of trying to force legislation before a proper investigation had been made to determine the facts. Burke apparently was surprised at this concerted opposition, for it was at this same session of Congress that Carter and Hastings had supported similar legislation for the Osages and had strongly condemned the Osage guardianships. They found several reasons to explain this apparent inconsistency, but it was a fact that the Osages all lived in one county and that their exploitation was not of state-wide political importance.[28]

Meanwhile the publication of the Sniffen pamphlet had reverberations in Oklahoma that at the time seemed important. Late in February more than four hundred Indians gathered at Tulsa to form a state-wide protective association against further exploitation. Five Tribes and West Side Indians alike were represented, and the colorfully blanketed Osage or Pawnee sat next to men like Victor Locke who were leaders in the white man's society. Copies of the pamphlet were distributed,

[26] *Indian Affairs in Oklahoma,* pp. 1-32; *Muskogee Times-Democrat,* February 6-12, 1924.

[27] *Congressional Record,* LXV, 2221, 4460-64, 5774; LXVI, 330, 3498.

[28] *Muskogee Times-Democrat,* February 15-19, 27, March 3, 22, 31, April 5, 10, May 1, 1924.

and a strong determination was expressed to secure corrective action instead of the resolutions and oratory into which so much Indian enthusiasm had evaporated.

Concerted action, however, seemed impossible. Some of the Indians present at this meeting were among the leading politicians of the state, and the temptation to further the interests of candidates in this election year was too strong to be resisted. Obviously the Indians could defend themselves only through political action, for the county judges who permitted the spoliation were elective officials, as were the members of the legislature and the members of Congress who refused them protection; but the introduction of political issues into their meeting divided them hopelessly on general principles foreign to Indian matters. Even if they could have subordinated all other considerations to the welfare of their people, it would not have been easy to agree upon a remedy. Should they fight the Indian Bureau for its stupid routine, its unimaginative and arbitrary control, and its financial muddling? Or should they seek greater Bureau protection to deliver them from the infamous power of the probate courts? They created a permanent organization, the Oklahoma Society of Indians, and indorsed the bill before Congress providing for an investigation, and the Frye Bill before the state legislature. After this innocuous action they adjourned.[29]

The Frye Bill was also the outgrowth of the recent revelations. It was sponsored by E. M. Frye of Sallisaw, Republican state senator, appointive Chief of the Cherokees, and perennial candidate for the Five Tribes Superintendency. As originally introduced it limited guardians' compensation to $50 a month, but this drastic restriction was modified. As finally enacted it forbade anybody to serve as guardian if he was financially indebted to the judge, if the judge became pecuniarily liable to him, or if he had rendered financial aid to the judge in his campaign. Money belonging to minors and incompetents could be invested only in real estate or first mortgages on real estate,

[29] *Ibid.*, February 26, 27, 1924.

in Federal, state, or municipal bonds, and in stock of Oklahoma building and loan associations. Auditors' compensation was limited to $25 a day. Guardians were to receive not more than 3 per cent for collecting oil and gas rentals and royalties, and not more than 10 per cent for collecting real estate rents and other income; and no guardian was to receive more than $4,000 for his services in one year. Attorney's fees were limited by a maximum of $50 a month for estates valued at not more than $50,000, $75 a month for estates between $50,000 and $75,000, and not more than $100 a month for estates of more than $75,000; but contingent fees based upon contracts for the recovery of property, approved by the court or in unrestricted cases by the Department, were not included in this limitation. If joint guardians were appointed, the total compensation should not exceed that paid to a single guardian. Any minor about to attain his majority against whom a petition of incompetency had been filed was given the right to have the question determined by a jury trial.[30]

Many people sincerely believed at first that this law would curb guardianship abuses, but it is impossible to discover any material reduction in administrative costs or any noticeable improvement in the guardianship system after its enactment.[31] The county courts generally held that it did not restrict their right to fix the guardians' compensation, that the percentage limitation applied only to *collections* and not disbursements.[32] Only the $4,000 limitation had any meaning under this interpretation, and this could be evaded by special allowances for extraordinary services.[33]

The *Muskogee Times-Democrat* published an editorial June 12, 1924, that attracted wide attention. It stated that approximately fifty wealthy restricted Indians were living outside the state or drifting from place to place afraid to establish a resi-

[30] *Ibid.*, February 20, March 9, 1924; State of Oklahoma, *Session Laws of 1923-24*, pp. 100-2.

[31] *Muskogee Times-Democrat*, March 15, 20, 1924.

[32] *Ibid.*, December 3, 15, 1924; June 22, October 20, 1925.

[33] *Survey of Indians in the United States*, XIV, 6335-36.

dence. Muskogee with its desirable living conditions and the convenient location of the Agency was the logical place for them to settle if they could be protected from persecution; and the writer suggested action to correct the guardianship system for the benefit of the Indians and the prosperity of the town. The county and district judges immediately wrote to express their complete endorsement of this "very able editorial."[34]

A year later the same newspaper stated that approximately ten million dollars had been lost to Muskogee by this short-sighted policy of driving its wealthy residents into exile, and it published a partial list of wealthy Negroes and Indians that had recently settled in other states and totaled their estimated fortunes. All these people were well known to local residents, for battles for control of their estates had filled the newspapers. Many of them had broken away from their guardians only after years of legal struggles, personal harassment, and even physical hazard. Others had not been so fortunate; and they were still subject to every form of personal humiliation and legal coercion that could possibly be employed to keep their property under local jurisdiction.[35] In 1931 when Federal Judge John C. Pollock was at Muskogee to hear one of the involved suits in which a young freedman was fighting to secure possession of his property, he said he had become convinced that at least a hundred wealthy allottees would like to live in Muskogee if only they dared to settle there.[36]

But while newspapers and judges were making these damaging assertions, the House committee made its investigation. The hearings took place in November 1924. The members were Homer P. Snyder of New York, Sid C. Roach of Missouri, Milton C. Garber, an Oklahoma Republican from the West Side, and W. W. Hastings. Hastings for the most part remained quietly in the background while the affairs of his state were under investigation, but he made a determined fight to keep the Wallen report out of the record; Garber went out

---

34 *Muskogee Times-Democrat*, June 12, 1924; *Indian Affairs in Oklahoma*, pp. 487-89.
35 *Muskogee Times-Democrat*, May 2, 1925.          36 *Ibid.*, March 4, 1931.

of his way to express his personal confidence in certain judges when specific charges were brought against them; and Snyder and Roach entered into a violent defense of all state officers and institutions. During the whole proceedings the efforts of the committee to avoid discovering anything were unique even in Indian investigations. In advance the members expressed their confidence in the courts, during the hearings they impugned the integrity of all who presented evidence to the contrary, and at the close they solemnly exonerated them of all wrong.[37]

Throughout the investigation Hastings condemned the probate attorneys for inactivity. No doubt he was right. Ever since they began their work under such favorable auspices in 1914 their authority had been progressively undermined until their legal position was so precarious that it was necessary for them to avoid antagonizing the judges. They still had the right to represent restricted Indians in probate matters, but an unfriendly judge could set his guardianship hearings upon days when it was impossible for them to be present because of conflicting duties in another county. The oil royalties collected by the Agency from restricted land were paid out to the guardian only with the approval of the probate attorney; but the Indian Office was using this power with extreme caution, and the county judges and guardians had already begun to challenge it in the courts. The probate attorneys, of course, had no authority over the guardian's management of unrestricted funds belonging to restricted Indians; and partition sales and the approval of fullblood conveyances, except with a few judges who maintained a policy of voluntary cooperation, were regularly carried out without notice to any Departmental representative.[38]

The tenure of the probate attorneys, moreover, rested upon political preferment, which in eastern Oklahoma was inextric-

---

[37] *Indian Affairs in Oklahoma*, pp. 1-26, 64, 158, 244, 249, 251, 255, 259-63, 345-47, 351-54, 379-84, 406-7, 455-58, 474-77.

[38] *Ibid.*, pp. 56-85, 146-49, 172-86, 197-207, 250-59, 265, 357, 420, 432, 460-62, 477-86; *Muskogee Times-Democrat*, September 13, 1923.

ably entangled with guardianship rivalries. They were themselves too vulnerable to local influence to resist the terrific pressure that was placed upon them. Hastings charged them with incompetence. Possibly he was right again. Considering the manner of their appointment it would have been a miracle if they had all been men of outstanding qualifications. The last Indian Appropriation Act had attempted to correct this condition by requiring a competitive examination by the Civil Service Commission. Though all had taken the examination, they had not been officially notified of their rating. Hastings on his return to Washington discovered that two had failed and that several others had made very low grades. Even the two who failed were continued under "temporary" appointment pending the selection of eligibles. Apparently only the most perfunctory attention was ever paid to the merit requirement, for one of the attorneys who failed to pass the examination was still holding his position in 1930.[39]

Obviously the number of Indians who were in need of probate protection had greatly declined. Most of the allottees had already attained their majority, and the guardianship business was now largely confined to rich adults who had been declared incompetent. The investigation disclosed, however, the extent to which a few real estate dealers controlled large tracts of agricultural land, often by forged leases or no lease at all. State and county officers usually refused to prosecute; the land barons were often deeply entrenched in political influence and public favor, and it was unpopular to put the county to the expense of protecting a group who paid no taxes. If the probate attorneys attempted to clear the land by a civil suit, the Indian had no money to pay the cost or even to travel from his distant mountain home to testify. If a *bona fide* lessee attempted to secure the land from the Indian, he was confronted by forged instruments and harassed by lawsuits until it was easier to abandon the field to the "lease grafter."[40]

[39] *Indian Affairs in Oklahoma*, pp. 495-96; Kappler, *Laws and Treaties*, IV, 430, act of June 5, 1924; *Survey of Indians in the United States*, XIV, 5496-97, 5939.
[40] *Indian Affairs in Oklahoma*, pp. 76-78, 108-46, 264-95, 306-10, 426.

The committee really tried to elicit information regarding one charge in the Sniffen pamphlet—that there was collusion between judge, guardian, and merchandise dealer; but they found no specific proof. This matter was so subtle and went through so many ramifications that it was almost impossible to discover.[41]

Charges against the Federal officials were also made before the investigating committee in the Jackson Barnett and Maud Lee Mudd guardianships and the Exie Fife divorce case.[42] These three cases were eventually to shake political circles in Oklahoma and Washington and break the armed truce that had been established between the state and the Department.

The final report of the committee completely exonerated everybody in the Interior Department even as it vindicated the probate courts, and sternly admonished Sniffen and his associates for publishing unsubstantiated rumors. But after "whitewashing" everybody connected with the system it strongly condemned the system itself. It found that the approval of fullblood conveyances by the county court furnished no protection to the Indians; that the unrestricted agricultural leasing invited forgery and blackmail, and was "indefensible from any standpoint of trusteeship"; and that "reprehensible" practices were carried on in the oil districts by professional guardians.[43] Since Congress was more responsible for the system than for the conduct of the individuals connected with its administration, this investigation, superficial as it was, should have furnished a basis for some constructive legislation.

Hastings attempted such legislation during the session of 1924-1925. His bill provided every possible safeguard in the approval of fullblood conveyances—public notice, the right of the probate attorney to appear, hearings in open court, and a compulsory interval of thirty days from the death of the de-

[41] *Indian Affairs in Oklahoma*, pp. 26, 341, 494; *Muskogee Phoenix*, August 7, 1923; *Muskogee Times-Democrat*, July 9, August 28, 30, 1923; February 18, 1924; March 21, June 21, 1925; June 29, 1926; *Okmulgee Daily Democrat*, May 1, 1929.
[42] *Indian Affairs in Oklahoma*, pp. 448-55, 460-63.
[43] *House Reports*, 68 Cong., 2 Sess., No. 1527.

cedent. It made agricultural leases subject to approval by the county court after notice to the Agency. It provided that all transactions involving Indian land should be judicial rather than ministerial. It provided for compulsory notice to the Agency in proceedings for the appointment of guardians for restricted Indians, and the right of either party to transfer cases involving estates exceeding $25,000 in value to the Federal District Court.[44]

The Department opposed this bill, and continued to support the measure introduced during the previous session, "restoring to the Secretary of the Interior the exclusive jurisdiction and control of the funds, lands, and other property of the restricted Indians." Even after making allowance for possible Agency influence, it is apparent that the Indians themselves desired such legislation, for it was endorsed by the Creek Baptist Association, the Kee-too-wah Society, and the Oklahoma Society of Indians. But the deadlock between the Department and the Oklahoma delegation prevented the passage of either bill, and by the next year the effect of the Wallen report, the Sniffen pamphlet, and the House investigation had evaporated.[45]

A law supported by the State Bar Association for the improvement of land titles was secured that winter by the Oklahoma delegation, but it made only one reform in county court procedure. It provided that the approval of fullblood conveyances should be made in open court. It extended the state statute of limitations to Indian land transactions. It gave either party to a suit involving land of restricted Indians the right to serve notice upon the Five Tribes Superintendent; and the United States might then intervene and remove the suit to the Federal courts, and in event of such notice and not otherwise the United States would be bound by court judgments.[46]

[44] *Congressional Record*, LXVI, 3498-3501.

[45] *Ibid.*, LXVI, 3501; *Indian Affairs in Oklahoma*, pp. 416-17, 481-82, 489-93; Commissioner of Indian Affairs, *Annual Report*, 1925, p. 30; *Muskogee Times-Democrat*, October 2, 1925.

[46] *Muskogee Times-Democrat*, October 2, December 11, 1925; *Congressional Record*, LXVI, 3497-98; LXVII, 6517-19; Kappler, *Laws and Treaties*, IV, 518-20.

Meanwhile the fight between Oklahoma politicians and the Indian Office was assuming serious proportions, particularly over the fight to control the property of Jackson Barnett. This one famous case illustrates so many of the conflicting forces in eastern Oklahoma society that it presents almost a complete cross-section of the influences surrounding oil-rich Indians.

Barnett was an illiterate Creek, who had been left an orphan at an early age, had grown up without any known relatives, and had lived the uneventful life of the conservative fullblood. He had belonged to the Snake faction, and had been arbitrarily given an allotment by the Dawes Commission. In 1912 a field clerk assisted him to lease this land to an oil company, but a rival company succeeded in establishing his incompetency before the Okmulgee County court and secured a lease from Carl J. O'Hornett, who was appointed as guardian. When the two leases were submitted to Kelsey for approval, he decided that Barnett was incompetent only in the sense that he was an illiterate fullblood; and the field clerk appealed his case to the district court and had his incompetency set aside. But O'Hornett continued to act as guardian and a compromise settlement was subsequently made between the rival lessees.[47]

The wells drilled on Barnett's allotment proved to be the most spectacular producers in the Cushing field. Royalties poured in to the Agency to be invested in liberty bonds or paid out to O'Hornett for the Indian's living expenses, and the quiet old man became nationally known in headlines as "The World's Richest Indian." He continued to live in a shack in the woods on the outskirts of Henryetta indifferent alike to publicity and wealth.

But in 1919 with the consent of his guardian, the county court, and the Department he gave $25,000 to build a Baptist church in Henryetta. Sells at this time made a personal investigation; he talked the matter over with the Indian, and became convinced that he understood and desired to make the gift. As soon as this donation became known, eastern Oklahoma Bap-

47 *Survey of Indians in the United States,* IV, 1542-76, 1625-35, 1646-47, 1722.

tists began to say that Barnett could easily give their denomination $200,000; as one Muskogee pastor expressed it, "if we do not get this money the lawyers and the department will get it as they have always done." In December 1919 it was reported that the Baptists had sent a committee to present the matter of a donation to Commissioner Sells. The following February Superintendent Parker said that he was expecting early Departmental approval of a plan to devote half of the Indian's accumulated $1,500,000 to charitable purposes. The program then included the construction of a great Indian hospital at Henryetta.[48]

But other plans were afoot for the investment of Barnett's wealth. In January the old Indian disappeared, and O'Hornett and the Agency officials were thrown into consternation by the report that he had left with a woman bent on matrimony. County officials were notified, and attempts at marriage were foiled at Holdenville and Okemah by the refusal of the county clerks to issue a license. O'Hornett and the Agency force searched the state, and finally succeeded in returning the Indian to his home. Three weeks later he disappeared again. The same frantic search was made; but the couple eluded their pursuers, and the marriage was triumphantly accomplished in Coffeyville, Kansas, and followed a little later, to make sure, by a similar ceremony in Missouri. Sells worked with O'Hornett to annul the marriage, but it soon became apparent that the old Indian was happy with his wife. The guardian and the Department agreed to dismiss the suit, and the Barnetts returned to Oklahoma.[49]

Mrs. Barnett made no attempt to debauch or bully the lonely old Indian, but she began to show him how to enjoy the material comforts of his great wealth. The couple, with Mrs. Barnett's sixteen-year-old daughter, came to the Agency in May

[48] *Ibid.,* 1637-42; *Muskogee Phoenix,* December 15, 1919; *Muskogee Times-Democrat,* February 9, 1916; February 21, 1920.

[49] *Muskogee Phoenix,* January 31, February 23, 24, 26, 1920; *Muskogee Times-Democrat,* April 7, October 4, 1920; *Survey of Indians in the United States,* IV, 1637-38.

frankly to ask for a larger allowance. At that time they were receiving $650 a month, and the Agency did not consent to increase the amount.[50]

Burke and Locke came into office the following year. The Barnetts continued to make plans to advance their scale of living. They wished to build a palatial residence in Muskogee but County Judge Hugh L. Murphy of Okmulgee County threatened to withhold his approval of the expenditures of all Indian estates if the Barnetts were permitted to remove from his jurisdiction. Locke talked with the Indian apart from his dominating wife, and decided to grant his request; he said he desired no trouble with any county judge, but he believed Barnett should choose his place of residence—"The old man has but a few years yet to live at the most, and he should be allowed to use his money as he wants to within reason." He raised the Indian's allowance from $650 to $1,000.[51]

While the Agency and the judge were negotiating, the Barnetts loaded their household goods into a truck and fled by night to Muskogee. They purchased an attractive house and filled it with comfortable furniture. A temporary truce seems to have been made, with O'Hornett and Murphy approving an allowance for living expenses of $2,500 a month. At the same time O'Hornett came before the Okmulgee County court and asked for money to defend the estate against "designing influences" in Muskogee.[52]

On July 8, Murphy announced a definite break with the Indian Office because of a conflict over the control of the Bruner estate. Richmond Bruner had died a few months before, leaving about $114,000 at the Agency in cash and Government securities. The estate was in litigation between three persons each claiming to be sole heir, and an appeal was also pending to remove the administrators whom Murphy had appointed. The Agency therefore refused temporarily to turn the funds over to the administrators, and Murphy angrily an-

[50] *Muskogee Times-Democrat,* May 26, 1920.
[51] *Muskogee Phoenix,* August 7, October 4, 15, 25, 1921.
[52] *Ibid.,* October 15, 20, December 6, 1921; May 13, 1922.

nounced that his court would no longer recognize the Muskogee office, Commissioner Burke, the Creek attorney, or M. L. Mott, who had been Burke's close friend ever since the events following the presentation of the Mott Report and who was supposed to be Burke's unofficial adviser in Oklahoma Indian affairs. The Department thereupon began to ignore O'Hornett and to pay the Barnetts' allowance to them directly; and in October Secretary Fall promulgated new regulations by which guardians might be disregarded in the payment of funds to restricted Indians.[53]

The plan of Sells and Parker to devote a portion of Barnett's money to philanthropic purposes had been abandoned upon his dramatic marriage, but now it was revived in a form to recognize Mrs. Barnett's right in the estate. Liberty bonds held by the Department to the amount of $1,100,000 were appropriated as follows: a trust of $550,000 was created for the benefit of the American Baptist Home Mission Society, which would pay Barnett a yearly income of $20,000 for the remainder of his life; another trust of $200,000 was created for Mrs. Barnett, to pay him $7,500 a year; and $350,000 was to be paid to Mrs. Barnett in cash. It afterwards developed that $137,500 of Mrs. Barnett's cash payment was destined to go to her attorney, Harold McGugin of Coffeyville, for services extending back to the time of the marriage, and that $15,000 was paid to M. L. Mott for his services at the time of the settlement. The illiterate Indian affixed his thumb mark to the deed of gift, December 15, 1922.[54]

Ambitious plans were immediately launched for thirty-nine new buildings at Bacone, to be completed within the next three years. At the same time O'Hornett's attorney instituted suits

[53] *Ibid.,* June 1, July 9, 1922; *Muskogee Times-Democrat,* April 4, July 6, 1923; *Indian Affairs in Oklahoma,* pp. 452-53; *Congressional Record,* LXVI, 336; *House Reports,* 68 Cong., 2 Sess., No. 1527, pp. 11-12; *Survey of Indians in the United States,* III, 1037-1311, 1320. The Indian Office released its control early in 1923 as soon as the heirship was determined. The estate was immediately dissipated, and the heir received only $584. Murphy, however, had retired from office at the beginning of 1923.

[54] *Survey of Indians in the United States,* III, 1037-1311; *Guthrie Daily Leader,* November 7, 1939; *Supreme Court Reports (Law),* LXXIII, 1385-89.

to enjoin the Agency from disbursing any of the Indian's money without an order from the Okmulgee County court, and asked the Department to approve an appropriation from the estate to recover the Liberty bonds. Persons claiming to be relatives represented by attorneys under contracts carrying enormous contingent fees also began to appear from all sides to protest against the gifts on the ground that such a settlement ignored the rights of possible heirs.[55]

A Muskogee reporter went to interview the old Indian. In the temporary absence of his wife and stepdaughter he had been sleeping placidly rolled in his blankets before the fireplace of his luxurious house. He talked freely of his recent gifts. "Well they give me lot over here near Sapulpa an' they find oil well on it. Lot of money. I get plenty money long as I live an' they say no use to have 'em fight over it after I'm dead. So we fix it so there won't be none lef'."[56]

Early in 1923 the Barnetts settled in Los Angeles. Sensational stories were told of their flight, and of the magnificent residence that Mrs. Barnett purchased in California. O'Hornett surrendered his empty title in June 1924, and the court appointed Elmer S. Bailey of Henryetta as his successor. The next month a trust company was appointed by the California courts upon petition of Mrs. Barnett, and the Department ignored Bailey and paid the allowance to this Los Angeles guardian. It was believed that Burke planned to make this a test case to challenge the whole system of guardianships for restricted Indians.[57] The feud between the Department and the local courts had reached this stage at the time of the House investigation in 1924.

The Department also found itself in difficulties regarding the Maud Lee Mudd guardianship, but here instead of a conflict there was a close connection between the guardian and the

[55] *Survey of Indians in the United States,* III, 53-54; *Muskogee Phoenix,* February 2, 15, 18, 1923; *Muskogee Times-Democrat,* August 20, 1923.

[56] *Muskogee Phoenix,* February 9, 1923.

[57] *House Reports,* 68 Cong., 2 Sess., No. 1527, p. 17; *Muskogee Times-Democrat,* May 31, August 20, 1923; February 2, 16, June 21, 1924.

Department. It was not a Five Tribes case, for the girl was a Seneca minor under the jurisdiction of the Quapaw Agency in the extreme northeastern part of the state; but as the small tribes attached to this agency occupied only fractions of counties they had been placed under the protection of the Five Tribes probate attorneys. There was at that time no regulation forbidding a probate attorney to serve as guardian of Indian minors, and William Simms, the probate attorney, became the guardian of this girl by appointment of the county judge. When T. A. Chandler retired from Congress, Simms appointed him as his attorney. O. K. Chandler, a mixed-blood Cherokee, not related to T. A. Chandler, was serving as Quapaw Superintendent. He opposed the payment of a fee to Chandler and disallowed some items in Simms' report of disbursements for the girl's living expenses. He was soon removed from the Quapaw Superintendency; and he blamed Simms and Chandler for this circumstance, and he became the unrelenting enemy of Burke. Congressman Howard used this story in his attack on the Indian Office.[58]

Another incident cited by Howard was the Exie Fife divorce case. Exie was a young Creek girl, whose head apparently had been turned by a sensational discovery of oil on her Creek County allotment in 1922. She married Berlin Jackson, a farm boy of the neighborhood, but within a short time she sued him for divorce. She and Jackson made an agreement by which he would receive a $15,000 settlement. Unlike most rich Indians she had no guardian, but as a restricted allottee she had to obtain Wallen's consent to any expenditure of her funds. She employed T. A. Chandler and other attorneys to represent her, and these men working with Jackson's attorneys and with the consent of the principals, raised the amount of the settlement to $50,000 and secured Wallen's approval. Wallen also approved modest fees to the girl's attorneys for their slight labor

[58] *Muskogee Times-Democrat,* March 1, 25, April 2, 3, 1924; June 9, September 18, December 19, 1925; January 5, 15, 16, June 1, 1926; May 13, 1927; *Indian Affairs in Oklahoma,* pp. 450-51; *Survey of Indians in the United States,* XIV, 5995-6021; *Congressional Record,* LXV, 1427-28, 1447.

in securing an uncontested divorce. But Jackson retained only $15,000 of his $50,000 and turned the remainder over to be distributed among the attorneys of both sides. The girl proved unable to keep a secret, and the story became public early in 1924. It was never shown that Wallen knew of the advance agreement when he approved the settlement, but the incident contributed to the agitation against the Indian service.[59]

All through 1925 eastern Oklahoma was filled with rumors of Wallen's approaching removal, and political trades for the appointment of his successor. Unseen forces also were at work to arouse the Indians against Commissioner Burke; frequent meetings were called to pass resolutions and ready-made protests on convenient cards were distributed through the mail to be signed and sent to President Coolidge. Other meetings were held to protest against the protesters, and the Oklahoma Society of Indians in a tumultuous session at Ponca City overwhelmingly defeated a resolution condemning the Indian Office. In April the Republican organization for the Second Congressional District, apparently influenced by several Okmulgee politicians who had figured prominently in Indian litigation and guardianships, drew up ten charges of malfeasance against Wallen and presented them to Coolidge, Work, Harreld, and Pine.[60]

This concerted attack on the Indian service sprang from a variety of motives. Bitter enmity had been aroused against the Agency by Burke's announced intention of breaking up the profitable guardianship business so far as it involved restricted Indians; the preparation and publication of the Wallen Report, the attempt to secure Congressional legislation abolishing the control of Indians by the probate courts, and the refusal in some instances to pay out restricted money to guardians had been a challenge to entrenched greed. The tangled political re-

---

[59] *Muskogee Phoenix,* September 17, 1922; *Muskogee Times-Democrat,* July 3, 1923; January 22, February 5, 12, March 14, June 20, 1924; August 3, 1926; January 25, 1927; August 30, 1930; March 23-25, November 7, 1931; *Survey of Indians in the United States,* XIV, 1322-23.

[60] *Muskogee Phoenix,* February 3-August 17, 1925.

lationships that had brought about Wallen's appointment gave instability to his position; other politicians needed the place for *their* henchmen. Moreover there was an uneasy feeling that all was not well with the Indian service, that too many trades had taken place in the appointment of the Superintendent and the more important Agency positions, in the probate attorney force, and in the boarding school faculties. And the attack against Burke was part of a larger fight that had been instituted by John Collier of the American Indian Defense Association and several others against many unjustifiable practices of the whole system of Indian administration, practices that ran back for many years, for which Burke was not personally responsible, but which he had accepted and made no effort to correct.

Secretary Work finally requested the Board of Indian Commissioners, as a neutral body not connected with Burke's office or local state politics, to make an investigation. The Commissioners reported that they found nothing wrong with Burke's policy in Oklahoma or Wallen's administration of the Agency. Wallen had not been alert in the Exie Fife divorce case, but they were convinced of his personal integrity. But they found a demoralizing atmosphere of suspicion and hostility resulting from the fact that the Superintendent was a spoils appointee and therefore subject to constant attack by the opposite party or hostile factions of his own party; and they recommended repeal of the law of 1914 making the office political.[61]

But in April 1926, eastern Oklahoma was suddenly thrown into a furor of speculation by the temporary removal of Wallen and his assistant pending a searching investigation of all administrative details of the Agency. A number of changes were made at the same time in the Agency personnel and the boarding school faculties. In May a Federal grand jury returned a number of indictments for transactions involving Indian land. Politicians began hopefully grooming their fa-

[61] *Ibid.*, October 6-17, 1925; *Congressional Record*, LXVII, 3049-52; Board of Indian Commissioners, *Annual Report*, 1926, pp. 10-20.

vorites in the race to secure Wallen's position, at the same time that the air was filled with rumors of his approaching reinstatement.[62]

The Government finally dropped the charges regarding the land transactions. The attorneys who participated in the division of the Exie Fife divorce fees were eventually convicted of conspiracy and fined. Wallen was never reinstated, but the Indian Office had had enough of factional fights between rival politicians, and temporary assignments to the position of acting Superintendent were made from the general Indian service or the Muskogee office. Local political leaders, especially Senator Pine, were deeply incensed at this slight.[63]

Pine also entered into violent championship of the local courts and guardians in the Barnett case. By the end of Burke's term of office no less than twenty-one important suits had been instituted in defense of this one indifferent old man, who slept through more trials, submitted to more mental examinations, and unwittingly created more personal and political enmities than any other Indian in the whole complicated history of Five Tribes guardianships.

Bailey instituted a suit in the United States District Court in New York to set aside the Baptist donation, which was held by a trust company there, and to secure control of the property as guardian. The Department of Justice intervened to set aside the gift, but to return the property to the Department of the Interior. Although the Department of Justice suit was technically in favor of Burke's own office, Burke covertly fought it and assisted the Baptists in every possible way. The gift, however, was invalidated on the ground that Barnett had been incompetent to understand the nature of the transaction and that the Commissioner's supervisory control over Indian prop-

[62] *Muskogee Times-Democrat,* April 26-August 18, 1926; *Muskogee Phoenix,* April 23-May 6, September 9, 1926.

[63] *Muskogee Times-Democrat,* January 31, March 19, 21, 26, May 7, 12, 17, August 3, November 3, December 9, 22, 1927; January 9, 25, December 14, 1928; January 21, November 14, 1929; August 30, 1930; *Muskogee Phoenix,* January 30, September 12, 1927; November 15, 1929; *Tushkahomman,* September 24, 1935; *Survey of Indians in the United States,* III, 1154, 1253, 1382.

erty did not authorize him to give it away. A similar suit in the District of Columbia to set aside Mrs. Barnett's trust with the Riggs National Bank was also successful. Suits to recover the cash were instituted in California against Mrs. Barnett and in Oklahoma and Kansas against her attorneys; and so far as the courts have passed upon these questions judgments were secured for the return of this property to the estate. But the Oklahoma courts and guardians never recovered their jurisdiction; the state Supreme Court decided that the appointment of O'Hornett and Bailey had been invalid, and the Federal courts regularly returned the recovered property to Department control. The feud between the Justice and Interior departments reached serious proportions in 1928 when a Federal grand jury at Muskogee was called to investigate criminal charges against Fall, Burke, and the beneficiaries of the gifts; but the Department of Justice suddenly dropped the matter just before the date set for the investigation.[64]

The case was fully investigated by a committee of the United States Senate in 1928-1929. Senator Elmer Thomas, a West Side Democrat who had succeeded Harreld in 1926, defended Burke's action, but Pine was bitterly hostile. The old man himself was brought in and questioned. Many courts had pronounced him incompetent, and in the legal meaning of the word there is no reason to doubt their judgment; but there was nothing about his appearance before the committee to justify the frequent popular reference to his "demented" or "idiotic" condition. He was an illiterate with an illiterate's limited concepts, but he spoke intelligently of matters within his experience. He could not be made to say that he had been coached for the hearing by his wife or Commissioner Burke, and it was apparent that he was content in his marriage. An attempt was made to show that he was held in gilded captivity in Califor-

---

[64] *Supreme Court Reports,* LXXIII, 546; LXXV, 1385-89; *Survey of Indians in the United States,* IV, 1718-27; *Muskogee Times-Democrat,* April 5, 1934; *Daily Oklahoman,* January 26, 1936; November 28, 1937; *Guthrie Daily Leader,* November 7, 1939.

nia, but he would not say that he desired to return to Oklahoma; he said, "I want to see some more; I want to hear some more before I go back." An amusing passage occurred between him and Senator Pine, who was trying with feverish insistence to prove him feeble-minded. Whether with the deep and shrewd humor of the fullblood or with uncalculating simplicity, the Indian discomfited the Senator, and the dialogue ended as follows:

"SENATOR PINE.   Do you know the difference between a $20 and a $5 bill?

"MR. BARNETT.   Yes; I have one in my pocket here—a twenty.

"SENATOR PINE.   You have a twenty?

"MR. BARNETT.   Yes [taking bills from his pocket]. Do you know? [Laughter.]

.   .   .   .   .   .   .   .   .

"MR. BARNETT.   [addressing Senator Pine].   What is the matter with your forehead? You have got sweat on your forehead . . . and all like that [indicating].

"SENATOR PINE.   I do not understand you.

"MR. BARNETT.   You have sweat on your forehead, and all blood;[65] it is swelled up as big as my finger [indicating].

"SENATOR PINE.   A little swelled, is it?

"MR. BARNETT.   Yes.

"SENATOR PINE.   All right Jackson."[66]

As the hearings progressed, Burke apparently lost his temper or his judgment, and made a melodramatic assertion that Pine and several Oklahoma Department of Justice officials who owed their positions to Pine's patronage were members of a conspiracy to destroy his office because of Pine's unsatisfied hunger for spoils. The committee investigated this charge, but Burke was unable to furnish proof, and Pine and his protégés were formally exonerated.[67] Affairs were in this state of open hostility when the Coolidge administration ended.

[65] Blood veins?         [66] Survey of Indians in the United States, IV, 1542-76.
[67] Ibid., III, 1313-88; IV, 1541-42; Muskogee Times-Democrat, March 13, 1929.

The Barnett litigation dragged wearily on. In 1934 the marriage was annulled by the Federal court in California, but Mrs. Barnett was allowed to continue managing the house and the expenditure of the $2,500 monthly allowance. Shortly after, the old man died. Inside of two days Mrs. Barnett, the state of Oklahoma, and nine "cousins" had presented their claims to the estate. Shortly after a "nephew" appeared, to be followed soon by a "son," and before the year had ended, by a "daughter." By the beginning of 1935 two hundred "heirs" had sprung up in Oklahoma, California, Kentucky, New Mexico, Tennessee, Indiana, and Ohio. A "wife" with two children arrived on the scene a little later. By this time people named Barnett in various parts of the United States were receiving communications from attorneys pointing out a previously unsuspected relationship to this rich Indian, and offering to defend their interests. The number of claimants eventually reached about one thousand.

The trial took place before Judge Robert L. Williams in the Federal District Court at Muskogee. It attracted a great deal of attention because of the picturesque character of the testimony and the magnitude of the financial interests involved. The decision was announced December 16, 1939. It was based upon the integrity of the Dawes rolls, and recognition was accorded to thirty-four claimants, mostly fullbloods, who were descended from one Siah Barnett, listed as the father of Jackson. A motion for a rehearing was filed by the disappointed claimants, and it seems probable that the litigation will continue for years and possibly exhaust the estate before it is ended. A number of criminal prosecutions have already grown out of the trial as several of the witnesses have been indicted for perjury and forgery of the tribal court records.[68]

[68] *Muskogee Times-Democrat*, April 5, May 29-31, June 2, 9, December 4, 1934; January 10, 1935; June 30, 1938; *Muskogee Phoenix*, September 27, 1935; *Daily Oklahoman*, May 2, 29, 1935; March 24, May 17, 1936; October 19-26, 1937; July 19, August 20, December 16, 1939; January 13, 1940; *Guthrie Daily Leader*, June 25, 1935. The writer has been informed by people named Barnett who claimed no relationship to Jackson Barnett that they had received offers from attorneys.

The Federal judge in New York who set aside the Baptist trust once characterized Barnett as a "shuttlecock in a game of battledore in which the stakes are high." The same might have been said of the Five Tribes Indians in general after their own institutions were destroyed. But shortly before 1930 the influence of a new policy began to appear in Indian administration.

CHAPTER XIII

# The New Trend

AFTER a generation of systematic reduction of the Indians' property by robbery through the courts and consumption through the Bureau, and progressive degradation of the Indian spirit by the destruction of native institutions and the substitution of a benevolent despotism, it began belatedly to dawn upon those who were responsible for the policy that the Indians were not exactly prospering under its execution. With the shrinking of their holdings the Indians were no longer regarded by patriotic builders of commonwealths as obstacles in the march of empire and by land-grabbers as profitable subjects for large-scale exploitation. With this complication removed, a few people were at last ready to admit that here was a problem too difficult to be solved by the easy grant of American citizenship and personal freedom, which had been urged with such Fourth of July eloquence by Oklahoma politicians and land dealers, or by adopting the Bureau's glib advice to eliminate local control. For the first time since the agitation that preceded the creation of the Dawes Commission an honest and sincere attempt was made by Congress and the Indian Office to study the situation from the standpoint of the Indians themselves. Attempts at remedial legislation were bitterly opposed, however, partly by the old predatory interests and partly because the matter was too complicated for unanimous agreement.

Some success was achieved in eliminating the spoils system, the most demoralizing single influence in Five Tribes administration. In the House committee hearings on the Interior Department Appropriation Bill in the fall of 1928, Assistant Commissioner Meritt pointed out the fact that the Superintendent at Muskogee was the only one in the service whose tenure was political, and recommended an amendment to correct the condition; and the chairman of the Indian Welfare Division of the General Federation of Women's Clubs, the secretary of the Eastern Association of Indian Affairs, Charles J. Rhoads of the Indian Rights Association, and the secretary of the National Civil Service Reform League wrote to Chairman Cramton insisting that the reform be carried out. Senator Pine fought the measure, but it was enacted with the assistance of Hastings and Howard. The scandals of the preceding eight years were largely responsible for securing this change.[1]

With the passage of this act a dead calm settled upon Five Tribes administration. Adrian M. Landman of Boston and New York, who had had twelve years' experience in the Indian service, was appointed as Superintendent in 1931. He immediately made a rapid series of visits to outlying fullblood settlements, and began an intensive program of agricultural education and social work.[2] He showed himself so indifferent to political considerations that even at the present time his party affiliation is a matter of conjecture.

Senator Gore, who succeeded Pine in 1931, made a strong attempt after the national Democratic victory the next year to restore the political status of the Superintendent, but he was unsuccessful. He did eliminate the civil service requirement for the probate attorneys, but no wholesale dismissals took place. The Republican appointees were allowed to remain under the status they had acquired in 1924, but vacancies that occurred in the force after 1933 were filled by political appointment.[3]

When Hoover became President, he disregarded the usual political considerations and appointed Charles J. Rhoads as

[1] Subcommittee of House Committee on Appropriations, *Interior Department Appropriation Bill for 1930* (Washington, 1928), p. 1241; *Congressional Record,* LXX, 550, 923-24, 1846-50; *Okmulgee Daily Democrat,* March 13, 1929; *Muskogee Times-Democrat,* December 27, 1928; January 7, 1929; *Statutes at Large,* XLV, 1583, act of March 4, 1929.

[2] *Muskogee Times-Democrat,* January 24, February 14, March 30, April 4, 1931.

[3] *Congressional Record,* LXXVI, 3626; LXXIX, 6681; *Statutes at Large,* XLVII, 825; J. H. Finley, Personal Interview, October 4, 1935.

Commissioner of Indian Affairs, and Joseph Henry Scatter-
good as his assistant. Both men were wealthy Quaker bankers
and philanthropists of Philadelphia, and both had been active
in reconstruction work in France. Their administration has
been severely condemned by some friends of the Indians because they did not immediately effect a revolutionary reform in
the Indian Office; but it is apparent in examining any detail
of their work that they made a consistent effort to improve the
service by the appointment of qualified persons. They also
showed a more sympathetic attitude than any of their predecessors toward the Indians' collective system of land tenure.[4]

For some time philanthropic friends of the Indians had
been inclined to question the wisdom of the general allotment
policy that they had once advocated with such uncritical fervor. The Board of Indian Commissioners, which was so largely
responsible for the breaking up of the communal holdings,
admitted in 1929 that the Dawes Severalty Act had been a
failure, and that its general effect had been the loss of the
Indians' property as soon as it passed under individual tenure.
Some members of Congress also began to express doubts as to
the good results of the system.[5] This tendency became a definite
administrative policy after the election of Franklin D. Roosevelt in 1932.

Oklahoma Democrats hoped to name a local man as Commissioner of Indian Affairs, but as usual they failed to agree
upon a candidate and the appointment went to John Collier,
executive secretary of the American Indian Defense Association. Collier was the first Commissioner who ever approached
his problem from the sociological and scientific point of view;
and he believed in the encouragement of native arts, the protec-

[4] Commissioner of Indian Affairs, *Annual Report*, 1926, p. 8; 1930, pp. 7-11; 1931,
pp. 9-11; *Interior Department Appropriation Bill for 1931*, pp. 123-27; *Muskogee
Phoenix*, March 19, 1930; *Muskogee Times-Democrat*, April 8, 11, 1929; January 19,
May 14, 1931; *Congressional Record*, LXII, 1051-53, 1809-13; Board of Indian
Commissioners, *Annual Report*, 1930, pp. 15-16. See Robert Gessner, *Massacre*
(New York, 1931), *passim* for hostile criticism of Rhoads' administration.

[5] Board of Indian Commissioners, *Annual Report*, 1929, pp. 5, 25; *Congressional
Record*, LXXV, 7936-37.

tion of Indian religion and tradition, and the preservation of all group relationships. He regarded the extinction of the tribal governments and the forcible breaking up of the communal holdings as a crime against the spirit of a people, and a gigantic economic blunder that had reduced the Indians to poverty. This complete reversal of Indian policy was actively supported by Secretary Harold L. Ickes and by President Roosevelt.[6]

The influence of the scientific spirit in formulating Indian policy was also manifested in a number of surveys that were carried on in the Five Tribes from 1926 to 1930. For the first time systematic attempts were made to discover the actual condition of the Indians and to enact legislation upon the basis of that knowledge.

The first step was a census by the Department. The population of the Five Tribes had never been known. The statistics secured by the Federal enumerators at the regular decennial census were always incomplete. The Dawes rolls with their overlapping enumerations of "newborns' had never been intended as census statistics, and they also contained the names of thousands of white and Negro citizens over whom the Department exercised no control; but every year the Commissioner's report carried these totals as the population of the Five Tribes. During the House investigation of 1924 Hastings demanded to know the exact number of restricted allottees, and when Wallen by a combination of guesses set the figure at 17,410 Hastings challenged the statement. The House Committee on Indian Affairs then directed Burke to take a census. This enumeration was completed in 1926; it showed that 9,100 fullbloods and 2,286 restricted mixed-bloods enrolled by the Dawes Commission were still living. The Agency officials thus learned for the first time the number of enrolled Indians for whom they were responsible, but they were still completely in the dark as to the generation born since 1906. As late as 1930, the agriculture and extension agent at the Musko-

[6] Secretary of the Interior, *Annual Report*, 1933, pp. 68-85; *Muskogee Times-Democrat*, January 28, December 22, 1932; *Congressional Record*, LXXVIII, 7807; John Collier, "Indians at Work," *Survey Graphic*, XXIII (June, 1934).

gee office gravely informed a Senate committee that he had 101,000 Indians to instruct in farming methods.[7]

In 1927 the Department undertook a survey of the restricted Indians regarding property, occupations, living conditions, education, etc., and the same year investigators appointed by the Institute for Government Research to make a comprehensive and impartial survey of all Indians in the United States visited the Five Tribes region. Both groups reported the deplorable conditions of ignorance, poverty, and disease that existed in the neglected hill settlements; and the legal specialist of the staff appointed by the Institute for Government Research described again the legislative system under which the exploitation of the Indians had been carried on. He also confirmed the impression that had been given by the House investigation of 1924, that the probate attorneys were devoting much of their time to the routine clerical work of approving requests of guardians for expenditures and were not active in defending the Indians in the courts.[8]

The findings of the Institute for Government Research were published in 1928. Before the publication, members of Congress frequently expressed their impatience to secure these data, and after the bulky volume appeared they quoted from it freely in considering Indian legislation. The immediate result was increased appropriations for boarding school rations and public health and social work for the Indians throughout the United States.

The Senate Committee on Indian Affairs next undertook a comprehensive investigation of the conditions of the various Indian tribes. The inquiry extended over several years, and included the investigation of the Jackson Barnett case previ-

---

[7] *Indian Affairs in Oklahoma,* pp. 410-12, 427; Commissioner of Indian Affairs, *Annual Report,* 1926, p. 25; *Survey of Indians in the United States,* XIV, 5958-60.

[8] Superintendent, Office Files, Report of C. L. Ellis, 1927, pp. 9-10, 13-14; *Muskogee Times-Democrat,* April 18, 1927; Meriam, *The Problem of Indian Administration,* pp. 484-88, 748, 756, 799-803. See also a similar characterization of the probate attorneys in a report made by the General Accounting Office (*Senate Docs.,* 70 Cong., 2 Sess., No. 263, pp. 106-7).

ously mentioned, and a visit to the Five Tribes area in November of 1930.

Chairman Lynn J. Frazier of North Dakota, Burton K. Wheeler of Montana, and Pine and Thomas of Oklahoma were the members who conducted the Five Tribes survey. They held open hearings at Durant, Idabel, Muskogee, Okmulgee, and Wewoka, and received testimony from all classes of people, especially fullblood Indians; they inspected the Government and tribal boarding schools in which Indian children were maintained under contract; and they drove out into the Cherokee hills and visited the squalid homes of that remote region. For the first time in the history of Congressional investigations of Indians they made a sincere attempt to discover the welfare of Five Tribes allottees; and although they were frequently unfair in blaming the Indian service for conditions that Congress had created, they appeared genuinely anxious to correct legislative defects.[9]

They found the entire hill country menaced by famine. A prolonged drought had ruined the Indians' scanty food crops, and the general financial depression made it impossible for them to secure work. The Seminoles, because of the recent oil discoveries in their country, were not actually starving, but in the rest of the fullblood settlements throughout the Five Tribes area the Indians were living on one or two meals a day of cornbread and gravy or cornbread and a native drink made of parched corn. Several deaths had already occurred from starvation disguised under such euphemisms as "undernourishment" or "diseases due to insufficient nutrition," and there was every indication that great numbers would starve to death before spring.[10]

The only remedy the Cherokees had to offer was the settlement of several outstanding claims against the United States, and the distribution of the proceeds. The Choctaws and Chick-

---

[9] *Survey of Indians in the United States,* XIV, 5881-82, 5918-23, 6374, 13697-13722; *Congressional Record,* LXXIV, 1927, 2638-54.

[10] *Survey of Indians in the United States,* XIV, 5322-24, 5351-52, 5696-5702, 5714-15, 6035-36, 6250, 6265-66, 6289.

asaws held a convention and appointed delegates to request an advance per caput payment to be charged with interest against their coal and asphalt and any future settlement of their claims. C. L. Ellis, who had been acting as Superintendent, saw no solution except the sale of oil leases and individual holdings; and the depression had destroyed the lease market and made it impossible for the Agency to sell portions of the Indians' allotments. The more thoughtful Indians seemed to believe that the only constructive and permanent solution lay in intensive social work to show the indigent how to become self-supporting and the rich how to live wisely. The Seminole Indian Protective Association presented a petition asking that some of the royalty money from their boarding school ground should be used for the construction of a hospital and the employment of a field matron to carry on social work throughout the tribe.[11]

The Agency also furnished the committee with detailed and specific information showing that the approval of fullblood conveyances was still largely perfunctory; that few judges notified the probate attorneys of guardianship hearings and that the looting of estates was still the rule; that the Agency was never notified of partition proceedings and that the victims of these forced sales often received no money at all; and that "lease grafters" still controlled much of the restricted land through widespread forgery and intimidation.[12] The members of the committee, especially Senator Wheeler, appeared completely dumfounded when the legal foundations of the hideous system were disclosed, and Senator Thomas promised to introduce bills prepared by the probate attorneys to correct it.[13]

Senator Thomas' willingness to cooperate in legislation to protect the Indians illustrates a tendency that had been increasingly apparent since about 1926. With the shrinking of the Indians' holdings the exploiting business was largely concen-

---

[11] *Ibid.,* XIV, 5700, 5724-28, 6250-51, 6254-55, 13697-13722.
[12] *Ibid.,* XIV, 5427, 5458-94, 5617-32, 5677-79, 5688, 5941-44, 6334-41, 6351-53.
[13] *Ibid.,* XIV, 5936-39, 6364-67, 6633-37; Indian Office Files, 3067/30 Seminole 160.

trated in the hands of a few guardians and attorneys in the oil districts, and a few real estate dealers of the Choctaw-Chickasaw country who monopolized agricultural leasing and inheritance sales. The members of Congress therefore had a constituency which although still determined enough to be dangerous was no longer unanimous in demanding a free hand with the Indian property. On the other hand was the cumulative influence of the recent surveys. As a result, although some Congressmen followed the old policy, the entire delegation no longer rose as a unit to fight any legislation increasing Federal supervision or limiting the power of the local courts or the right of the Indians to dispose of their property. These conflicting influences are fully shown in the legislation to extend the restrictions beyond 1931.

For a number of years after the McCumber Amendment and the act of 1908 had set the date for the expiration of the restrictions it was assumed by the Department that some mysterious process would make the Indians entirely competent by that time; but in 1922 the Board of Indian Commissioners began to advise the extension of the trust period, and by 1925 and 1926 it was apparent that the Indian Office and various organizations of Five Tribes Indians were working to the same end. The survey made by the Agency in 1927 was undertaken primarily for the purpose of convincing Congress to extend the restrictions, and the report of the Institute for Government Research issued a solemn warning against the inevitable "carnival of dissipation, fraud, and oppression," that would occur at the expiration of the trust period.[14]

In 1926 Charles D. Carter attempted to secure legislation that would protect the Indians and at the same time satisfy the land hunger of his white constituents. His bill provided that the restrictions should be extended for sixteen years on an

[14] Board of Indian Commissioners, *Annual Report*, 1922, pp. 7-8; 1926, pp. 10-13; *Muskogee Times-Democrat*, September 25, 1925; November 17, 1926; Superintendent, Office Files, Report of C. L. Ellis, 1926, p. 6; *ibid.*, 1928, letter forwarding report; *Congressional Record*, LIX, 7893; Meriam, *The Problem of Indian Administration*, pp. 19, 48, 94, 747-48, 800-4.

eighty-acre homestead for each enrolled fullblood Indian, and that without waiting for 1931 the remaining land should be immediately sold on a deferred payment plan at public auction to the highest bidder.

This first concession ever made by an Oklahoma legislator to the restrictions policy raised a storm of protest. Carter made every attempt to avert the wrath of his constituents by showing that it was a bill for the *removal* of restrictions. He said that the Indian Office was in favor of extending the restrictions on all Indian land, and that a majority of Congress was in full sympathy with the policy; hence his bill was "about the best compromise obtainable." As to the "incidental feature," the extension of restrictions on the homesteads, the amount of land was too small to offset the benefit of throwing the remaining land upon the tax rolls. The Department census of 1926 showed only 3,476 living Choctaw-Chickasaw fullbloods still owning restricted allotments; their homesteads, therefore, would comprise only 278,080 acres, only about 2.5 per cent of the area that once constituted the Choctaw-Chickasaw domain.[15]

But Carter was defeated upon this issue in the Democratic primary by Wilburn Cartwright of McAlester, and forced to retire from Congress after serving his district continuously since statehood. It is impossible to determine whether he had introduced his ill-starred bill to prevent more drastic legislation, as he told his constituents, or whether he was making a cautious effort to protect the Indians. The latter is the more probable, for after his defeat he used all his influence to further legislation to extend the restrictions. When a much stronger bill was pending in 1928, he telegraphed to Cramton that if it should be defeated "and these helpless full-blood Indians left at the mercy of the scheming grafters, it means that most of the original owners of [the] entire domain of this State will be reduced to penury."[16] Carter was one of the ablest men who

---

[15] *Congressional Record*, LXV, 10828-29, 11590-91; *Daily Ardmoreite*, April 13-15, June 20, 24, July 7, August 6, 1926.

[16] *Congressional Record*, LXIX, 8582, 8584.

ever represented Oklahoma in Congress, and there is no question of his personal integrity, but he had yielded much to political expediency and there is ironical significance in the fact that his belated attempt to protect his people should have ended his political career.

Cartwright fought the measure with great determination. He read letters from his "great avalanche of mail" to show how the Indians were pleading to be released from Bureau control; the examples he selected, however, were from white men—an attorney, a banker, a lumber dealer, a real estate dealer, etc.—several of them from the West Side. Fletcher B. Swank, a west side Representative, also opposed the bill, and Howard attempted to amend it by a $10,000,000 Federal appropriation to the state to reimburse it for the loss in taxes.[17]

The legislation was enacted May 10, 1928. It extended the restrictions upon land owned by original allottees of one-half or more Indian blood for twenty-five years—to April 26, 1956; but in accordance with the advice of Secretary Work it repealed the preference right by which inherited homesteads were held for the benefit of heirs born too late to receive allotments. It limited the tax exemption on these restricted holdings to one hundred and sixty acres to be selected by the Indian or the Secretary, and it provided that minerals should become subject to taxation April 26, 1931. This latter provision was void so far as Seminole and Cherokee homesteads were concerned, for the agreements with those tribes had exempted the Seminole homestead "in perpetuity" and the Cherokee during "the time such homestead is held by the allottee." It became necessary therefore for the Agency to separate the oil income off the homesteads of Seminoles and Cherokees from the rest of their oil income.[18]

[17] Congressional Record, LXIX, 7892-93, 8582-84; Muskogee Times-Democrat, April 7, 1928; Okmulgee Times-Democrat, March 25, 30, 1928.

[18] Kappler, Laws and Treaties, I, 664, 788; Statutes at Large, XLV, 495-96, 733-34; XLVI, 1108-9; Superintendent, Office Files, Report of A. M. Landman, 1932, pp. 10-11; Congressional Record, LXIX, 7892-93.

In 1929 land speculators went out through the fullblood settlements and purchased for a mere pittance the shares of inherited land belonging to heirs born prior to March 4, 1906. The object, of course, was to force the sale of the land through partition proceedings as soon as the restrictions in favor of the unenrolled heirs should expire. Since these older heirs were unrestricted except as to county court approval of the sale, it was the opinion of some attorneys that such conveyances were legal. The speculators were especially active in securing these instruments from the Choctaw fullbloods conveying land in the agricultural counties of the old Chickasaw district. The probate attorneys instituted suits to set the deeds aside, but the speculators planned to appeal and keep the cases in the courts until April 26, 1931, and then secure new deeds.[19]

The Indians themselves desired the extension of the restrictions. When the Senate committee visited Oklahoma in 1930, a number of them expressed their gratitude for the act of 1928, and nearly every real Indian who appeared at the hearings asked that it be extended to protect their unenrolled young people. A Cherokee from the hills beyond the Grand River expressed a characteristic view when he said:

"We have some of these old folks who have restricted lands, and they leave it up to me to say this about the restricted land: The old folks are going to die pretty soon. . . . We are thinking. I have talked it over and over. Just leave the restrictions on it and not let anybody, the State or anyone else, take the restrictions off the land.

". . . We have not very much land now. If we keep on selling it piece by piece, after a while the Indians will not have any land in this country, not one piece left. Now, what are we going to do? Are we going to be turned out like hogs or something like that?

". . . If we do not have but 1 acre, we could live there until we starved to death or just die."[20]

---

[19] *Congressional Record*, LXXIV, 3957; *Survey of Indians in the United States*, XIV, 5495-97, 5671, 5678.

[20] *Survey of Indians in the United States*, XIV, 6277.

Commissioner Rhoads and Secretary Wilbur attempted during the following session of Congress to secure legislation to protect the unenrolled Indians from the spoliation that would almost certainly occur in April, and to clarify an uncertainty in the law of 1928 by providing that the extension of restrictions should apply also to funds held by the Department. The measure was supported by Hastings, but opposed by Cartwright and Tom D. McKeown, whose district included the Seminole country. It passed both houses, but it became joined with a measure for the creation of trust estates. When it was returned to the Senate in the closing hours of this short session with this feature eliminated, Thomas was conducting a filibuster in the interest of an oil tariff and there was no opportunity to consider it. Thomas apparently had been in favor of it, but during his seventeen hours' speech on a variety of subjects he was asked if he knew the Extension of Restrictions Bill had passed the House and he answered by a sweeping condemnation of the whole measure.

Probably the Oklahoma members of Congress were not sorry that the bill encountered this snag in its passage, for during the last few days of the session they had received a deluge of letters and telegrams of protest from their constituents. On March 2 the state legislature also adopted a resolution declaring that "said bill does by its terms prevent the handling and managing of such property by local state and county agencies and places the same entirely under the control and management of the Secretary of the Interior and deprives such Indian heirs of the protection of home government and places it at long range and beyond their personal reach," and memorializing Congress "to not inflict upon the state and the Indian citizenship of the state this burden which we believe to be unjust."[21]

[21] *Congressional Record*, LXXIV, 1437, 1581, 3956-58, 5003, 6485, 7219-22, 7268 ff, 7312-13; LXXVI, 2288; *House Reports*, 71 Cong., 3 Sess., No. 2188; State of Oklahoma, *Session Laws of 1931*, pp. 395-96.

If the twenty-eight million dollars in accumulated oil royalties held by the Department for individual restricted Indians had passed into the hands of guardians throughout the Five Tribes area the result can be easily imagined; but pending judicial determination the Federal officials took the position that the restrictions did not expire upon such funds. Landman also made every possible effort to protect the unenrolled Indians from the anticipated orgy of land sales. He and the probate attorneys and the field clerks held conferences with the Indians; he succeeded in enlisting the support of nearly half of the county judges in the adoption of rules governing the sales; and he appealed to the public, requesting individual citizens to report to the Agency any fraudulent transaction that should come under their notice. It is impossible to discover how many young landless Indians lost their shares of their parents' allotments at this time. The only available statistics show the number of fullblood sales of inherited land during the fiscal years 1931-1932 and 1932-1933. The number is 466 and 245 respectively. Obviously these figures leave a gap from April 26 to July 1, 1931, when the sales were probably the greatest; they omit the sales by all heirs but fullbloods; and they include the sales by enrolled fullbloods. The Department attempted through the activity of the probate attorneys to secure fair prices for the land where the county judge permitted such cooperation, but the demoralized condition of the land market made all prices very low. It appears, however, that the same condition discouraged the land buyers and decreased the number of sales.[22]

In 1931-1932 an attempt was made to secure the legislation that the filibuster had defeated the previous session. Hastings worked very earnestly for the measure, but apparently he was opposed by every other Representative from Oklahoma, especially Cartwright, Swank, and Wesley E. Disney, a new mem-

[22] Commissioner of Indian Affairs, *Annual Report*, 1932, pp. 22-23; 1933, p. 98; Board of Indian Commissioners, *Annual Report*, 1931, p. 20; *Muskogee Times-Democrat*, April 25, 27, 1931.

ber from Tulsa. Again the provisions for extending the restrictions passed both houses, but again the bill was defeated by failure to agree on other provisions.[23]

The legislation was finally enacted January 27, 1933. The law provided that all funds then held by the Secretary or coming into his hands thereafter, belonging to "enrolled or unenrolled" Indians of the Five Tribes of one-half or more Indian blood should remain under his jurisdiction until April 26, 1956, and that when the entire interest in restricted land should be acquired by "inheritance, devise, gift, or purchase, with restricted funds, by or for restricted Indians," it should remain restricted and tax exempt during their lifetime until the same date, except that no individual should hold more than one hundred and sixty acres under this tenure and that minerals should be subject to state and Federal taxation. It also authorized the probate attorneys to represent any restricted Indian of the Five Tribes before any county or appellate court of Oklahoma and provided that no fullblood conveyance of inherited land should be valid except when approved in open court after notice according to the probate rules of 1914, and that the probate attorneys should have the right to appeal such cases to the district court.[24]

At that time two guardians of unenrolled Indians were suing to compel the Secretary to release accumulated royalties inherited by their wards. The courts now decided that since the money had been in the possession of the Secretary when the law was passed it became subject to the extended restrictions. The act therefore protected the vast accumulated royalties that the Secretary was holding for individual Indians.[25] At the same time the control of this money by the Agency was not altogether satisfactory, because of the disproportionate amount of time

---

[23] *Congressional Record,* LXXV, 1956, 8163-70, 8222, 13998-99, 14145, 14171.

[24] *Statutes at Large,* XLVII, 777-79.

[25] *Federal Reporter,* Second Series, LXIV, 979-83, Court of Appeals for the District of Columbia, April 3, 1933; Secretary of the Interior, *Annual Report,* 1933, p. 97.

required to protect the interests of a few rich Indians. The same law therefore attempted to relieve this situation by elaborate provisions for the creation of trust estates.

The Department had taken the initiative by establishing the ill-fated Jackson Barnett trust. This was followed in 1925 by a $200,000 trust for Eastman Richards and $250,000 for Richards' daughter, Mrs. Jeanetta Barnett, and early in 1926 by a $300,000 trust for Mollie Davis. In the absence of specific legislation authorizing the creation of trusts from restricted funds, the Department after the unfortunate experience with Jackson Barnett adopted the method of removing the restrictions and the Indian immediately used his newly conferred competence in accepting the trust agreement.[26]

The first three of these trusts had been approved and several more were pending when the Indian Commissioners made their investigation in 1925. They recommended the plan at that time and again in 1926, and their reports met instant favor with eastern Oklahoma financiers and bankers, who hoped to secure the trusts for their own firms. As soon as Thomas entered the Senate he began working actively with Commissioner Burke to secure legislation specifically authorizing the Department to establish these trusts and providing safeguards to prevent the use of undue influence in creating them and to destroy all incentive to break them. When Rhoads became Commissioner, he was already favorably disposed toward the plan because of his own experience as a banker and trust executive, and he and Thomas worked together during succeeding sessions of Congress. The Senate committee that visited Oklahoma in 1930 made every effort to secure information on the subject, and the evidence indicated that in spite of obvious dangers these trusts apparently would place the great wealth of oil-rich Indians beyond the reach of destructive litigation.[27]

[26] Survey of Indians in the United States, XIV, 6497-6514; Attorney General, Official Opinions, XXXVI, 98-100.

[27] Congressional Record, LXVII, 3049-52; LXIX, 7144, 7337-38; LXX, 2290, 2476-77, 2731-33, 5163; LXXIV, 6485, 7312; LXXV, 500, 3642, 4601; Muskogee

The law finally secured by Senator Thomas in 1933 authorized the Secretary to permit any Indian of the Five Tribes to
create a trust out of his restricted property for his heirs or any
other beneficiary designated by him. The creation of the trust
would not operate to remove the restrictions, and the corpus of
the trust and the income would not be subject to alienation or
incumbrance or debt liability during the restricted period. The
trustee should be required to render an annual account to the
Secretary and to the beneficiary of the income. The trust agreement would be irrevocable except with the consent of the Secretary, but if it should be set aside by court order, the money
would return to the supervision of the Department. The Attorney-General was authorized to institute suit to cancel the trust
if evidence of fraud should appear, and the Federal courts
were given exclusive jurisdiction. All agreements for the creation of trusts made before this law was enacted were declared
void unless already approved by the Secretary, and trust companies were forbidden to pay any commission except to their
regular employees for any influence in securing the approval
of the trust. Trusts were limited to twenty-one years beyond
the death of the last surviving beneficiary.[28]

Secretary Ickes and Commissioner Collier came into office
soon after the enactment of this law. The new administration
acted with extreme caution, but several trusts were eventually
approved. Then in December 1938 the Secretary requested the
Department of Justice to take steps to cancel seven trusts totaling $2,805,000 held by one Kansas City company, upon the
contention that the man who had acted as its agent in obtain-
ing the consent of the Indians was not a regular employee
within the meaning of the act. Suits to break these trusts were
instituted in the Federal District Court April 17, 1940. As

*Times-Democrat,* January 30, 1926; August 13, September 14, 1929; *Muskogee
Phoenix,* December 12, 1926; *Survey of Indians in the United States,* XIV, 6024-26,
6039-79, 6376-81, 6476-6560, 6604-5; *Senate Reports,* 70 Cong., 1 Sess., No. 918;
72 Cong., 1 Sess., No. 221; *House Reports,* 70 Cong., 1 Sess., No. 1358, Part 2.

[28] *Statutes at Large,* XLVII, 777-79.

matters stand, it is too early yet to pass judgment upon the utility of the trust plan of investment for oil-rich Indians.[29]

All this legislation—the extension of the restrictions, the enactment of rules governing county court procedure, and the careful regulation of trust agreements—represent the gradual reaction from the old policy of "turning the Indians loose." The same influences slowed up and finally stopped the individual removal of restrictions.

In 1927 Congress at the request of the Department passed a general law authorizing the cancellation of fee simple patents issued to Indians without their consent before the expiration of the restrictions in their original patents. The Interior Department Appropriation Act of the same year still carried the anachronism of a competency commission to the Five Tribes, but it had not been used the previous year, and the next year the appropriation was discontinued. In 1928 the Muskogee office sent the questionnaire previously mentioned to the field clerks regarding the welfare of the unrestricted Five Tribes Indians, and at the same time Assistant Commissioner Meritt stated to a Senate committee that Lane's "misguided philosophy of life and his misinformation about Indians" had caused thousands of Indians throughout the country to lose every foot of their land. The conditional removal of restrictions from Five Tribes allottees and the sale of their land through the Agency almost ceased; and when Ickes and Collier came into office this complete reversal of previous practice became a fixed policy of the administration. Indian land is now sold only when acreage in excess of the quarter-section limit is about to be lost through tax sale.[30]

[29] Secretary of the Interior, *Annual Report,* 1933, p. 98; *Muskogee Times-Democrat,* March 22, 25, 1933; *Daily Oklahoman,* December 14, 1938; February 2, 22, 1939; April 18, 1940.

[30] Commissioner of Indian Affairs, *Annual Report,* 1931, p. 38; Secretary of the Interior, *Annual Report,* 1933, pp. 98, 100; *Statutes at Large,* XLV, 204; Kappler, *Laws and Treaties,* IV, 932-33; Senate Committee on Indian Affairs, *Survey of Conditions of the Indians in the United States* (Washington, 1928), pp. 14, 34; *Survey of Indians in the United States,* XIV, 5639; *Interior Department Appropriation Bill for 1930,* pp. 743-45; Superintendent, Office Files, Report of A. M. Landman, 1935, p. 10.

Ickes and Collier also secured the passage of the Wheeler-Howard Act, soon known as the Indian Reorganization Act, in 1934. In its original form it went almost the whole way back to the system of communal land tenure and tribal autonomy which the Federal Government had been working for more than two generations to destroy. It was greatly modified before its passage, but it prohibited further allotment of lands still held under tribal tenure, extended the trust period of restricted allotments until further legislation by Congress, authorized the appropriation of two million dollars a year for the acquisition of land for landless Indians, authorized the organization of tribal corporations with the privilege of accepting relinquishments of the title to allotted land in exchange for cash or shares in the corporation, established a system of credit for Indians with authorization of a ten-million-dollar revolving fund, permitted the organization of tribal governments with control over tribal funds and the expenditures of the Indian service, exempted qualified Indians from general civil service competition in appointments to positions in the Indian service, authorized the establishment of a student loan fund for training Indians in college and trade and professional schools in order to fit them for leadership among their people, directed the Secretary to apply conservation principles to forests and range lands belonging to Indians, restored the undisposed surplus and ceded lands on hand to tribal ownership, and forbade the approval of any sale, devise, or gift of restricted land except, with the consent of the Secretary, to the tribe.[31]

The Oklahoma delegation worked as a unit against the application of this law to Oklahoma. Hastings, himself a Cherokee citizen who had achieved distinction in a mixed society, made a masterly analysis of its provisions and an able defense of the old Indian policy. He believed in protection of the Indians' property and in social and educational training to fit them for United States citizenship; this measure, he said,

[31] *Congressional Record*, LXXVIII, 7807; *Statutes at Large*, XLVIII, 984-88; *Daily Oklahoman*, December 16, 1935.

would keep them in a state of perpetual inferiority and permanently prevent their assimilation. The Oklahoma press fought the bill with a virulence reminiscent of the old battle against the restrictions and the defense of the probate courts. Some important missionary organizations were also hostile, because Collier was believed to be too sympathetic toward native religion.[32]

Indian opinion was divided. Ben Dwight, appointive Chief of the Choctaws, able and brilliantly educated, was strongly in favor of the legislation; and a Choctaw convention held at Goodland endorsed it with only two dissenting votes. Apparently Chickasaw and Creek gatherings also approved it, and the fullblood Kee-too-wah Society claiming 6,000 Cherokee members passed resolutions of unqualified support. On the other hand members of the different tribes formed an irregular federation and worked actively against its adoption. While the measure was pending, Collier came out to Oklahoma to discover if possible the sentiments of the Indians. More than 2,000 members of seventeen tribes met him at Anadarko, and in a closed session from which the general public was excluded, he entered into an informal discussion of his policy while interpreters simultaneously translated the proceedings into the different languages. If the reports of the meeting by a uniformly hostile press can be trusted, this representative gathering rejected his plan. Apparently too much water had flowed under the bridge since the Five Tribes Indians had stood as a unit to prevent the destruction of the system which Collier was now trying in a measure to revive.[33]

The Oklahoma delegation succeeded in excluding Oklahoma Indians from the main provisions of the act, especially the formation of tribal organizations and collective land hold-

---

[32] *Congressional Record*, LXXVIII, 9265-71, 11126; *Muskogee Phoenix*, March 8, 21, 24, 25, October 5, 1934; *Muskogee Times-Democrat,* November 2, 1934.

[33] *Muskogee Phoenix*, March 13, 18, 21-25, 1934; *Congressional Record*, LXXVIII, 11741-42.

ings. They were eligible to participate in such individual benefits as student loans and appointments to the Indian service.[34]

But while Thomas was working to defeat the application of the measure to Oklahoma he said that he would endeavor before the next session of Congress to discover the real sentiments of the Indians. He invited Collier to join him, and in October the two men visited a number of Indian gatherings, Collier defending the Wheeler-Howard Act and Thomas opposing it. Again if accounts in the public press upon such a controversial subject are to be trusted, the Indians upon the whole opposed the extension of the law to the state. But Collier and Thomas, unlike their predecessors in the Indian Office and in Congress, were sincerely seeking to discover the wishes of the Indians rather than to impose some policy upon them by external force, and during these conferences they acquired a familiarity with the situation that they hoped would enable them to draft constructive legislation.[35]

When Congress convened in January, Thomas became chairman of the Senate Indian Affairs Committee, and Will Rogers of Moore and Oklahoma City, who had entered Congress in 1933, occupied a similar position in the House. The bill introduced by Thomas and Rogers as the result of the conferences with Indian groups was not a Department measure, but it was actively supported by Ickes and Collier. The provisions relating to the Five Tribes were as follows:

It accepted the existing educational system of paying tuition to public schools for the attendance of Indian children and continuing the boarding schools; and it pledged Congress to establish additional day schools and hospitals sufficient to provide adequate educational and hospitalization facilities for Oklahoma Indians. It continued the power of the Secretary to remove restrictions, and it gave rejected applicants the right of appeal to a Federal court. Before the expiration of any restrictions on Indian land, the President was empowered to extend the restricted period at his discretion. The Secretary was authorized to acquire land through purchase or assignment, including restricted land held by Indian owners, to

[34] *Congressional Record*, LXXVIII, 11744; *Statutes at Large*, XLVIII, 984-88.

[35] *Muskogee Phoenix*, October 5-16, 1934; *Daily Oklahoman*, October 16, 1934; *Tushkahomman*, April 9, 1935; *Congressional Record*, LXXVIII, 11126.

be held in trust by the United States for the communal use of any tribe, band, or group of Indians. Such land was removed from the jurisdiction of the state courts; the assignment to individual use, the ownership of im-,provements, and the leasing to third parties were to be subject to regulations prescribed by the Secretary. Indians living on such land were given authority to adopt constitutions and receive charters of incorporation, with the right to participate in the revolving credit fund of the Wheeler-Howard Act, and to exercise such powers as the Secretary might delegate in the management and control of the land, the administration of any services formerly performed by the Department, and the regulation of the affairs of the corporation and its members. Any Indian tribe or band, whether residing on communal land or not, was also given the right to organize for the control of any rights, claims, or property already belonging to the group. Any ten Indians were authorized under certain regulations to form cooperative credit, producers, consumers, marketing, and land-management associations, and the Secretary was directed to create an Oklahoma Indian Credit Corporation to receive an appropriation from the Federal treasury to be loaned to these local cooperative units. The Secretary was given exclusive jurisdiction over the estates of deceased restricted Indians, the approval or disapproval of wills, the determination of heirs, the partition of land and other property, and the settlement of claims against the estate. No guardian was to be appointed by the courts of Oklahoma for restricted Indians except on petition approved by the Secretary. Small fees were to be charged by the Department for the management of restricted property.[36]

The bill thus attempted to modify the general principles of the administration to conform to the situation in Oklahoma, where the Indians were distributed throughout the population. It aimed to destroy the opportunity for local exploitation of Indian property, and to enable the unassimilated Indians who so desired to return to a system of local self-government and communal land tenure similar to the lost tribal organization; but it held the ultimate purpose of releasing all Indians into the general citizenship of the state.

The bill instantly aroused angry opposition in Oklahoma. The state legislature passed a resolution condemning the pos-

[36] *Tushkahomman,* March 5, 1935; *Congressional Record,* LXXIX, 2709, 2776, 6665-67. The bill also contained provisions regarding Indians of less than one-half Indian blood, but these provisions were inapplicable to the Five Tribes because Indians of that class were entirely outside Departmental jurisdiction.

sible extension of restrictions, the removal of the probate jurisdiction from the state courts to the Department, and the
purchase of land with title vested in the United States and
therefore exempt from taxation. Super-patriots even discovered
the hidden hand of Red Russia behind the measure, and Collier was forced to defend himself before the House Indian Affairs Committee against charges of communism, atheism, and
sedition.[37]

Again the real sentiment of the Indians is difficult to determine. They were distributed throughout the citizenship of the
state, or isolated in remote settlements, and their tribal unity
was gone. Their opinion was subject to misinterpretation by an
over-enthusiastic Indian Office, or misrepresentation by a ven-
omously hostile press. Apparently, however, they were overwhelmingly in favor of the measure; for it was calculated to fit
the psychology of the conservative fullblood, and a large number of the prominent educated group from whom the opposition might have been expected to come, supported it.[38]

After drastic amendments to satisfy Oklahoma objectors,
the bill—now known as the Oklahoma Indian Welfare Act—
became a law June 26, 1936. The section abolishing guardianships for restricted Indians and giving the Department control
over partition and the determination of heirs has been eliminated. Oklahoma Indians are authorized to adopt constitutions
and receive charters of incorporation giving them the right to
engage in business, administer tribal property, elect officers,
and manage local affairs; and the Secretary is empowered to
purchase land under the general provisions of the Wheeler-
Howard Act and hold it in trust for such incorporated groups.
The act also permits the organization of Indians into voluntary cooperative associations for purposes of marketing, consumers' protection, or land management, and authorizes

[37] *Muskogee Phoenix,* September 27, 1935; *Tushkahomman,* April 9, 16, May 14,
June 4, August 27, 1935; June 10, 1936.
[38] *Tushkahomman,* March 5-26, April 16, May 14, 1935.

Congress to appropriate two million dollars for loans to such associations.[39]

Field men were immediately appointed to assist the Indians in drawing up charters of incorporation and to prepare bases for the extension of credit to cooperative associations. By the end of the fiscal year 1938-1939 the Indians had formed twenty-four credit associations, which with the approval of the Agency had made 350 individual loans. In addition, twelve fullblood Cherokees near Stilwell had entered into a community organization for the purpose of growing strawberries and other fruits and vegetables, and had borrowed $2,800 of which $600 was repaid the first year. Apparently the work has progressed slowly and cautiously, but it may be the means by which the Indians will eventually attain a satisfactory economic status.

It is highly improbable that any of these five extinct Indian republics will ever collect its scattered members and regain its lost autonomy, but there is an apparent tendency of the full-bloods to form smaller groups under the Act. The lead has been taken by the Creeks, the most tenacious of all the tribes in holding to the native ways. Their ancient "town" organization, which was actually a separate tribe in a federal union, had persisted through more than a century of constitutional development before allotment and had survived all the disintegrating influences of the allotment period; and it now forms a convenient unit for community action. In 1939 two of these "towns,"—Thlopthlocco and Alabama-Quassarte—adopted constitutions and articles of incorporation for the purpose of acquiring communal land, borrowing money for town enterprises, and caring for indigent members. The people of Kialigee Town have initiated similar action. The Euchees, always the most conservative of Creek groups, have been seeking to reestablish their identity as a separate tribe, and among the Cherokees the Kee-too-wahs are working for the same recognition. It is too early yet to evaluate the effect of this movement; but it is apparent that the two constitutions that have been

[39] *Statutes at Large,* XLIX, 1967-68.

adopted were not superimposed by white men, for they are in harmony with fundamental Creek institutions.[40]

Although Oklahoma opposition was still strong enough to defeat the provisions of the Indian Welfare Bill that related to probate matters and restrictions, the state lost one principle that it had stubbornly defended since 1908. A law—also passed in 1936—gave the Department supervision over agricultural leasing of restricted land belonging to enrolled or unenrolled Five Tribes Indians of one-half or more Indian blood. This law has delivered the Indians from forged leases, it has materially increased the amount of their rentals, and it is hoped that it will give them the opportunity of training in business transactions. In a more practical and narrow sense it should do away with the absurdity of supporting them by public charity while a few real estate dealers monopolize their land.[41]

Many of the Five Tribes Indians have, in fact, become public charges. Even before the general depression brought them from destitution to starvation a tendency was apparent to seek gratuity appropriations to elevate their condition by health, educational, and social work. This tendency was part of the general policy of increased expenditure for welfare work that followed the survey by the Institute for Government Research.

The Five Tribes Indians are now receiving adequate medical care. In 1930 a small general hospital was completed at Claremore in the Cherokee country, and early in 1936 more than a million dollars in Works Progress Administration funds was allocated for the construction of large hospitals or annexes at Talihina, Tahlequah, and Claremore. Most of the buildings were completed during the next two years, and Congress appropriated $341,300 for maintenance during the year 1939-

[40] Oklahoma-Kansas Regional Office of the Indian Service (Oklahoma City, Oklahoma), Office Files; Department of the Interior, *Constitution and By-Laws of the Thlopthlocco Tribal Town Oklahoma* (Washington, 1939); Department of the Interior, *Constitution and By-Laws of the Alabama-Quassarte Tribal Town Oklahoma* (Washington, 1939); Department of the Interior, *Corporate Charter of the Alabama-Quassarte Tribal Town Oklahoma* (Washington, 1939).

[41] *Statutes at Large*, XLIX, 1135; Superintendent, Office Files, Land and Money Division.

8. Typical Dwelling of Five Tribes Indians in the 1930's. Direct assistance was required to save the Indians from starvation.

1940. Until very recently the field medical service was limited to the part-time work of a nurse attached to one of the boarding schools and to the unskilled efforts of the general field workers; but in January 1938 a comprehensive public health program was inaugurated, and at the close of the succeeding fiscal year eight physicians and six nurses were employed in this work. Each of the boarding schools now has a contract physician and either a nurse or a ward attendant to care for the health of the students.[42]

In 1930 the general field service was strengthened by the addition of trained workers. Graduates of agricultural colleges began to instruct the Indians in gardening, stock raising, farm methods, and terracing, and to organize farm clubs among the adults and the so-called "4-H Clubs" among the boys and girls. Their work in fact is similar to that of the county agricultural agents that has proved so effective in white communities of the state except that it requires more patience and personal guidance. Home demonstration agents with specialized college training were also sent out to instruct the Indian women in cooking, canning, and sewing, and a few social workers trained in case methods began the almost hopeless task of elevating the sodden life of the fullblood communities.[43]

More direct assistance has been required to save the Indians from starvation. During the year 1929-1930 the acting superintendent reported that $706.03 had been spent for relief, and that many of the aged and indigent would have died without this help. In the more desperate emergency of the following winter the Federal Government was helpless to care for the most destitute class, the Indians whose restrictions had been

[42] *Statutes at Large,* XLV, 1582, 1640; XLVIII, 375; *Survey of Indians in the United States,* XIV, 5600, 5695-5711; 6229, 6280, 6306, for example; Commissioner of Indian Affairs, *Annual Report,* 1930, p. 302; Superintendent, Office Files, Report of Superintendent 1930, p. 88; Report of A. M. Landman, 1939, pp. 325-31; *Tushkahomman,* November 5, 1935; March 31, 1936; *Daily Oklahoman,* December 6, 1935; March 20, 1936; February 20, 1938; *Statutes at Large,* LIII, 707.

[43] Through the courtesy of Mr. Arthur I. Gilkison, Chief of the Extension Work, the writer met and talked with several of the field workers, examined reports, photographs, and Indian handwork, and with Mrs. Orpha M. Young visited Indian settlements and observed the work of the home demonstration agents and social workers.

removed, and the local government in spite of the proud boast of the early days of statehood was completely unable to cope with the situation. But the Red Cross came to the rescue with its disaster program, Agency and Red Cross officials worked together, and during the winter an average of over three thousand families received weekly assistance. The army also turned over a large amount of unused clothing to the Agency. The relief was limited almost entirely to the Cherokees, Choctaws, and Chickasaws; oil-rich individuals among the other two tribes aided their relatives and friends, and very little outside assistance became necessary. When spring came, the Agency started a garden campaign and the worst of the crisis was past.[44]

Subsequent needs of the Indians have been cared for mainly by the various work relief projects that became such a familiar feature of American life during the Roosevelt administration. It was Landman's opinion in 1939 that 50 per cent were in need of relief. According to his estimate for the fiscal year 1938-1939, old age pensions were paid to seven hundred individuals; $67,093.83 was expended for work relief for 840 families; $111,000 was allocated for the construction of rehabilitation projects; $292,993.61 was used to maintain camps of the Civilian Conservation Corps with an average enrolment of 325; and direct relief—carloads of discarded army clothing and bedding and $12,150.08 in cash—was distributed to 468 families. Some of these rehabilitation projects embrace comprehensive schemes for community settlements, but it is still too early to estimate the value of this program.[45]

While Commissioner Collier was attempting through legislation and administrative policy to create the opportunity for group action in economic matters, the Indians began to revive their tribal governments. This movement came partly as the

[44] Superintendent, Office Files, Report of Superintendent, 1930, pp. 7, 88; Commissioner of Indian Affairs, *Annual Report*, 1931, p. 28; *Muskogee Times-Democrat*, January 16, 1931; *Congressional Record*, LXXIV, 1926; *Survey of Indians in the United States*, XXVI, 13720-22.

[45] Superintendent, Office Files, Report of A. M. Landman, 1939, pp. 327, 417, 439, 442, 446-47.

result of definite encouragement from the Indian Office, and partly because the Indians had been so freely consulted with regard to legislation that they felt the need of an agency for the expression of opinion.

The Creek "towns" began to send representatives to a monthly meeting in the old capitol at Okmulgee or at the New Town Church northwest of that city to deliberate on tribal matters. In the fall of 1934 delegates from each of the "towns" met for the first tribal election of Chief since the election of Pleasant Porter. They chose Roley Canard, who was thereupon appointed by the President. The Seminole organization of an elective Chief and a Council of representatives from the bands, which had existed unregarded so many years, now received the recognition of the Indian Office. In 1935 George Jones was elected as Principal Chief, and this action was subsequently confirmed by the President. The Choctaw custom of holding conventions for united action on tribal matters was officially recognized by Collier when he authorized the calling of a convention at Goodland in June 1934. The old county and district organizations had been broken up by allotment, but delegates were apportioned among seventy-one Choctaw neighborhoods according to estimated population. This convention created an Advisory Council of eleven members, which, like the old tribal legislature, meets the first Monday in October and for special meetings at the call of the Chief. Leading citizens of the state comprise its membership, and it began immediately to take a very active part in promoting tribal interests. The old capitol, which had stood vacant for many years, has been restored by tribal funds, and serves as the place of meeting. W. A. Durant is the Principal Chief. In 1939 upon the death of Douglas H. Johnston, Floyd E. Maytubby was appointed as Governor of the Chickasaws—in this case without action by the tribe. Only the Cherokees have no tribal organization.[46]

[46] *Tushkahomman,* April 9, June 11, July 30, October 15, 1935; *Muskogee Times-Democrat,* May 27, 1924; September 4, 1934; *Daily Oklahoman,* August 14, 1938; July 23, 27, 28, 1939; *Guthrie Leader,* October 18, 1939; Superintendent, Office Files,

Unofficial Indian societies still meet for the formulation of Indian policy and the expression of Indian opinion. The Kee-too-wah Society through its ceremonials exercises an influence deeply religious in its nature upon the Cherokee fullbloods. The Choctaw-Chickasaw Treaty Rights Association after its victory in the tax suits continued its existence to work for the fulfilment of the agreements in the sale and distribution of the tribal property. The Choctaw-Chickasaw Protective League also maintains a healthy and active existence.[47]

The respectful hearing accorded these Indian organizations represents a new spirit in Indian administration just as the encouragement given to communal ownership shows a complete reversal of Federal policy. The success of the new system is highly problematical; the forces set in operation more than a generation ago by the creation of the Dawes Commission may have become too strong to be reversed. A study of the present Indian population with an inventory of their spiritual and material possessions may assist the reader to answer this question.

Report of A. M. Landman, 1935, pp. 4-7; 1939, pp. 3, 291-92; Indian Office Files, 3067/30 Seminole 160.

[47] *Tushkahomman,* March 5, 12, October 29, 1935; April 28, 1936; *Daily Okla-homan,* July 27, 1939.

# CHAPTER XIV

# The Present Situation

THE Federal census of 1930 apparently was more nearly complete than previous enumerations of the Indian population. It showed 72,643 Indians of the Five Tribes living in Oklahoma. The distribution through the former Indian Territory varied from a few hundred living in the western agricultural counties of the Chickasaw Nation to 4,931 in Adair County, where the Indians constituted one-third of the inhabitants. The total population of the state was 2,396,-040, of which 20,082 were Indians other than Five Tribes.[1] It should be pointed out that the Federal census lists as Indians only persons of appreciable Indian blood.

In 1931 the Agency for the first time made an enumeration of the Indians under its jurisdiction with their unenrolled children. This count showed 7,211 families of 27,924 individuals. Apparently it did not include allottees of one-half or more Indian blood whose restrictions had been removed, or the descendants of such unrestricted Indians.[2]

These Indians still own 1,604,664 acres of restricted land, of which 92,895 acres is in excess of the 160-acre limit and is therefore subject to taxation.[3] This amount—about 222 acres to a family—seems generous enough, but an unknown number of Indians whose restrictions have been removed are entirely landless. Much of this restricted land, moreover, is mountainous and unfit for farming, or it is far from the Indian's home. Much of it was once covered with fine timber, but virtually all

---

[1] Commissioner of Indian Affairs, *Annual Report,* 1931 p. 39; *Fifteenth Census of the United States,* III, Part 2, 541, 550-56, 573.

[2] Superintendent, Office Files, Report of A. M. Landman, 1931, p. 1.

[3] *Tushkahomman,* January 28, 1936. These are 1936 figures; later statistics do not seem to be available at the Superintendent's office.

the timber of commercial value has been cut. Most of the land is suitable for grazing, but according to the state law, which places the matter under local control, the hill counties usually have free range; and since the Indian is unable to fence his holdings, herds belonging to white men are very generally turned loose upon his pasture.[4]

Many Indians make little effort to make the best of the poor resources that they have. W. M. Wallace, probate attorney for McCurtain, Choctaw, LeFlore, and Pushmataha counties, told the Senate committee in 1930 that at least 90 per cent of the Choctaws in that section lived in the country on their own or their relatives' land, and that perhaps one-fourth of that number tried to raise a little corn, cotton, or fodder. Of the small number who did attempt to farm, he said that not more than one-fourth owned work animals or one-tenth owned milch cows, but a considerable proportion owned hogs, which ran almost wild in the woods. Most of the Indians leased their land and depended mainly upon the meagre rentals, upon an occasional windfall from the sale of an inherited allotment, and, if they were fortunate enough to own land in the Chickasaw counties, upon oil leases. The number supporting themselves upon their farms by their own efforts was "negligible."[5]

In 1934 a survey of the entire membership of the Five Tribes was undertaken as a Civil Works Administration project for the relief of unemployed college graduates, and 6,582 families comprising 25,407 individuals were visited before the work was discontinued. The survey apparently was very carefully made, but the totals and averages are somewhat misleading because of the disproportionate prosperity of a very few persons, and because more than half the cases investigated were white or of less than one-fourth Indian blood.

The individual cards are therefore more revealing than the statistical summary. The Indians usually remembered the amount of land they had owned and its ultimate disposition. In many cases it had been lost through forgery, a supposed

---

[4] *Survey of Indians in the United States,* XIV, 5680, 6470-72.  [5] *Ibid.,* XIV, 5680.

lease that turned out to be a deed, manipulation of the records, or guardian's sale; in other cases there had been a fair sale, possibly with inadequate consideration, but with the consent of the owner; but regardless of the nature of the transactions the Indians were progressively impoverished. One family selected almost at random may be regarded as typical. The data were secured in March, 1934:

The man was a Creek fullblood, aged 63. He had reached the fourth grade in school, and was therefore a product of the tribal educational system. He owned no land. He had sold 80 acres of his allotment for $800, and the remaining 80 for $4,000. He had inherited and sold the following land: one-third interest in 160 acres for $500; another one-third interest in 160 acres for $500; an inheritance, amount unknown, for $400; an inheritance, amount unknown, for $300; 80 acres for $300; 80 acres for $500; and an inheritance, amount unknown, for $500. He had earned nothing in 1933, and had no income whatever; but he had raised $37 worth of garden produce for home consumption.

The wife was a Seminole fullblood, aged 65, who had reached the second grade in school. She had sold 40 acres of her allotment for $150, and 5 acres for $500 as nearly as she could remember; and 165 acres of inherited land for an unknown amount. She still owned 75 acres of her allotment, and 40 acres of inherited land. She had received $32.50 for the rental of her land during 1933, which with the $37 worth of garden produce raised by her husband constituted the family living. The couple owed $20 for groceries.

They lived in a four-room frame house in fairly good condition on a paved highway. They had twelve peach trees in the yard. They owned one horse worth ten dollars, 11 hogs, 25 chickens, and 7 geese. They had an automobile, but no farm implements; a plow and a wagon, which they had once owned, had been stolen. Their household goods consisted of a victrola, a trunk, a stove, two tables, six chairs, a bench, two beds, two cupboards, and a sewing machine. Their stored food consisted of 550 pounds of meat which they had dried. They burned wood from the farm, and had a wagon load on hand. The appearance of the farm and house was good. They had enough bedding, but their clothing, although neat, was inadequate. They had never received any relief.

Living with them was a widowed daughter, aged 32. She had reached the third grade in school. She had two children, aged ten and nine, from her deceased husband, and a third aged eighteen months which was apparently illegitimate or the child of a divorced husband. She had worked as a domestic 300 days during 1933, and had received 25 cents a day for her work. She still owned the 40-acre allotment, which had been her share as a Seminole "newborn," and 12 acres which she had inherited from her husband. She had sold the following inherited land: 13 acres for $150; 40 acres for $900; 8 acres, which she had mortgaged for $10, and had lost through foreclosure because she had been unable to find and pay the man who held the mortgage; and 3 acres for $176. She had received no agricultural rental from her land, but had received $52 from an oil lease through the Agency. With the $75 which she had earned as a domestic, her total income for 1933 was therefore $127. She owned no personal property except a bed and a trunk and very inadequate bedding and clothing. She was in debt for $22.45. Her two older children were in the fourth and first grades in school. They each owned 12 acres of land, which they had inherited from their father, and each had received an income of 66 cents during 1933. The youngest child owned no property.

The old couple had another widowed daughter aged 39. She had reached the third grade in school. She still owned 80 acres of her original allotment, and 3 acres of inherited land. She had sold 40 acres of her allotment for $1,150, 40 acres of inherited land for $1,500, and oil royalty from her three acres for $30. During 1933 she had received $83 from rentals, and raised $10 worth of farm and garden produce for home consumption. She had 600 pounds of dried meat on hand and 24 quarts of canned vegetables. She lived in a six-room house, in fairly good condition, on a hard surfaced highway. She had 9 fruit trees in the yard, too young to bear. She owned 2 mules worth $250, 1 milch cow, 3 hogs, 25 chickens, 3 turkeys, and 5 geese. She had a harness, but no farm machinery. In her house were a radio, a stove, a table, 6 chairs, a davenport, 3 beds, 2 cupboards, a trunk, and a sewing machine. Her clothing and bedding were adequate. She burned wood from her farm, but had none on hand. The appearance of the house, yard, garden plot, and livestock was classed as fair. She had had no relief, but she was in debt to the extent of $500. She had three children classed as fullbloods, aged 10, 9, and 5. The two older ones were in the first grade in school. The children owned no land.[6]

Such homely details of living are more revealing than the statistical totals of the Agency reports, because the latter are inflated by the huge cash balances of a few wealthy Indians. In order to correct the misleading impression of these figures Landman issued a public statement in April 1931, showing that although the Agency held about $28,000,000 for approximately 28,000 restricted Indians it was distributed as follows: 171 wealthy individuals averaged $137,000 each; 10,234 aver-

[6] Superintendent, Office Files, office of Arthur I. Gilkison, Cards 6546, 6547, 6566.

aged $440, and the remaining 18,000 had no cash balance at all.[7]

Landman reported $22,921,231.34 as the cash balance on hand to the credit of individual restricted Indians in 1939. He reported the year's income at $2,799,605.92, of which the principal items were as follows:[8]

| | |
|---|---:|
| Agricultural and other surface leases | $ 99,081.06 |
| Oil and gas | 1,280,356.73 |
| Miscellaneous mining leases | 2,811.35 |
| Land sales | 62,111.07 |
| Interest on bonds and cash balances | 415,450.57 |
| Semi-annual interest distribution | 275,261.18 |
| Sale of Government securities | 113,200.00 |
| Indian Credit Associations | 163,256.72 |

Because of the general depression in the oil and gas industry, leasing declined during the 1930's. The most active year was 1935 when an important new field was developed in the eastern Chickasaw and the western Choctaw counties. In 1927 the Department discontinued the practice of selling oil leases through individual bargaining—a practice that had brought many charges of favoritism in behalf of certain companies—and sales are now held at the Agency, and the lease is awarded after competitive bidding. Landman reported in 1939 that 809 leases were in force.[9]

The field clerks continue to a large extent to supervise the disbursements of individual Indians. With the collapse of the huge oil incomes of the Twenties these expenditures no longer run into fantastic figures. The decline during the last half of the past decade has been especially noticeable; the total dropped from $2,698,984.85 during the fiscal year 1934-1935 to $259,-296.12 during 1938-1939. The most important items for these two years are as follows:[10]

[7] *Muskogee Times-Democrat,* April 24, 1931.

[8] Superintendent, Office Files, Report of A. M. Landman, 1939, pp. 19, 219, 269.

[9] *Ibid.,* pp. 249-53; *Tushkahomman,* January 28, 1936.

[10] Superintendent, Office Files, Report of A. M. Landman, 1935, pp. 8-9; 1939, p. 79.

|                                        | 1934-1935      | 1938-1939    |
|----------------------------------------|----------------|--------------|
| Cash payments                          | $1,310,264.83  | $150,325.26  |
| Houses and living expenses             | 682,306.78     | 43,369.83    |
| Farms, improvements, livestock, etc.   | 202,837.36     | 22,619.42    |
| Automobile and upkeep                  | 106,969.16     | 13,927.88    |
| Attorneys' fees                        | 60,549.61      | 401.97       |
| Cost of litigation, judgments, etc.    | 36,348.38      | 588.90       |

But even in these last days there are still some oil-rich Indians. Some through a fortunate combination of steady character, uncomplicated title to their estates, and accidental freedom from rapacious guardians manage to live normal and satisfying lives. Enos Wilson, who upon the death of Jackson Barnett succeeded to the newspaper title of "The World's Richest Indian," was an example of this class. Wilson was a Creek foundling, brought up and educated by an Okmulgee banker, who acted as his guardian. After he attained his majority, oil wells began to spout gold from his barren allotment, and his fortune mounted rapidly. He lived quietly at "Peak Castle," a magnificent residence which he built about fifteen miles from Okmulgee, and suffered no wrongs and committed no escapades to win him a newspaper headline. When he died in 1937, he was mourned by both Indians and whites.[11]

The Burgess family, a Seminole family, fills more nearly the popular conception of oil-rich Indians. In 1930 Mrs. Jeanetta Tiger Burgess came from her palatial home near Konawa to complain to the Senatorial committee of the straits to which she had been reduced by the miserly policy of Acting Superintendent McMillan. He had cut her monthly allowance to a mere $1,000; had subtracted her last month's gasoline bill, $95, from her current check instead of making an extra allowance as she had requested; and refused to approve the purchase of a new Pierce-Arrow. She had purchased two automobiles, a Ford and a Chrysler, for which she was paying by instalments from her allowance, and she owned a Chevrolet truck, but the Pierce-Arrow which she had persuaded McMillan to let her purchase

---

[11] *Daily Oklahoman*, April 15, 1936.

three years before, had reached the venerable stage where she had to "grind it" to make it start.

When Senator Wheeler volunteered some good advice about thrift, she answered:

"THE INTERPRETER. She says while she has a little money she likes to enjoy life like anybody else. Hereafter she says she could not use that money."

Senator Wheeler then warned her that she would spend all her money and be reduced to living in a tent. She replied:

"THE INTERPRETER. She says she has been in a tent all her life. That is the way her mother and father lived. If she had to go back like that, it would not be anything new to her. She says she was brought up on the Indian food and don't know anything about the modern white man's food. Osvfke and things like that were common in her tent. She says she was brought up on plenty of wild animals, wild turkey, and prairie chicken, and squirrels. Now there is not any such thing as that, not even rabbits."

McMillan stated that the $1,000 monthly allowance represented virtually all of the income from Mrs. Burgess' oil royalties and $219,000 in Liberty bonds. The Burgesses were steady upright people, not given to intemperance or any kind of dissipation; the money was not squandered, but was used mainly to feed the fullbloods of the tribe, who flocked to their hospitable table. "We have been severely criticized for disbursements in connection with some of the rich Indian accounts, but the disbursements are not for the family; they are for the whole countryside. That is what they need their truck for, to haul out the groceries."[12] It was people like the Burgesses who made it unnecessary for the Red Cross to expend money for relief that winter for the Creeks and Seminoles.

The kind of rich Indians that fill newspaper headlines—not so much now as formerly, however—was referred to by the harassed Landman in 1932. "A certain class of our wealthy Indians keep the [probate] attorneys, as well as other em-

[12] *Survey of Indians in the United States,* XIV, 5836-47.

ployees, in a constant fever of damage claims resulting from debts, automobile accidents, love and marital entanglements, and crimes. There is also the detail of ordinary determination of heirs, administration of estate and guardian supervision. After it all comes the harrowing details, and often bitter argument, incident to the settlement of attorneys' fees."[13]

Indian litigation still exists in eastern Oklahoma, but it no longer dominates its legal history. But a new type of litigation began when the tribes finally won their long fight to refer questions involving treaty violations and Federal administration of their property to the Court of Claims. The Oklahoma delegation in Congress had supported these reasonable tribal demands for an accounting for many years; but they had to overcome the opposition not only of economy advocates but the special hostility of the Mississippians, who tried to block all legislation unless the Mississippi Choctaws should be given the status of a nation and the right to sue. But Burke was more friendly to such legislation than any of his predecessors, and the jurisdictional acts were passed in 1924.[14] With the approval of the Department the tribes then made contracts with attorneys, and fifty-nine suits were filed, with claims running into hundreds of millions of dollars and involving almost the entire history of the relations between the tribes and the Federal Government.[15]

Only a few of these cases have been decided. Some have been won by the Government, but it is already apparent that regardless of the welfare of the Indians it would have been more profitable for the United States if a strict accountability had been observed in administering their affairs. In 1933 the Creeks won a judgment for $144,106.01 for the illegal educational expenditures previously mentioned, and other unauthorized

---

[13] Superintendent, Office Files, Report of A. M. Landman, 1932, p. 17; *Daily Oklahoman*, April 12, 1940.

[14] *Congressional Record*, LX, 2904, 4021, 4335; LXV, 8621; Kappler, *Laws and Treaties*, IV, 403-4, 414-17, 450-52, 550; *Statutes at Large*, XLV, 1229-30; XLVII, 137-38.

[15] *Survey of Indians in the United States*, XXV, 13549-51; *Congressional Record*, LXXII, 11098-11100; Secretary of the Interior, *Annual Report*, 1933, p. 98.

disbursements, and in 1938 they won $296,011.42 for a strip of land along their western boundary opened to homesteaders in Oklahoma Territory through a faulty survey. In 1935 the Court of Claims awarded the Seminoles $1,317,087.27 for illegal use of their tribal funds, especially for the schools, and for general errors in accounting; but this case has not yet (1940) come to a final judicial determination.[16]

Other judgments are expected to follow soon. Because of the complicated nature of these claims and the claims of other Indian tribes, bills have been introduced in Congress within the past few years for the creation of a special Indian claims court or commission,[17] but no legislation has been enacted. The effect of the prolonged delay has been extremely demoralizing to the Indians. The denial of justice for so many years in cases where they had a good cause has led them to build up fantastic claims without foundation and to discontinue their productive efforts in the expectation of realizing enormous wealth at some future time.[18]

Three of the tribes own very little property except what they may eventually recover from the claims. The Cherokees' total tribal property consists of 365.87 acres of land for which the Government has never been able to find a purchaser. The Creeks still own 306.84 acres of unsold land, two boarding school plants, and the 57 recovered town lots in Tulsa and Muskogee. The Seminoles own only the Mekusukey school ground, still producing some oil and valued in 1935 at $30,000.[19]

The Choctaws and Chickasaws are still the unwilling owners of 381,077.05 acres of unsold coal and asphalt valued at $10,088,649.67. The thirty-year leases made under the Atoka Agreement have all expired, few new leases have been secured,

[16] *Court of Claims Reports*, LXXVIII, 455-505; LXXXII, 135-61; LXXXVII, 280-81; *Tushkahomman*, May 7, 1935; *Daily Oklahoman*, September 13, 1939.

[17] *Muskogee Times-Democrat*, January 3, 1930; *Daily Oklahoman*, June 15, 1935; *Tushkahomman*, March 19, May 14, 1935.

[18] For example, *Muskogee Times-Democrat*, January 3, 8, 1930.

[19] Superintendent, Office Files, Report of A. M. Landman, 1939, pp. 286-87.

and recent attempts at sale have been unsuccessful. The Agency reported $30,691.88 collected in coal royalty during the fiscal year 1938-1939. Since 1925 only one mining trustee has served to represent both tribes.[20]

The tribes also own 21,186.24 acres of unsold or forfeited land and 303 town lots forfeited or reserved for the coal lessees, and a small amount in deferred payments on their land sales is still outstanding. In 1939 their tribal property including the minerals was valued at $10,425,301.67. The Federal Government also pays the Choctaws an annuity of $10,520 in fulfilment of the land cession treaties of the early nineteenth century, which is equivalent to a considerable capital investment.[21]

The possession of this property still exposes the two tribes to the designs of citizenship claimants. Bills are introduced in every session of Congress for the benefit of the "court citizens" or the Mississippi Choctaws or for general revision of the rolls. Since the probability of winning some of the cases before the Court of Claims became apparent, similar attempts to revise the other rolls, especially the Cherokee, have developed.[22]

Ever since the work of the Dawes Commission attracted national attention to the wealth of the Five Tribes Indians, swindlers have worked upon the credulity of the general public by arousing in the minds of white people false hopes of enrolment. A typical member of this fraternity began working in western Oklahoma and Texas when Congress passed the jurisdictional acts in 1924. He collected $25-fees from his dupes, and promised to secure their enrolment as Choctaws, and obtain for each a cash payment of $28,500 and 160 acres of agricultural or 40 acres of oil land. The authorities found it easy

---

[20] Superintendent, Office Files, Report of A. M. Landman, 1939, pp. 218, 285; *Congressional Record*, LXXII, 8503-4, 10437-39, 11734-36; *Statutes at Large*, XLV, 737-38; XLVIII, 1240; Secretary of the Interior, *Annual Report*, 1933, p. 102.

[21] Superintendent, Office Files, Report of A. M. Landman, 1939, p. 285; *Statutes at Large*, LIII, 728; Kappler, *Laws and Treaties*, II, 87-88, 192-94, 212-13.

[22] For example, *Congressional Record*, LXXV, 777, 1279, 1280, 12072; LXXVIII, 1037; LXXIX, 630, 975, 1040; *Tushkahomman*, May 26, 1936.

to collect evidence from his victims, but the swindler himself had disappeared.[23]

It is easy to set these schemes in operation because the general public has never understood and does not now understand that Indian descent, no matter how well authenticated, did not entitle one to tribal citizenship. When the Senatorial committee visited Oklahoma in 1930 several apparently honest and truthful people appeared and presented their claims to enrolment by stating facts that completely destroyed their case.[24] At the present time if one will spend a few hours at the Agency, he is almost certain to meet some of these deluded people, usually humble people with every appearance of sincerity. They have no noticeable Indian characteristics, but in their family tradition is an Indian ancestor. Their family was living outside the Indian Territory at the time of the enrolment, perhaps had been living outside for generations, and neglected to present their claims. They have now learned that the tribes own immense tracts of land, and have come to enroll and receive an allotment. The sinister influence behind these inquiries is that at least part of these people reveal the fact that they are the dupes of sharpers. Moreover, the constant agitation to reopen the rolls is a menace to any tribe so long as it has property to guard or claims that may be enforced against the Federal Government.

Since the estates of three tribes are virtually closed, and the coal mines belonging to the other two no longer produce large royalties, the tribal revenues have almost ceased. But small appropriations of Choctaw, Chickasaw, and Creek funds are made to pay salaries to the officials and the expenses of councils and conventions. These expenditures during the year 1938-1939 were as follows: Choctaw, $28,234.79; Chickasaw, $7,-377.46; and Creek, $672.66. The attorneys who are pushing the claims under the jurisdictional acts are working under contingent fee contracts. The tribes no longer bear any of the cost

23 *Muskogee Times-Democrat,* August 28, 1924.
24 *Survey of Indians in the United States,* XIV, 6209-16, 6235-41.

of education; the last appropriation—the Choctaw—was discontinued in 1937.[25]

As a result of the general increase in expenditures for Indian education the sum paid for public school training rose in 1929 from the $150,000 to which it had dropped during the 1920's. It reached $400,000 in 1931-1932 and remained close to that figure during the remainder of the decade, standing at $398,000 for the year 1939-1940. Strictly speaking, this appropriation is not confined to the Five Tribes, for it includes also the small tribes attached to the Quapaw Agency. The expenditure is justified by Congress upon the ground that the state is entitled to assistance in educating Indian children as long as part of the Indian land is not subject to taxation.

Nine education field agents and five school social workers under a supervisor at the Agency visit the schools, apportion the funds, and distribute relief to needy children. Until the school year of 1938-1939 no distinction was made regarding the quantum of Indian blood; hence it was impossible to concentrate upon the fullblood settlements most in need of educational effort, and the public schools of the state were paid tuition for the attendance of many nearly white "Indians" whose parents had long ceased to hold any tax exempt allotments. But at the present time the welfare of the Indians rather than financial assistance to the school districts has become the major consideration: the appropriation is limited to those children who are at least one-fourth Indian by blood, and it is required that one-half the tuition money be expended upon an "enrichment program"—vocational training, 4-H Club work, the purchase of equipment, etc. During 1938-1939 the public school districts received $286,407.76 as tuition for 9,946 children, an average of about 22 cents for each day's attendance of an Indian child. A portion of the money was used to purchase clothing, school lunches, text books, etc., for needy children.[26]

---

[25] Superintendent, Office Files, Report of A. M. Landman, 1939, p. 233; *Statutes at Large*, XLIX, 190; L, 584.

[26] Superintendent, Office Files, Report of A. M. Landman, 1939, pp. 391-92; *Statutes at Large*, LXVI, 298, 1134; XLVII, 107, 680; XLVIII, 374; XLIX, 190;

An increasing amount of the appropriation has been used for the establishment of special Indian day schools in the full-blood settlements. When the tribal schools were taken over by the state, only one of the old neighborhood schools remained—the Redbird Smith School in a Cherokee settlement—and proved too useful to be discontinued. But the Indian Office did not favor this type of school, believing at first that the public schools would soon take charge of Indian education, and later that the specialized training of the boarding school was the answer to the problem. In 1930 Hastings, who was on the committee in charge of Indian appropriations, insisted that more schools of the Redbird Smith type should be established, and he secured a special authorization for the use of $10,000 for that purpose. Later in the year when the Senatorial committee visited Oklahoma several of the more thoughtful persons from the Indian settlements recommended this kind of school. The present administration is fully committed to the establishment of these special schools to be used also as neighborhood centers, with shop, domestic science equipment and a community garden.

Highly qualified teachers of Indian blood were employed for this work, and ten of these schools were established. In 1937 Congress authorized the use of $21,500 of the public school appropriation for this purpose, and the number of schools has now increased to fifteen. During the year 1938-1939 there was a total enrolment of 409 Indians—267 Cherokees, 48 Choctaws, 48 Chickasaws, and 46 Creeks—and 77 of the underprivileged white children living in these remote communities. The grade level attained by these children shows an appalling retardation, but the attendance, although irregular, is far above that of the usual fullblood neighborhood. With a frank acknowledgment of the seriousness of the situation the teachers in these special schools are now attempting with a real missionary zeal to raise the educational and social level of a

L, 584; LII, 310; LIII, 706; *Tushkahomman*, May 21, 1935; *Interior Department Appropriation Bill for 1931*, pp. 539-44.

group that has been almost completely neglected for a generation. As a result the whole spirit of some of these retarded
Indian communities has become alert and hopeful.[27]

The enrolment in boarding schools has steadily decreased
since 1932. The schools and their locations are as follows:
Carter Seminary for girls, Ardmore; Euchee Boarding School
for boys, Sapulpa; Eufaula Boarding School for girls, Eufaula; Jones Academy for boys, Hartshorne; Wheelock Academy for girls, Millerton; Sequoyah Orphan Training School,
boys and girls, Tahlequah. The Federal Government owns the
Sequoyah school, but the other plants still belong to the tribes.
The Sequoyah school carries its pupils through high school
graduation; the others run only to the ninth or tenth grade, and
two of them make use of the public schools except for the children in the lower grades. Congress made a total appropriation
of $417,625 for these six schools for the year 1939-1940, and
an undetermined additional amount was expended for the maintenance of Five Tribes young people sent to Chilocco and
Haskell. Most of the children selected for boarding school attendance are fullbloods.[28]

These schools are imposing in their physical plants, and attractive to the visitor in the fine spirit of their faculties and the
apparent contentment of the children; but the Congressional
appropriations secured for this highly specialized institutional
training are not entirely free from the suspicion of "pork." It
costs more to maintain four children at one of these schools
than it costs, by using agencies already in existence, to support
one of the special Indian day schools with its service to an
entire community.

The total capacity of the six schools is 1,075 children, and
290 additional young people are maintained under contract in

[27] *Interior Department Appropriation Bill for 1931,* p. 544; *Statutes at Large,*
XIV, 5684; Superintendent, Office Files, Report of C. L. Ellis, 1927, pp. 101-2;
Report of A. M. Landman, 1935, pp. 32-33, 37; 1939, pp. 407-9; Supervisor of
Indian Education, Office Files (Oklahoma City), Report of George C. Wells,
1934, pp. 6-11, 32, 146; 1935, p. 17; *Tushkahomman,* March 5, May 21, 1935.

[28] Superintendent, Office Files, Report of A. M. Landman, 1939, pp. 350-74, 415;
*Statutes at Large,* LIII, 706; *Tushkahomman,* September 10, 1935.

Presbyterian and Roman Catholic institutions and in the Murray State School of Agriculture. The church schools also enroll 180 young Indians for whom no tuition is paid, and about 100 are attending state and denominational colleges and universities. The school statistics for 1938-1939 showed 13,825 children of one-fourth or more Indian blood between the ages of six and eighteen; of these, 12,856 were enrolled in school, and an additional 783 whose ages were beyond this scholastic limit were attending school or college.[29]

It is too early to evaluate the results of the new educational policy. Only the future will show whether the children now in school are being adequately prepared to take their place in the society into which their parents were so suddenly thrust upon the dissolution of the tribal governments. It is clearly apparent that the educational policy of the past generation has not been successful; and the net result of allotment is that after the impoverishment of the Indians the United States has assumed the entire financial burden as well as the responsibility that the tribes were forced to relinquish in 1898.

The total expenditures of the Federal Government for education, field service, health, and Agency administration for the Five Tribes reached $2,270,206.89 for the year 1938-1939.[30] These disbursements, of which one of the largest single items is paid to the public schools for tuition, should much more than compensate the state for the Indians' tax exempt holdings, since these holdings have now shrunk to 1,511,769 acres of almost worthless land and the oil production from Seminole and Cherokee homesteads held by original allottees.

It is unquestionably true that a much larger proportion of Federal appropriations than formerly is used for the welfare of the Indians. The work of the Dawes Commission and much of the early work of the Agency consisted in placing their land under a tenure that would expedite its settlement by white people. Later the Agency was almost exclusively occupied in

[29] Superintendent, Office Files, Report of A. M. Landman, 1939, p. 390; *Statutes at Large*, LIII, 706.

[30] Superintendent, Office Files, Report of A. M. Landman, 1939, p. 227.

trying to save a little of the Indians' property, a policy that gave the rich Indians a disproportionate amount of its services. During the whole period, both territorial and state, the Federal agencies were used largely for the benefit of political spoilsmen. But within the past few years, especially since 1928 and more particularly since 1930, an increasing tendency has been shown to administer the service for the benefit of the forgotten Indians in the hills. This mission calls for greater spiritual understanding and more highly trained intelligence than the former policy; and although too many Agency employees are still content to perform routine duties and remain in ignorance of the history and institutions of the people they are supposed to serve, the personnel is constantly improving. One very striking change that has taken place in the Agency force during the past five years is the large proportion of Indians holding positions in the service.

The workers have lost in optimism as they have gained in knowledge. A field clerk reported to the Superintendent in 1928: "the progress that our allottees are making is far from satisfactory. Our allottees seem to lack initiative, and they do not seem to understand conditions as they exist, and are more or less backward in adjusting themselves to these conditions. This is a condition which, we will frankly admit, we do not know how to combat within any limited length of time. The only solution we have to offer is education and the force of circumstances, aided by advice, precept, and example." A probate attorney stated to the Senate committee in 1930: "There may be some remedy or method whereby these wards of the Government can be placed upon a plane of industry, self-support, and independence. If so, the originator or inventor of the beneficent scheme should speedily appear in order that the current fast ebbing may be reversed."[31]

Unquestionably the policy of destroying the Indians' institutions and suppressing the traits that once made them strong has degraded an overwhelming majority of the fullblood

[31] *Survey of Indians in the United States*, XIV, 5652, 5680.

group. But the waves of white influence that flooded the lowlands will almost certainly reach these isolated hills; and the Indians' chance of survival still depends upon their ability to face the inundation. If the present attempt to understand and use their genius for collective effort, the revival of racial self-consciousness through free consultation rather than arbitrary rulings, and instruction in the white man's economic techniques will restore the hope and confidence of former days, the lost fullbloods in the hills may yet be saved.

# BIBLIOGRAPHY

## SOURCE MATERIAL

### I. *Manuscript Collections*

Acts of the Choctaw Nation, 1885, 1896-1910. Phillips Collection, University of Oklahoma. Norman, Oklahoma.

Cherokee Papers. Phillips Collection, University of Oklahoma. Norman, Oklahoma.

Commissioner of Charities and Corrections. Office Files. Oklahoma City, Oklahoma.

Commissioner of Indian Affairs. Office Files. Washington.

Department of the Interior. Indian Territory Division Files. Washington.

Five Tribes Papers. Oklahoma State Historical Society. Oklahoma City, Oklahoma.

Fort Smith Papers, United States Court and Indian Territory. Phillips Collection, University of Oklahoma. Norman, Oklahoma.

Muskogee County (Oklahoma) Register of Deeds. Records. Muskogee, Oklahoma.

Oklahoma-Kansas Regional Office of the Indian Service. Office Files. Oklahoma City, Oklahoma.

Secretary of the Interior. Office Files. Washington.

Superintendent for the Five Civilized Tribes. Office Files. Muskogee, Oklahoma.

Supervisor of Indian Education for Oklahoma. Office Files. Oklahoma City, Oklahoma.

United States District Court, Eastern District of Oklahoma. Court Records. Muskogee, Oklahoma.

### II. *Official Documents*

#### 1. FEDERAL DOCUMENTS

Attorney-General. *Annual Reports,* 1913-1922 (Washington, 1913-1922).

Attorney-General. *Official Opinions,* Vol. XXXVI (Washington, 1932).

Board of Indian Commissioners. *Annual Reports*, 1885 (*House Exec. Docs.*, 49 Cong., 1 Sess., No. 109), 1900, 1901, 1912-1916, 1922, 1926, 1929-1931 (Washington, 1901-1931).

Bureau of the Census. *Extra Census Bulletin, The Five Civilized Tribes in the Indian Territory* (Washington, 1894).

————. *Fifteenth Census of the United States*, Vol. III (Washington, 1933).

————. *Fourteenth Census of the United States*, Vol. III (Washington, 1922).

————. *Indian Population in the United States and Alaska* (Washington, 1915).

————. *Population of Oklahoma and Indian Territory 1907* (Washington, 1907).

————. *Thirteenth Census of the United States*, Vol. III (Washington, 1913).

————. *Thirteenth Census of the United States, Abstract with Supplement for Oklahoma* (Washington, 1913).

Commission to the Five Civilized Tribes. *Reports*, 1894-1904 (Washington, 1894-1904).

Commissioner of Indian Affairs, Department of the Interior, Secretary of the Interior. *Annual Reports*, 1890, 1893-1933 (Washington, 1890-1933).

*Congressional Record*, Vols. XXIX, XLI-LXX, LXXII, LXXIV-LXXVI, LXXVIII-LXXX (Washington, 1897-1936).

Department of the Interior. *Education of Indians in Oklahoma* (Washington, 1922).

————. *Constitution and By-Laws of the Alabama-Quassarte Tribal Town Oklahoma* (Washington, 1939).

————. *Constitution and By-Laws of the Thlopthlocco Tribal Town Oklahoma* (Washington, 1939).

————. *Corporate Charter of the Alabama-Quassarte Tribal Town Oklahoma* (Washington, 1939).

House Committee on Appropriations (Subcommittee of). *Interior Department Appropriation Bill for 1930* (Washington, 1928).

————. *Interior Department Appropriation Bill for 1931* (Washington, 1931).

*House Docs.*, 58 Cong., 2 Sess., Nos. 528, 556, 575, 614.

House of Representatives, Committee on Indian Affairs. *Indians of the United States*, Vol. III (*Investigation of the Field Service*) (Washington, 1920).

————. *Investigation of the Administration of Indian Affairs in Oklahoma* (Washington, 1924).

House of Representatives, Committee on Indian Affairs. *Withholding Certain Lands from Allotment in the Creek Nation* (Washington, 1915).

*House Reports,* 61 Cong., 3 Sess., No. 2273, Vols. I, II; 68 Cong., 2 Sess., No. 1527; 70 Cong., 2 Sess., No. 1358, Part 2; 71 Cong., 3 Sess., No. 2188.

Jones, W. A. *Regulations* (Approved by E. A. Hitchcock, December 5, 1902).

Kappler, Charles J. *Indian Affairs, Laws and Treaties,* Vols. I-IV (Washington, 1904-1929).

Mott, M. L. *A National Blunder* (Probably published at Washington, 1924).

Senate Committee on Indian Affairs. *Survey of Conditions of the Indians in the United States* (Washington, 1928).

————. *Survey of Conditions of the Indians in the United States,* Vols. III, IV, XIV, XXV, XXVI (Washington, 1929-1932).

*Senate Docs.,* 54 Cong., 1 Sess., No. 182; 57 Cong., 1 Sess., No. 381; 58 Cong., 2 Sess., Nos. 106, 169, 189; 60 Cong., 2 Sess., No. 707; 61 Cong., 1 Sess., No. 89; 62 Cong., 3 Sess., No. 1139; 70 Cong., 2 Sess., No. 263.

*Senate Reports,* 53 Cong., 2 Sess., No. 377; 59 Cong., 2 Sess., No. 5013, Vols. I, II; 70 Cong., 1 Sess., No. 918; 72 Cong., 1 Sess., No. 221.

United States. *Statutes at Large,* Vols. IV, XXVI, XXIX, XXX, XXXIII, XXXIV, XXXVI, XXXVII, XLVI-LIII (Boston, Washington, 1880-1939).

### 2. OKLAHOMA STATE DOCUMENTS

Childers, C. C. *How Oklahoma Collects Taxes* (Compiled for the Legislature, January, 1925).

Commissioner of Charities and Corrections. *Reports,* 1909-1916, 1924 (Oklahoma City, Guthrie).

————. *Monthly Bulletin,* Vol. I, Nos. 5, 9 (Oklahoma City, 1912).

Corden, Seth K., and Richards, W. B. *Oklahoma Red Book,* Vol. II (Oklahoma City, 1912).

*Journal of the House of Representatives of the Extraordinary Session of the Third Legislature of the State of Oklahoma* (Shawnee, no date).

*Journal of the House of Representatives of the Regular Session of the Fifth Legislature of the State of Oklahoma* (Oklahoma City, no date).

*Journal of the Proceedings of the Senate of the Extraordinary Session of the Second Legislature of the State of Oklahoma* (Guthrie, 1910).

*Journal of the Proceedings of the Senate of the Extraordinary Session of the Third Legislature of the State of Oklahoma* (Shawnee, no date).

*Journal of Senate of the Fifth Legislature of the State of Oklahoma* (Oklahoma City, no date).

Snyder, Henry G. *The Compiled Laws of Oklahoma* (Kansas City, 1909).

State of Oklahoma. *Session Laws,* 1909, 1910, 1910-1911, 1913, 1915, 1916, 1919, 1923-1924, 1931 (Oklahoma City, Guthrie, 1909-1931).

### 3. COURT REPORTS

*Cases Decided in the Court of Claims of the United States,* Vols.. XXXVIII, LI, LII, LVII, LXII, LXXVIII, LXXXII, LXXXVII (Washington, 1923-1939).

*Federal Reporter,* Vols. CLIV, CLXIV, CLXXI, CLXXIX, CLXXXVII, CXCII, CC, CCXXXV, CCLXXIII; Second Series, Vol. LXIV (St. Paul, 1907-1933).

*Indian Territory Reports, Cases Determined in the United States Court of Appeals for the Indian Territory,* Vol. V (Parsons, Kansas, 1906).

*Pacific Reporter,* XCV, CIV, CX, CXIV, CXXXI, CXL, CXLIV, CLI, CLII, CLV, CLXII, CLXVI, CLXIX, CLXXIII-CLXXV, CLXXXII, CLXXXIV, CLXXXIX, CXC, CXCII, CXCIV, CXCV, CXCVIII, CCIV, CCVII, CCXVIII, CCXIX, CCXXIII, CCXXIV, CCXXXII; Second Series, Vol. II (St. Paul, 1909-1931).

*United States Reports, Cases Argued and Decided in the Supreme Court of the United States,* Vols. XXV, XLVII, XLVIII, LIV-LVI, LIX, LXI-LXVI, LXXII, LXXIII, LXXV (Rochester, 1905-1931).

### III. *Contemporary Publications*

#### 1. PUBLICATIONS OF SOCIETIES, ETC.

*Democratic Nominees for State Office* (Campaign Document, 1910). Phillips Collection, University of Oklahoma. Norman, Oklahoma.

Lake Mohonk Conference. *Reports,* 1904, 1913-1915 (Philadelphia, 1904-1915).

Oklahoma and Indian Territory Bar Association. *Proceedings of the Third Annual Meeting,* 1906. Phillips Collection, University of Oklahoma. Norman, Oklahoma.

Oklahoma Bankers' Association. *Proceedings of the Eight Annual Convention,* 1904. Phillips Collection, University of Oklahoma. Norman, Oklahoma.

#### 2. NEWSPAPERS

*Adair County Republican.* Stilwell, Oklahoma, 1913, 1914.

*Antlers News.* Antlers, Oklahoma, 1906.

*Ardmore Statesman.* Ardmore, Oklahoma, 1912.

*Caddo Herald.* Caddo, Oklahoma, 1905.

*Cherokee County Democrat.* Tahlequah, Oklahoma, 1912.

*Chickasaw Capital.* Tishomingo, Oklahoma, 1904.

*Daily Ardmoreite.* Ardmore, Oklahoma, 1926.

*Daily Oklahoman.* Oklahoma City, Oklahoma, 1911, 1913, 1934-1940.

*Guthrie Daily Leader.* Guthrie, Oklahoma, 1936, 1939.

*Hugo Husonian.* Hugo, Oklahoma, 1913.

*Idabel Democrat-Record.* Idabel, Oklahoma, 1911, 1912, 1916, 1917.

*Indian Citizen.* Atoka, Oklahoma, 1895-1898.

*McAlester Daily News.* McAlester, Oklahoma, 1908, 1912.

*McAlester News-Capital.* McAlester, Oklahoma, 1926.

*McCurtain Gazette.* Idabel, Oklahoma, 1911.

*Muskogee Daily Phoenix.* Muskogee, Oklahoma, 1896, 1905-1935.

*Muskogee Democrat.* Muskogee, Oklahoma, 1905.

*Muskogee Evening Times.* Muskogee, Oklahoma, 1904.

*Muskogee Times-Democrat.* Muskogee, Oklahoma, 1907-1938.

*Nowata Star.* Nowata, Oklahoma, 1913-1915.

*Okmulgee Daily Democrat.* Okmulgee, Oklahoma, 1929.

*Okmulgee Daily Times.* Okmulgee, Oklahoma, 1923.

*Okmulgee Times-Democrat.* Okmulgee, Oklahoma, 1928.

*Sapulpa Evening Democrat.* Sapulpa, Oklahoma, 1912-1915.

*Sapulpa Evening Light.* Sapulpa, Oklahoma, 1911.

*Sapulpa Evening News.* Sapulpa, Oklahoma, 1914.

*Sapulpa Herald.* Sapulpa, Oklahoma, 1914-1918.

*Seminole Capital.* Wewoka, Oklahoma, 1904-1910.

*Seminole County Capital.* Wewoka, Oklahoma, 1912.

*Seminole County News.* Seminole, Oklahoma, 1908, 1909, 1913.

*Standard-Sentinel.* Stilwell, Oklahoma, 1911-1915.

*Tulsa Daily World.* Tulsa, Oklahoma, 1913.

*Tushkahomman.* Stroud, Oklahoma, 1935, 1936.

*Vinita Weekly Chieftain.* Vinita, Oklahoma, 1903, 1904.

*Wagoner County Courier.* Wagoner, Oklahoma, 1913.

*Wagoner County Record.* Wagoner, Oklahoma, 1913, 1914.

*Wewoka Democrat.* Wewoka, Oklahoma, 1907-1914.

*Wewoka Herald.* Wewoka, Oklahoma, 1905.

### 3. MAGAZINE ARTICLES

Collier, John. "Indians at Work," *Survey Graphic,* Vol. XXIII (Concord, New Hampshire, 1934).

Dawes, Anna Laurens. "An Unknown Nation," *Harper's Magazine,* Vol. LXXVI (New York, 1888).

Godfrey, J. H. "Suggestions for an Oklahoma Investigation," *Quarterly Journal of the Society of American Indians,* Vol. I (Washington, 1913).

McAdam, Rezin W. "An Indian Commonwealth," *Harper's Magazine,* Vol. LXXXVII (New York, 1893).

Valentine, Robert G. "Making Good Indians," *Sunset Magazine,* Vol. XXIV (San Francisco, 1910).

4. BOOKS

Evans, Charles, and Bunn, Clinton Orrin. *Oklahoma Civil Government* (Ardmore, Oklahoma, 1908).

Meserve, Charles F. *The Dawes Commission and the Five Civilized Tribes* (Philadelphia, 1896).

Thoburn, Joseph B., and Holcomb, Isaac M. *A History of Oklahoma* (San Francisco, 1908).

IV. *Personal Interviews*

Finley, J. H. Muskogee, Oklahoma, October 4, 1935.

Gilkison, Arthur I. Muskogee, Oklahoma, September 27 ff, 1935.

Nicholson, Henry. Muskogee, Oklahoma, December 17, 1935.

Mills, Lee. Pryor, Oklahoma, September 27, 1935.

Young, Mrs. Orpha M. Muskogee, Oklahoma, September 28 ff, 1935.

SECONDARY MATERIAL

Abel, Annie Heloise. "Proposals for an Indian State," *Annual Report American Historical Association,* 1907, Vol. I (Washington, 1908).

———. *The American Indian as Participant in the Civil War* (Cleveland, Ohio, 1919).

———. *The American Indian as Slaveholder and Secessionist* (Cleveland, Ohio, 1915).

———. *The American Indian under Reconstruction* (Cleveland, Ohio, 1925).

Beckett, A. L. *Know Your Oklahoma* (Oklahoma City, 1930).

Bledsoe, S. T. *Indian Land Laws* (Kansas City, 1909).

Debo, Angie. *The Rise and Fall of the Choctaw Republic* (Norman, Oklahoma, 1934).

Foreman, Carolyn Thomas. *Oklahoma Imprints* (Norman, Oklahoma, 1936).

Foreman, Grant. *Advancing the Frontier* (Norman, Oklahoma, 1933).

———. *Indian Removal* (Norman, Oklahoma, 1932).

———. *The Five Civilized Tribes* (Norman, Oklahoma, 1934).

Gessner, Robert. *Massacre* (New York, 1931).

Harman, Robert. *Hell on the Border* (Fort Smith, Arkansas, 1898).

Johnson, Roy M. *Oklahoma History South of the Canadian,* Vol. I (Chicago, 1925).

Kellog, Laura Cornelius. *Our Democracy and the American Indian* (Kansas City, 1920).

La Moore, Parker. *Pat Hurley* (New York, 1932).

Langworthy, Henry P. *Indian Land Titles* (Tulsa, Oklahoma, 1914).

Leupp, Francis E. *The Indian and his Problem* (New York, 1910).

Meriam, Lewis, and Others. *The Problem of Indian Administration* (Baltimore, 1928).

Moorehead, Warren K. *Our National Problem* (Privately printed about 1913).

———. *The American Indian in the United States* (Andover, Massachusetts, 1914).

Schmeckebier, Laurence F. *The Office of Indian Affairs* (Baltimore, 1927).

INDEX

# INDEX

Adair County, 232, 379; land transactions in, 227-9

*Adair County Republican,* 228

Adams, John Quincy, 121

Adams, Samuel, 212

Adams, Spencer B., 39

Agency employees, number, 9, 63; characterization of, 201, 278-80, 394. *See* also Federal employees, Spoils, Union Agency

Agreements, negotiation of, 23-4, 32-5; Atoka, 24, 33, 35, 64, 65, 85, 97, 387; Seminole, 32, 35, 64, 85, 211; Creek 33-4, 64, 75, 86-7, 121; Cherokee, 34-5, 64, 85, 87; Choctaw-Chickasaw Supplemental, 35, 39, 41, 51, 79-80, 210, 261; Creek Supplemental, 35, 85, 87, 88-9, 134, 208-9, 211; restrictions in, 90; tax exemption in, 164; abrogation of, 283-4, 298; interpretation of, 301. *See* also Treaties

Agricultural land, 6, 11, 16, 95, 98, 114

Agriculture, Indian, in tribal days, 3, 14-15; Indian, after allotment, 51, 127-30, 279, 380-2; training in, 278-9, 375

Alabama, 155

Alexander, M. L., 189, 237

Allen, J. Weston, 239

Allen, R. C., 251-3, 256

Allotment, in East, 5, 42; agitation for, by whites, 19-30; Seminole, 48-9; Creek, 49-50, 273-6; Cherokee, 50, 98-9; Choctaw and Chickasaw, 50-1, 95-8; contests, 52; refusal to accept, 53-8, 127-30, 152-6; Mississippi Choctaws, 97-8; assistance of real estate dealers, 94-9; freedmen, 98; to children, 103-4; feeling of Indians toward, 127-31; attempt to cancel Creek, 273-6

American Indian Defense Association, 22-3, 327-30, 336-7, 345, 353

Anadarko, 369

Appraisal of land, 41, 47-8, 260

Ardmore, 27, 93, 98, 107, 112, 131, 143, 149, 204, 244, 269, 286, 319, 392

*Ardmore Statesman,* 211

Arkansas, 134, 138, 267

Arkansas law, 19, 117, 301-2

Asp, Henry, 141

Asphalt, 35, 65, 79-82. *See* also coal land

Atkins, Tommy, 274

Atoka, 50, 77, 95

Attorneys, of Choctaw and Chickasaw freedmen, 26, 42, 151, 269; of tribes, 38-41, 63, 100, 112-13, 124, 196, 226, 232-7, 241, 246, 249, 251-3, 259, 269, 321, 386, 389; of Mississippi Choctaws, 43-4; of citizenship claimants, 45, 269; of Four Mothers, 54, 297; of individual allottees, 115-16; of guardians, 191, 242-7, 305 ff.; of claimants to oil land, 275-6; of Treaty Rights Association, 297-8; of Barnett claimants, 342, 349; of Exie Fife, 343-4, 346. *See* also Probate attorneys, Bar associations

Automobiles, 288, 320, 322, 328, 384-5

Autonomy, 5, 161-2. *See* also Government, tribal; State Government

Bacone College, 137, 325-6, 341-2, 346-7

Bailey, Elmer, 342, 347

Baker, William A., 198-9, 232, 246-7

Ballinger, Richard A., 264

Baptists, 7, 137, 325-6, 337-9, 341, 346-7

Bar associations, 137, 226, 243, 329, 337

Barnard, Kate, 222, 231, 246, 308, 310, 311; defense of Indian children, 184-92; McCurtain County investigation, 225-7; hostility to, 238; speech at Lake Mohonk, 240; recommendations regarding probate attorneys, 248; creation of people's lobby, 254-6; retirement, 257

Barnes, Cassius M., 141

Barnett, Jackson, 294, 336, 338-42, 346-50, 365, 384

Barnett, Jeanetta, 365

Barnett, Mrs. Jackson, 338-42, 346-9

Bartlesville, 87, 111, 131, 206

Bassett, Mabel, 308

## DATE DUE